THE IDEOLOGIES OF CLASS

THE IDEOLOGIES OF CLASS

Social Relations in Britain
1880–1950

ROSS MCKIBBIN

Oxford   New York

OXFORD UNIVERSITY PRESS

1991

Oxford University Press, Walton Street, Oxford OX2 6DP

Oxford New York Toronto
Delhi Bombay Calcutta Madras Karachi
Petaling Jaya Singapore Hong Kong Tokyo
Nairobi Dar es Salaam Cape Town
Melbourne Auckland
and associated companies in
Berlin Ibadan

Oxford is a trade mark of Oxford University Press

First published 1990 by Oxford University Press
First issued as an Oxford University Press paperback 1991

British Library Cataloguing in Publication Data
McKibbin, Ross
The ideologies of class: social relations in Britain
1880–1950.
1. Great Britain. Working classes, history
I. Title
305.5620941
ISBN 0–19–285243–4

Library of Congress Cataloging in Publication Data
McKibbin, Ross.
The ideologies of class: social relations in Britain, 1880–1950/
Ross McKibbin
p. cm.
Reprint. Originally published: Oxford: Clarendon Press, 1990.
1. Working class—Great Britain—History. 2. Social classes—
Great Britain—History. I. Title.
HD8390.M37   1991   305.5'0941—dc20   90–25984
ISBN 0–19–285243–4

Printed in Great Britain by
Biddles Ltd.
Guildford and King's Lynn

In Memoriam

E. K. B.
(1902–1978)

PREFACE

THIS book in its intellectual concerns is a successor to my published doctoral thesis, *The Evolution of the Labour Party* (Oxford, 1974), and is in some senses what I would like to have written then. Although that thesis argued a case which, on the whole, I still think to be right, it did so often implicitly and sometimes by assertion. In these essays I hope to make the case more explicitly; they all, therefore, start from the same question as my thesis—what was the social character of the British working class in the period we conventionally think it to be most 'mature', that is from the 1880s to the early 1950s, when about 75 per cent of the population were manual-working wage-earners or people who depended on them. In my doctoral thesis I tried to answer that question by looking at the development of the Labour Party at a significant moment in its history, 1910–24. But that necessarily meant a narrow approach. It excluded much that we would need to know about the working class and it omitted almost everything to do with the working class's relations with the rest of society. Yet the development of the working class was itself partly determined by the behaviour of other social classes. Historians for their part necessarily observe the working class very largely through the eyes of these other classes. Thus my original question has been an evolving one and each step has suggested another, so that a book which begins with the working class and ends with the not-working class is less strangely organized than it appears. The book has two structural themes: an interior one, the political and social character of the British working class; and an exterior one, the relationship of that class to society and the state. It also has a chronological theme: the two world wars.

The essays are not published in the order they were written, though the last was written last. The first three, 'Why was there no Marxism in Great Britain?' (1984), 'Arthur Henderson as Labour Leader' (1978), and 'The Franchise Factor in the Rise of the Labour Party' (1976; written jointly with Colin Matthew and John Kay and reprinted here with their permission) are ideological and political, concerned with the particular set of circumstances in which British working-class politics was conceived. The second three, 'Working-class Gambling in Britain, 1880–1950' (1979), 'Work and Hobbies in Britain, 1880–1950' (1983), and 'Class and Poverty in Edwardian England' (1978) are studies of working-class social life, although 'Class and Poverty' also analyses what we might call 'official' perceptions of the working class and thus acts as a bridge to the final three essays. All of them, 'The Economic Policy of the Second Labour Government, 1929–1931', (1975), 'The "Social Psychology" of Unemployment in Inter-war Britain' (1987), and 'Class and Conventional Wisdom; the Conservative Party and the "Public" in Inter-war Britain' (1988) look at the relationship between the working class and the state and the working class and the not-working class in the inter-war years. All of them represent working-class defeats, or the working class coping with defeat. The essay on the second Labour government suggests (amongst other things) that the structure of power and ideological interest within Britain did not permit the adoption of alternative policies and I still see no reason to doubt this conclusion. The essay on inter-war unemployment follows logically from the previous two. Many of the psychological studies of inter-war unemployment, though they claimed to be scientific, differed little in their assumptions from the Edwardian culture of poverty literature and were similar, perhaps to a surprising extent, to the 'official' view of the working class. Equally, the unemployed were central to the fall of the second Labour government and their status tells us much about the political structures of British society. The final essay, 'Class and Conventional Wisdom', attempts to explain the most visible of these defeats—the remarkable electoral success of the Conservative Party in the inter-war years. The essay argues that once people were required to declare themselves for or against the organised working class, as they increasingly were after 1918, the Conservatives were able to mobilize the 'public', the constitutional classes, who in the inter-war years were a large majority of the adult population, against a particular conception of the working class.

All the essays have undergone some rewriting except the last essay, which is entirely new. In the fourth, sixth, and eighth essays the rewriting has been substantial, to the extent that the sixth bears a new title. It was originally called 'Social Class and Social Observation in Edwardian England' but has been revised to incorporate its argument within the debate on the so-called 'culture of poverty'. A change of title, therefore, seemed appropriate. In the other essays rewriting has been more slight and designed to unify what were originally scattered articles.

There are many who have directly or indirectly helped me in the preparation of this book. I should like to thank Asa Briggs, Martin Ceadel, Peter Ghosh, José Harris, Brian Harrison, Michael Hart, Boyd Hilton, Janet Howarth, Jo Innes, Paul Johnson, John Kay, Tim Mason, Ken Morgan, John Prest, John Rowett, and Pat Thompson. I should also like to thank the convenors of and participants in seminars at the Universities of Cambridge, Liverpool, London, Oxford, and Warwick, where several of these essays were presented as papers. I must mention separately Angus Macintyre and Keith Thomas, who read parts of the book in manuscript, Philip Waller, who also read some of the text and encouraged me to bring the essays together, and, finally, Colin Matthew to whom I owe a particular debt of gratitude.

R. I. McK.

ACKNOWLEDGEMENTS

EIGHT of the chapters in this book were written, in somewhat different form, as either articles or essays, and I am grateful for permission to reprint them. Chapters 1 and 3 appeared in the *English Historical Review*, 99, April 1984, and 91, October 1976; Chapter 2 in the *International Review of Social History*, 23, Part I, 1978; Chapters 4 and 7 in *Past and Present*, 68, August 1975, and 82, February 1979 (world copyright reserved, Past and Present Society); Chapter 5 in J. M. Winter (ed.), *The Working Class in Modern British History* (Cambridge University Press, Cambridge, 1983); Chapter 6, as 'Social Class and Social Observation in Edwardian England', in the *Transactions of the Royal Historical Society*, 28, 1978; Chapter 8 in P. J. Waller (ed.), *Politics and Social Change in Modern Britain* (Harvester Press, Brighton, 1987).

CONTENTS

ABBREVIATIONS

COS	Charity Organisation Society
GWR	Great Western Railway
ILP	Independent Labour Party
LCC	London County Council
LPLF	Labour Party Letter Files (in the Labour Party Headquarters)
LRC	Labour Representation Committee
NLF	National Liberal Federation
PP	Parliamentary Papers
PRO	Public Record Office
Q, QQ	Question, Questions
TUC	Trades Union Congress
SDF	Social Democratic Federation
SPD	Sozialdemokratische Partei Deutschlands (German Social Democratic Party)

1

Why was there no Marxism in Great Britain?

IN 1906 Werner Sombart published a famous essay *Why is there no Socialism in the United States?* He was, in practice, asking not so much why there was no socialism as why was there no mass working-class party.[1] His question was implicitly and explicitly comparative: what were the differences between the United States and Germany? He did not perform a similar exercise for Britain and Germany, partly because the contrasts were much less obviously striking. Yet no one in the pre-1914 international labour movement could miss them; the predominant British working-class party, the Labour Party, was understood to be unique in Europe. It was admitted to the Second International by a contrived formula—that it and its attached unions objectively advanced the political interests of the working class—which was only just compatible with the Marxist or 'rejectionist' ideology shared by nearly all the major European working-class parties. The extent to which these parties could or should 'reject' the political systems in which they were compelled to work was, it is true, a matter of great controversy; equally, there were serious disputes within the Labour Party over the extent to which it was or should be 'socialist'. Nevertheless, despite this, both the European parties and the Labour Party entrenched their ideological differences: the first reaffirmed their nominal rejectionism while the other continued to exclude a programmatic socialism and any candidate who ventured to stand as a 'socialist'. They thus devised antithetical 'resolutions' to their ideological dilemmas.

In these circumstances Sombart's question might more fruitfully be asked of Britain than of the United States. Britain was similar enough to the Continent to make the differences more puzzling; between America and Europe the contrasts were, in fact, too

[1] W. Sombart, *Why is there no Socialism in the United States?*, ed. C. T. Husbands (Macmillan edn.; London, 1976).

apparent to allow much of a problem. It is, therefore, the purpose of this chapter to pose the question of Britain: why was it that, before the First World War, political Marxism's classical moment, Britain alone of the major European states produced no mass Marxist party, why groups—like the Social Democratic Federation—which could claim at least a vulgar Marxism were either absorbed into the Labour Party or became mere sects without a significant following? It is proposed to answer this larger question by examining four subsidiary ones: how far did the structure of the work-force encourage a sense of sameness and collectivity amongst its members; to what extent did the associational culture of the British working class accelerate or impede the transmission of rejectionist ideologies; how far did that class feel itself excluded from civil society; and finally, to what degree did it possess a leadership which could articulate and direct a specifically socialist working-class politics?

Before 1914 nowhere in Europe was seemingly more likely to produce a mass working-class party than Britain. In 1901 about 85 per cent of the total working population were employed by others, and about 75 per cent as manual workers. The agricultural sector was almost exiguous: slightly less than 12 per cent of the male population worked in agriculture, horticulture, and forestry and the number was declining. In the broadest sense Britain was unquestionably a working-class nation. But on closer analysis the huge British proletariat disperses itself, and its 'collective' element becomes remarkably thin. There are several ways by which this can be shown. If we take trade union membership as a reasonable index of collectivity we find that in 1901 of an employed work-force of 13.7 million, little under 2 million, about 15 per cent, were union members. The effective number is probably somewhat higher since this figure includes among the work-force children and adolescents who were not eligible for union membership.[2] Even so, it is clear that about 80 per cent of the male work-force was non-unionized; the female work-force outside cotton was almost entirely non-union. By 1914 the proportion unionized was significantly higher—25.8 per cent—but on the eve of the war three-quarters of the male work-force was still non-unionized,

[2] H. Clegg, A. Fox, and A. F. Thompson, *A History of British Trade Unions since 1889* (Oxford, 1964), 466.

while the proportion of women workers in unions remained tiny.[3]

By itself that 25 per cent—4 million workers—could have constituted a formidable proletarian vanguard; but there is no simple identity between union membership and political inclination. Indeed, we know pretty well what union opinion was. In 1913 legislation which reversed the Osborne Judgement required union members to vote on the establishment of a political fund;[4] many did not vote at all and of those who did 40 per cent voted against affiliation to the Labour Party. Only in one union, the Engineers, was the ideological character of the Labour Party an issue and in that union alone can we assume that some of the opposition to affiliation came from the left. In other unions, in so far as the argument had a clear point, it was the 'socialism' of the Labour Party which was objectionable.[5] Even if we simply leave aside those who did not vote at all we ought perhaps to exclude from a 'collectivist' reckoning about 40 per cent of the unionized work-force. By the index of a politically sympathetic union membership it seems likely that a working-class party hoping to exploit 'collectivist' sentiments among the working class could mobilize at most about 20 per cent of the male work-force. Since, however, this conclusion presupposes an inert working class incapable of responding to leadership or agitation, or even of exercising judgement, the question should perhaps be reformulated: was the *potentially* 'collectivist' work-force larger than that apparently available to a working-class party? In 1897–8 the number of men who came within the sphere of the Chief Inspector of Factories was 4.5 million. If we add to this the 300,000 who were employed by the railways—a generous addition since many of those were railway labourers who had little sense of class or occupational solidarity—and the 730,000 who worked in coal or shale mining, the number is still less than 6 million, about 35 per cent of the work-force.[6] However, it is clear from the growth of the unskilled workers' unions (which recruited men outside the trades already mentioned) that we must add more to the total. How much? The most impressive gains in union membership between 1901 and

[3] Ibid.; for the problems of organizing women, 469–70.
[4] See H. Pelling, 'The Politics of the Osborne Judgement', *Historical Journal*, 25. 4 (1982).
[5] M. Beer, *A History of British Socialism*, ii (London, 1920), 340–4.
[6] Chief Inspector of Factories, *Report, 1897–8*, PP (1900), xi. 1 (Cd. 27), 249.

1914 were, in fact, in those occupations where union 'density' was already high.[7] The general unions, moreover, had not maintained the impetus of the early 1890s. They were organizing notoriously unreliable trades very vulnerable to cyclical fluctuations and with a highly mobile and easily fragmented work-force. They were, on the whole, occupations where stable work relations were untypical.[8] The general unions claimed 350,000 members in 1890 but there is little evidence they enrolled that number. Before 1911, in any case, that was certainly their peak. The comparative failure of the general unions in the unskilled trades implies that any political party would, at least, have as much difficulty organizing them; and implies the same reason, the dispersion and instability of the work-force.[9]

The same was even truer of the working class in the service sector, the most rapidly growing part of the Edwardian economy. There was that vast and unnumbered race who worked for themselves or others on a catch-as-catch-can basis: vendors of all kinds, porters, carters, operators on the doubtful fringe like bookies' runners, and even, to some extent, dockers. In many ways they had what we take to be the essential characteristics of the Edwardian working class, yet in them a collective sense of class was aetiolated almost to non-existence: on the contrary, a jaunty and attractive individualism was essential to their lives.[10] While they were fairly well aware of where they stood on the social ladder, they were almost entirely outside a conventional political culture. Indeed, their occupational world of chance and quick-wittedness was in many ways absolutely opposed to collectivist politics. An enforced but much more desolating individualism was equally representative of the new servants of the service sector: clerks, shop assistants, attendants, warehousemen and storemen. The British shopocracy created a real proletariat: individuals disorganized, over-disciplined and isolated both from each other and the outside world. W. Johnson, secretary of the Shop

[7] Clegg *et al*. 468–9.

[8] E. J. Hobsbawm, 'General Labour Unions in Britain, 1889–1914', in *Labouring Men* (London, 1964), 179–97.

[9] This was Charles Booth's view. See C. Booth, *Life and Labour of the People in London*, 2nd ser., iii (London, 1903), 403.

[10] Ibid. 269–70; G. Stedman Jones, 'Working-class Culture and Working-class Politics in London, 1890–1900: Notes on the Remaking of a Working Class', *Journal of Social History*, 7 (1974).

Assistants' union, told the 1891 Royal Commission on Labour how this could be so. Why was it so difficult to organize shop assistants and warehouse clerks? The average clerk and assistant, he replied,

goes into the business at an early age. Indeed, from the time he goes in as a rule he is shut from all communication with the world and he does not know really the changes that are taking place around him. He does not read the daily papers . . . But how [he was asked] is it that intelligent men cannot combine as well as working-men who have less education and less intelligence?—Because working-men have the opportunity for social intercourse with each other and for discussing these matters, which shop-assistants have not.[11]

The whole apparatus of the advanced service sector worked against most sorts of common activity, let alone working-class politics. It was wracked by status anxieties, and the young men and women who entered it were subjected to often dislocating pressures from socially ambitious parents. Politically, it encouraged either an insurance agents' Liberalism (of the sort that compelled Lloyd George to exclude funeral benefits from the National Insurance Act[12]) or a rather craven Toryism, or no politics at all.[13] Although in the government sector (the Post Office particularly) and in the Co-operative Societies there was some advance in organization, private commerce remained almost immune from working-class politics,[14] rendered so not only by the action of employers but by the social environment of its occupations. It seems difficult to argue, therefore, that the potential support for a class-conscious working-class politics was very much greater than its measurable support. It is unlikely that unskilled or service sector occupations which were so resistant to unionization would be much more susceptible to conversion by an ideologically specific political party, particularly as so many of the trades encouraged or demanded an individualist view of the world.

If, however, we are interested in the extent to which the work-force felt a sense of sameness, it is not enough to know what they did, we must know where they did it and in whose company. We

[11] Royal Commission on Labour, *Minutes of Evidence*, PP (1893–4), xxxiv. QQ [Questions] 31, 120–2.
[12] Bentley B. Gilbert, *The Evolution of National Insurance in Great Britain* (London, 1973), 326–40.
[13] For a Marxist analysis, see F. D. Klingender, *Clerical Labour in Britain* (London, 1935), 11–24.   [14] Clegg *et al.*, 469.

must try to assess how far it was an aggregated working class and what might be the political consequences of its aggregation or dispersal. It is a commonplace that the industrial organization of the British economy was small-scale. In 1898–9 the average British workshop employed only 29.26 male employees.[15] In textiles the average was rather higher, 35.6 male employees; in non-textile plants slightly lower, 28.45. Employment in heavy industrial units was by this definition equally fragmented. 'Shops' or 'departments' in iron and steel mills employed on average 237.5 men and in all metal founding concerns 55.65. In heavy engineering (outside ships) the average was 67.7, and in ship- and boat-building itself 240.4. Averages, of course, can be misleading, but an analysis of the employment size of British firms emphatically confirms them. In the Edwardian period there were 100 firms employing more than 3,000 people and on a generous estimate their total of employees was 700,000—or, allowing for a fair number of women employed in textiles, about 5 per cent of the male work-force.[16] This is unquestionably a low proportion but one which itself has to be modified. The figures represent size of firm and not size of plant. Thus the country's largest 'firm', the Cotton Spinners' Association, itself hardly a firm in the accepted sense, with 30,000 employees, was distributed throughout dozens of plants of widely divergent size, many of them very small. Furthermore, the list includes all the major railway companies, which were *sui generis* organizationally (the 1901 census recognized nine categories of railwaymen[17]) and whose employees were deeply divided by craft and status, the Royal Dockyards (the second largest employer), state-owned and worked by men interested in jingoism, and the Co-operative Wholesale Society (the tenth largest employer), which had a unique character. There were, in fact, only four 'heavy industrial' firms employing more than 10,000 people: Armstrong Whitworth, Vickers, John Brown, and Stewarts and

[15] Chief Inspector of Factories, *Fourth and Fifth Annual Returns: General Summary of Persons Employed in Factories, 1898–9,* PP (1902), xii. (Cd. 1300), 1–30.

[16] Christine Shaw, 'The Large Manufacturing Employers of 1907', *Business History*, 25. 1 (Mar. 1983), 42–60; for capital size of firm, see P. L. Payne, 'The Emergence of the Large Scale Company in Great Britain', *Economic History Review*, 2nd ser., 20 (Dec. 1967), 519–42.

[17] Population Census of the United Kingdom, PP (1903), lxxxiv. 1, 206–7.

Lloyds.[18] The typical British workshop was probably no smaller than continental ones; what is important is the decidedly small scale of plant in the mainlines of the industrial economy. The great yards of Barrow and Tyneside, even Alfred Williams's locomotive and coach-building works in Swindon or Lady Bell's forges in Middlesbrough were exceptional;[19] and they, by American or German standards, or indeed, the standards of St Petersburg or Turin, were small beer. Furthermore, in those firms where the units themselves were comparatively large, size was qualified by complicated systems of employment and sub-employment. This meant, as a rule, that relations between employer and employee were either close (if direct) or endlessly mediated by working sub-employers (like the butty-men at Stephenson's of whom Arthur Henderson was one) which probably tended to undermine a collective sense of class. This was true even of the mines and partly accounts for the persistence of radical Liberalism in many of the fields. Characteristic here, for example, were the checkweighmen, elected by the miners but who became, in effect, agents of both employer and men. Barnet Kenyon, successively Liberal, Labour, and Liberal MP for Chesterfield, 1913–29, was only the most vibrant example of the type.[20]

Now it is certainly not true that size *necessarily* encourages the transmission of political radicalism or that smallness impedes it. By one model the reverse could be true: smallness brings men together and lubricates political communication. French syndicalism (though probably not French Marxism) seems to have benefited from the small scale of French industry, and it is noticeable that the Social Democratic Federation, the closest approximation Britain then had to a Marxist party, flourished in Burnley, a town of small textile plants. Historical circumstances, however, alter cases, and it is arguable that the structure of British industry presented a Marxist party with the worst of two worlds. Because the patterns of employment were so fragmented and localized, political communication and group loyalties became multilinear: men could unite against masters; equally they could unite with

[18] The number is six if the Royal Ordnance Factories and Guest, Keen & Nettlefold are included.

[19] Alfred Williams, *Life in a Railway Factory* (London, 1915); Florence, Lady Bell, *At the Works* (2nd edn.; London, 1911).

[20] For Kenyon, see R. Gregory, *The Miners and British Politics, 1906–1914* (Oxford, 1968), 156–67.

them. Fragmentation facilitated the movement of powerfully articulated ideologies which worked against a 'rejectionist' Marxism[21] as much as it impeded working-class politics: the structure of the economy thus tended to narrow the base of a political collectivism by partly diffusing and partly absorbing working-class consciousness. On the other hand, the effects of scale in distancing men from employers and uniting them in a common alienation were equally diminished. It is likely, for example, that the work experience of men employed in the hundred largest firms—given their dispersal—differed little from the rest of the work-force but likely also that it differed significantly *amongst* that 5 per cent— between (say) cotton spinners and shipwrights in the Royal Dockyards.

This had predictable political consequences. The success of the Hornbys in Blackburn,[22] Chamberlain in Birmingham, or Sir Howard Vincent in Sheffield (who, like Chamberlain, held his city for the Tories even in 1906) demonstrates how the structure of industry could foster a political affinity between masters and men.[23] When Baldwin told the House of Commons that, as a boy, he knew by name every man who worked in Baldwin's iron works (Bewdley) he was invoking a political reality and not (or not only) uttering a Tory platitude.[24] To many foreign observers this was Britain's exemplary achievement. 'Nowhere', Schulze-Gaevernitz wrote,

do we meet the social pessimism so familiar in Germany, nowhere the belief among the lower classes that salvation can only come through the overthrow and destruction of the existing order . . . Amongst the English working classes, the economic investigator never meets that deep-seated mistrust which makes the German workman regard every man in a good coat as an enemy, if not a spy.[25]

This suggests that the clientele likely to patronize a specifically

[21] For these ideologies, see below, 17–32.

[22] P. F. Clarke, 'British Politics and Blackburn Politics', *Historical Journal*, 12 (1969).

[23] For both Birmingham and Sheffield, see D. Smith, *Conflict and Compromise: Class Formation in English Society, 1830–1914* (London, 1982). More generally, see the important study by Patrick Joyce, *Work, Society and Politics* (Brighton, Sussex, 1980).

[24] HC Deb. 6th ser., 839–41 (6 Mar. 1925).

[25] G. von Schulze-Gaevernitz, *Social Peace: A Study of the Trade Union Movement in England* (London, 1893), p. xx.

working-class party based upon an occupational solidarity was a comparatively small one and even smaller if the party were Marxist or quasi-Marxist. We might wonder, therefore, whether a communitarian solidarity might not have better concentrated and expressed class-consciousness. There has always been some evidence that it could: 'Poplarism' and, more recently, Clay Cross, were strong affirmations of parochial as well as class-loyalty. Furthermore, the geographical separation of the classes was probably the most important feature of nineteenth-century urban development. Yet no political party was able to exploit community, except in a limited way. Why was this so?

The first reason lies in simple poverty. Poverty had a number of fairly obvious results. The sheer struggle for survival demanded so much time and physical energy that there was little left of either for any kind of active politics. In addition, the instability and overcrowding of lower working-class domestic life, however affectionate family relations were, discouraged a sense of collectivity. In such conditions, R. A. Bray wrote, 'people drift apart, the one from the other, until the common life becomes little more than a sorry farce.'[26] Poverty also implied mobility, which implied votelessness; the poorer the areas the more gross the disfranchisement.[27] The consequence was that nearly half the male working class could not participate even in the elementary act of voting in parliamentary elections; only a negligible number of working-class women could vote in municipal elections and none at all, of course, in parliamentary ones.[28]

The second reason comes from the sexual division of labour. A high degree of communitarian solidarity to some extent presupposes sexual solidarity: that the prime loyalties of a husband were to his family and neighbourhood. But it is doubtful if they were. The first interests of women (even if they worked) were children and household. Men took pleasure in their families (Margaret Loane thought they spoilt their children[29]) but they were often rather passive members.[30] In so far as they had

---

[26] R. A. Bray, 'The Boy and the Family', in E. J. Urwick (ed.), *Studies of Boy Life in our Cities* (London, 1904), 37–8. [27] See below, 72–81.
[28] M. G. Sheppard, 'The Effects of the Franchise Provisions on the Social and Sex Composition of the Municipal Electorate 1882–1914', *Society for the Study of Labour History Bulletin*, 45 (Autumn 1982), 22.
[29] M. Loane, *From their Point of View* (London, 1908), 108–10.
[30] Ibid. 144–56.

communitarian loyalties it was to male friends and to male associations and activities. It is difficult to know how far husbands thought of their wives as companions (or vice versa), but it seems unlikely that many couples shared the same social or political interests, particularly as the disfranchisement of women reinforced the view that politics was a male preoccupation. Lady Bell thought that Middlesbrough women were

on the whole . . . curiously devoid of public spirit or interest in outside affairs . . . At the most acute moment of the Free Trade discussion, for example, in which most of the workmen—not all—took one side or the other, the women, almost without exception, seemed quite indifferent. When they were asked what their husbands' views were, the majority had not an idea . . . and had no views of their own upon it.[31]

Nor, she thought, was the wife much involved in her husband's job: 'I cannot say what the attitude of the working woman in other countries is towards her husband's work, but my impression is that, for the most part, the wife of the English workman is quite detached in interest from it.'[32] Eglantyne Jebb suggested the same was true of Cambridge women, as much by their own choice as their husbands':

Many of the most respectable women among the poor regard it as a credit to themselves that their lives are bounded by their household cares. How often one hears them say in a tone of pride that they never go anywhere except perhaps to church on Sunday, and that they never speak to anyone! And, indeed, with their limited horizon conversation with their neighbours is likely to lead to nothing but gossip and scandal.

The result of this is easy to see. The husband does not find an interesting companion in the wife whose range of topics is bounded by the four walls of her home, and if he wants rational intercourse he seeks it elsewhere.[33]

Doubtless domestic pressures also drove men out of the house and into the company of friends (which often meant workmates), but the surviving evidence points to the overwhelming importance to men of the workplace: home was where they lived, work was where they had their social being. Even if men disliked their work it was unusual for them to dislike the workplace and the social

---

[31] Lady Bell, 324.　　　　　　　　　　　　　　　　　　　　　[32] Ibid.
[33] E. Jebb, *Cambridge: A Brief Study in Social Questions* (Cambridge, 1908), 139.

relations dependent upon it.[34] As long as the domestic and social lives of men and women were so divorced and while women remained excluded from formal political activity it is hard to see how a neighbourhood loyalty could override an occupational one.

Finally, tensions within working-class communities almost certainly undermined local solidarity. While these communities were notoriously characterized by extraordinary mutuality they were also marked by backbiting, gossip, and a jockeying for social superiority. If this was true, as Robert Roberts suggests, of parishes whose members were alike in most 'objective' ways,[35] it was truer still of communities where there were real differences of income and status.[36] All working-class communities were equally affected: single-status ones by the usual neighbourhood disputes (between those who kept the front step washed and blacked and those who did not, for example[37]) while multiple-status communities displayed real social distances and much hostility between their members.[38] The somewhat monolithic appearance the working class presented to strangers concealed divisions which were at least as intense within communities as they were within the work-force. Communal loyalties were, therefore, ambiguous; they were inert rather than active, and defensive rather than aggressive. Some of this changed after 1918—and was changing before 1914—but in the Edwardian period high mobility, wide disfranchisement, and irregular employment introduced a chaotic element into the politics of working-class neighbourhoods. C. F. G. Masterman described it in a hyperbolic but not unfair way:

Outside the Metropolitan Gasworks at the dinner hour, and in Peckham High Street after nightfall, a cloud of mingled, confused oratory and invective rose to the unconscious stars; as six or seven meetings, each within easy earshot of each other, shouted in hoarse accents women's votes or cheaper food or the rights of the publican. Wagon loads of pictorial illustration wedged their way through the coagulated masses of South London, now lit with fierce glare of torches, now disguised as an illuminated fire-engine pumping truth upon Liberal mendacities; now loaded with slum children, looking, it must be confessed, exceedingly happy and healthy, but dolorously labelled 'Victims of the Public-house

[34] See below, pp. 148–9.
[35] R. Roberts, *The Classic Slum* (Pelican edn.; Harmondsworth, 1974), 17–18, 47.
[36] Bray, in Urwick, *Studies of Boy Life*, 13–21.   [37] Roberts, 37.
[38] See Arthur Morrison, 'Behind the Shade', in *Tales of Mean Streets* (London, 1894), 115–27; H. Bosanquet, *Rich and Poor* (London, 1896), 4–5.

Monopoly'. Hysteria, as in all such deliriums, was never far away; women shrieked aloud at meetings, and had to be removed; madness fell upon a boy of twelve, and he stood on the top of a barrel, talking Tariff Reform.[39]

Furthermore, we might argue that a proletarian communitarian solidarity can *only* exist to the extent that class solidarity exists; otherwise communitarian and class solidarities are simply antithetical. We are thus back where we began: the prime determinant of political allegiance was work and the political mentality it imposed on the work-force. That mentality was the first obstacle to the development of a political party which presupposed a unified and ideologically unique working-class interest. The proportion of working men lumped together in *Grossbetriebe*, combined by a common deprivation which outweighed unequal privileges, and well distanced from employers, the proportion which a party based upon class ideologies and appealing to collective sentiments could hope to exploit was, on a priori as well as measurable grounds, at most half and in practice much less than half of the whole. Against that, small workshops, which might have incubated a rejectionist party, were even more likely to breed working-class variations of already existing ideologies. Marxism lost all ways.

The second theme to be examined is how the associational life of the British working class stood in relation to a rejectionist political ideology. It could be supposed—certainly on the German model—that the success of a party based upon such an ideology almost demanded a working class without an already established associational culture, one whose organizing energies—political energies in the broadest sense—could be utilised and directed by the party. This condition did not exist in Britain.

The first reason for this is the rural origin of so many working-class pastimes. Most sports, things to do with sports, religious affiliations, and many hobbies were simply late nineteenth-century souvenirs of country life. Memories of a rural past had material significance even for a working class increasingly taught to believe that the country was alien and almost comic.[40] Rural reminders were embodied in the physique of the towns: millions of cottages

---

[39] C. F. G. Masterman, *The Condition of England* (London, 1909), 128–9.

[40] Margaret Phillips, *The Young Industrial Worker: A Study of his Educational Needs* (London, 1922), 24.

in thousands of villages. Only in Scotland and in parts of London and Liverpool were the working classes herded continental-style into flats and they, in turn, created the closest Britain has come to a proletariat. Arguably, these souvenirs helped to familiarize a newish working class with industry, provide a comforting associational structure for urban life and diminish that catastrophic alienation which overtook much of an ex-peasant work-force on the Continent. The second reason is rising real wages. In his study of the United States Sombart argued that high real wages in themselves partly accounted for the absence of socialism in America.[41] As a general rule, this seems doubtful. At a certain wage-level socialism presumably becomes unattractive, but it would be a crude sociology that put much weight on wage-levels as such. For one thing, the governing wage-rates in pre-1914 Britain had nowhere near reached a point where socialism must become unattractive; for another, wage-rates as absolute factors acquire significance only as tokens of rights or comparative status. Rising real wages in themselves do not eliminate a sense of injustice; if they do it is only when circumstances deny men the power of comparison. In one area, however, they are pertinent. British wages did permit more or less everything that made up late nineteenth-century working-class pastimes: the development of organized hobbies, mass sport, popular betting, a modest domesticity, and the commercialization of much working-class entertainment. They gave the working classes a certain autonomy, an opportunity to choose between alternative activities not available to any other European work-force; and the choice was at least partly their own. The result was that any working-class party had to compete with an existing working-class culture which was stable and relatively sophisticated. For this wage-rates were partly responsible.

What was the political function of the associational culture? Gareth Stedman Jones has trenchantly argued that it was regressive. He suggests that the radical artisanal culture of mid-nineteenth-century London had degenerated by the end of the century into an inward-looking, apolitical culture, preoccupied by sport, betting, the music-hall, etc. Above all, he concludes, it ceased to be a work-centred culture.[42] This thesis is questionable in several ways: London is not Britain; it is unlikely that its radical

[41] Sombart, 105–6.   [42] Stedman Jones, 484–6.

artisans were any more characteristic of a political culture than autodidact socialists were fifty years later or any other self-selecting group that leaves its impress on history; it is doubtful if the British working class as a whole did cease to be work-centred. I have argued that the occupational life of the British workman did not much decline and that, in so far as it did, there were compensations within the workplace.[43] Furthermore, work was often the focus of those innumerable clubs and hobbies (including sport) that were as characteristic of the working class as the boozy jingoes who staggered off to the music-hall. There were, in fact, two kinds of alternatives to political action, a passive one (which Stedman Jones isolates and treats rather pejoratively) and an active one which bred dogs and pigeons, grew flowers, raised canaries, founded angling clubs and cycling societies, put the factory or local football team together (or seized it from the possession of middle-class patrons), preached in church/chapel, attended Pleasant Sunday Afternoons, or forgot what it learned at the fourth standard but amazed the middle classes by its knowledge of football, racing, or even cricket (a sport few urban working men actually played before 1914).

Religious activities performed the same kind of quasi-political associational function. The extent to which the early leadership of the Labour Party was specifically Christian is well known, but it is worth stressing how far that inhibited a 'continental' politics in Britain. Ideological incompatibilities were probably less significant than social ones: religious affiliation threw working-class church-goers into the company of the middle classes and encouraged an egalitarian bonhomie. As Dückershoff wrote of Northumberland: 'The middle and the working classes are on very friendly terms. This is because they are brought together in clubs and religious organisations; and then, too, there is the general equality.'[44] What religion gave with one hand it took away with the other. Its structures helped to familiarize the working classes (or some of them) with political behaviour and gave an acceptable—though utterly conventional—ethical force to working-class politics. However, it also gave its practitioners a firm foothold on the status quo. Arthur Henderson, Ben Tillett's famous 'Gospel-Temperance-

[43] See below, pp. 152–7.
[44] E. Dückershoff ('A German Coal Miner'), *How the English Workman Lives* (London, 1899), 55.

Liberal election agent' is a good example.[45] His political career was much assisted by Wesleyanism; from it he learned his rhetoric, his ability to run meetings and his personal and mental stability. However, it also gave him a good place in society and meant that most of his closest friendships were made within the bosom of the chapel. His political colleagues might have been his brothers but they were not his friends.[46]

But it was not apolitical or inert culture. It is true that those who had enough surplus income frequented—and that is clearly the right word—the music-hall and increasingly the cinema. Who, however, was deceiving whom in commercialized entertainment is unclear: working men and women clearly enjoyed it and many found it intellectually stimulating as well.[47] Yet going to the cinema does not eliminate other activities: a comparatively rich associational culture simply scattered and localized political ambitions. Men could wish to be elected either to a trades council or secretary of a pigeon-breeding society: one had to be comparatively unusual to do both. Which a man chose was as much a matter of temperament as anything else; the required qualities did not differ, although the ambitions in some cases did. The fact that politically ambitious individuals were often suspect and sometimes disliked (understandably in certain instances[48]) perhaps further depreciated party-political action while making alternatives more attractive. Stedman Jones is clearly right that strictly political activities occupied only a small part of working-class life, but it was a life in the broadest sense political—the *same kind* of people who founded pigeon-breeding societies also founded the Labour Party, and, though certainly unusual, it was possible for the same person to do both: Arthur Henderson was (indirectly) a founder of Newcastle United, a prominent figure in lawn bowls, one of the country's leading lay Methodists, as well as the chief organizer of the Labour Party;[49] Will Thorne, MP for West Ham (South), was, at least as a younger man, an active boxer (proud nephew of the Birmingham professional 'Mouse' Wilson), athlete, and cyclist for

---

[45] B. Tillett, *Is the Parliamentary Labour Party a Failure?* (London, 1908), 8.
[46] See below, pp. 42–65.
[47] For an assessment, see A. Freeman, *Boy Life and Labour* (London, 1914), 133–9; C. E. B. Russell and E. T. Campagnac, 'Poor People's Music-Halls in Lancashire', *Economic Review*, 10 (July 1900), 306–7.
[48] Stuart Macintyre, *A Proletarian Science: Marxism in Britain, 1917–1933* (Cambridge, 1980), 205–8.   [49] See below, pp. 42–65.

whom party politics was something of an anticlimax; W. J. Davis of the Brassworkers, one-time chairman of the parliamentary committee of the TUC, was not only its historian but also the country's leading authority on nineteenth-century token coinage. For most, however, 'political' energies were dispersed amongst a profusion of associational activities which might be party politics but, as a rule, were not. Working-class associations were thus not merely complementary to party-political action: they were competitive with it. They were also competitive in another sense. Working men were relatively successful in expelling the middle classes from working-class leisure life, against feeble middle-class attempts to resist;[50] there was, for example, nothing before 1914 like the Business House Sports movement of the 1930s, a real attempt at incorporation.[51] This diminished the allure of a political movement which tried to emphasize, as the SDF did, the necessary moral and political isolation of the proletariat. It is partly for these reasons that a 'socialist culture' could not be created in Britain as the SPD was supposed to have created one in Germany.[52] Furthermore, some of those Labour leaders who were the strongest actual proponents of such a culture (or, at least, some elements of it) were those whose own associational lives were least likely to produce it. It is hard to imagine a continental equivalent of Arthur Henderson, not even among the revisionists, yet he was more committed to the 'purity' of working-class politics than most.

The constraints upon the development of a Marxist or quasi-Marxist party which have been examined so far have been primarily structural and only indirectly ideological. Yet the most powerful constraint upon any political party, the most salient determinant of its character and success, is the formal ideological environment in which it grows. We might agree that the British work-force was large but scattered and the pattern of industry ensured reasonably close and easy-going class relations. Yet an important, if comparatively small, part of the work-force was not

[50] P. Bailey, *Leisure and Class in Victorian England* (London, 1978), *passim*, esp. 169–82.

[51] This was a movement—embodied in the National Council of Sport in Industry and Commerce—to encourage loyalty to the firm by the lavish provision of sporting and recreational facilities. It was particularly strong in the 'new' industries of the South and the West Midlands. For the character of the Council, see its journal *Sport in Industry* (1938–9).

[52] On this see P. Nettl, 'The German Social Democratic Party 1890–1914 as a Political Model', *Past and Present*, 30 (April 1965).

so scattered and the conditions in which it worked by no means facilitated 'mateyness' between masters and men. Structurally, there seems no reason why it should not have been more attracted to a rejectionist ideology. In practice, however, all members of a society inherit assumptions and attitudes with which they live and which they modify only in part. The past, however it reaches us, shapes our present actions, and as individuals or as groups we can merely struggle to reformulate our own histories: as Marx admitted, the past 'weighs like a nightmare on the brain of the living', and it weighed no less heavily on the 'brain' of the British working class. It inherited traditions which both burdened and liberated it, an ambiguous set of social values which it shared with other classes and which gave legitimacy to institutions and sentiments whose ideological power precluded a revolutionary rhetoric or strategy.

The stability of British society was due, Bagehot thought, to the deferential nature of its people. Deference was procured by dazzle. They

defer to what we may call the *theatrical show* of society. A certain state passes before them; a certain pomp of great men; a certain spectacle of beautiful women; a wonderful scene of wealth and enjoyment is displayed, and they are coerced by it . . . The climax of the play is the Queen: nobody supposes that their house is like the court.[53]

Much suggests that Bagehot was right. Crown and, as well, parliament possessed an ideological hegemony which, if anything, increased throughout the century. The acceptability of both to the working class underwrote the existing status-order and preserved the country's institutions and class-system more or less intact. But in 'deferring' to an inherited status-order how much did the working class extract in return? It was not a question that Bagehot posed directly but which is, nonetheless, inescapable.

The extent to which the working class was attached to the monarchy is surprising but not inexplicable. The monarchy was widely disliked before 1837 and Queen Victoria's widowed seclusion after 1861 contributed to the republicanism fashionable among radicals in the early 1870s. But in her later years, she combined regular and much reported attention to public duties with dignified (and quite subtly advertised) domesticity. There can

[53] W. Bagehot, *The English Constitution* (Fontana edn.; London, 1963), 248.

be no doubt that the Crown was able to mobilize an extraordinarily powerful common sentiment for which it is difficult to find an analogy elsewhere. Why should the working classes have shared this sentiment? One answer—that they were taught to—seems invalid. They were not taught to, at least not in the same way as (say) Germans and Russians were 'taught' to respect their emperors. Furthermore, in those countries where crown-worship was most frantic the crowned head usually came to a sticky end—which suggests that conditioning alone will not be effective. Another answer—that the monarchy came to embody 'certain fundamental moral standards' and 'the sacredness of communal life and institutions'—has been given by Edward Shils and Michael Young.[54] Yet this, as Steven Lukes argues, is distinctly crude Durkheimery, presenting 'an excessively simple answer' to an exceedingly complicated problem.[55] (What are the fundamental moral values? How do we know that society is agreed upon them? Why should the monarchy embody them?) Some of the Shils–Young argument is probably true but most of it is truistic, and undemonstrable. One explanation is that the withdrawal of the Crown from overt political life was largely complete by the end of the nineteenth century; its role thereafter was increasingly of a high ceremonial character which was emotionally pleasing and politically uncontentious. Equally, however, it can be argued that the monarchy simply exchanged one overt political role for another. Whereas at the beginning of the century the Crown was an active agent in ordinary political life, necessarily partisan and thus often unpopular, by the end it had apparently become the even-handed guarantor of the class-neutrality of Parliament, the institution which ensured that the rules of the game would be followed. This was acceptable to all classes: to the politically strong because the Crown undoubtedly represented a conservative force; to the politically weak because they, more than any, had an interest in seeing that the rules *were* followed. How far this new role was cultivated and how far allocated by circumstances is a matter of judgement: the private views of individual monarchs continued to be partisan and largely predictable, though (usually) private. In any case, the Crown assumed that was its role; after the

[54] E. Shils and M. Young, 'The Meaning of the Coronation', *Sociological Review*, 1 (1953), 80.
[55] S. Lukes, *Essays in Social Theory* (London, 1977), 62–4.

1923 elections and on the eve of the formation of the first Labour government the King's private secretary, Lord Stamfordham, wrote that the King 'will be interpreting the general feeling of the country, that, true to British ideas, the Government, whoever they should be, should have a fair chance'.[56] Even the private language of the Crown had, therefore, become engrossed by the stylized vocabulary of 'fairness'.

Either way the change of political role was effected with success. Keir Hardie's attacks on the monarchy did him no good at Mid-Lanark in 1888,[57] and his later criticisms of it were not particularly popular. More embarrassingly representative were the views of Will Crooks. Speaking in South London as Edward VII lay dying, he invited his listeners to begin the evening by singing 'God Save the King', and continued:

I am one of those men who perhaps know rather more intimately than the majority of men something about the King. I feel, and I know, at the bottom of my heart that he is the greatest statesman that the world possesses at this moment . . . You may say, What makes you care for him more than for other men? . . . The King is above men, he is above Party; in fact, he is a father to the lot of us, and smiles down upon us all.[58]

One measure of this successful change was the readiness with which imperial honours were accepted by the working class. While it is true that there were many in the Labour movement deeply hostile to baubles as, indeed, to the rituals of parliament, they were, in practice, a minority.[59] From the moment David Shackleton was knighted (1917),[60] the path to honours was broad and rosy: knighthoods, garter knighthoods, baronies, viscountcies, earldoms (two, Attlee and A. V. Alexander), an infinity of lesser awards. The willingness to dispose and to receive certainly suggest a highly integrated working class, as it was in some senses (although not, as I shall argue, in all).[61] The acceptance of honours, however, did not necessarily imply an abandonment of class; for most of the

[56] H. Nicolson, *King George V* (London, 1952), 384.

[57] K. O. Morgan, *Keir Hardie* (London, 1975), 29.

[58] G. Haw, *The Life Story of Will Crooks M.P.* (London, 1917), 301–2.

[59] Aneurin Bevan was one, at first; see M. Foot, *Aneurin Bevan*, i (London, 1962), 104. Dislike of peerages could have a vestigial Radical character. Henderson refused one in 1931 and MacDonald himself declined one after his defeat in 1935.

[60] It is, of course, true that Shackleton was by then no longer an MP but permanent secretary of the new Ministry of Labour.

[61] See below, pp. 26–32.

recipients no class was involved: they were a class-neutral representation of the idea of the nation. Elsewhere in the British diaspora this was not so. Where the neutrality of the Crown was suspect, as it was, for example, in Australia, the honours system was far more suspect. Acceptance of a knighthood by an active member of the Australian Labour Party normally meant immediate expulsion.

If the legitimacy the monarchy gave the existing social system was quasi-hieratic it was parliament which clothed it with a functional one. While there was in the early part of the nineteenth century some talk of alternatives to parliament, there is surprisingly little evidence that such alternatives were seriously considered.[62] On the contrary, it was the manner by which parliament was elected which was at issue. By the end of the nineteenth century few doubted that a representative parliament was the proper focus of working-class aspirations. Thus a 'reformed' parliament had the same resonance in the ninetenth century as a 'free' parliament had in the seventeenth. The nineteenth century re-established the hegemony of parliament by rewriting and vulgarizing its history in a Whiggish-democratic direction, by enthroning the doctrine of representation of people instead of interests and by elaborately formalizing its procedures on the basis of strict fairness. Despite residual suspicions and the fears of many that working-class MPs would be lost to their class, only the most sectarian working man denied that parliament was the repository of the liberties of the people. Thus Jack Lawson, a miner and Labour MP for Chester-le-Street, could write of the Speaker of the House of Commons:

Elected by Members, with time-tested, keenly-scrutinised qualities, Mr. Speaker, whoever he be by name, embodies the hardly won liberties of the people—even to the executing of a king; he asserts the prerogatives and privileges of the Commons, is the champion of the Opposition and the minorities, the guide of debates and the whole work of Parliament.[63]

There is in this description both an ideological and a calculating element: it embodies the supremacy of parliament and the rules of the game as an ideological value, parliament as it would like to see itself, as well as the real helpfulness of parliament to people who were all too likely to find themselves in opposition and in a

---

[62] T. M. Parsinnen, 'Association, Convention and Anti-Parliament in British Radical Politics, 1771–1848', *English Historical Review*, 88 (1973).

[63] J. Lawson, *A Man's Life* (London, 1932), 145.

minority. This calculation should not be dismissed: it is easy to see why such a clearly rule-governed body should be attractive to a politically inexperienced and defensive class operating within a society whose political institutions were largely made by others. Thus parliament preserved its hegemony.

The place of parliament in the public mind was endlessly reinforced by the ceremony of elections and by the rapid growth of the so-called 'local parliaments' which familiarized young men of the lower middle and working classes with parliamentary manners. While the franchise was a political asset objectively worth possessing, elections themselves were crucial to the official ideology of Britain; they enhanced social stability and were a ritualized confirmation of a received form of political life. As Lukes has written:

Participation in elections can plausibly be interpreted as the symbolic affirmation of the voters' acceptance of the political system and their role within it. The ritual of voting draws their attention to a particular model of 'politics', of the nature of political conflict and the possibilities of political change. Moreover, it both results from and reinforces the belief, in which there is normally little truth, that elections give them an influence over government policy.[64]

He probably underestimates the influence of individual voters as members of a class, but the general proposition must surely be right. The demand for the vote, the emphasis upon the instrumentality of enfranchisement, made it difficult to conceive of any other form of political action as legitimate, or, indeed, of any other form of political action. The obvious alternative, the 'political' strike, though certainly talked about, was for the great majority simply 'unconstitutional' and therefore illegitimate.

Voting and elections gained even more ideological acceptability when, like parliament, they became assimilated to the rules of the game. Elections had always been exciting and, if contested, recognizably part of the great British sporting tradition. The (partial) elimination of corruption from parliamentary elections accompanied the (partial) elimination of corruption from sport, and sport and elections remained consciously linked activities: thus the introduction into political discourse of metaphors borrowed from sport, a passion common to all classes—'fair play'

[64] Lukes, 72.

(appropriated by most European languages), 'below the belt', 'not cricket', 'Queensberry Rules', etc.—made a breach of the rules additionally unthinkable.[65] While the assimilation of politics to sport was doubtless in part the consequence simply of the way of life of the politically predominant classes, it was also actively encouraged by them. It was typical that Baldwin should have resigned in 1929, although the elections gave no party a majority, on the ground that it would have been 'unsporting' not to have done so.[66] The effect of this was twofold: by emphasizing the play-element in politics and the rules of the game the sphere of political action was severely circumscribed; anything outside the rules was necessarily unlawful. The fact that the rules were (on the whole) strictly followed made the need to contemplate alternatives even less pressing. The popularity of the local parliaments had much the same result. Inspired originally by the Oxford Union, they meticulously followed parliamentary procedure and their debates were often reported in the local papers. Their role in legitimating parliament can hardly be overrated; it was in the St Pancras parliament, for example, that the young Ramsay MacDonald learned his Erskine May: 'Now below the gangway, now above it, sometimes he consults the Speaker and gets behind the chair, then he is in close "confab" with the Clerk of the House; again he consults the leader of the Opposition.'[67] John Hodge, elected Labour MP for Gorton in 1906, recorded that his experience 'as the Speaker of a Parliament Debating Society' made him

very well acquainted with the forms and procedures of the House. That experience I found exceedingly useful in these early days, with the result that I made no false step so far as the forms and ceremonies to be observed were concerned, although many of the new Members from all Parties in the House were continuously falling into errors of form and custom which created great hilarity amongst the old hands.[68]

These societies not only habituated future working-class leaders to parliamentary decorum, they threw them in with the politically ambitious from the lower middle classes—and sometimes even

[65] For a discussion of this, see P. M. McIntosh, 'The British Attitude to Sport', in A. Natan (ed.), *Sport and Society* (London, 1958), 21.
[66] Nicolson, 435.
[67] D. Marquand, *Ramsay MacDonald* (London, 1977), 23.
[68] J. Hodge, *Workman's Cottage to Windsor Castle* (1931), 152.

more: Ostrogorski claimed to have seen in a West End parliament a morganatic cousin of the Queen holding the office of first lord of the admiralty.[69] While the parliaments encouraged working men to think about politics and gave them experience in public speaking they did so in a highly stylized and derivative way. Ostrogorski thought the 'conventional character' of the parliaments 'weighs heavily' on them:

it lessens their value as instruments of *political education*, by accustoming their members to *play a part*, to strike an attitude for the gallery. And what makes things worse is that they have not even got to create their parts; for the pieces which they act are exactly the same as those performed on the great national stage of the House of Commons, and they simply copy the actors on that stage and imitate their gestures, their tones, making them more emphatic if possible.[70]

The extent to which the working classes lost their autonomy in these institutions should not be exaggerated; like so many associations of this kind they were often successfully colonized by them, but the behaviour they were taught undoubtedly came from the heart of the ruling class.

Crown and parliament, dazzle and fairness: to these T. H. Marshall added a third 'familiar instrument of modern democracy'— 'patriotic nationalism'.[71] How far did a sense of nationality act as a socializing agent upon the working class? Common sense would suggest that it did but the evidence *that* it did is thin, or thinnish. It is questionble how far the Empire mattered to the working classes—though the areas of white emigration probably did—and attitudes to its imperial wars were distinctly ambiguous.[72] Alfred Williams was genuinely distressed at how little adolescent boys at the GWR works at Swindon knew or cared about the Empire.[73] The state made little attempt to teach people to be British as (say) the Third Republic tried to turn out little Republicans. It is exceptionally difficult to do for British textbooks what Dominique

---

[69] M. Ostrogorski, *Democracy and the Organization of Political Parties* (London, 1902), i. 417.

[70] Ibid., 417. For a closer study, see B. Jerrold, 'The Manufacture of Public Opinion', *Nineteenth Century* (June 1883), 1085–92.

[71] T. H. Marshall, *Citizenship and Social Class* (Cambridge, 1950), 41.

[72] This is Richard Price's qualified conclusion; R. Price, *An Imperial War and the British Working Class* (London, 1972), *passim.*   [73] Williams, 157.

Maingueneau has done for French precisely because they were probably written with little except primitive instruction in mind.[74] But of course this might have been so because no one felt the need to inculcate a sense of nationality, that nationality was simply a casual assumption of everyday life. It is hard to escape the conclusion that a sense of being British was widely and positively felt in the working classes—and that was partly why imperial honours were acceptable to them.[75] Margaret Loane thought they were not particularly xenophobic, but that their knowledge of being British implied attitudes to the outside world, sometimes of contempt, usually of indifference. These attitudes, she thought, they undoubtedly shared with all other classes.[76] The working classes were everywhere *en fête* for Victoria's jubilees and the sovereign was the excuse for open self-satisfaction at being British and not foreign.[77] The degree to which people felt themselves part of a wider nationality presumably varied but it is difficult to deny that most were at least partly sensitive to it—and the stereotypes of other nationalities were fully fledged in the popular culture.[78] 'Nationalism', unlikely in any case to be much shared by the Scots or the Welsh, was feeble; an awareness of a common British ancestry was rather strong. Furthermore, all classes drew upon and appealed to the same stock of vulgarized catchphrases: 'an Englishman's home is his castle', 'British justice', 'rights of a free-born Englishman', etc. These had not only a highly individualist political implication but, as well, a strong national sensation of shared rights born of a unique history.

We can, therefore, establish a working class which was highly dispersed by occupation, having (appearances notwithstanding) a fairly low level of communitarian solidarity, following a number of competing associational activities and highly conditioned by inherited ideologies which emphasized a common citizenship, the fairness of the rules of the game and the class-neutrality of the major institutions of the state. These ideologies were themselves legitimated by an overwhelming public ceremonial (at all levels of

[74] D. Maingueneau, *Les Livres d'école de la Troisième République* (Paris, 1979), 47–73, 99–101.
[75] See above, p. 19.
[76] M. E. Loane, *An Englishman's Castle* (London, 1909), 33–4.
[77] See e.g. Roberts, 92–3, 182.
[78] F. Zweig, *The British Worker* (Harmondsworth, 1952), 53.

political life and in which the working classes freely participated[79]) which actually became more formal and elaborate at the end of the century than it had ever been. It was, consequently, perfectly possible for the working class to draw a distinction between the 'interests of labour', which might be aggressively pursued, and a received idea of the nation which could be accepted more or less uncritically. James Mawdsley, for example, was very obviously a representative of labour on the 1891 Royal Commission on Labour; yet he was not just a Tory but a Conservative parliamentary candidate.[80] He was, in addition, as a commissioner almost always in agreement with other representatives of 'labour' (who were in their own politics either Liberal or 'Labour') and with the future Liberal president of the board of trade, A. J. Mundella (an employer). On what was already becoming the central question of the day there was not a pin to put between them: they differed only in the general way they looked at the world. How successfully this state system reproduced itself is strikingly illustrated in a justly famous passage from J. R. Clynes's memoirs. Remembering the audience with the King in 1924 when MacDonald was sworn in as prime minister, he wrote:

As we stood waiting for His Majesty, amid the gold and crimson magnificence of the Palace, I could not help marvelling at the strange turn of Fortune's wheel, which had brought MacDonald the starvelling [*sic*] clerk, Thomas the engine-driver, Henderson the foundry-labourer, and Clynes the mill-hand, to this pinnacle behind the man whose forebears had been Kings for so many splendid generations. We were making history . . .

The King first created MacDonald a Privy Councillor, and then spoke to us for some time. He gave us invaluable guidance from his deep experience, to help us in the difficult time before us, when we should become his principal Ministers. I had expected to find him unbending; instead he was kindness and sympathy itself. Before he gave us leave to

[79] There is little evidence, for instance, of Labour councillors dispensing with mayoral chains of office or gowns: Henderson's 1903 electoral address at Barnard Castle was headed by an illustration of him in full-fig as mayor of Darlington. There were, of course, certain other lines that were crossed only with difficulty. No Labour ministers wore court-dress after the experience of the first Labour government.

[80] At Oldham in July 1899, where he stood in a double by-election in tandem with Winston Churchill. Both lost. For a 'Marxist' view of Mawdsley, see Engels to G. V. Plekhanov, 21 May 1894, in *Karl Marx and Frederick Engels on Britain* (Moscow, 1953), 536–7.

go, he made an appeal to us that I have never forgotten: 'The immediate future of my people, and their whole happiness, is in your hands, gentlemen. They depend upon your prudence and sagacity.'[81]

And Clynes, though undoubtedly a 'moderate', was an old member of the ILP and by no means a deferential working man.

Prima facie, therefore, a modified form of Bagehot's analysis seems right. The combination of pomp and fairness might alone explain the failure of Marxism (or any other form of rejectionism) to mobilize a mass following. This ideological pattern by itself almost entirely distinguished Britain from most of the continental countries: while their political systems were theatrical enough, they were also plainly arbitrary and 'unfair'. But Bagehot provides only half an answer. His view, or one associated with it, suggests a passive working class and concentrates exclusively on its socialization. Yet it gives no explanation for the behaviour of the political preponderant classes—why, for example, admit fairness and not use coercion?—nor any account of the results of their behaviour. But it is entirely arguable that the traditions, catch-phrases, and ideological fragments that shaped working-class politics also helped to shape the politics of all other social classes. It is further arguable that the freedom of the middle and upper classes to *choose* one political strategy as against another was thereby limited by these historical imperatives, while, equally, the ability of the working classes to modify the social and economic relationships they inherited was proportionately enlarged.

In the first place, if a system acquires its legitimacy partly by the strictness with which the rules are applied, the rules must be binding on both sides. Even before parliament was opened to the working classes a more or less punctilious adherence to its forms was observed. At the same time as the 'political' classes succeeded in confining the working class to institutions they devised, they necessarily eliminated a number of political possibilities that might otherwise have been open to them. They could now no more breach the rules of the game than anyone else. As Engels noted in the celebrated Introduction to the 1895 edition of *The Class Struggles in France*, once the ruling classes had placed politics on the basis of contract, coercion became both rhetorically indefensible

[81] J. R. Clynes, *Memoirs* (London, 1937), i. 343–4. See Rothstein's comments on this attitude to monarchy: T. Rothstein, *From Chartism to Labourism* (London, 1929), 293.

and politically risky.[82] The problem of this apparently universal truth is that it was true of Britain alone. In the second place, the acceptability to all classes of these vulgarized ideological precepts— 'free-born Englishman', etc.—gave an almost irresistible attractiveness to the stereotype of the upstanding and no-nonsense British working man. It was admissible even to the chief actor in Bagehot's theatrical show. In a homiletic letter to her daughter, the crown princess of Prussia, Queen Victoria lamented the milieu in which the future Kaiser was being raised ('your position in Prussia, living always in a Palace with the ideas of immense position of Kings and Princes etc.') and added:

The Germans must be very different from the English [working classes] and above all from the Scotch . . . But I fear they are, from what dear Papa often said, and the English even are in that respect, especially in the South—for in the North they possess a good deal of that great independence of character, determination, coupled with real high noble feelings, which will not brook being treated with haughtiness. The Germans have less of this.[83]

Whether the British working man actually possessed that 'great independence of character' is hardly relevant: that he was believed to, and that it was desirable that he should, is so. Assertions of that independence—trade unions, strikes, a wish to be elected to parliament, no 'kow-towing' to management—all the features, in short, of a bloody-minded and ill-disciplined work-force thus became as legitimate as the political assertions of any other class and as difficult to deny.

Once this stereotype of the British working man had been absorbed into the larger stereotype of the nation, the state was more or less compelled to withdraw from the sphere of industrial relations. Any attempt to give the market generally or bargaining in particular a legal or punitive framework infringed the understood basis of the state's stability: such a framework would have required the recasting not simply of employer–employee relationships but of the idea of the nation itself. While the state succeeded in defining and narrowing the conventions of the class struggle, it became increasingly sensitive to charges of class inequality even in

[82] F. Engels, Introduction to K. Marx, *The Class Struggles in France 1848 to 1850* (Moscow, 1952;, 41.

[83] Queen Victoria to the Crown Princess of Prussia, 11 Feb. 1871, in F. Ponsonby (ed.), *Letters of the Empress Frederick* (London, 1928), 123.

areas, the enforcement of compulsory education, for example, where it was determined to act and where it had significant working-class support. It was reluctant to interfere in the pleasures of the people and was usually driven to it (as in the case of gambling) only when there was pressure from *all* classes to do so.[84] And if the pressure became intolerable the inevitable royal commissions or select committees could be so rigged that every interest gained equal representation and no recommendation which impelled the state to partisan action could be agreed.[85] Indeed, the rituals of the great royal commissions imitated the rule-governed institutions from which most of their members were drawn and almost certainly reinforced the hegemony of parliament and the rules of the game. By 1875 the necessary withdrawal of the state from bargaining was generally complete. The British unions were given a freedom of action unique in Europe and (as far as I know) in the world, unencumbered by law or opinion. In part, Disraeli's 1875 legislation (actually, legislation drafted by the preceding Gladstone ministry) was simply an element in that corporate pluralism which was characteristic of the Liberal state; but the legislation not so much endowed the unions with rights as extended to them an almost archaic corporate immunity. The unions claimed and received the kind of associational privilege previously allowed to many upper- and middle-class institutions, such as Oxford and Cambridge colleges, West End clubs, and army messes. Whereas these self-governing bodies, however, ruled themselves within a clear legal framework, the unions notoriously operated within no framework at all. There was no other way the state could guarantee fairness in that area where the working classes were determined that fairness should prevail: any law was worse than no law.[86] Civil society thus promoted its own stability by subverting the coercive powers of employers. As Ernst Dückershoff noted:

[84] See below, p. 135.

[85] All Victorian royal commissions to some extent confirm the point, but it is best made by the chaotic report of the Royal Commission on the Depression of Trade and Industry, with its nightmare of amendments, dissents, and dissents to dissents. The commission, appointed by Salisbury's minority 1885 government, would, in the hopes and fears of many, reopen the fiscal question. The commission, as its personnel made entirely predictable, came to no conclusion, either on the fiscal question or the depression.

[86] I am grateful to Dr Mark Curthoys here for permission to read his unpublished paper, 'Under Sufferance: Trade Unions and the Law, 1846–1866'.

The attitude adopted in England is what is right for one side is justifiable for the other side. *Politics are not in question.* There are only two sides in a strike—the strikers and their employers. Such hatred and mutual rage as in Germany is not to be met with. The capitalist employs the same means as there, but he is not backed up in the same way by the authorities.[87]

Dückershoff is here adopting the definition of politics which the ideology and apparatus of the British state was designed to confirm: the exclusion of the market from 'politics', and a 'politics' that permitted a viable class-neutral state. 'Politics' might be religion, the Empire, home rule, about which working men could and did differ amongst themselves, as other classes differed amongst themselves. It did not embrace relations of labour and capital since that would engage one *class* against another, and even on a prudent calculation the risks were too great. In 1875 Alfred Marshall thought that a 'combination of capitalists' could still 'conquer' the unions but concluded that 'it is doubtful if it could do so without introducing social anarchy'.[88] It is unlikely that the capitalists would have had the goodwill of the state in such an enterprise.

In practice, although the hand of employers was unquestionably weakened by a neutral state, they complied with and to some extent welcomed its neutrality. As late as 1951 Zweig was disconcerted to discover how reluctant employers were to criticize the unions, even in private.[89] But this reluctance long pre-dated 1951. The Count of Paris, writing in 1869, thought that the 'peace treaty' signed between masters and men in that decade represented the liberation of the market from (more or less) all restraints; that, indeed, it restabilized society—'cette liberté, en effet, est la sanction de toutes les autres'.[90] Employers had plenty of opportunities before the 1891 Royal Commission on Labour to air grievances and a number did. Some professed themselves helpless before the unions and shed crocodile tears; but many asserted the positive value of unions and were reluctant to contemplate a change in the law, a reluctance shared by the commissioners.[91] To

[87] Dückershoff, *English Workman*, 25. Italics mine.
[88] Quoted in J. K. Whitaker (ed.), *The Early Economic Writings of Alfred Marshall* (London, 1975), ii. 351.
[89] F. Zweig, *Productivity and Trade Unions* (Oxford, 1951), 9.
[90] Louis-Philippe d'Orléans, Comte de Paris, *Les Associations Ouvrières en Angleterre (Trades-Unions)* (Paris, 1869), 308–16.
[91] See, for example, the evidence of J. P. White, Royal Commission on Labour, *Minutes of Evidence*, PP (1892), xxxiv. QQ 7608–15.

Shadwell, attitudes to unions marked off British employers from all others:

Nothing has struck me more in the course of this investigation than the remarkable difference in attitude towards trade unions displayed, in private, by employers in this country and in the others. I have not heard a single word in favour of trade unions from any employer in Germany or America . . . employers [there] hate and dread the unions. In England I have met no such feeling at all. I have heard the unions unfavourably criticised and sometimes condemned, but without bitterness; I have far more often heard from employers and managers fair and even friendly expressions of opinion.

One 'great captain of industry' told him that union leaders were 'very nice', better still 'sensible men'.[92] Shadwell wrote just after the height of the employers' counter-offensive, of which he was well aware, and his comments nicely demonstrate why it was so feeble. The engineers' lock-out (1897–8) was the employers' only major victory (and that not complete),[93] while the series of decisions culminating in Taff Vale did not, in fact, follow or even suggest an all-out attack on the American model. Employers' strategies were as inhibited by their fear of bringing 'politics' into industrial relations and by the same received ideological traditions as their purported political representatives. If, for example, one of the most dogmatically individualist of the Charity Organisation Society's ideologues, Helen Bosanquet, could see virtue in the propensity of the British working man to enrol in trade unions and co-ops then, one might say, all was lost.[94] Certainly much was lost. Even if employers had been ready to embark on a war against the unions, their allies were unreliable. They could (as ever) count on part of the judiciary but they were (as ever) deserted by parliament: the House of Lords passed without demur the Trades Disputes Act (1906) at a time when it was wreaking havoc on the rest of the government's programme.[95] The peers, like most others, were anxious to keep the market out of 'politics'. In any

---

[92] A. Shadwell, *Industrial Efficiency* (London, 1906), ii. 330–1.

[93] Clegg *et al.* 165–7; also Dückershoff, 56–7.

[94] H. Bosanquet, *The Strength of the People* (London, 1902), 104–6.

[95] Much to the annoyance of those who were looking for a weapon against the Lords. Bertrand Russell wrote to Elie Halévy: 'I wish the Lords would reject the Trade [*sic*] Disputes Bill; that might give a real chance of getting them abolished, as it would rouse fury. But I fear they have too much sense' (Russell to Halévy, 11 Oct. 1906). I am grateful to Dr Colin Matthew for this quotation.

case, it is unlikely that employers would have wanted such a war even if it had been in their interest to wage one: their 'objective' needs were persistently frustrated by their 'subjective' images of British society.

It is within this context alone that we can understand the centrality of free trade finance to the political economy of the British working classes. It is a truth, not perhaps sufficiently emphasized by historians, that the free trade fiscal system had, before 1914, an ideological value for the working class beyond any conceivable socialist doctrine. While 'socialism' meant little, if anything, to most working men—though that does not mean they were necessarily hostile to it—after 1903 there was hardly one who did not have a 'view' of the fiscal question; and the great majority appear to have been hostile to any modification of free trade.[96] At first sight, this is surprising. Chamberlain, after all, specifically advocated tariff reform as an employment policy: 'Tariff reform means jobs for all.' As a political device it was aimed directly at the working-class electorate.[97] No doubt much working-class opposition to protection was simply material: 'cheap food' was an effective counter at a time of inflationary pressure on real wages. But that alone hardly explains the intensity of the opposition; even the class-harmony of Birmingham was disturbed. W. J. Davis of the Brassworkers, the personification of vertical loyalty, was so outraged at Chamberlain's action that he was only with difficulty dissuaded from standing against him in West Birmingham.[98] The ideological power of free trade lay in its analogy to unfettered collective bargaining; both stood for the same conception of politics. It is true that Peel and Gladstone understood by free trade something other than its later vulgarizers. But their assumption— that it was a self-regulating fiscal mechanism beyond merely contingent politics—was not so different from that of their successors. For them, too, it represented the exclusion of 'economics' from 'politics' but in terms which turned out to be unexpectedly favourable to the working class. Free trade finance increasingly became a technique by which market capitalism was

[96] For this generally, see P. Adams, 'Tariff Reform and Popular Politics, 1903–06', unpublished thesis (Oxford, 1982).
[97] See, for example, Chamberlain's speech at Liverpool, 27 Oct. 1903, in C. W. Boyd (ed.), *Mr. Chamberlain's Speeches* (London, 1914), ii. 199–218.
[98] W. A. Dalley, *The Life Story of W. J. Davis* (London, 1914), 310–11; Adams, 326–8.

justified to working men, to such an extent that the 1905 Liberal government undertook a substantial programme of redistributive legislation in order to shore it up. Like the post-1875 industrial regime, 'free trade' permitted the relative autonomy and propriety of working-class politics and confirmed that no other class could govern against the working class. Tariff reform, however, proposed to reunite the political and economic systems and, despite Chamberlain's personal disavowals, threatened the enforcement of a new social discipline. It was the closest to a continental political strategy Britain had ever reached; its failure meant the failure not only of a policy that would have subordinated the working class under a new fiscal–industrial order but the failure of any working-class ideologies—Marxism, for instance—which also argued that the country's political and economic systems should be reunited.

Bagehot's belief, therefore, that the working classes were induced to defer to a political system dominated by the upper middle classes and manipulated by a combination of theatricality and parliamentary rituals is only partly true. The theatrical element no doubt promoted social stability but largely by divorcing itself from that area of social relations—labour and capital—where there was least value consensus. It is inconceivable, for example, that the British monarchy could have perpetuated itself so successfully if, like the German and the Russian, it had associated itself with the ambitions of an authoritarian state and a determined *patronat*. The British working class clearly liked (and likes) dazzle, but normally on its own terms. Further, such a view seriously underestimated how peaceful a weapon 'fairness' can be in the hands of politically inferior classes. It permitted the working class to exert a political pressure on the state while making it more difficult for employers to enforce an order of production they increasingly felt to be necessary. In both cases a Marxist ideology was undermined: the ideological predominance of crown, parliament, and nationality inhibited the evolution of the idea of an alternative social system while a libertarian pattern of industrial relations obstructed that sense of fear and resentment which was so characteristic of workers' attitudes on the Continent.

A fourth conceivable condition for the emergence of a Marxist party is an active 'socialist' leadership whose own values and way of life are largely outside and hostile to the ruling values of civil society. If that is indeed a necessary condition, then it is possible that the absence of a significant quasi-bourgeois leadership helped to ensure that any working-class party would be grounded not on a universal proletarian consciousness but on working-class sectionalism; and there is an important element in both Marx's and Marxist thinking which has always argued that this would be so. It is certainly the case that there were few in the leadership of the labour movement who stood radically outside the existing class structure or who felt much alienated from it. The Edwardian Labour Party was overwhelmingly working-class in its social origins; it was one of the few European working-class parties where there was an almost exact social identity between its leadership and those likely to support it. Nothing suggests that middle-class influence was important in its rank and file, and the parliamentary party was wholly working-class. Of the fifty-one individuals who sat as official Labour MPs between 1900 and 1914 all were of working-class birth. They were, it is true, different kinds of working men but only three did not begin their lives as industrial labourers: Ramsay MacDonald, a pupil teacher; Philip Snowden, an assistant revenue officer (but the son of a weaver) until he contracted spinal TB; and Frank Goldstone (MP for Sunderland, 1910–18) who was an elementary schoolteacher and sponsored by the National Union of Teachers. No MP had any sort of university education and only MacDonald was born of parents not of the industrial working classes.

Could a different political élite have changed the ideological character of the Labour Party? It is difficult to know how to answer such a question. Notoriously Britain did not have an intelligentsia, and the educational system was not designed to provide one.[99] Anyway, a single variable does not rate as an argument. Nevertheless, the sort of men who were so prominent in European socialist parties—marginal bourgeois, journalists, 'theoreticians', professional orators—were comparatively rare in Britain. In the Parliamentary Labour Party the two who came closest to the type were MacDonald and Snowden. Both were autodidacts;[100] both became journalists and full-time propagandists; both were theoreticians of an eclectic kind—MacDonald was, in Henderson's words, 'the brains of the party'; both were very hostile

[99] For an excellent discussion of this, see T. Nairn, *The Break-Up of Britain* (Verso edn.; London, 1981), 33–8 and *passim*.
[100] For an evocative account of this, see Marquand, *MacDonald*, 21–2.

to the old-fashioned Lib-Lab'ism which, in one form or another, was still the base of working-class politics. The ILP was the obvious home for men like these, and it is not surprising that the ILP was a more energetic proponent of 'independent' Labour politics than men who came from the fairly stable social relationships of which Lib-Lab'ism was a product. But the attitudes of men on the margin are necessarily uncertain. MacDonald and Snowden, for example, spectacularly deserted their class in 1931 when the old Lib-Lab'ism (using the term generically) held firm. It is only a short step from journalism and oratory to middle-class styles of life and from that to a contempt (scarcely concealed in MacDonald's case) for working-class narrowness and stupidity. All Labour leaders and presumably much of the active rank and file were subject to similar pressures. There was always assumed to be a body of culture that people ought to know, and the autodidacts assumed it more than most.[101] This culture was very largely grounded on the classic texts of English literature, and it is surprising the extent to which they were known.[102] Similarly, the periphrasis of much working-class speech was, as Margaret Loane suggested, an attempt to master what was thought to be polite language:[103] the change in status of many a Labour leader can be measured by the transformation of his literary style.[104] To the

[101] Macintyre, 69–75.

[102] A good example of this is provided by the debate on the Labour newspaper the *Daily Citizen* at the 1912 Labour Party conference. This paper was in competition with George Lansbury's quasi-syndicalist *Daily Herald*. In the course of the debate a reference was made to 'two "Richmonds" in the field'. It is clear from the context that speakers understood the allusion—it is to *Richard III*—and knew its source (Labour Party, *Report of the Annual Conference*, 1912, 79–81). It is almost inconceivable that such an allusion would be understood today by any number at a Labour Party conference, or at the conference of any other party or professional organization.

[103] Loane, *From their Point of View*, 82. See also below, pp. 182–3.

[104] During the course of the Barnard Castle by-election (1903) when Arthur Henderson (the Labour Representation Committee candidate) was scarcely known to Ramsay MacDonald, he wrote to MacDonald asking him to speak in the constituency in order 'to give your humble a lift' (Henderson to MacDonald, 25 May 1903, LPLF, LRC 9/181). Henderson would never have used such an arch and uncertain phrase a few years later when his written manner became much more matter-of-fact and professional. In Robert Tressell's *Ragged Trousered Philanthropists*, the socialist hero and Tressell-figure 'Owen' (notoriously) speaks received standard English while his non-socialist workmates communicate in various forms of a debased demotic. It is plain, furthermore, that Tressell regarded such speech as a sign of a political incompetent. Since this is one of the few Leninist tracts in British socialist literature and is so unsympathetic to the working class the

extent that working-class leaders were drawn away from their class it was not just, as Michels argued, via a bureaucratic mobility,[105] nor, as Parkin has recently suggested, through the influence of the company they kept,[106] but as a result of the social and cultural assumptions on which they were raised.[107] In such a milieu, for as many who were attached to a 'bolshevik' strategy and who could have provided a kind of revolutionary vanguard, there was an equal number who simply found working-class politics futile. Either way, a potential *déclassé* leadership was composed of men who were alien to industrial working-class life or were ineluctably leaving it.

Even if all other conditions had been equal, however, it is unlikely that much of the working class would have followed such a revolutionary leadership. The structure of the work-force imposed a representational incoherence on working-class politics which even the most single-minded leadership could probably not have overcome. Furthermore, a specifically 'socialist' leadership was suspect not so much because it was socialist but because it was middle-class. The *ouvrièrisme* of the British working classes

novel's popularity is almost inexplicable. (For this, see A. Swingewood, *The Myth of Mass Culture* (London, 1977), 50–8.) Tom Bell recorded that at Socialist Labour Party education classes the 'student would study *Wage Labour and Capital* at home. At the class we would read it over paragraph by paragraph, round the class. The practice aimed at helping students to speak fluently and grammatically' (quoted Macintyre, 73). The apparently necessary expression of working-class politics through bourgeois forms of speech has, of course, always preoccupied Marxist leaders. See Trotsky's revealing essay, 'The Struggle for Cultured Speech', in L. Trotsky, *Problems of Everyday Life* (New York, 1973), 52–6. The notion of polite speech also caused tension in the Parliamentary Labour Party. Will Thorne's easy-going memoirs abandon their geniality only once—when he records Philip Snowden's criticisms of his 'mispronunciation of the English language' (W. Thorne, *My Life's Battles* (London, 1925), 218–19).

[105] R. Michels, *Political Parties* (New York, 1962), 81–202.
[106] F. Parkin, *Class Inequality and the Social Order* (London, 1972), 130–4.
[107] See J. R. Clynes's account of the purchase of a sixpenny dictionary: 'How I pored over that dictionary! . . . I skipped all the ordinary words. The rest I wrote down and repeated over and over again, syllable by syllable. I worked through the dictionary for months from A to Zymic . . . I have that dictionary to this day; I still look upon it as the foundation-stone of my fortunes' (*Memoirs*, i. 34). Also Jack Lawson: 'My own books—a few dozen. History on one shelf, poetry another; fiction here, classics there. My own books in my own room . . . There is worn, old, brown-leaved Gibbon, four volumes of him; real morocco-backed Shakespeare and the Bible; ragged Tennyson; and Milton and stiff and tough and inviting as his lines. All my own' (Lawson, *A Man's Life*, 79). More generally, see B. Harrison, *Peaceable Kingdom* (Oxford, 1982), 162–5.

(whatever else can be said of it[108]) was an attempt to protect the integrity of working-class life. In many ways introverted and defensive, that life was also characterized by a high degree of associational independence.[109] The late nineteenth-century working class had absorbed numberless organizations founded for their benefit by the bourgeoisie and had then gone on to found numberless more of their own, one of which was the Labour Party. That they were not middle-class was one of their more desirable features. It is easy to see why so many working-class leaders, having freed themselves from direct middle-class tutelage, were reluctant to accept it again in the guise of socialism. They knew that bourgeois often entered working-class politics for reasons of their own and that the life assumptions of middle-class socialists were middle-class. The extreme hostility shown by many trade unionists in 1917–18 to the provision of individual membership of the Labour Party (that is, to the possibility of large-scale middle-class membership) was not simply the last cry of a decaying Lib-Lab'ism but a declaration of the political and cultural competence of the British working man. In the circumstances 'socialism' became either just a vulgarization of or derived from existing 'progressive' doctrines[110]—the ILP—or instrumental to the industrial needs of certain unions, nationalization, for example.[111] A full-blown Marxism was not the only or the least likely victim: syndicalism was another and more likely one. The latter had some popular support and the powerful traditions of the trade unions to exploit, but it disintegrated before the continuing preponderance of parliamentarism and the sectionalism of the working class. Tom Mann's flight to Australia personified its failure. He has no monument in Britain; in Australia he has given his name to the large and splendid headquarters of the Australian engineering workers' union. The working classes had enough in common to hold a working-class party together but not much else. An anodyne ethical socialist rhetoric was thus acceptable because it contained no commitments which might disturb any particular working-class interests.

[108] S. Macintyre, 'Socialism, the Unions and the Labour Party after 1918', *Society for the Study of Labour History, Bulletin*, 31 (Autumn 1975), 101–11.
[109] See above, pp. 12–14.
[110] R. McKibbin, *The Evolution of the Labour Party* (Oxford, 1974), 91–106.
[111] E. Eldon Barry, *Nationalisation in British Politics* (London, 1965), 78–125.

The character of the Labour Party was determined by the structure of the work-force and the ideologies which it inherited. Neither of these favoured the development of a Marxist party. The relations of production, rather than aggregating and collectivizing the work-force as Marx suggested they would, in fact scattered it throughout an industrial and mercantile structure where the collectivized part of the work-force was a small part of the whole. This diminished a sense of likeness in the work-force and the social hostilities that usually accompany aggregation. In smaller industrial units relations between employer and employee, though not informal and by no means necessarily amiable, were often close and frequently easy-going. The political product of that was more likely to be a hybrid Lib-Lab'ism than anything else since Lib-Lab'ism was the perfect representative of a politically independent working class following the rules of the game learned from their social superiors. In other parts of the economy, most obviously in the service sector, communication between working men was often poor or non-existent. At the same time many working men were individualist by occupation or temperament, and such individualism was not, except in one or two places, overridden by an active sense of community. This cultural and vocational diversity was typified and enhanced by the unions. Craft-pride, real and legitimate if exaggerated, was deeply divisive and more than one local Labour Party foundered on disputes between 'skilled' and 'unskilled' unions.[112] The status-consciousness which accompanied craft-pride undermined working-class *esprit de corps* as much as it did that of any other class. Technological changes worked on both. They not only disturbed relations between employer and employee, they threw the working class on the defensive and, by encouraging a general *sauve qui peut* attitude, further disrupted working-class solidarity.[113]

This affected the Labour Party in three ways. First, it meant that the Party found itself as often arbitrating between warring sections of the labour movement as representing them.[114] Second, it frequently led to intractable disagreements within the Labour Party over major policies—the eight-hour day, nationalization, national insurance, compulsory arbitration, an enforceable basic wage, etc. Finally, it ensured that the unions' interest in the Party

[112] McKibbin, 36–7.   [113] For example of this, see Williams, pp. 36–7.
[114] McKibbin, 32–43.

was only intermittent. In the Edwardian period the Party was useful to them but no more than that: in an unregulated system of industrial relations the main business of the unions was direct negotiations with employers. The Labour Party was tied to the unions but they would guarantee it neither continuous support nor obvious direction. Yet the structure of the work-force evidently did not obstruct the growth of *a* working-class party or of unions which enrolled a significant fraction of the work-force. It was probably as effective in keeping men out of working-class politics altogether as in impeding the development of a Marxist party. On balance, associational and ideological impediments to a rejectionist party were almost certainly more powerful ones. The 'leisure' activities of the working classes were a formidable competitor to party politics not because, as so many British politicians alleged, they acted as a narcotic—the evidence for that is very slight[115]— but because they dissolved the proletariat into clubs, societies, informal association, sporting loyalties, and private hobbies and put many working men outside the activities and claims of the official political parties. For some men politics was their hobby but for most it was not. Associational interests did not weaken working-class politics as such nor were they incompatible with them, but they partly ensured that politics would be based upon male group solidarities—and therefore fractious, partial, and self-absorbed.

The second of these two impediments was received ideological tradition. The working classes inherited an ideology of rights which was both permissive and restraining: it increasingly allowed the vigorous pursuit of working-class interests within the economy while confining the working class to ceremonial and conventional institutions whose ideological pre-eminence was based upon fairness and adherence to the rules. To the extent that civil society reproduced itself it was the reproduction in all classes of the ideological predominance of these institutions. The consequence of this was unique to Britain. The substantial exclusion of the market from politics gave the British working class rights and immunities shared nowhere else, while it restrained the employing class from adopting the industrial techniques of its continental counterparts. In the major European states the social discipline of the labour force was assumed to be fundamental to the stability of

[115] See below, pp. 148–58.

the state, and both coercion and incorpation were deployed in an attempt to achieve that. In Britain, on the contrary, it was assumed that such attempts would undermine the stability of the state. In consequence the existing political institutions commanded a near-unanimous support while there were growing differences about the working of the market. We should, of course, not exaggerate these differences: a real free-for-all in the market could hardly have failed to undermine an agreed conception of 'politics'. Furthermore, the structure of the economy localized industrial relations—at least in the nineteenth century—in a way that employers could more or less comfortably live with. But not as comfortably as ideally they would have wished: by adhering to a universally acceptable definition of politics, the upper middle classes preserved the forms of their hegemony while sacrificing much of the substance. Yet it is doubtful if they had much choice. As much as the working classes they had inherited a status-order and ideologies which encouraged the assertion of rights and enfeebled efforts to deny them.[116] The growth of a Marxist party in this country would have required employers to behave in a way that most would and could not do. The result was a highly cohesive but poorly integrated nation; the unchallenged predominance of crown and parliament legitimated both the state and the decaying authority of the industrial upper middle classes.

At the same time there was no environment from which a revolutionary working class could emerge. The territorial codes which governed all British corporate life were extended to it. It was mostly left to its own devices and given many opportunities to subvert the 'free' market. Relations with other classes, although usually good-natured and often intimate in a peculiar way, were also formal and egalitarian. There was little of that dangerously

[116] This subject has been suggestively treated by John Goldthorpe. Drawing on categories derived from T. H. Marshall's notion of 'citizenship', Goldthorpe argues that the class-system in all industrial capitalist societies is underpinned by a status-order largely pre-captitalist in origin but which the market constantly undermines— 'the phenomenon of prestige itself decomposes.' This decomposition, he continues, has gone further in Britain than elsewhere, but only because the British working class is most 'mature'. In many ways a most fruitful analysis, it nevertheless, like Marshall's, exaggerates the universality of this development. Historically, what distinguishes Britain is the comparative ineffectiveness with which this decomposition has been delayed. Historically, other countries were more adept at rendering their work-forces docile. (J. H. Goldthorpe, 'The Current Inflation: Towards a Sociological Account', in F. Hirsch and J. H. Goldthorpe (eds.), *The Political Economy of Inflation* (London, 1978), 197–9.)

volatile paternalism encouraged on the Continent and, given how comparatively ungoverned market relations became, it is doubtful how far much of the work-force can be called deferential. It 'deferred' only within a system of politics whose boundaries largely excluded matters upon which the work-force might not be expected to defer. As an explanatory category, therefore, 'deference' explains very little.

There was thus no overwhelming grievance which could have united the working class against civil society. The leaders of the working class found themselves as restrained as employers: the work-force was no more willing to have its market rights infringed by the leaders of the Labour Party than by anyone else. Those leaders who disliked sectionalism or who took the 'wider view' (as it was called) were repeatedly disappointed. This was recognized at the time. Masterman wrote of the 'English working men' that he is

much more allied in temperament and disposition to some of the occupants of the Conservative back benches, whose life, in its bodily exercises, enjoyment of eating and drinking, and excitement of 'sport', he would undoubtedly pursue with extreme relish if similar opportunities were offered him. Figures like Mr Snowden, with his passionate hunger for reform, like Mr Henderson, with his preaching of religious and ethical ideals in Wesleyan Chapels, like Mr George Barnes or Mr Jowett, with their almost pathetic appeals to rational argument in the belief that reason directs the affairs of the world, are figures in whose disinterested service and devotion to the work of improvement any class might be proud. But in their excellences as in their defects they stand sharply distinct from the excellences and defects of the average English artisan. They care for things he cares nothing for: he cares for things which seem to them trivial and childish.[117]

Furthermore, since the people it could hope to represent did not necessarily stand in a common relationship to society or, except in

[117] Masterman, *Condition of England*, 142–3. See also G. K. Chesterton's Introduction to Haw, *Will Crooks*. Most working men, Chesterton suggested, were 'rather more like the Duke of Devonshire than Keir Hardie'. The austerity and pedantry of Labour MPs 'may remind us of our duties; but it does not remind us of the Walworth Road'. Will Crooks, he continued, was the only Labour member 'who symbolises, or who ever remotely suggests the real labouring men of London' (pp. xv–xvi). Though arguing an important point, Chesterton, like Masterman, probably exaggerates the lack of identity between Labour members and the working classes. In any case, Crooks, though undeniably possessing a touch of the Walworth Road, was deeply hostile to drinking and gambling, two of its principal activities.

a general way, to each other, the leadership of the Labour Party was compelled to attenuate the ideological rigour of its politics almost to vapidity. Two of the prime assumptions of any Marxist party—a rejection by much of the working class of existing social institutions and a belief in the unity of 'economics' and 'politics'— simply did not hold. The Labour Party was not free to choose between Marxism and reformism but only between varieties of reformism.

2

Arthur Henderson as Labour Leader

ARTHUR Henderson[1] was the only member of the industrial working classes to lead a British political party.[2] He was the only trade-unionist to lead the Labour Party, and, as well, one of the only two active Christians to do so. In the history of the Labour Party's first thirty years he seems to have a centrality shared by no other man.[3] But what constitutes his centrality is a genuine problem, and both his contemporaries and his colleagues were aware of it. J. R. Clynes once wrote: 'I would not class Mr Henderson as a type, but as one quite unlike any any other of his colleagues.'[4] In this chapter I would like to test his judgement, to examine both Henderson's 'typicality' as a historical figure in the labour movement and the significance of his career as a labour leader.

Henderson's personality and habits tell us something about the psychological and physical aptitudes he brought to the labour

[1] Arthur Henderson (1863–1935), born in Glasgow, but moved to Newcastle-on-Tyne in 1871. Apprenticed as iron-moulder. Joined the Friendly Society of Ironfounders in 1883, and eventually became a union organizer. Circulation manager of the *Newcastle Evening News*, 1893. Secretary-Agent to Sir John Pease, Liberal MP for Barnard Castle (Durham), 1896. Elected to both Durham and Darlington Councils as a Liberal. Mayor of Darlington, 1903. MP for Barnard Castle (Labour), 1903–18, and MP for Widnes, Newcastle East, Burnley, and Clay Cross, 1918–35. Three times chairman and chief whip of the Parliamentary Labour Party; secretary of the Labour Party, 1911–34; leader of the Labour Party, 1931–2. President of the Board of Education, 1915–16; paymaster-general (labour adviser to the government), 1916; Minister without portfolio in the War Cabinet, 1916–17; led ministerial mission to Russia, 1917, and resigned shortly after his return: Home Secretary, 1924; Foreign Secretary, 1929–31; president of the World Disarmament Conference, 1932–5.

[2] I am thinking here of the leadership of the Labour Party as established after 1922. Before that date the chairmanship rotated, and was important only when Ramsay MacDonald held it, 1911–14.

[3] I have discussed this elsewhere, see R. McKibbin, *The Evolution of the Labour Party* (Oxford, 1974), 124–5.

[4] In an Introduction to Edwin A. Jenkins, *From Foundry to Foreign Office: The Romantic Life-Story of the Rt. Hon. Arthur Henderson* (London, 1933), p. vii.

movement. In appearance and dress he followed fashion scarcely at all, except to trim his moustache during the war. He had a 'clean face, clean collar, clean cuffs, umbrella, and Pleasant-Sunday-Afternoon respectability'.[5] He invariably wore a bowler hat. Compactness, neatness, cleanliness, were inseparably associated with him. Even the psychologist employed by the *Daily Sketch* could not fail to notice it: 'He has a high appreciation of the value of time, is very methodical . . . while he has a perfect horror of strife.'[6] These characteristics led easily to parody or condescension. G. K. Chesterton once suggested that the state could be a 'very small number of men in good black coats, in charge of all the telephones and all the police . . . Mr Arthur Henderson will probably be one of them.'[7] Yet they were the public face of indispensable qualities he later brought to the Labour Party.

They were not, however, the only characteristics that Henderson presented to his movement. He was all his life a leading Wesleyan Methodist and temperance enthusiast. Born to Congregational parents, he was in his adolescence converted to Wesleyanism by the famous evangelist 'Gypsy' (Rodney) Smith—who, in his turn, claimed to have been converted (at the age of eleven) by Sankey.[8] Henderson at no time questioned his faith: twice president of the national council of the Brotherhood Movement, and an energetic lay preacher, he absorbed nearly all of the values of institutional nonconformity at its height and decline. Furthermore, his only (so to speak) intellectual influences were religious ones. In his reply to the questionnaire sent by W. T. Stead to the Labour MPs of the 1906 parliament, Henderson disclosed no formative reading other than the Bible (his 'best book') and the sermons of Wesley, Spurgeon, Talmage, and Hughes.[9] He was by no means the only one in that band of brothers to find his best book his best guide, but the narrowness of his reading was even in this company unusual. It appears from other sources that he had read the

[5] Alex Thompson, *Here I Lie* (London, 1937), 193.
[6] *Daily Sketch*, 16 Aug. 1917.
[7] *Daily Herald*, 22 Mar. 1913.
[8] See H. M. Murray, *Sixty Years an Evangelist* (London, 1935), 82. It is alleged that Henderson publicly attested his conversion at an open-air meeting.
[9] *The Review of Reviews*, 33 (1906), 574. Henderson always acknowledged Spurgeon's influence. Spurgeon was a powerful and compelling evangelist, whose collected sermons alone went through 23 editions. He occupies 9 full pages in the British Library's catalogue of printed books.

American pastor George D. Herron,[10] and, of course, Benjamin Kidd.[11] Spurgeon, Herron, and Kidd: exactly what one would expect from a man whose reading in the 1890s was utilitarian and designed to provide radical sermon-fodder.

Although (presumably) his religious and political lives developed from the same traits of personality and cultural influences, both reinforced each other. His religion cohered with his political ideology, while his missionary activities were easily adapted to the organizational techniques required by a party still very much in its evangelical phase. His styles of speech and writing were clearly manufactured in the pulpit, and, particularly during the war, when 'political' preaching relieved intense emotional pressures, he often used sermons as a way of speaking publicly to current political questions.

The rigid teetotalism was inherent to his religious vocation. In 1910 he told a (doubtless sceptical) audience that he, too, had once drunk and gambled, but that he had abandoned both drink and gambling shortly after conversion.[12] This seems improbable since his conversion was largely of a nominal kind. His family, though not Wesleyan, was pious and chapel, and held conventional chapel views about vice. Henderson took his temperance seriously, and it was the closest he came to 'political' nonconformity. He stayed wherever he could, often at the cost of personal comfort, at temperance hotels, and he was an active member of the United Kingdom Alliance and other temperance organizations. It caused difficulties in his political career; though temperance was acceptable to much of the labour movement, it was unacceptable to another part, and Henderson came dangerously close to being damned as a canter.[13] Furthermore, it was one question upon which he was not prepared to compromise: he could see no sense in transforming capitalism 'to a democracy penalised and paralysed by drink'.[14] Even so it was not until the 1920s that Henderson's

[10] See, for example, A. Henderson, 'Christianity and Democracy', in E. T. Whittaker *et al.*, *Man's Place in Creation, and other lectures delivered in the Central Hall, Manchester* (London, 1905), 28–48.

[11] For the flavour of Herron's writings, see his essay 'Economics and Religion', in *Social Meanings of Religious Experiences* (London, 1897), 49–84. For Kidd, see his 'The Function of Religious Beliefs in the Evolution of Society', in *Social Evolution* (London, 1895), 97–117.

[12] Jenkins, *From Foundry to Foreign Office*, 3.   [13] See below, pp. 48.

[14] Quoted by H. J. Fyrth and H. Collins, *The Foundry Workers* (Manchester, 1959), 124.

adherence to temperance appeared crotchety. In 1928 there was an embarrassing incident when he resigned from the party election committee because the 'drink question' was excluded from the manifesto—and he was only *just* asked to return.[15]

The constancy and importance of these elements in his life made any clear discontinuities in his political developments unlikely to start with. Thus change, when it did occur, was almost imperceptible. All his life Henderson was an advanced radical of the old style, but his radicalism in time became encrusted with habits and patterns of thought collected elsewhere.

It could hardly be otherwise: he grew up in an enfolding radical atmosphere, and at every stage of his early career he had Liberal patrons who advanced him politically. At first it was Stephenson's, the great Newcastle heavy-engineering firm, which promoted him to local politics, then the Newcastle Liberal machine under Robert Spence Watson, then the Pease family (large shareholders in Stephenson's), and then, in his union, Fred Maddison. He had every reason to be grateful to the Liberal Party, and he always was. From Spence Watson's influence he never escaped,[16] and it is arguable that Henderson's later and almost exclusive turn to international relations, which is more surprising than it seems, given his own parochialism and industrial background, was partly due to the pacifist radicalism which he absorbed from Spence Watson and his circle. It was they who arranged his election to the Newcastle council in 1894 and attempted to get him to parliament as John Morley's running mate in 1895. In this they failed, but too much has been made of their failure.[17] There is no evidence to

[15] Hugh Dalton, *Call Back Yesterday* (London, 1953), 172. After he became Foreign Secretary, men of the world like Dalton and Philip Noel-Baker coaxed him into drinking a glass of wine with his evening meal. On most other matters of morals he held orthodox nonconformist views. He was a signatory of the minority report of the 1912 Royal Commission on Divorce, and he supported liberalizing divorce legislation thereafter. In the 1906 parliament he seconded a resolution to permit marriage to the deceased wife's sister—a typical piece of anti-Anglicanism. At the Labour Party head office he always turned a blind eye to the sexual unorthodoxies of the staff, however obvious.

[16] See P. Corder, *Life of Robert Spence Watson* (London, 1914).

[17] In 1892 the Liberals had lost one of the two Newcastle seats they had held. This was assumed by Spence Watson and others to be due to the reluctance of working-class voters to support middle-class Liberal candidates. In March 1895, therefore, they induced the Liberal and Radical Association to select Henderson as the second Liberal candidate. But the Liberal One Thousand refused to acquiesce, and they nominated instead 'one James Craig'. M. A. Hamilton, *Arthur Henderson* (London, 1938), 30. Mrs Hamilton implies that Craig was a nonentity. He was, in

support Mrs Hamilton's contention that Henderson had 'seen the cloven hoof. The sight was not forgotten.'[18] It would have been surprising if he had been selected. He was only 32, young for a parliamentary candidate not indigenous to the ruling classes, relatively unknown, and unmoneyed. Liberal bigwiggery made up for the loss and, as consolation, he happily accepted Sir Joseph Pease's offer of the agency-secretaryship of the Barnard Castle constituency.[19]

At the same time his trade-union career was also advancing. By 1903, he was, indeed, the parliamentary candidate of his union, the Friendly Society of Ironfounders.[20] Much ambiguity was involved in this selection. The Ironfounders were under as much pressure as the other unions to secure parliamentary representation, but their approach was circuitous and prudential. They resolved that their candidate was to be 'allowed a free hand . . . so long as he votes with the labour party on matters pertaining to the welfare of the union'.[21] Furthermore, even if Henderson's politics were not well known before his nomination, they were widely broadcast by his opponents during the selection ballot. He was clearly the candidate of the union's Liberal wing, and Fred Maddison, the union's president, openly agitated on his behalf. Though the candidacy was (more or less) understood to be an independent Labour one, Henderson did not feel obliged to give up his position in Barnard Castle, nor did he imagine that any conflict was involved.

Similarly, it seems clear that Henderson's election as MP for Barnard Castle (in succession to his Liberal employer) involved no

---

fact, the former Liberal MP for the city and much better known than Henderson. It is unlikely that Henderson much regretted the outcome. Both Morley and Craig were defeated, and the balance of the votes suggests that Henderson would have been as well. Furthermore, he liked Darlington (and Barnard Castle) more than Newcastle, and would no doubt have agreed with his employer and last patron, Sir J. W. Pease, when he told his son Jack: 'I hate the Newcastle low political standard. "What shall we pocket? in grog? and money?" My Dalemen are a superior article.' J. W. Pease to Jack Pease, 11 Oct. 1900, Gainford Papers 12B, Nuffield College, Oxford. For further details of Henderson's earlier career see A. W. Purdue, 'Arthur Henderson and Liberal, Liberal–Labour and Labour Politics in the North-East of England, 1892–1903', *Northern History*, 11 (1976 for 1975).

[18] Hamilton, 30.

[19] Not only were the Peases large shareholders in Stephenson's, but Jack Pease was then MP for Tyneside. [20] For his union career, see below, pp. 52–3.

[21] Fyrth and Collins, 110.

ideological conflicts, but did not involve conflicts of name and loyalty.[22] His union felt the same conflicts: he even doubted whether he would be allowed to stand as 'an unadjectival Labour candidate',[23] and both panicked when it was clear that he would have a Liberal opponent.[24] Henderson won because he could find no graceful way of not standing at all. Even then he was reluctant to sign the constitution of the Labour Representation Committee (LRC), and did so only after three months' wavering.[25]

Henderson's transition from the Liberal to the Labour Party was gentle and demanded no abrupt philosophic shift: not for nothing was Keir Hardie excluded from the Barnard Castle contest.[26] It is important that the nature of this transition be understood: it was, in the first instance, an institutional and not a political one. In the case of Henderson and the Ironfounders it was made by men who remained advanced radical in tendency, but who knew that if they wanted parliamentary representation they would have to arrange it themselves. Henderson, unlike Richard Bell and a number of miners' MPs, was (nearly) always loyal to the LRC as an institution, but his politics remained recognizably Liberal–radical in type. This was the subject of more or less discreet ILP criticism,[27] and more open attack from other quarters.

There was plenty for his critics to get their teeth into. His maiden speech was in support of free trade,[28] and he had to be coerced by the executive of the LRC into not appearing on 'neutral' (that is, Liberal) platforms.[29] He defended that action with spirit.

[22] For an account of the by-election campaign, see P. Poirier, *The Advent of the Labour Party* (London, 1958), 196–206.

[23] H. L. Barrett to J. R. MacDonald, 29 Mar. 1903, LPLF, LRC 8/68.

[24] See Robert Morley (president of the Workers' Union) to MacDonald, 19 Mar. 1903, LPLF, LRC 7/285; H. H. Hughes to MacDonald, 20 May 1903, LPLF, LRC 9/208.

[25] Minutes of the National Executive of the Labour Party, 17 Dec. 1903.

[26] J. R. MacDonald to A. Henderson, 3 July 1903, LPLF, LRC LB/2/280. According to MacDonald, Hardie felt his exclusion 'very keenly'; see also K. O. Morgan, *Keir Hardie* (London, 1975), 135. Henderson many years later told Cripps, quite untruthfully, that the exclusion was done with Hardie's 'complete understanding and approval'. Dalton Diaries, 29–30 Jan. 1934, Dalton Papers, London School of Economics.

[27] Bruce Glasier thought Henderson 'a humbug', while Hardie later found his leadership of the Labour Party 'reactionary and timid'. L. Thompson, *The Enthusiasts* (London, 1971), 143, 156.

[28] H. C. Deb. 4th ser., cxxix, 1237–41 (12 Feb. 1904).

[29] Minutes of the National Executive of the Labour Party, 30 June 1904.

Unless our independence has to become isolation, it is essential that the votes of Labour men and especially Trade Unionists—if we are to retrieve our 'legal position'—should be cast by the advice of the Committee [the executive of the LRC] into such channels as will help to secure our object . . . It is remarkable that such a demonstration of feeling should have taken place simply because we pursued the same policy at an election as has been followed by almost every Labour Member and Candidate for some time past. In nearly every constituency in the agitation against Protection, against Chinese Labour, against the Licensing Bill, most of us joined with other citizens in our protest against the Government policy on these questions.[30]

It was the policy of the 'neutral platform', which was practised until the outbreak of the war—and then, of course, after it even more—that lent sting to Tillett's polemic, *Is the Parliamentary Labour Party a Failure?* Despite its crudity, the activities which it condemned were all too recognizable. 'Some of [the PLP's] leading members . . . have stumped the country, subservient to the Nonconformist–Temperance–Liberal Party, ignoring the great tragedy of starvation as represented by the millions unable to find work or food.'[31] As for Henderson, when he was 'a "Gospel–Temperance–Liberal election agent" he was of little public importance, in spite of his multiple offices: but the Labour Party has increased his influence and his value to the bourgeois "Temperance" party.'[32] Tillett himself, of course, was also a crank on the drink question—as on much else—but Henderson, like Shackleton and, indeed, Snowden, left himself open to attacks of this kind, because they were often in part true.[33]

The 'neutral platform' equally provided Victor Grayson with his opportunities in 1908 and 1909. Grayson argued that the Labour MPs in parliament failed to diminish unemployment, not because they were tied to the government for tactical reasons, but because their political objectives were the *same* as the government's. This

[30] Draft Report of the Friendly Society of Ironfounders on Harborough and Devonport Elections, LPLF, LRC 18/92.

[31] B. Tillett, *Is the Parliamentary Labour Party a Failure?* (London, n.d.), 3.

[32] Ibid. 13.

[33] And given that both Shackleton and Henderson were devout nonconformists, the attacks could scarcely not be. See also Bruce Glasier on Henderson: 'His eternal appearances on Temperance and Methodist platforms and the absence of a single proclamation from him of a leadership order gives countenance to those miserable hints and accusations in the *Dispatch* and elsewhere that the party is becoming merely a Liberal tail.' Quoted in Morgan, *Keir Hardie*, 220.

was certainly unfair. The Parliamentary Party had worked hard on unemployment legislation in difficult circumstances; on the other hand, it is not hard to detect in Henderson's attitude a feeling that unemployment was an issue secondary to other great radical causes. Thus he told Arthur Ponsonby, who had urged on him the need to meet the Lords with forces undivided, that 'the position you take . . . largely represents my personal opinion . . . I am afraid, however, if the Government were to appeal during the present year without attempting to provide permanent remedies for Unemployment—it would divide the forces that ought to attack the Lords unitedly.'[34]

There is no evidence that his radicalism was much modified before the war, though there were important changes of emphasis. Only one aspect of his behaviour before 1917 is perhaps surprising and that is his reaction to the outbreak of the war. It is perfectly conceivable that he could have taken the same attitude as John Morley, John Burns, and Arthur Ponsonby (who all resigned from the Liberal government), or, indeed, MacDonald. He had the same political background, he lived in the same political world, and the Quaker–radical influences in Newcastle and Darlington were intensely pacifist. If, like Burns necessarily, or MacDonald by choice, he had inhabited an almost exclusively middle-class milieu, he might have behaved as they did. But the union connection was strong enough to push him into supporting the war, and it is probably true that, outside those who regarded themselves specifically as socialists, the working class was quite as military-minded as the bourgeoisie: within the labour movement perhaps more so.

Henderson's behaviour during the war was, therefore, always ambiguous. He continued to call himself a 'pacifist',[35] and only once descended into the contemporary style.[36] He certainly believed that German militarism was responsible for the war, but

[34] Henderson to Ponsonby, 22 Jan. 1909, Ponsonby Papers C 658, Bodleian Library, Oxford. See also the Master of Elibank's testimony, dated 14 Apr. 1910. His relations with Henderson were based upon 'cordiality and trust'. A. C. Murray, *Master and Brother* (London, 1945), 48.

[35] See, for example, *Daily News*, 11 Jan. 1915.

[36] 'There are·some people who thought that it did not matter . . . whether England or Germany came out victors in the war . . . Such people took up tremendous risks. Was any man going to see his child butchered and his wife dishonoured without retaliating? He did not believe it!' *Yorkshire Observer*, 1 Jan. 1915.

he also believed that it was caused by diplomats and practitioners of the balance of power: that Sir Edward Grey shared guilt with Bethmann-Hollweg.[37] He always argued that the 'unmoral' use of German military force had to be defeated, but, as well, that the processes of arbitration and conciliation that he already knew so well would have to supersede the old diplomacy.

It was perhaps the continuing strength of pacifist radicalism in his own make-up as much as the internal evolution of the Labour Party that forced him out of Lloyd George's government in August 1917.[38] The only letter of congratulation on his resignation that remains in his papers came from his old friend the Revd Tom Sykes, secretary of the national council of the Brotherhood Movement, who wrote: 'Toryism dies hard in this ancient land and is the unscrupulous enemy which needs the "knock-out"—and will get it. I do not mean quite political Toryism, but rather the superior castle-spirit and its press organs.'[39] Why this letter alone was preserved is not clear, but the old-fashioned democracy of its sentiments accorded well with Henderson's own radicalism and that of the circles in which he continued to move. Thus in 1919 he was recalling the glad days of 1909 and 1910, when Lloyd George 'drew his inspiration from advance radicalism', when he 'had the interest of the popular masses at heart', and before he became the 'apologist of the class interests which he formerly denounced with more pungency and fervour then any statesman of our time'.[40] In 1920 he was reminiscencing nostalgically of Campbell-Bannerman,[41] and in 1921 he announced, with a last Gladstonian gasp, that the great issue of the next election would be Ireland.[42]

His increasing absorption in League of Nations affairs must be seen in the same way. He showed no sign of regarding the international working-class movement as an alternative to those conciliating institutions traditionally advocated by British Liberals. Henderson, rather, tried to use the strength of international

[37] *Northern Echo*, 15 Jan. 1915.

[38] For Henderson's resignation, see J. M. Winter, 'Arthur Henderson, the Russian Revolution and the Reconstruction of the Labour Party', *Historical Journal*, 4 (1972); more generally, C. F. Brand, *British Labour's Rise to Power* (London, 1941).

[39] Sykes to Henderson, undated but almost certainly Aug. 1917. LPLF, Henderson Papers, HEN/13/1.   [40] Labour Party Leaflet, no. 44 (1919).

[41] B. J. Matthews (ed.), *World Brotherhood* (London, 1920), 105.

[42] *Manchester Guardian*, 28 Aug. 1921.

socialism to buttress these institutions. As early as January 1915 he had concluded that 'the mischievous effects of . . . the balance of power must be superseded by a congress of nations . . . The functions and powers of the Hague Tribunal must be extended, and it must have the assistance of a permanent council of conciliation, and advice with the machinery of arbitration must be speeded up.'[43] At the meeting of the rump Second International in January 1919, he alone in that disputatious gathering spoke to what he called 'practical purposes'.

We ought to say to the governments that all their Balances of Power, however scientifically arranged, have failed. Their standing armies have not served to save our children from slaughter. Their secret diplomacy resulted in disaster . . . We should say to Paris; 'all this must be revolutionised immediately by a League of Nations *now*.'[44]

The continental delegations could hardly have been less interested. He completed the circle to his maiden speech in 1904 when he told a Swiss paper fifteen years later that the League 'can only succeed in so far as all obstacles to world commerce—customs barriers, for example—are abolished and replaced by a policy of free trade'.[45] As he did with domestic policy, so in international affairs he saw the working class as now the only effective support of policies which were in the interest of society generally, but which before the war might have been promoted and defended by a vigorous middle-class radicalism.

Everything that has been said about Henderson so far points to his viewing British society as one based upon harmonious class-relations: a social harmony in which class-antagonism would be diminished by an even-handed state on the one side, and by conciliation and arbitration on the other. Although he spoke increasingly after 1917—as did all labour leaders—of 'democratic control of industry', he did not even then assume that the organization of capitalist industry would change significantly. And, at every stage, his attitudes were, of course, shaped and

[43] *Nottingham Daily Express.* 5 Jan. 1915.
[44] Stenographic Report of the Reconstruction Meeting of the Second International at Berne, 26–8 Jan. 1919.
[45] Quoted in *Le Populaire*, 30 Jan. 1919.

hardened by a social Christianity that was—to use more recent terminology—specifically class-collaborationist.

In the 1880s Henderson had entered a craft and a union that encouraged such attitudes. The foundries were still fairly small-scale, and even when they were not, labour was organized in a hierarchic and personalized way that allowed the diffusion of an essentially middle-class radicalism—or, at least, a radicalism that was organized in a bourgeois-dominated political party. Henderson, as a 'butty-man' in a firm like Stephenson's, where relations between men and masters were, on the whole, genial, and where union officials were cultivated by management, could scarcely have escaped its effects. His union, the Ironfounders, was Liberal in its leadership and in its political tendencies, and, although this Liberalism was increasingly contested within the union, Henderson was not one of the dissidents. He was, on the contrary, a protégé of Fred Maddison, the union's Lib–Lab president.

In 1892, after nine year's membership of the Ironfounders, he was elected a district delegate, and in 1894 became secretary and senior workers' representative of the North East Conciliation Board. This body, established during the 1894 engineers' strike, revealed his great skills and patience as industrial negotiator. When a similar board was established in Lancashire under the 1898 Act, he was nominated as workers' representative there. Thereafter, he was a public advocate of arbitration: as such he strongly opposed the establishment of the General Federation of Trade Unions as likely to encourage and intensify industrial disputes.[46] Until the early 1920s much of his time was spent in industrial conciliation: he nearly always acted for his own union, and frequently for others as well. His involvement was often such to exclude his party work altogether, to the annoyance of coming men like Hugh Dalton, anxiously arranging their political futures.[47] Before the war, he was a senior negotiator of the railway strike (1911) and of the great Dublin strikes of 1913. Though there was much evidence to suggest that the unions had not done particularly well from arbitrated settlements in this period,[48] Henderson agreed to be a member of the Industrial Council (1912–13), and,

---

[46] Fyrth and Collins, *Foundry Workers*, 102.

[47] Dalton Diaries, 27–9 Mar. 1922.

[48] See J. H. Porter, 'Wage Bargaining under Conciliation Agreements, 1860–1914', *Economic History Review*, 2nd ser. 23 (1970), 474–5.

apart from Sir George Askwith himself, he was one of the few to believe that it could work.[49]

His attitude to industrial relations was, in fact, double-sided. Clearly his aptitude as a negotiator was valued by the unions, and he owed his place in the movement to them—but he had a general view of industrial relations which was almost totally unrepresentative of that of the unions; his was, in the broadest sense, *political*. He always argued for the 'Australian' system of compulsory arbitration—in 1909 he and Will Crooks even introduced legislation to enforce it—but it was repeatedly rejected by the unions and finally disposed of at the 1911 TUC.[50] It was political in the sense that he conceived solutions as necessarily external to the disputes: the overriding interest was that of the community or the state and not that of the disputants. Since the state must be involved, so must the Labour Party as the political wing of the labour movement. He was thus sceptical of the unions' capacity to take the 'broad view', and he saw himself, and his party, as in a position to take the 'broad view', and equally he saw himself, and his party, as in some way representing the community. In September 1913, from Dublin, he wrote: 'It will take a stiff fight to get sense into both sides,'[51] and in November (also from Dublin) he deplored the way the unions had excluded the party from negotiations: 'The Parliamentary Committee [of the TUC] are in possession and you know what that means.'[52] The refusal of the TUC to make use of the Joint Board[53] maddened him: 'The whole of the blame must rest with them and not with us.'[54]

The war did not much change all this. He let compulsory arbitration go, sensibly enough, but the other sides of the policy were grasped even more tightly. They had three closely related characteristics: a reassertion of the overriding interest of the community, a continued rejection of industrial action as against conciliation, and an emphatic opposition to 'direct action', to the

[49] See Lord Askwith, *Industrial Problems and Disputes* (London, 1920), 198–9: I. G. Sharp, *Industrial Conciliation and Arbitration in Great Britain* (London, 1950), 298–302.
[50] *Report of Proceedings at the Annual Trades Union Congress, 1911*, 229–31.
[51] Henderson to J. S. Middleton, 17 Sept. 1913, LPLF, LP/HEN/08/1/89.
[52] Henderson to Middleton, 13 Nov. 1913, LPLF, LP/HEN/08/1/100.
[53] An organization comprising both the political and industrial wings of the movement and designed to co-ordinate action between the two.
[54] Henderson to Middleton, 18 Nov. 1913. LPLF, LP/HE/08/1/103.

political use of the strike. His view that the interest of the community was superior to all others was strengthened by his experience of the war and the Russian Revolution—he was, of course, in Russia in May and June 1917. In February 1917 he said that 'capital and labour had often in the past, in the settlement of their differences by lock-out or strike, forgotten that there was a third party, the community, whose interests were being seriously endangered . . . If the State recognized that it depended on capital and labour, he hoped capital and labour would recognize their obligations to the State.'[55] He urged the same thing on those Russians who cared to listen to him: there should be a 'truce as between two extremes';[56] as in this country, the 'state should act as a buffer between two warring sections.'[57]

But if the community were to be protected from the consequences of industrial strife, the state had to do more than act as a buffer. It had to establish what he called (and what the Labour Party in 1918 became committed to) 'democratic control' of industry. He did not, of course, mean by this any necessary structural change in the organization of industry. He meant the development of the conciliation services that he had known before the war, and particularly the development of the Whitley councils. In June 1918 he admitted ('as a result of his experience in connection with the Conciliation Boards') that 'difficulties would arise in applying the principles of the Whitley Report to many industries, especially those that are unorganized.' But if labour and capital

could come together in a spirit of toleration . . . all concerned in the conduct of industry would profit, and the community would be saved from the recurrent industrial troubles so deplorably frequent in the pre-war years . . . Co-operation is the key word of the Whitley Report . . . Co-operation or disastrous strife, reconstruction or revolution . . . The idea that the relationships between capital and labour must necessarily be antagonistic must be abandoned on both sides.[58]

Even by the end of 1920, when it was obvious that Whitleyism would, at best, have only very modest success,[59] he was continuing

---

[55] *Yorkshire Post*, 19 Feb. 1917.
[56] Henderson to R. W. Raine, 19 June 1917, LPLF, Henderson Papers, HEN/1/29.
[57] Henderson to T. W. Dowson, 19 June 1917, ibid., HEN/1/30.
[58] *Brighton Herald*, 29 June 1918.
[59] See J. B. Seymour, *The Whitley Councils Scheme* (London, 1932), 94–105.

'to attach much importance to the working of the Whitley Council scheme. As a method of Industrial councils the Whitley councils have very great value.'[60]

It is less clear what 'democratic control' meant in concrete terms. It seemed to imply a moral rather than a structural change. Men would have to behave towards each other decently, with mutual respect and courtesy. He was certain, however, that the old forms of deference and class exclusiveness would have to disappear.

The dream of some employers that they will be able again [after the war] to get a docile and contented army of workers, who will readily accept a position of subordination and take orders 'mechanically' from their superiors, is a vain dream. The desire of a few less enlightened employers to destroy the trade-union movement, to expel from industry the trade union 'agitator' . . . is an even vainer desire.[61]

The possibility of moral change was, of course, in some sense confirmed by the requirements of his own religion. Thus at an ecumenical conference in September 1921, he said that the

Churches should endeavour to secure the reconciliation of the workers actually engaged in industry, and the humanizing of all the conditions of their employment . . . The Church must assert the fact that the worker was first of all a man, with a human claim to full life, entitled to an adequate minimum of leisure, of health, of education, of subsistence, and an opportunity to develop all the faculties he possessed.[62]

In practice, however, this was also what he demanded from the Labour Party. It was not, as he saw it, a 'class' party: 'Labour is in politics, not in the interests of a class, but to further the interests of the community as a whole. The Labour Party is . . . a national people's party'.[63] Class prejudice was for others: the propertied classes' fears of Labour were, therefore, 'unreasonable fears'.[64] The Labour Party could be their party as well, but only if they accepted that organized labour had as much right to power and representation as organized capital. When, for example, he complained of the 1918 and 1924 parliaments as 'class' parliaments, he did not really mean that capital was over-represented, but that

---

[60] 'The Problem of Permanent Industrial Peace', *Financial Review of Reviews*, Dec. 1920, 378.   [61] Ibid. 367.

[62] *The Times*, 17 Sept. 1921.   [63] *Ploughshare*, Dec. 1919.

[64] *Manchester Guardian*, 20 Mar. 1920.

labour was under-represented, and that narrow and unenlightened interests were perpetuating the old system of social snobbery and class arrogance. The Labour Party was to so order society that this behaviour would no longer be possible.

Equally, Henderson had a quite specific conception of the Labour Party's place in the wider labour movement, and it presupposed (as it had before the war) the primacy of political action over industrial and the party over the unions. He never doubted the continuing effectiveness of parliamentary democracy, nor did he doubt that 'direct action' was just his old enemy 'syndicalism',[65] under a more fashionable name. In September 1919 he told his own union that 'to endeavour to force upon the country and upon the Government by illegitimate means the policy of a section of the entire community—involves the abrogation of Parliamentary government, establishes the dictatorship of the minority and might easily destroy eventually all our constitutional liberties.'[66]

He argued this at greatest length in an important set-piece exchange with Robert Williams, the secretary of the Transport Workers, in September 1920. It occurred on the eve of the miners' 'datum line' strike (15 October 1920) and the possible resurrection of the Triple Alliance. Henderson had already made known his fear that Lloyd George would use the occasion to dissolve parliament and that Labour could only lose such an election. Williams answered this, stating flatly that Labour should take whatever industrial action was necessary—'as far reaching and as constructive as the Government appears to be doing'.[67] Henderson then replied (unusually for him) in a lengthy gloss circulated to the members of the national executive of the Party. He began by questioning Williams's contention that 'virile pressure on the industrial side' had done Labour (at least) no electoral harm.

I believe 'direct action' propaganda . . . has been definitely harmful and

[65] See his gleeful letter to J. S. Middleton: 'We had the finest conference at Newcastle I have yet attended. The delegates filled the floor space and crowded into the gallery . . . Two or three syndicalists did not get a look in as Wilkie ruled them out of order every time.' Henderson to Middleton, undated but clearly 1913, LPLF, uncatalogued. This was a conference held before the ballots required by the 1913 Trade Union Act. The syndicalists were opposed to 'balloting in' and, indeed, to almost any other form of support for the Labour Party.

[66] Friendly Society of Ironfounders, *Monthly Report*, July 1919.

[67] Williams to Henderson, 15 Sept. 1920, LPLF, uncatalogued.

has had the effect of frightening away many voters who were inclined to support Labour . . . I hold the view that the coquetting [*sic*] with Bolshevism and the 'direct action' propaganda has prevented our reaping the full fruits of a promising strategical position . . .

I have always been a strong advocate of the closest possible measure of co-ordination between the industrial and political wings of the Movement. Unfortunately this has yet to be achieved, for in actual practice there is a lamentable lack of cohesion except on rare and isolated occasions, and such instances . . . of real unity and co-operation have been . . . of a temporary character . . .

It is impossible to regard the establishment of the Miners' claim and the defeat of the coalition government as separate and unrelated as Mr Williams presents them, yet the Miners' claim has been kept strictly in the hands of the industrial wing, as though it had no relation or bearing on the political situation . . .

In the present case the political wing has been completely excluded from participation in the trade union consultations and conferences. Now Mr Williams suggests co-ordination of all our forces for the final stage of the struggle. As soon as there is a possibility of the venue being changed to the political arena, the political wing is invited to seek the co-operation of the industrial wing. It seems to me that it would have been a far better policy if the closest co-operation between the two wings had been established as soon as it became apparent that the fight might become more than a Miners' fight . . . I am strongly of the opinion that a general election on the issue which Mr Williams suggests would be disastrous . . . We would suffer, I believe, a very severe reverse—both industrially and politically.[68]

This is an elaborate and revealing exposition of his own position, though characteristically it is a tactical rather than an ideological statement. Yet, while it is certainly true that direct actionism was in time abandoned by the unions as a political weapon, this was something that evolved on its own account, and not because of Labour Party pressure. The political wing never gained primacy; never even gained the equality that he had urged in reply to Robert Williams, and the unions continued to follow a policy of industrial sectionalism which effectively excluded the Party. In 1926, for example, it might as well have not existed, and the relationship between the unions and the Party established after 1931 was hardly what Henderson wanted.[69] Similarly all attempts

---

[68] 'Notes on Mr Williams's letter by the Secretary', Sept. 1920, LPLF, uncatalogued. 　　　　　　　　　　　　　　　　　[69] See below, 64–5.

to make the post-1918 National Joint Council[70] a super-executive of the labour movement failed—as they had done before the war. It is probably true that Henderson's turning away from industrial policy to international affairs was as much a result of this depressing failure as of the influence of pre-war radicalism.

In summary, it must be concluded that Henderson's politics moved in a continuous and fairly unbroken way. Even the war seems to have done remarkably little to alter his view of the world—and this is not surprising in a man who was already 50 when it broke out. It is not hard to imagine him acting and thinking in exactly the same way had he remained within organized Liberalism. What had moved ahead with speed, however, was his view of Labour's part in the promotion of the old causes. Whereas before 1914 he could genuinely have believed that it was the Labour Party's function to push the Liberal Party in the direction that they both wanted to go, after 1917 he was convinced that the organized labour movement itself must be the vehicle of social improvement. This was a real development and the 1918 reorganization of the Labour Party was the physical symbol of it.[71] It is this development that sharply distinguishes Henderson from MacDonald. MacDonald had always been a socialist. He believed, that is to say, in the inevitability of society's evolution to collective forms of life. But he never believed that the working class would necessarily hasten this evolution: on the contrary, he had long before concluded that the ignorance and parochialism of the working class could actually obstruct it. It was this that made his departure from the Labour Party in 1931 so easy.

How far, then, was Henderson a 'type', and how representative was he of his class as a political interest? In the first place, he was certainly an example of the *homo novus* of politics, a man who, in Weber's words, had chosen politics as his 'vocation'. Men of Henderson's stripe 'take the organization in hand. They do so either as "entrepreneurs"—the American boss and the English election agent are, in fact, such entrepreneurs—or as officials with

---

[70] As its name implies, a joint council made up of representatives of the Parliamentary Labour Party, the National Executive of the party and the General Council of the TUC.

[71] See McKibbin, *Evolution of the Labour Party*, 91–111.

a fixed salary.'[72] Henderson was successively agent *and* official, but his career would not have been possible without the division of labour within politics that was everywhere apparent at the end of the nineteenth century, and nowhere more so than in the great working-class parties of Western and Central Europe. As such he was certainly a type of socialist leader, 'the Jouhaux, Hendersons, Merrheims, Legiens and Co'.[73] He shared their characteristics— sobriety, ambition, conscientiousness, toughness—as well as their administrative gifts.

The middle and upper classes observed them with both admiration and distaste. In 1915 Bruce Glasier, a leading bourgeois member of the ILP, described Henderson as 'clever, adroit, rather limited-minded . . . domineering and a bit quarrelsome—vain and ambitious'.[74] The daughter of the British ambassador in St Petersbourg had reason to note these characteristics more closely (Henderson had been sent there with a brief to replace her father, amongst other things). She compared the *ancien régime* with this figure from the new order: his father 'slim, upright, unmistakably patrician . . . with only a slight twist round his nostrils, a twist which we all knew signified a certain distaste and fastidious disapprobation. Mr Henderson, on the other hand, square, thick set, rather red in the face looked completely out of place . . . listening with a complacent smile to the little speech of welcome Prince Lvoff was making.'[75]

Robert Michels developed a powerful theory of political oligarchy from the careers of such men, and his picture of the conventional socialist organizer, though drawn from men like Ebert, Scheidemann, and their party, could equally be drawn from Henderson and his party. Michels pointed to the fatiguing character of the organizer's life, the endless demands made upon him by the masses, and the magnetic attractions of a leader who was a parliamentarian as well.[76] Henderson acknowledged this— 'it is very stiff night after night speaking from two to three

---

[72] M. Weber, 'Politics as a Vocation', in H. H. Gerth and C. Wright Mills eds.), *From Max Weber* (London, 1948), 102.
[73] V. I. Lenin, *Left-Wing Communism: An Infantile Disorder* (Moscow, 1970), 46. [74] Thompson, *Enthusiasts*, 206.
[75] M. Buchanan, *The Dissolution of an Empire* (London, 1932), 210–11. For these purposes Lenin must be regarded as upper-class. See his comments in *Left-Wing Communism*, 46–7.
[76] R. Michels, *Political Parties* (New York, 1962), 91.

hours'[77]—but it was, in fact, his vocation. As a political 'entre-preneur' Henderson was instantly recognizable. Hugh Dalton found him at first meeting 'eminently a politician',[78] and Fritz Adler once gently chided him for taking up a position which, as 'an old politician', he should have known was too inflexible.[79]

Henderson's aptitudes within a bureaucratic organization are easy to see. He had psychological and physical resilience, internal poise and self-confidence, and a mind sufficiently narrow not to worry too much about the world, yet expansive enough to show him where it was moving. He had immense capacity for work, and he developed a sureness of touch in dealing with his party that was almost unique.[80] Weber sometimes saw professional political action as not much more than the creation of systems of patronage.[81] We may well dispute this, yet it is undeniable that the Labour Party created such a system and that it was indispensable in Labour's growth. In turn Henderson was indispensable in the creation of the system: he recognized faces, organized votes, found money, and put the right men in the right jobs—that it was done so without financial corruption is an even more remarkable achievement. In the long run, it was the most important gift he left his party. Neither MacDonald nor Hardie could have done so.

On the other hand, he lacked many of what Michels rather quaintly called 'accessory qualities of leadership'.[82] He was not a real orator, was no literary stylist—indeed, wrote nothing sustained at all—and he had few of the external 'qualities' possessed by, say, MacDonald. Yet this alone suggests some of the reasons why Michels almost certainly misconceived the relationship between leaders and masses in the labour movement. Michels argued that the political identities between leadership and rank and file were undermined by the upward social mobility of the leadership, via an essentially bureaucratic-bourgeois organization. But in Henderson's case at least, political divisions between the leader-ship and the rank and file were subordinated to or concealed by social identities, by shared styles of life and expectations. Between Henderson and the movement there were three of these identities.

[77] Henderson to Middleton, 13 Nov. 1913, LPLF, Middleton Papers, un-catalogued. [78] Dalton Diaries, 26 Nov. 1919.
[79] Stenographic and Confidential Minutes of a Conference between the Vienna Union and the National Executive of the Labour Party, 19–20 Oct. 1921.
[80] For illuminating details, see Hamilton, *Henderson*, 221–5.
[81] Weber, 'Politics as a Vocation', 221–5. [82] Michels, 98–104.

First, his pattern of life. Throughout his career he remained palpably working-class, and this was never spurious, as it was increasingly, for example, in the case of J. H. Thomas. He had easy relations with people of all classes, but the essentially working-class nature of his life never changed.[83] Henderson certainly represented the respectable strain in working-class life, but this was a very powerful one, and it was one reason why Henderson was so popular. The bohemianism cultivated by some middle-class socialists never went down well in the labour movement, and its cultivators showed ignorance of working-class values. Similarly, Henderson's habit of not inviting colleagues to his home—something resented by bourgeois socialists like Dalton—was equally characteristic of his class. The 'homeliness' was important:[84] it can be argued that the demoralization of the Labour Party in 1929–31 was less than it could have been partly because so many members of the government were identifiably of the same class as the people they represented. This is no longer true of the Labour Party.

The second identity was his sense of loyalty to and solidarity with his class. Although he strongly disapproved of a number of working-class political and industrial habits, he rarely tried to override them, and the few times he was 'off-side' with his movement were the occasions of severe mental distress. Thus after his resignation from the government in August 1917, he wrote to Walter Runciman, the Newcastle shipowner and former Liberal minister: 'I have paid the penalty of trying to serve two masters, the government and the Labour Movement. I got wrong with one in seeking to be loyal to the other. Yet if I had to go through it again the only thing I would do would be tender my resignation a little earlier.'[85] His attitude to the breakup of the second Labour government in 1931 was rather different since he did not feel the same conflict of loyalties. But the absence of conflict is itself revealing. By mid-August 1931, when almost everyone was admitting of the need to think 'nationally' (that is, adopt those policies urged by Labour's political opponents[86]), Henderson 'launched out into eloquence on the inadequacy of the unemployed

---

[83] Hamilton, *Henderson*, 220.
[84] E. Wertheimer, *Portrait of the Labour Party* (London, 1929), 183.
[85] Henderson to Runciman, 17 Aug. 1917, Runciman Papers, University of Newcastle. [86] See below, pp. 218–24.

grants and all that we had said for thirty years'.[87] He allowed the government to collapse, and with it almost all his hopes in international affairs, rather than 'get wrong' with the movement.

Unity of the movement and, by implication, class solidarity became his chief political tactic. 'He will always be on the side of the compact majority. His gospel is the gospel of making the best of both worlds', the *Labour Leader* argued during the war.[88] This was certainly a fair criticism; on the other hand, his fear of divisions in the working class and the fracturing of the organized labour movement was intense: 'unity is the great need of the moment' was one of his clichés.[89] After the collapse of 1931 this fear was even more deeply felt. By July 1934 the founder-figure of post-war social democracy was the only member of his party's executive to take seriously the United Front. 'The influence of Fascism has aroused great feeling throughout the entire working class movement. So strong is the opposition to War and Fascism that . . . we may expect that our own forces will be more than ever divided.'[90] That might have come from a Comintern handout. Similarly, he persuaded himself that the Incitement to Disaffection Act (1934), aimed at Mosley, would be used 'against our people'.[91]

Finally, his own reformism, political geniality, and his rather ill-defined sense of goodwill to all men associated with him the dominant strain in Britain left-wing traditions, even if it is possible to make too much of this. Henderson was very much a man of the North-East and his politics had a distinctly regional quality. Advanced radicalism, temperance, class-harmony, and Methodism were characteristic: 'No PM no MP.'[92] He obviously did not come

[87] MacDonald Diaries, 17 Aug. 1931, PRO.

[88] *Labour Leader*, 1 June 1916.

[89] See, for example, Henderson to Camille Huysmans, 26 July 1920, LPLF, International Files.

[90] Henderson to Middleton, 21 July 1934, LPLF, Middleton Papers.

[91] Ibid. He was not above exploiting his well-known sacrifices for the movement as a political tactic. He clearly used his sufferings in 1917 as a weapon to force through the constitutional changes of 1917–18: 'a certain door-mat for example is now being used very effectively as an altar-cloth.' Report by Edward Magegan on the Jan. 1918 Conference of the Labour Party, circulated to the Cabinet, 4 Feb. 1918, Cabinet Papers 24/42/3609, PRO.

[92] i.e. 'No Primitive Methodist no Member of Parliament'. For the social and cultural background of Co. Durham, see R. Moore, *Pit-men, Preachers and Politics* (Cambridge, 1974), 140–90. Dr Moore, however, inaccurately notes that Henderson 'held the Barnard Castle seat for Labour, unsponsored. He had agreed to support the Lib–Labs. in 1903' (p. 183). Henderson was, of course, the sponsored candidate of the Ironfounders and sat as a pledged member of the LRC.

from the great sinful cities, with their alcoholic, sporting, and church-and-king traditions, and he was for much of his career uneasy in them. They, in turn, as we have seen, were suspicious of him.[93] Nevertheless, as I shall suggest shortly, these differences came to be of decreasing importance, and by 1931 he was as representative of the rank and file as any individual leader could be. In the end, he owed his leadership of the Labour Party to his capacity to identify himself with the general aspirations of the labour movement, and to skills in formal organization, which were more highly developed in him than in any other labour leader of his generation.

There are a number of general conclusions that can be drawn from Henderson's career. First, that for a large number of Labour men, of whom Henderson here is plainly one, it was possible for a sense of an independent working-class movement to develop without any significant ideological shift taking place. For much of his life, even when he was well-established as a Labour leader, he continued to inhabit the same political world as most Liberals and to hold the same values. This is why it was so easy for individual Liberals to enter the Labour Party after 1918 without undergoing ideological conversion. Now what was true of Henderson was not necessarily true of other Labour leaders, but it was true enough of the labour movement to emphasize how subtle and complicated was the relationship between Labour and the older political parties.

Second, that the effect of the First World War on men like Henderson was also a subtle one. That it quite unexpectedly catapulted him into the leading place in the British left, that is to say, in British progressivism, and that he exploited this place with great skill, was due, so far as *he* was concerned, to structural rather than ideological changes in British politics. The widening of the franchise and the decisive position of the unions within the war economy had overturned the old relationship between the Labour and the Liberal Parties. He knew that there was no going back to 1914; but this did not mean that the old political progressivism should not continue. This explains his attempts to woo former Liberal–radicals into the Labour Party, and his comment to C. P. Scott that if 'good radicals' wanted to continue the good

[93] See above, pp. 47–8.

work they could most effectively do it in the Labour Party.[94] Thus, although Henderson was certainly influenced by the collectivist thought of the war years, he regarded it as an extension of rather than as a break with the pre-war radicalism.

Third, that Henderson must be seen as a representative transitional figure. Before 1914 he was identifiable as a former Liberal, and a Liberal from a particular part of the country. This was, as we have seen, an important element in his political personality, and it also helped to determine the way that other members of the Labour Party reacted to him. Furthermore, the pull of religion and temperance was in the direction of middle-class Liberalism, and was certainly a divisive force in the labour movement. Increasingly after 1918 this was no longer true. Although they were as much a part of Henderson's life as ever, they did not define his place in the movement in the same way. He was thus able to act as a bridge from the decidedly fragmented working-class party of 1914 to the more integrated party of the 1930s.

But the final conclusion is perhaps the most important one. In almost every way the labour movement developed against his wishes. On the industrial side, his view of arbitration and conciliation was quite unacceptable to the unions, whatever the lip-service, and they applauded his efforts to introduce into international relations those institutions they would not have at home. Henderson deeply resented the way they behaved. Furthermore, the great unified political–industrial labour movement—his heart's desire—was never, and could never have been constructed. It represented a political conception of working-class industrial behaviour that was also unacceptable to the unions. The complicated bodies established in the 1920s at all levels to impose unity on the movement either did not work at all or were dismantled in the 1930s.[95] Indeed, Henderson was one of the few labour leaders to hold such a monolithic conception of the working class and he held it in face of all the evidence about that class's dynamics.

Yet even he was disabused in 1931. At a joint meeting of the national executive of the Labour Party and the general council of the TUC on 10 November 1931, he sat in acquiescent silence as

[94] T. Wilson (ed.), *The Political Diaries of C. P. Scott* (London, 1970), 316–17.
[95] For this, see McKibbin, *Evolution of the Labour Party*, 245.

Walter Citrine, the secretary of the TUC, lectured him on the history of the Labour Party:

The TUC did not seek in any shape or form to say what the Labour Party was to do, but they did ask that the primary purpose of the creation of the Labour Party should not be forgotten. It was created by the Trade Union Movement to do things in Parliament which the Trade Unions found ineffectively performed by the two-Party system.[96]

In other words, the Party could do as it liked until it affected the particular interests of the unions, and then it was to do as it was told. Though Henderson came in to the Party as a trade-unionist, that was a conception of the Party's function of which he profoundly disapproved.

This, in turn, suggests more generally that Michels seriously overestimated the ability of a party leadership to determine the political nature of the organization it leads. It may well be true that Henderson had an occupational interest in the supremacy of the Labour Party over the unions; it may also be true, as Michels argued, that an oligarchical leadership necessarily becomes divorced from its mass support: the very qualities that characterize this leadership are those most often absent in the industrial working class. Furthermore, many labour leaders, Henderson included, had typically 'middle-class' attitudes to certain aspects of working-class social life—to drinking and gambling, for example. But equally, as Henderson's own career demonstrates, the political leadership was there on sufferance. He had bureaucratic skills which the labour movement needed, and these, together with his delicate sense of loyalty, made him the labour leader *par excellence*. Yet at no time was he able to impose his own ideologies (so to speak) on his party: his leadership—like MacDonald's—was always organizational and rhetorical. Thus, in 1931, when the leadership of the Party stood, on the whole, for one set of policies, and the unions for another, the leadership was powerless to do anything other than either 'betray' or submit.[97] MacDonald 'betrayed', but took no significant part of the labour movement with him. Henderson submitted, and so kept his leadership, but that was now little more than administrative and formal.

[96] Minute of a Joint Meeting of the General Council of the TUC and the National Executive of the Labour Party, 10 Nov. 1931, filed in the 1931 volumes of the minutes of the National Executive.   [97] See below, pp. 220–3.

3

The Franchise Factor in the Rise of the Labour Party*

(written with Colin Matthew and John Kay)

THE literature on the rise and fall of the Liberal Party is voluminous and inconclusive. We believe it is inconclusive because it usually assumes British politics to be structurally static. We wish to suggest that changes in the structure of British politics are at least as significant as chronological developments: in other words, that the changes in the franchise are at least as significant as the effects of the First World War.[1] On the evidence presented to date, after all, the post-war difficulties of the Liberal Party are paradoxical and difficult to explain. In practice, the problems are such that nearly all historians are forced to argue that the First World War was decisive in fragmenting the Liberal Party's support and in leaving the way clear for Labour. But the 'war' argument has never been satisfactorily demonstrated. Undoubtedly it is not easy to compare the pre- and post-war electoral situations, but we

[1] The authors would like warmly to acknowledge the research assistance of Miss Sue Curry, and the help of the Board of the Faculty of Modern History of Oxford University, which made a grant towards her efforts.

* This chapter differs somewhat from the others, in part because it was jointly written, in part because it provoked a considerable critical literature. Much of that literature, however, is concerned only with the franchise as such and leaves aside the wider question of a political culture which was to us as important as the technicalities of the vote. None the less, it might be helpful for those readers who are interested if the more important contributions were noted here. P. F. Clarke replied to us ('Liberals, Labour and the Franchise') and we replied to him in *English Historical Review*, 92 (1977), 582–9 and 589–90. J. P. D. Dunbabin ('British Elections in the Nineteenth and Twentieth Centuries: a Regional Approach', *English Historical Review*, 375 (1980), 241–67) argued, rather as André Siegfried did for France, that there were marked regional continuities in the historical support for the 'party of movement' and the 'party of resistance' and that these continuities were independent of franchise changes. M. W. Hart ('The Liberals, the War and the Franchise', *English Historical Review*, 97 (1982), 820–32) suggested that we had depreciated the significance of the war and that there was no way of knowing whether a fully enfranchised working class would in fact, have voted Labour in significant numbers before 1914. D. Tanner ('The Parliamentary

should at least attempt such a comparison: to argue that, since comparison is difficult, historians must resort to inference and guess is clearly absurd. In this article we will suggest that too little attention has been given to the size of the Edwardian electorate, and the effect which it had on the form and nature of Edwardian politics. Furthermore, this electorate, created in two stages by the Reform and Redistribution Acts of 1867–8 and 1884–5 and by a number of ancillary minor Acts, has not adequately been compared with its successor, a product of the 'Fourth' Reform Act of 1918.[2] Such a comparison may provide the necessary data to explain the Liberal Party's decline. We will also suggest that the Liberals were wedded to the forms of the 1867–1914 political community as their opponents were not, that the ideologies of both the Labour and Conservative Parties made them better able to exploit a fully democratic franchise, and that these things were true before 1914 as well as after the war.

Of all countries with a more or less representative system of government in 1914, the United Kingdom and the kingdom of

Electoral System, the "Fourth" Reform Act and the Rise of Labour in England and Wales', *Bulletin of the Institute of Historical Research*, (1983), 205–19) strongly took the view that the old electoral system did not discriminate particularly against any class and that, therefore, the 1918 Act could not in itself have peculiarly benefited Labour. J. Turner ('The Labour Vote and the Franchise after 1918: An Investigation of the English Evidence' in P. Denley and D. Hopkin (eds.), *History and Computing* (Manchester, 1987)) argued on the basis of a computer analysis that the Labour Party did not gain from the franchise changes but that the Conservatives did. He also seemed to argue, however, that the newly enfranchised *were* primarily working-class, as we had originally suggested. Finally, K. D. Wald, *Crosses on the Ballot: Patterns of British Voter Alignment since 1885* (Princeton, 1983), also on the basis of computer analysis, attempted to demonstrate (with much evidence) that it was not so much franchise changes as the declining salience of religion which was likely to be responsible for the decline of the Liberal Party.

It is not possible to comment here on this literature except to say two things. First, it is clear that as a whole, however critical they are of our original essay, its authors are in no sense in agreement with each other. While not perhaps entirely intact, our argument still stands, therefore, if only for negative reasons. Second, our essay tried to explain *why* it was that the Liberal Party could not mobilize the post-1918 electorate as well as the Conservative or Labour Parties—and that it could not do so seems indisputable. We offered a political-cultural explanation which still seems to us more satisfactory either than no explanation at all or one which loads all the explanation on to the First World War. (Colin Matthew has further developed our view in H. C. G. Matthew, 'Rhetoric and Politics in Britain, 1860–1950', in P. J. Waller (ed.), *Politics and Social Change in Modern Britain* (Brighton, 1987), 34–58.)

[2] We have excluded Ireland from our discussion as far as possible.

Hungary alone did not have manhood suffrage.[3] Yet with one of the most limited electorates in Europe, the United Kingdom was widely regarded by contemporaries (or, at least, by British contemporaries) as a mature democracy—and this was even true of some well-known progressive politicians who failed to recognize that while the expectation of what 'democracy' meant had changed, the system remained the same. In July 1885 Chamberlain wrote that 'government of the people by the people . . . has at last been effectively secured by the two measures which together constitute the great achievement of Mr Gladstone's second administration.'[4] Sir Henry Maine agreed: 1884 had begun an era of 'unmoderated democracy'.[5] But this was not merely a Liberal delusion. Ten years after this another democratic paladin, Keir Hardie, stated flatly that 'there is no need now to fight the battle of the franchise. Our fathers did that, and today only the details remain to be adjusted.'[6] In Robert Tressell's novel *The Ragged Trousered Philanthropists*, a work often regarded as an accurate portrayal of Edwardian working-class life, the following exchange is recorded.

'Presently when there is an election, you will go and vote in favour of a policy of which you know nothing . . . You are not fit to vote.'

Crass was by this time very angry.

'I pays my rates and taxes', he shouted, 'an' I've got as much right to express an opinion as you 'ave . . .'[7]

[3] The point is made generally—not, though, about Hungary—in W. L. Arnstein, 'The Survival of the Victorian Aristocracy', in F. C. Jaher (ed.), *The Rich, the Well Born and the Powerful: Elites and Upper Classes in History* (Chicago, 1973), 220–1. The Hungarian aristocracy did not fail to take the point. See the comments of Count Julius Andrassy during the Hungarian suffrage crisis of 1905–6, A. J. May, *The Hapsburg Monarchy*, 1867–1914 (Cambridge, Mass., 1968), 359.

[4] In his Preface to *The Radical Programme* (London, 1885), p. v. Gladstone, typically, was more accurate and more revealing. In 1887 he wrote that the country 'is in principle a self-governing country. This principle, indeed, though fully recognized, has until lately been only applied to practice in a manner extremely partial and fitful. Even now it is still struggling out of its swaddling clothes, and probably nothing better than a more or less effective approximation to an acknowledged law is in the nature of things attainable.' 'Electoral Facts of 1887', *Nineteenth Century* (Sept. 1887).

[5] Sir Henry Maine, *Popular Government* (2nd edn.; London, 1886), 92.

[6] J. Keir Hardie, 'The Independent Labour Party', in A. Reid (ed.), *The New Party* (London, 1895), 258. Hardie's naïvety about electoral statistics is clearly shown in A. Rosen, *Rise Up Women* (London, 1974), 23.

[7] R. Tressell. *The Ragged Trousered Philanthropists* (London, 1965; 1st 1914), 24.

But Tressell's 'philanthropists' were all peripatetic house-painters, the majority of whom almost certainly would not have been able to vote at all: a view confirmed by the novel's emphasis on the frequent 'flittings' of both lodgers and householders.[8] From the other—Tory—side, Reynolds and the Woolleys, in their sympathetic study of the Edwardian working class, argued that the only objectionable feature of the structure was plural voting but that otherwise electoral access was universal.[9]

Memory also can play tricks, even to the sharpest observer. Thus Robert Roberts, in his reminiscences of Salford slum life, attributes to the world war significant changes in voting habits. 'Dyed in the wool Tories,' he writes, 'who had voted Conservative since getting the franchise, were talking now not "Liberal" but "Labour".'[10] Many, no doubt, did vote Tory before 1914, but in Salford North (evidently Roberts's constituency) only 53 per cent of the adult male population was on the register, and it seems a fair assumption that the very poorest—the classic slummies, the frequent flitters—against whom the pre-1918 system most obviously discriminated—had never voted for any party.

Similar comments are legion; the point may be obvious but it is, nevertheless, one frequently ignored, even when most relevant. Henry Pelling, for example, in his *Social Geography of British Elections*, while mentioning the case of Tower Hamlets, does not discuss levels of enfranchisement elsewhere, though he provides the reader with more or less all other relevant information. Two assumptions have persisted about the post-1885 British electorate. First, that it was essentially democratic, and that, if there was injustice, it was, in Lowell's words, an injustice that 'affects individuals alone. No considerable class in the community is aggrieved.'[11] Second, that political parties were, *ex hypothesi*, already acting in a democratic arena and that their function was the mobilization of a mass electorate. It was, for instance, Ostrogorski's aim to show how they went about it. The extent to

---

[8] Almost certainly the only voter in that motley bunch would have been the foreman.

[9] S. Reynolds and B. and T. Woolley, *Seems So!* (London, 1912), 147. Their West Country working-class subjects, many of them fishermen, were, it is true, more likely to have been on the registers than the industrially employed.

[10] R. Roberts, *The Classic Slum* (Manchester, 1971), 178 and 178 n.

[11] A. L. Lowell, *The Government of England*, 2 vols. (New York, 1910), i. 214.

which politicians worked on the basis of these assumptions will be examined later.

Even a brief examination of the electoral system as it worked in 1910 shows that both of these assumptions are wrong. Rosenbaum then claimed that it was intended 'to produce a sort of electoral college . . . the members of this college are constituted not by election, but by selection; and not merely by selection, but by the elimination of those who may not be members.'[12] It automatically eliminated paupers, estimated by Rosenbaum as 472,000 in 1910; living-in servants (except in Scotland), 205,000; any son living with his parents who could not claim exclusive use at any time of his own room;[13] lodgers in rooms whose unfurnished rental was less than £10; as well as peers, lunatics, and, of course, women. The pre-1867 notion of the vote as a trust, a view shared both by J. S. Mill and Palmerston, remained. Thus the section on 'Life and duties of the citizen' in Arthur Acland's 'Evening School Code' of 1893 described 'the vote as a trust as well as a right'.[14] Inept citizenship led to the loss of the right, as a 1905 local government order showed: parents claiming school meals for their children under the order lost their right to vote.[15] That right was, in fact, still something dependent on a successful claim to possession. Conceptually, therefore, it differed little from the pre-1867 situation. This was because the nineteenth-century Reform Acts had widened the membership of the electorate, but had not fundamentally altered the nature of the franchise system: the right to vote was a privilege purchased through property, whether by its occupation, its ownership, or, in the case of the servant franchise, by an economic relationship to an owner of property. Many franchises were of great antiquity. It was not even known how many there were. But of the seven chief franchises only two, and those of little numerical significance—the freeman and the

---

[12] S. Rosenbaum, 'The General Election of January, 1910 and the Bearing of the Results on Some Problems of Representation', *Journal of the Royal Statistical Society*, 73 (1910), 473. Almost all serving soldiers and sailors were also excluded.

[13] This was plainly a middle-class franchise: very few working-class bachelors would have had a bedroom to themselves.

[14] See G. Wallas, *Human Nature in Politics* (London, 1920), 191–2.

[15] Because the feeding was done by the Boards of Guardians. See Bently B. Gilbert, *The Evolution of National Insurance in Great Britain* (London, 1973), 108–9. Striking could also lead to disfranchisement, for a long strike often made many strikers paupers; see, e.g., Hardie on some 4000 disfranchised Merthyr miners in 1900, in K. O. Morgan, *Keir Hardie* (London, 1975), 114.

university franchise—were not directly linked to the ownership or occupation of property.[16] As J. R. Clynes observed, the Speaker's Conference proposals of 1917 introduced for the first time an approximation to the view that 'the right that a man has for a vote is that he is a man.'[17]

The system also did more than exclude specific categories, important though these exclusions were. On 1 January 1910 there were 7,659,717 men on the rolls (including Ireland).[18] By allowing for 450,000 plural voters, Rosenbaum calculated that the total number of men *not* on the register was 4,665,000.[19] Dilke, an old hand at this game since the 1884-5 conferences, thought he underestimated the number of plural voters,[20] and J. R. Seager, the Liberal national agent, privately estimated them in 1912 at 520,000.[21] Neal Blewett, whose work has done so much to draw our attention to this question, concludes that there were 'at least half a million plural voters'.[22] A figure of 500,000 would, therefore, probably not be an exaggeration. This means that J. A. Pease's guess, made when drafting the 1912 bill, that there were in that year 4.6 million voteless men, is probably an underestimate, and the figure is probably closer to 4.8 million.[23] Whatever the exact number, it seems likely that at least 4.5 million men who would have been enfranchised had the 1918 terms applied were not eligible in 1910.

Who were these men? Certain specifically excluded categories, such as those on outdoor relief, can be calculated with some certainty. For the mass, however, it is difficult to be at all specific

[16] The five franchises important for registration levels were: Property (40s. freeholders, etc.); Occupation (property of £10 yearly value); Householder (occupier as owner or tenant of a separate dwelling, the landlord not being resident); Service (occupier of a separate dwelling by virtue of office or employment); and £10 Lodgers. For these, and an elegant exposition of the complexities of franchises and registration, see Neal Blewett, 'The Franchise in the United Kingdom, 1885-1918', *Past and Present*, (Dec. 1965); much illuminating detail will be found in P. F. Clarke, *Lancashire and the New Liberalism* (Cambridge, 1971), 427-9, and P. Thompson, *Socialists, Liberals and Labour: The Struggle for London 1885-1914* (London, 1967), 68-72.

[17] HC Deb. 5th ser., xcii, 530 (28 Mar. 1917).   [18] Rosenbaum, 473.
[19] Ibid. 475.
[20] Discussion of Rosenbaum's paper, *Journal of the Royal Statistical Society*, 73 (1910), 520-2.
[21] Memorandum by J. A. Pease, Gainford Papers, 64, Nuffield College, Oxford.   [22] Blewett, 'Franchise', 31.
[23] Memorandum by J. A. Pease, Gainford Papers 64.

in the post-poll book era. Few works on individual constituencies make even tentative estimates,[24] while other area studies or trade union histories hardly seem aware of the problem, though Clegg, Fox, and Thompson were the first historians to draw attention to it at a national level.[25]

A geographical analysis of levels of enfranchisement in 1911 immediately reveals a pattern.[26] England and Wales, nationally, show an obvious difference between boroughs and counties—a level of 59.8 per cent for the boroughs, 69.9 per cent for the counties. In Scotland the levels are both lower and closer: 57.3 per cent and 62.5 per cent. But the national figures conceal important differentials. In the towns the scale runs from 79.7 per cent in Inverness Burghs, 78.6 per cent in Montgomery Boroughs,[27] 75.3 per cent in Birmingham Central to 40.6 per cent in Glasgow, Bridgeton, 39.3 per cent in Liverpool, Everton, and 20.5 per cent in Whitechapel. These are extremes, but at neither end are they isolated anomalies. Whitechapel is often assumed to be freakish, but the working-class areas of London, comprising a large number of seats, had the lowest levels of enfranchisement in the country, and the figures for seats within the conurbations generally were very low. In England and Wales, 32.6 per cent of borough seats (70, of which 34 were in London) had adult male enfranchisement levels of 57 per cent or less, while only 22 out of the 215 English and Welsh boroughs (most of them county towns like Taunton and Oxford) had an adult male level of 70 per cent or over. A very few industrial towns, for example Rochdale (71.1 per cent) and Halifax (70.6 per cent) have levels characteristic of the county towns, but they are exceptional. Manchester could be regarded as

[24] A partial exception is Roy Gregory, *The Miners and British Politics* (Oxford, 1968). See Appendix A (pp. 192–7) for an attempted electoral breakdown of mining constituencies, finding about 55% of adult miners enfranchised in the North East. See also Thompson, *Socialists, Liberals and Labour*, and C. Wrigley on Battersea in K. D. Brown (ed.), *Essays in Anti-Labour History*, (London, 1974).

[25] H. Clegg, A. Fox, and A. F. Thompson, *A History of British Trade Unions since 1889* (Oxford, 1964), 269–70.

[26] 1911 has been used as the basis for comparison since the *Census of England and Wales, 1911*, PP (1912–13), cxii. 13, Table 3, 'Parliamentary Counties and Boroughs' supplies electoral and male population figures. Scottish figures are taken from PP (1912–13), lxvii. 495; PP (1913), lxxx. 361; and tables on the cities in PP (1912–13), cxixx.

[27] Most of the amalgamated district burgh and borough seats in Scotland and Wales have high levels.

the norm, with 53.1 per cent.[28] In London, socially superior divisions are markedly high. The average for Clapham, Dulwich, Croydon, Hampstead, South Kensington, Norwood, and Strand is 66.1 per cent.

It will be noticed that the figures in Table 3.1(*b*), high though they are, are still below those of prosperous county boroughs (see Table 3.2).[29] Yet even the county borough levels are still only reaching the *average* of the rural districts. Some examples of enfranchisement in agricultural county seats (Table 3.3) show how wide was the overall differential.

Characteristic of the levels in mixed rural and suburban county divisions are, for example, Warwickshire (4 seats)—71.3 per cent; and Surrey (6 seats)—69.4 per cent. We may here notice that the English national record holder (apart from the obvious exception of the 548.0 per cent of the City of London)[30] was Pudsey, where 112.1 per cent of males over 21 were enfranchised. The relationship between such levels was not uniform: a number of these county seats (including Pudsey) were Liberal, although the majority were Tory, and, despite the work of Peter Clarke, it cannot be concluded that there is a general relationship between high enfranchisement and Liberal parliamentary representation.[31] The mining divisions, traditionally the safest of the Liberal county seats, nearly all had well below average levels of enfranchisement. In County Durham (8 seats), for example, the figure was 65.4 per cent. This differential was especially marked in Wales. In the five mining and steel divisions of Glamorgan[32] the figure was 55.6 per cent, but in twelve other predominantly rural Welsh county seats[33] it was 76.2 per cent.

It cannot be argued that substantial improvement in national enfranchisement levels could be achieved by registration drives, though this could help in certain constituencies. The levels of the January 1915 register—the last made up under the pre-1918 franchise and registration Acts—show only a marginal improvement on those of 1892, and if figures for the 1914 county and

[28] The figure for Manchester is 51.0% if suburban North-West is excluded.
[29] None of these tables makes allowance for plural voters.
[30] In 1911 the City had a total residential male population of 10,080, but 30,988 electors, the great majority of whom lived outside the constituency.
[31] See Appendix to this chapter.
[32] East Glamorgan, Rhondda, Gower, Mid- and Southern Glamorgan.
[33] Anglesey, Brecknock, Cardigan, Camarthen East and West, Denbigh East and West, Flint, Merioneth, Montgomery, Pembrokeshire, Radnor.

TABLE 3.1. *Enfranchisement in urban areas, 1911 (% of adult males)*

	Seats/members	%
(a) Examples of low enfranchisement		
Tower Hamlets	7	35.7
Bethnal Green	2	42.6
Devonport	1	47.9
Dundee	2	48.1
Southwark	3	49.4
Islington	4	49.4
Liverpool	9	49.8
Glasgow	7	52.4
Birkenhead	1	52.8
Manchester	6	53.1
Middlesborough	1	53.6
Warrington	1	53.6
Salford	3	53.9
Swansea district	1	54.7
Portsmouth	2	54.9
Southampton	2	55.6
Merthyr	2	55.7
Barrow	1	56.1
Cardiff	1	56.4
Morpeth	1	56.4
Stockton	1	56.4
Stoke	1	57.0
Hanley	1	58.3
Sheffield	5	58.5
(b) Examples of higher enfranchisement		
Kingston upon Hull	3	61.9
Birmingham	7	62.0
Wolverhampton	3	63.0
Oldham	1	63.1
Newcastle upon Tyne	2	63.4
Leeds	5	64.2
Bristol	4	67.4
Nottingham	3	67.4
Bradford	3	67.9
Edinburgh	4	69.1

TABLE 3.2. *Enfranchisement in county boroughs, 1911 (% of adult males)*

	%
Bath	68.6
King's Lynn	68.7
Cheltenham	70.7
Warwick and Leamington	73.1
Scarborough	73.1
Cambridge	73.6
Exeter	74.2
Oxford	75.0

TABLE 3.3. *Enfranchisement in agricultural counties, 1911 (% of adult males)*

	Seats	%
Somerset	7	79.4
Cornwall	6	80.7
Devon (incl. Ashburton)	6	81.3
Lincolnshire	7	84.1

borough populations were available, even this change would probably disappear. Table 3.4 shows the trends.[34] The register of January 1915, compiled from the overseers' lists of July 1914, may well have represented as high an enfranchisement level as could be

[34] Made up from the 1891, 1901, 1911 census tables, PP (1893–4), xx. 675, which allows comparison of the 1892 electorate with the 1891 population, and PP (1914–16), lii. 596. The England and Wales column includes university voters. The 1915 figure is calculated on the basis of the 1911 census using an adult male percentage of 57. On the basis of the 1914 male population estimate of Mitchell and Deane, *Abstract of British Historical Statistics* (1962), 10, the England and Wales figure is 66.4% (i.e. below the 1892 figure); no estimates for the 1914 borough and county populations have been found. Because of the rapidly declining birth rate throughout this period, it is important to calculate the *adult* male percentage; comparison on the basis of the all-male population is misleading. The following have been taken in this chapter as the percentages of males aged 21 and over: 1891, 51.7%; 1901, 54.4%; 1911, 56.0% 1915, 57.0%; 1921, 59.5%.

TABLE 3.4. *Adult males enfranchised in England and Wales (%)*

	Total	Counties	Boroughs
1892	66.9	73.2	59.7
1901	63.0	68.1	56.9
1911	65.6	69.9	59.9
1915	68.1	72.8	61.9

achieved under the old franchise and registration system; the war had begun before the revision courts began to sit, and the lists consequently went through the revising barristers' courts for the most part uncontested by the party organizations.[35]

After the 1918 Act enfranchisement levels quickly rose very high.[36] The preponderance of men as plural voters and the fact that women's enfranchisement depended upon a property qualification nevertheless ensured that almost everywhere female enfranchisement was markedly lower than male. By the autumn register of 1921,[37] the English adult male enfranchisement level was 94.9 per cent and only 39 out of the 509 constituencies in England and Wales had levels of less than 85 per cent for males over 21. Eight of these were in London; Chelsea (82.4), Hammersmith North and South (77.7, 84.4), Paddington South (80.6), St Pancras SE and SW (79.0, 74.7), Mile End (59.1), Whitechapel (57.1). A surprising number of the rest were in those county towns previously noted for high levels, but some of these are to be explained by such local anomalies as university terms or

[35] See W. E. Hume-Williams in HC Deb. 5th ser. lxxiii, 1857 (23 July 1915).

[36] Under this Act there were three franchises for men: one dependent on six months residence, another dependent on occupation of business premises of £10 yearly value, and the university franchise. The first enfranchised almost all adult men, the others allowed a plural vote, which could only be cast once. A proportion of females were also enfranchised, a woman over 30 being registered if a local government elector occupying property of £5 yearly value, or if occupying (in the pre-1918 sense) a dwelling house, or if married to a man similarly entitled to be registered. Since the register was now compiled twice yearly, the post-1918 local government register cannot be regarded as even an approximate indicator of how the old system would have been post-1918 had it not been reformed. See G. P. W. Terry, *The Representation of the People Act* (London, 1919).

[37] Taken from the *Census of England and Wales, 1921, General Report* Table 16, p. 24.

military and boarding-house absences: Oxford (82.4), Weston-super-Mare (84.7), Bournemouth (78.4), Aldershot (66.0), Epsom (82.5), Brighton (82.9), Hastings (82.2), Eastbourne (80.6), Salisbury (80.6), Carnarvon Boroughs (74.4). One, Cardiff, had a higher female than male percentage level (84.1 male, 85.0 female). Because plural voting continued, these figures do not give one man–one vote levels; 76 seats in England and Wales in 1921 had an adult male registration percentage of 100 or over.

The national increase was dramatic enough—from 68.0 per cent to 94.9 per cent in England and Wales—but for the urban areas of previous low enfranchisement the increase was in many cases spectacular, with the adult male level of enfranchisement being in some great cities almost doubled; Glasgow for example increased from 52.4 per cent to 101.3 per cent. The extensive redistribution of 1918 means that the 1921 constituencies of Table 3.5 cannot exactly be compared with those of Tables 3.1 and 3.3, but even allowing for the alteration in boundaries, the effect of the 1918 Act on urban and industrial areas is plain.

The geographical pattern of pre-1918 enfranchisement—and lack of it—is, therefore, fairly clear. It was high in rural areas, county boroughs, suburban divisions, spas, and watering places. It was particularly low in the cities, in constituencies of high mobility, and low generally in industrial seats. Although there are a few anomalies, these generalizations hold true for the vast majority of seats. As for its social characteristics, the old electoral system discriminated in the first place by sex: all women were excluded,[38] it discriminated by class, through plural voting on the one hand, and statutory and *de facto* disfranchisement on the other; it discriminated against the poorest; it discriminated against the most mobile; it discriminated against the youngest; it excluded between 40 and 45 per cent of the Edwardian adult male population, and in terms of the 1921 electorate this meant about 65 per cent of possible voters.

Is it now possible to analyse the Edwardian electorate further? Few national or local studies have tried, and those that do are not very reliable. A. K. Russell estimates that in 1906 75–80 per cent of the electorate were members of the working class,[39] but even a superficial glance suggests that this is a serious overestimate.

---

[38] Though under certain conditions they had the vote in local elections.
[39] A. K. Russell, *Liberal Landslide* (London, 1973), 19–21.

TABLE 3.5. *Examples from autumn register, 1921*
(% enfranchised)

	Number of seats	Adult males	Females aged 30 and over
Totals			
England	474	94.9	79.5
Wales (including Monmouthshire)	35	95.3	84.1
Scotland	70	94.1	79.2
Boroughs			
Glasgow	15	101.3	85.5
Sheffield	7	99.3	85.2
Merthyr and Rhondda	4	99.4	91.6
Birmingham	12	99.0	81.7
Edinburgh	5	99.0	87.0
Bristol	5	98.7	84.4
Leeds	6	97.5	82.8
Dundee	1	97.1	82.8
Liverpool	11	95.9	82.4
Salford	3	94.2	78.1
Manchester	10	93.8	81.7
London	61	93.4	79.9
Islington	4	92.1	81.0
Southwark	3	91.1	87.1
Bethnal Green	2	90.9	84.3
Stepney	3	66.9	64.7
Counties			
Durham	11	98.9	87.2
Cornwall	5	97.3	77.7
Warwickshire	4	95.1	76.5
Devon	7	94.8	73.4
Somerset	6	94.6	75.4
Lincolnshire	4	93.7	79.2
Surrey	7	90.1	70.4

According to Guy Routh, the *whole* of the Edwardian working class made up 79.67 per cent of the population.[40] But for Russell's calculation to be accurate there would have to be an absolute

[40] G. Routh, *Occupation and Pay in Great Britain, 1900–1960* (Cambridge, 1965), 4–5.

identity between the structure of the population and that of the electorate. Plainly this was not so. Blewett—on the basis of Routh's figures—judges that about 38 per cent of the electorate belonged to the middle class.[41] But given the high enfranchisement levels of suburban seats the registration of middle-class voters was perhaps greater than he allows for and the figure is probably more like 40 per cent or even higher: that is exactly twice the proportion the middle class bore in the electorate after 1918, when the structure of the male electorate and the structure of the male population largely conformed. Since, however, agricultural labourers are included in Routh's category of 'manual workers', even this must be a chancy sum. Pelling, for example, concludes that before 1914 89 constituencies (electing 95 members) were 'predominantly working-class in character'.[42] On redistribution the number of such seats would presumably have increased substantially, but in the Edwardian electoral system the industrial working class was probably not a preponderant element.

How was such a large proportion of the male working class excluded from the registers? Most observers persist in regarding such exclusion as merely the anomalous working of laws which in principle permitted universal access.[43] But access was in principle already denied to four categories of people; paupers, living-in servants, most of the military, and many sons living with parents. And while it is true that the very rigorous registration requirements attached both to the occupation and lodger franchises denied the vote to millions who might in theory have claimed it,[44] this was anticipated when the requirements were formulated in the first place.[45] It is hard to disagree with the Liberal agents when they told Pease that mass disqualification was inherent in the occupation

[41] N. Blewett, *The Peers, the Parties and the People* (London, 1972), 363–4.

[42] H. M. Pelling, *Social Geography of British Elections* (London, 1967), 419–20.

[43] This is the implication of Blewett's argument in 'Franchise' and *The Peers, the Parties and the People*, 358–64. See also Richard Rose, *Electoral Behaviour* (London, 1974), 482.

[44] For details, see Blewett, 'The Franchise', 34–43.

[45] A. Jones, *The Politics of Reform, 1884* (Cambridge, 1972), 133–5. See also Joseph Chamberlain's speech 'The Fruits of the Franchise', 29 Jan. 1885, *Mr. Chamberlain's Speeches* (London, 1914), i. 152. The long process of drawing up the register meant that it was very stale when it came into operation. This did not affect the enfranchisement levels, but it did affect a party's ability to mobilize its vote, if, as in Dec. 1910, a substantial proportion of its voters might have removed; see, e.g., Clarke, *Lancashire and New Liberalism*, ch. 5.

franchise.[46] It is hard, also, to avoid the conclusion that that is precisely why it was there.[47]

The complexities of registration were considerable, none more so than for the £10 lodger franchise, 'a mere agent's franchise' as Blewett has called it,[48] and in the large boroughs only 127,360 men were registered under it. Even more than the occupation franchise, it put a premium on registration and an effective constituency agent.[49] A successfully registered lodger was usually a small-scale triumph, and who after 1918 would have apostrophized his vote as Richard Le Gallienne, decadent friend of Wilde and Beardsley, did in 1895?

> There, in my mind's eye, pure it lay,
> My lodger's vote! 'Twas mine today.
> It seemed a sort of maidenhood,
> My little power for public good,
> Oh, keep it uncorrupted, pray.[50]

However, that this system was intended to be class-exclusive is unquestionable, and its effect was to disfranchise almost half the industrial working class.

[46] Memorandum by A. K. Durham (Southport) on behalf of Liberal Agents, Gainford Papers 67, (?) June 1912.

[47] One of the sharpest critics of the registration laws was Sir Charles Dilke's former secretary and a student of a genuinely democratic electorate, J. E. C. Bodley. He made the interesting point that 'the granting of the vote to women in municipal and other elections [perpetuated] the possession of property as the basis for electoral suffrage' and postponed the enactment of a uniform and 'unencumbered' franchise 'to the distant period looked forward to by politicians whose ideals need the genius of Swift or Aristophanes to do them justice'. J. E. C. Bodley, *France* (London, 1898), ii. 63–4.   [48] Blewett, 'Franchise', 41.

[49] For the significance of registration, see M. Ostrogorski, *Democracy and the Organization of Political Parties* (London, 1902), i. 373–82; H. J. Hanham, *Elections and Party Management: Politics in the Time of Gladstone and Disraeli* (London, 1964), 394–403. Grace A. Jones, 'Further Thoughts on the Franchise', *Past and Present*, 34 (July 1966), 134–8, emphasizes the importance of the registration agent by the end of the 19th c. For the work of the agent see particularly Arthur Henderson to J. R. MacDonald, 6 June 1903, LPLF, LRC 9/11; and more generally, A. Henderson and J. R. MacDonald, *Notes on Organization* (London, 1903). Despite Henderson's assertion that it was not the function of the registration agent merely 'to keep voters off the register' (Henderson and MacDonald, 17), it was in practice one of his main duties. Challenging the register before a revising barrister led to much ill-will, and was an inevitable consequence of laws both complex and obscure. But it also led to considerable ingenuity. Ostrogorski records the following exchange in the Islington Registration Court: '*The Revising Barrister*. A wise man would send his claim through both parties. *The Vestry Clerk*. or claim through his political opponents. *The Revising Barrister*. and give notice to his friends. *The Vestry Clerk*. and use his opponents' conveyances at elections.' Ostrogorski, i. 379 n.   [50] Reid, *New Party*, 275.

This may not necessarily have had consequences either for the sociology or the history of British political parties, but it is reasonable to suppose that it might. Yet until very recently this phenomenon went almost unnoticed. Ostrogorski, despite much on the absurdities of the registration requirements, never actually examined their effect, beyond concluding that 1829, 1832, and 1867 more or less completed the triumph of democracy.[51] Seymour at least assumed that democracy did not triumph until 1885.[52] These weighty, but erroneous, judgements have found their way into the conventional wisdom. Thus David Butler tells us that the 1884 Act 'went almost all the way to universal male suffrage',[53] while he and Donald Stokes assumed that the parents of their oldest cohort—the 'pre-1918' cohort—were enfranchised.[54] McKenzie and Silver are more directly inaccurate: they argue that the working class 'constituted a majority of the total electorate' after 1867, and that the last impediments were removed in 1884.[55]

Clegg, Fox, and Thompson drew attention to the national figures, and subsequently Blewett and Clarke have tried to come to terms with the implication of a limited electorate.[56] But only Clarke has inserted the consequences of franchise reform within his argument, and the success of this assertion is dependent, as we shall see, upon an assumption that is arguable and not proven when tested.[57] So far as we know, only Ivor Crewe, in a long review of Butler and Stokes, and Chris Chamberlain try to tackle

---

[51] Ostrogorski, 125–30, 578. But see Bagehot, who (in 1872) argued that the only question was how 'the few nominal electors—the £10 borough renters, and the £50 county renters were able to suborn the masses. W. Bagehot, *The English Constitution* (Fontana edn.; London, 1973), 249. Ostrogorski, Cadet deputy in the first Duma and a doctrinaire Russian liberal, would never have asked himself such a question.

[52] Charles Seymour, *Electoral Reform in England and Wales* (New Haven Oxford, 1915), 523.

[53] D. E. Butler, *The Electoral System in Britain since 1918* (Oxford, 1963), 5.

[54] D. E. Butler and Donald Stokes, *Political Change in Britain* (Pelican edn.; Harmondsworth, 1971), 66–73. The Butler–Stokes questionnaire contained no item on either enfranchisement or registration, and the historical dimension is perhaps the weakest part of this otherwise most important book.

[55] Robert McKenzie and Allan Silver, *Angels in Marble* (London, 1968), 9–10. It is unlikely, though, that this affects their conclusions, which stand or fall on other grounds.

[56] Clegg, *et al.*, 269–70; Blewett, *Peers, Parties, and People*, 358–64; Clarke, *Lancashire and New Liberalism* 103–29. Roy Douglas, 'Labour in Decline, 1910–1914', in Brown, *Essays in Anti-Labour History*, mentions the problem but ignores its implications.   [57] See Appendix to this chapter.

the consequences of the 1918 franchise changes, but in the first case only *en passant*, and in the second, by using national figures which are misleading and somewhat inaccurate.[58]

This survey of the nature and historiography of the pre-1918 electorate leads to the hypothesis which seems to us central: that it was the 1918 Representation of the People Act—the 'Fourth' Reform Act—which was of first importance in Labour's replacing the Liberal Party as the principal party of progress. Such a hypothesis must argue that the events of the war were only subordinate factors in this change, and that under a genuinely democratic pre-war franchise Labour would have been a more effective rival of the other two parties than it actually was. But we do not suggest that the Labour Party would necessarily have superseded the Liberals before 1914—it only *just* did so in the early 1920s and to ignore chronological developments would be absurd—but it is to suggest that the disproportion between their strengths would have been significantly less, and diminishing.

There is a negative and a positive reason for supposing that such a hypothesis might be true. The negative one is that the 'war' argument, though frequently embraced, has never been properly demonstrated, and in some cases not demonstrated at all.[59] It is easy to see why this should be. It would have to be shown that the war so significantly altered the structure of the British economy and habits of thought and expectation that the social basis of the pre-war party system no longer existed, or that the divisions within the Liberal Party themselves determined the post-war successes of Labour. Finally, such an argument must assume that in the event of manhood suffrage coming before 1914 the newly enfranchised would have voted for the same political parties in the same proportion as the existing electorate, even though the mass of the new voters came from different social classes. However, this assumption is not argued in any of the literature, let alone proved.

But the war was not responsible for any major structural changes in the economy, and it is hard to show that it altered

[58] Ivor Crewe, 'Do Butler and Stokes Really Explain Political Change in Britain?' *European Journal of Political Research*, (1974), 49–72; Chris Chamberlain, 'The Growth in Support for the Labour Party', *British Journal of Sociology*, 24 (1973), 474–8.

[59] For a discussion of this, see H. M. Pelling, *Britain and the Second World War* (London, 1970), 298–9.

popular attitudes.[60] This is true even of franchise reform itself, as is shown below. Furthermore, those who argue for the war's importance have also to argue that mass political behaviour is largely conditioned by the actions of a number of political élites—by events at Westminster—yet Clarke, who believes that the mass of the potential working-class electorate was Liberal and who explicitly asserts the crucial significance of the war, is nevertheless anxious to show that political behaviour is not conditioned by élites.

We know, however, that in 1914 Britain was the most industrialized country in Europe, with the largest hereditary working class, much of which was organized by a powerful and rapidly growing trade-union movement. It is hard to disagree with Sombart that growing division between capital and labour transformed the patterns of politics in Great Britain, as in Western Europe, by creating social classes that could not be contained within its traditional political organizations.[61] Furthermore, though Western European working-class parties had grown rapidly since 1890, there were important national differences, and Great Britain already had a Labour Party, the agency of a trade-union movement absolutely and relatively more numerous than any on the Continent.

It is hardly unreasonable, therefore, at least to examine the hypothesis that the growth of the Labour Party before 1914 was limited not by 'natural' social and political restrictions, but an artificial one: a franchise and registration system that excluded the greater part of its likely support.

The most effective test of the impact of the franchise changes on party strength would be to refight the 1922 election on the 1910 franchise.[62] This objective is frustrated by a combination of two

[60] Philip Abrams, 'The Failure of Social Reform: 1918–1920', *Past and Present*, 24 (1963), 59–62.

[61] W. Sombart, *Der Moderne Kapitalismus*, 3 vols. (Munich/Leipzig, 1917), iii. 1093–107.

[62] The extensive redistribution of 1918 left very few boundaries unchanged, and the boundaries of and in most cities were altered drastically; we have not been able to find enough comparable constituencies to attempt to compare pre- and post-1918 election results, nor have we attempted to incorporate changes consequent on redistribution into our analysis; Labour's benefit from redistribution appears to have been slight; see M. Kinnear, *The Fall of Lloyd George* (London, 1973), 52. Because of the complexity of party affiliations and cross-affiliation in 1918, and the fact that in many constituencies the major parties were not in opposition, we have chosen for purposes of comparison 1922 as the first representative post-war election.

factors—the major redistribution of constituencies in 1918 and the change in the nature and variety of contests which occurred. We therefore adopt a more circumstantial approach and assess the principal alternative hypothesis of the origins of Labour support— that Labour was the major beneficiary of the Liberal decline. This argument has recently been criticized by Chamberlain, who notes that the maximum Liberal vote achieved was 5.3 million in 1929. Liberal totals of 4.1 million in 1922 and 4.3 million in 1923 compare favourably with the pre-war maximum of 2.9 million in January 1910.[63] Chamberlain's view that 'it is very unlikely that Liberal supporters abandoned their party on any large scale' must, however, be exaggerated. When the size of the electorate is trebled, as in 1918, a party which fails to increase the number of its voters is doing very badly indeed. It is unlikely that the political preferences of the male and female members of households in which men were enfranchised before 1918 were markedly different and the Liberals might have expected a total of 5 million votes in 1922–4 and 6 million in 1929 from this group alone. The erosion of Liberal support is perhaps most marked in London, where in straight fights between Conservatives and Labour there is an average swing to the Conservatives of 6.1 per cent between 1923 and 1924. In three-cornered contests, the Labour share of the vote rises in 14 of 15 constituencies, by an average of 5.8 per cent, while the Liberal share falls catastrophically from 31.8 per cent to 17.8 per cent.

There can therefore be little doubt that there were substantial Liberal defections, some from those who were deprived of a Liberal candidate to vote for (the Liberals fought 477 seats in 1922—339 Asquithian and 138 Lloyd George Liberals—and only 346 in 1924), others from those who chose to give their vote to another party. Who benefited from these defections? Some suggestive evidence is provided by Butler and Stokes, who find that of those who recall their father's preferences as Liberal, 40 per cent now see themselves as Conservatives and 34 per cent as Labour voters: while among those whose own earliest preferences were Liberal, the split is 25 per cent Conservative, 19 per cent Labour.[64] This pattern is confirmed by more detailed analysis of the London pattern described above. There is a (low) correlation

[63] Chamberlain, 'Support for the Labour Party', 475.
[64] Butler and Stokes, *Political Change*, 307–8.

between Liberal losses and improvement in the Conservative performance relative to Labour, and the two seats in which the Liberal vote holds up best (Mile End and Lambeth North) are the only two in which the Conservative share of the vote declines.

An alternative approach is to examine the second preferences of frustrated Liberal voters: those who did not have a Liberal candidate to support. We have examined those English constituencies in which Liberals contested one or two, but not all three of the elections in 1922, 1923, and 1924, and have estimated what the result would have been in each case had the Liberals withdrawn from an election which they did in fact contest. This enables us to estimate what the Liberal voters would have done had they not voted Liberal—how many would have stayed at home, and how the rest would have divided between the other two parties.[65] The results are shown in Table 3.6.

It is possible that the differences we observe between different years are real ones: but it should be noted that if we have, for example, overestimated Labour's gains between 1922 and 1923 the result will be that we understate the number of Liberals who voted Labour in 1923 and overstate the number of Liberals who voted Labour in 1922. The pattern of the data suggests that this may very well be so. But whether or not it is so, the general position is clear. There is a committed Liberal vote, unwilling to vote for either of the other two parties, which amounts to around 25–30 per cent of the total number of Liberal voters. The breakdown of the remaining Liberal vote does not markedly favour one party or the other. There is some indication that Liberals in urban areas were more Conservative in their preferences, those in rural seats being more likely to vote Labour, but the differences are not great. If our statistical explanation of the differences between years is correct, we can reasonably average the percentage figures and suggest that the Labour and Conservative Parties each held about 35 per cent of Liberal voters' second preferences, with any marginal advantage going to the Conservatives.

Thus these different pieces of statistical evidence run strongly

[65] We have assumed that had a Liberal not intervened, the two-party swing and turnout change would have been the same as the average for seats in which there was no such intervention. This hypothetical result is compared with the actual result, and the difference between the actual and notional polls of each major party indicates the number of Liberals whose second preference was that party, while the difference in turnout indicates the number with no second preference.

TABLE 3.6. *Estimates of Liberal voters' preferences ('second pre ferences') where no Liberal candidate stood, 1922–1924*

1922 Liberals: vote in 1923

	Labour	Conservative	Abstention
Boroughs	9,187	28,541	14,893
Counties	15,592	17,967	15,747
Total	24,779 (24%)	46,508 (46%)	30,640 (30%)
1923 Liberals: voted in 1922			
Boroughs	27,811	29,039	24,683
Counties	71,906	29,056	49,676
Total	99,717 (43%)	58,095 (25%)	74,359 (32%)
1923 Liberals: vote in 1923			
Boroughs	101,584	104,192	49,981
Counties	39,671	19,980	41,341
Total	141,255 (40%)	124,172 (35%)	91,322 (26%)
1924 Liberals: vote in 1923			
Boroughs	5,911	8,708	5,146
Counties	17,150	18,139	8,920
Total	23,061 (36%)	26,847 (42%)	14,066 (22%)

against the hypothesis of a single, progressive vote which in the 1920s switched its allegiance from the Liberals to the Labour Party. The disintegration of the Liberal Party did not produce large net gains for either of its rivals, and it is slightly more probable that the Conservatives were the beneficiaries. But it is easy to see why the opposite has been assumed. If the Conservative and Liberal Parties are of roughly equal size, and Liberal support divides equally between the Conservatives and an emergent Labour Party, then one of the parties which result will be overwhelmingly larger than the other. Yet even in 1924, before this process was complete and in a bad year for Labour, the new party won 5.5 million votes as against 7.8 million for the Conservatives. This success can only be explained by supposing that Labour was able to mobilize some latent source of support which had not been available to the other two parties.

Such potential support certainly existed in the pre-war electorate. Of the 579 mainland constituencies, Labour contested only 77 in January 1910 and 56 in December, obtaining (in January) just over half a million votes. We have undertaken an analysis of the second preferences of Labour voters in 1910, on similar lines to that described above. Here there is a marked contrast between Lancashire and Scotland in both of which a significant proportion of the Labour voters appear to see the Conservatives as an alternative, and the rest of the country, where that proportion is negligible (Table 3.7). There is a minority of Labour voters who are not accommodated by either of the then major parties. This is confirmed by the behaviour of Labour voters in the two cases where two Liberal and one Labour candidate sought election in two-member constituencies (Table 3.8). (These Dundee and Portsmouth results are very different from those obtained in other two-member seats, where Labour and Liberal candidates were in co-operation rather than in conflict, and the degree of loyalty to the ticket was very high.)

Thus there is evidence of a latent Labour vote in the pre-war electorate, which could have been mobilized by more candidates. But it could not have been large. The greater proportion of Labour votes were obtained in seats where there was no Liberal opposition. Blewett has shown that in the 35 cases where Labour

TABLE 3.7. *Estimated second preferences of 1910 Labour voters (%)*

	Conservative	Liberal	Abstention
Lancashire and Scotland	30	53	17
Other	5	70	25

TABLE 3.8. *Second preferences of 1910 Labour voters (%)*

	Conservative	Liberal	Abstention
Dundee, 1906	14	48	37
Portsmouth, 1910	8	50	42

candidates fought three-cornered contests in 1910, Labour came bottom of the poll in 29, and obtained a median share of the vote of 22 per cent.[66] It is unlikely that the seats Labour contested were chosen at random, and if they had put up more candidates their share would certainly have been lower. An overall average share of 15 per cent would have given Labour under a million votes in 1910. Further, the turn-out in January 1910 (86.6 per cent) was the highest at any modern election. If the votes which were to bring Labour to power in the 1920s were not, in the main, being cast for the Liberals, there is little evidence that they were consciously withheld in the absence of an acceptable candidate.

Thus there was in the pre-war electorate no large pool of voters uncommitted to the existing major parties: nor was the subsequent weakening of those commitments a factor which gave net advantage to the Labour Party. It follows that the substantial post-war growth in Labour's relative strength must in large measure be attributable to the franchise extension and registration reform of 1918. It is difficult to assess how large that measure is—indeed the question is hardly a meaningful one, since the factors involved in the rise of Labour are not independent. Labour's acquisition of a substantial new basis of support was clearly a factor promoting the defection of Liberal voters to both right and left. Had the Liberal vote not been crumbling for what were, at least in part, other reasons, a larger proportion of the newly enfranchised electorate might have given them their support. We cannot say how many votes the introduction of universal franchise was worth to Labour, but we can say that it was a critical element in the emergence of the party as a major force.

Even the most tentative interpretations of these figures do not give much comfort to those who argue the existence of a single 'progressive' vote. Indeed, the more or less equal division of the Liberals between right and left suggests that the Liberal Imperialists were probably correct in their assumption that their party stood to lose equally in both directions.[67] The evidence thus suggests that the Liberals were unable to mobilize the fully enfranchised electorate as successfully as the Labour Party—or the Conservative Party. But the argument that the electorate was

[66] Blewett, *Peers, Parties, People*, 389–95.
[67] For this, see H. C. G. Matthew, *The Liberal Imperialists* (Oxford, 1973), 291–6.

polarized into 'right' and 'left' and that the Liberals as the party of the centre were bound to lose is only prima facie true. We could certainly agree that as the cleavage between capital (or management) and labour became a fundamental one, a party based upon organized labour seems likely to have emerged. As we suggested earlier, that argument is basic to our hypothesis. On the other hand, it is questionable how many of the new Labour voters saw themselves as specifically 'left', and in any case, full enfranchisement did the Conservatives—*the* party of property—little discernible harm.

Therefore, while we believe that many of the difficulties faced by the Liberal Party in the post-1918 era were intrinsic to the developments of British capitalism, we would argue also that its failure lay partly in its attitude to the political community and the nature of its political organization. This is seen at two levels: in the reluctance of the Liberals to take electoral organization seriously, and, more widely, in their incapacity to make the necessary 'demagogic' appeals to the mass electorate created by the 1918 Act.[68]

Attempts to reform the Liberal organization—or rather to set one up—almost always failed. Herbert Gladstone's reforms as whip seemed far-reaching, but in fact they succeeded only in raising the number of candidates and improving their finances immediately before the election. His scheme to increase the number of permanent agents, and to co-ordinate them by fourteen district agents, was rejected.[69] A district agent scheme was started in 1910 by J. A. Pease, but the agents were responsible to district federations set up under the same scheme, which seem to have been chiefly concerned with policy discussion rather than organizational detail. It is interesting that, on returning as party organizer in 1922, Herbert Gladstone did not blame the war for the collapse of organization, but rather the form of Pease's decentralized federation: 'If his [Pease's] scheme had had any

[68] Sir Robert Hudson, the key organizational figure in any Liberal revival, showed no awareness of any major change in his letter to Sir D. Maclean of 12 Jan. 1919, spelling out required changes; these amounted to a more effective NLF, an 'enlarged' publication department, 'special attention to be paid to (a) the women, and (b) the nonconformists' (Maclean MSS, Bodleian Library, Oxford, dep. c. 465, fo. 121).

[69] See T. O. Lloyd, 'The whip as paymaster: Herbert Gladstone and party organization', *English Historical Review*, 89 (1974), 798.

bones in it, it should have been a virile force when the L[iberal] C[entral] A[ssociation] fell to pieces in 1918. It had no power of initiation, it did nothing to stop the rot, it did not even propose a policy.'[70] The Liberals never seem to have contemplated a formal party structure, and the notion of party membership would probably have been seen as illiberal. It is true that organization was taken more seriously after 1906, but then fitfully and only by part of the leadership. As Sir Robert Hudson pointed out in 1907, the Liberal habit in many places of having agents only at election time was hazardous, and he complained publicly in 1910 that the first retrenchment was always in organization.[71]

Despite the recovery after 1902, the Liberals in the boroughs still depended on the caucus system, which, as Ostrogorski pointed out, was already in decline in the 1890s, on the *ad hoc* personal and commercial relationships of local businessmen and other self-selected bourgeois notables. This system, even at its most perfect, would have had difficulty in coping with the demands of a very much larger electorate, but the old organization had decayed, and there were only a few signs by 1914 that the Liberals had devised a new one, unlike the still small Labour Party, which regarded mass organization as the indispensable preliminary to later political success,[72] and the Unionists, who greatly strengthened their organization in the late Edwardian period.

This ambiguous attitude to organization was in part a product of a view of politics that was unique to the Liberal Party. More than the other parties the Liberals assumed that the electorate could be organized, not by extra-parliamentary agencies, but by an appeal to issues, to good sense, to active citizenship, to intelligent political interest, and to an articulate awareness of the content of legislation. It was the policy of 'filling the cup', of the Newcastle Programme, of the hunt for a New Liberalism, for an electorally successful social policy, for 'campaigns' (like the Land Campaign of 1912 onwards) that would excite the electorate. It is apparent equally in the earnestness with which the Liberal press tried to eschew 'stunts' and 'sensations'—the supposed chief characteristic

---

[70] Gladstone to Hudson, 3 Feb. 1923, BL Add. MS. 46475, fo. 37.

[71] J. A. Spender, *Sir Robert Hudson* (London, 1930), 119.

[72] For this, see R. McKibbin, *The Evolution of the Labour Party* (Oxford, 1974), 20–43. It is worth noting here that one of the principal reasons for reorganizing the Labour Party in 1917 was that the existing organization could not handle the electorate about to be created by the 1918 Act.

of the Tory press. The remarkable thing about this anachronistic system is that it should have lasted so long. It did so partly because the Edwardian electorate was as narrow as it was and so defined that a fair part of it would respond to appeals of this sort.

The Liberal Party saw itself—and it was seen by its opponents on the right—as the party of democracy and of a democratic electorate. Yet, consciously or not, the Liberals acted as if they were satisfied with the existing electorate, purified perhaps of some of its anomalies. In 1908 A. L. Lowell wrote that 'neither political party is now anxious to extend the franchise . . . and leading Liberals have come to realize that any further extension would be likely to benefit their opponents.'[73] On the other hand, in 1971 Clarke concluded that 'with the advent of class politics, the Liberals could no longer afford to perpetuate a system which over-represented their natural opponents and excluded many of their potential supporters. Yet the logical strategy—a fourth Reform Bill—was confounded by the Government's irresolution. In obstructing the claim for woman suffrage the Liberal Party risked being hoist with its own petard.'[74]

Not surprisingly, the truth lies somewhere between these two. In the 1906 parliament Labour members sponsored several private manhood suffrage bills, but the Liberal offering was a plural voting bill rejected by the Lords. J. A. Pease's bill of 1912, the Liberal's most serious effort, would have abolished most forms of plural voting and would have greatly improved registration procedures, adding about 2.5 million men to the electorate. The bill was, of course, killed by the 'Speaker's bombshell'—the ruling of January 1913 that women's suffrage (the so-called Conciliation Bill) could not be tacked on to it. It was not again presented and the cabinet weakly brought forward no other major franchise bill.[75]

It is clear from the evidence of Pease's papers, as well as from the general apathy in the House of Commons,[76] that the government and the Parliamentary Liberal Party cared little about

[73] Lowell, *Government of England*, i. 214.   [74] Clarke, 129.

[75] Much the best source for the history of the suffrage bill of 1912 is to be found in the papers of J. A. Pease (Gainford Papers 85 (Diaries) and 63 to 65).

[76] See the *Manchester Guardian*, 18 June 1912: 'Time was when a Reform Bill would not only have set the roofs of Bristol ablaze but kept members from their tea. We have changed all that. Tonight in a listless and half-empty House . . . a new Reform Bill was introduced.' The *Daily News* thought that 'the week-end habit was to blame' (18 June 1912).

the hill. Pease blamed Lloyd George for the torpor; and he certainly showed no interest in it.[77] Harcourt thought that the 'ship was simply carrying too much cargo'; the government's timetable was already so filled that it could not admit another 'big bill'.[78]

That was true—but the timetable showed priorities: a cabinet which in November 1912 put Welsh disestablishment far ahead of the fourth Reform bill hardly seemed seized of any particular need to advance the constitutional pale,[79] particularly if they believed that franchise extensions would have benefited them. The *Morning Post*'s comment on Pease's bill, that it would depreciate 'the standard of active citizenship',[80] though meant for the country vicarages, probably also reflected cabinet opinion, and certainly as a sentiment differed little from Grey's support in cabinet for payment of MPs (as it would rescue his constituents from the 'control of trade organizations'), or from Lloyd George's complaints of 'trade union dictation' in Wales.[81]

As Lowell suggested, the cabinet would probably have liked a simple plural voting bill. Pease, constantly obstructed in his attempts to bring in a large bill, was under pressure to produce a quick one. The Liberals had done a good deal of research into the effects of plural voting, though characteristically without reaching unanimity: the *Westminster Gazette* calculated that the Liberals stood to gain about thirty seats;[82] Pease that they stood to gain about nine.[83] But it was agreed that a plural voting bill would remove the only known bias against the Liberals in the existing structure. It was widely assumed that there would be such a bill. The secretary of the Labour Party, Arthur Henderson, told Ramsay MacDonald, on 'reliable authority', that the Liberal chief whip, Illingworth, had addressed the Liberal agents 'on the lines of "general election next year, and certainly not without the passing of the Plural Voting Bill" '.[84] But the cabinet could not even manage that. Pease's cajoling—he told the cabinet that the 1912 bill was the 'best method to secure Liberals in power and

[77] Gainford Papers 85, 27 Jan. 1913.
[78] Harcourt to Pease, 27 Dec. 1912, Gainford Papers 63.
[79] Gainford Papers 85, report of the cabinet of 20 Nov. 1912.
[80] *Morning Post*, 18 June 1912.
[81] Gainford Papers 85, 6 July 1910.
[82] *Westminster Gazette*, 30 Dec. 1910.
[83] Memorandum by J. A. Pease, 17 Jun. 1912, Gainford Papers 111.
[84] Henderson to MacDonald, 29 May 1914, LPLF, LP/MAC/09/1/73.

safeguard Peace of World, Free Trade—trusts of which we are custodians'[85]—came to nothing.

There is, of course, a danger of overinterpreting evidence. Cabinet apathy towards reform may only indicate that its importance was misunderstood or that the problem of the women's vote was genuinely felt to be insuperable. There is little *direct* evidence to show that the cabinet shrank from electoral reform because of fear of its electoral consequences. As is plain from J. R. Seager's well-known report to Elibank in November 1911, the secretaries of the Liberal federations were, on the whole, in favour of manhood suffrage: only the Western federation said that it would add to the rolls 'the loafer and the wastrel'.[86] But all to some degree recognized that there was an element of leaping in the dark: the Yorkshire Federation thought that the 'extensive enfranchisement' of young workers would benefit Labour and hurt the Liberals in industrial Yorkshire; the Scottish Federation argued that the enfranchisement of young men 'with no votes at present would give the Labour Party an enormous addition of strength'. Press reports suggest some Liberal anxieties.[87]

Action and priorities in politics are what in the long run matter; on this test the Liberals were not a franchise reforming party. On the contrary, there was constant dragging of feet. Typically, only the Labour Party turned up in force to vote for the bill in 1912, since it alone supported it in practice.[88]

Nor did the Liberals necessarily become enthusiastic or willing franchise reformers during the war itself. The huge numbers of men displaced by military and naval service, and by temporary changes in place of employment, meant that the franchise and registration system, based predominantly on property occupation and stability of domicile, very quickly broke down, as one of the first Acts of the war anticipated—the Electoral Disabilities (Naval and Military Service) Removal Act of 7 August 1914. Was a £10

[85] Notes for Cabinet on Franchise Bill, ? Jan. 1912, Gainford Papers 68.

[86] Report filed as PRO, Cab. 37/108/148, 16 Nov. 1911.

[87] See the report of the London commentator of the *Yorkshire Post*, 19 June 1912. 'Even in the Liberal clubs' he detected no 'enthusiasm' for the bill. The Party agents, he said, in 'the Metropolitan divisions, as in other constituencies' feared the influx of new voters. 'In every London constituency, I am informed, men qualified by the Bill can be found in thousands who have not hitherto aspired to a Parliamentary vote . . . Whether the change would favour the Radicals or the Unionists in London is a moot point, on which expert opinion is divided.'

[88] Henderson and MacDonald, *Notes on Organization*, 17.

lodger still a £10 lodger at Mons? Yes, because the war was
expected to be short: but what once he had survived to Gallipoli?
The lists for the 1916 register were compiled in the summer of
1915, but the process was stopped before the stage of the autumnal
revising barristers' courts was reached.[89] Politicians thus faced a
situation either of continuing to use the January 1915 register,
based on the lists of July 1914, or of attempting a wartime register,
or of starting afresh on a new franchise and registration basis. The
Asquith coalition went to very considerable lengths to avoid a
fresh start, attempting unsuccessfully 'the creation of some form of
ad hoc temporary or special register', but on the premiss of 'no
alteration in the franchise itself'.[90] Lloyd George in the debate in
March 1917 on the Speaker's conference proposals, observed in 'a
plain little talk' that in the period 1914–16 'every effort was made
to eliminate anything in the nature of a franchise proposal' and to
arrange a temporary register, until 'we were driven—absolutely
driven, perforce, by circumstances which were irresistible—to
appeal to you, Mr Speaker, to preside over a Conference.'[91] It had
proved impossible to unravel the tangled skein of the nineteenth-
century registration and franchise Acts. Registration could not be
dealt with separately from the franchises, and consideration of the
franchises necessarily raised the question of whether the registration procedure was not in itself an agent of disfranchisement.
Thus the twin guardians of the limited electorate of the nineteenth
century perished together. But it must be noted that the old system
was replaced only when it was broken beyond repair: in that sense,
the war undoubtedly did precipitate change.

'The new Act makes Great Britain one of the completest
democracies in the world.'[92] All three parties had to confront this
'complete democracy'; why did the Liberals lose most by it? In
part, as we have argued, the answer lies in the developments of the
British economy and of the social classes produced by it. In this
case the new electorate was probably less antipathetic to the
Liberals than indifferent to them, and there was probably little

---

[89] Elections and Registration Act 1915; see *HC Deb*. 5th ser. lxxiii. 1833 (23 July
1915).

[90] Asquith, in *HC Deb*. 5th ser. xcii. 463 (28 Mar. 1917) and ibid., lxxxv. 1453
(14 Aug. 1916).   [91] Ibid., xcii. 488, 490 (28 Mar. 1917).

[92] Terry, *Representation of the People Act*, p. xxi.

that the Liberals could do about that. The Liberal Party was not the party of organized labour, and even if there had been an opportunity for them to become such a party in the late nineteenth century, they had missed it. The refusal of local Liberal associations to adopt working-class candidates on a wide scale went far beyond mere tactical failure; it was a necessary consequence of the social structure of the Liberal Party and of its caucuses. Similarly, it seems fairly clear that the polarization of the electorate between right and left after 1918 was difficult to reverse, and the Liberal vote thus slowly disintegrated in the period under study here.

Yet, as we suggested, it is unlikely that the new Labour-voting electorate thought itself as being particularly 'socialist', and we know also that much of the working class was deeply Tory, by both instinct and allegiance. Thus, although the Tory Party perhaps suffered absolutely by the franchise changes, it did not do so relatively and, indeed, for much of the inter-war period it was the working class party *par excellence*.[93] We would suggest that the survival of the Conservative Party probably had something in common with the growth of the Labour Party under universal franchise. The question then becomes how far both these parties differed in their techniques from the Liberals.

The Labour Party, particularly its leadership, had inherited much from its Liberal past: democracy, progress, rationality, education, information. As much as any Liberal, MacDonald, Hardie, or Snowden believed that these ingredients, suitably mixed, would produce political success. In practice, however, the Labour Party never believed that the electorate could be mobilized by 'democratic rationalism'. While the Liberals devolved organization to their Federations (to Herbert Gladstone's later chagrin[94]), the Labour Party developed an authoritarian mass organization which drew its strength primarily from non-parliamentary and quasi-political organizations, the trade unions. 'Policy' never stood in the way of exploiting the diffuse, but intense, social consciousness of its adherents. In fact, its publicly stated policy was not much more than a collection of shrewdly contrived slogans

[93] See below, pp. 287–8.
[94] See particularly, Gladstone to Sir Robert Hudson, 3 Feb. 1923, BL Herbert Gladstone MSS 46475 fo. 37; also to Vivian Phillips, 26 Mar. 1924, 46475 fo. 261. Gladstone noted the NLF was 'almost useless for any sort of electoral organization', Memorandum of July 1925, Maclean MSS, Bodleian Library, Oxford, dep. c. 468, fo. 26.

attached to deeper and more subtle calls upon class-loyalty. Despite the traditions and aspirations of its leadership, Labour's politics were conducted in a pretty vulgar way. But, of course, the Tories conducted theirs in a vulgar way as well. From Disraeli's Crystal Palace speech onwards, the Tories had made a clear distinction between the rhetoric of electioneering and the construction of policy. Like the Labour Party, the Conservatives had it both ways. They were the party of those who wished to preserve property. But they were also the party of hierarchy and respectability: as such they won the support of much of the working class by powerful appeals to existing social and cultural relationships.[95] Both parties combined, on the one hand, a precise class self-interest, with, on the other, a less sharply defined and thus more compelling appearance.

But the Liberal Party was by its nature almost incapable of such a combination after 1918. This is not to say that the Liberals were never up to the kind of 'demagogic' appeals that its competitors were making. The party that had in the past denounced Bulgarian Atrocities, Established Churches, Landlords, Randlords, Dear Food, and Big Navies was clearly not above sloganeering. It was widely believed, however, that the old cries were being used to less and less effect, and the so-called new Liberals were probably—though not certainly—right to believe that they should be replaced. But they proposed to replace them with a style of politics that demanded an informed and intelligent electorate. They proposed to base their appeal on a programme of parliamentary legislation whose chief content would be specific items of social reform. Nevertheless, it is important to understand that this was not as much a break with the past as it seemed. At least ideally, the Liberal leadership had always believed that Liberalism was a rational doctrine adhered to by rational men: in no other way can the eclectic Newcastle Programme or the policy of 'filling the cup' be understood. Thus a man like Asquith, who had no special interest in social reform as such, could, as R. B. McCallum noted, 'only calculate what men ought reasonably to think'.[96] However much the Liberal leadership differed over particulars they all believed that calculation and good sense would move men, and

---

[95] For further discussion of this see below pp. 259–93.

[96] R. B. McCallum, *Asquith* (London, 1936), 128–9. See also Matthew, *Liberal Imperialists*, 289–92.

they despised Toryism, not so much because it was conservative, but because it pandered to the lowest appetites of the electorate.[97]

Nevertheless, even those Liberals favourable to mass enfranchisement understood the possibly debilitating effect of manhood suffrage on the calculation and good sense of the electorate. Thus, as one way out, the possibility was aired of raising the legal age of voting. Herbert Samuel in *Liberalism, its Principles and Proposals*, the Koran of the advanced Liberals, noted nervously that the abolition of the lodger franchise would admit to the registers young men whose judgement was 'immature' and whose 'influence would be dangerous'. He suggested that the 'question of raising the age of citizenship at the same time that the other qualifications are lowered is perhaps worth more attention than it has yet received'.[98] We have seen that several of the Liberal federation secretaries also feared the consequences of giving the vote to large numbers of young men,[99] and J. A. Pease, when drafting the 1912 bill, declared himself in favour of 23 or 25 as a minimum age, and hoped that the cabinet might follow him.[100] That, of course, was a political impossibility, and the trend of the times was utterly against such proposals. The Liberals were left, therefore, either with the apparently failed Liberalism of the old style, or with the new social policy.

Yet it is doubtful if social policy, however well conceived, was likely to be more successful with a mass electorate than the old catch-phrases. For such a programme expected in democracy just those qualities most conspicuously absent from it—knowledge and a well-developed political intelligence. But to that there is one caveat. A progressive Liberalism might have survived if the electorate had possessed at least some of these qualities—that is, if it had remained as limited as it was in 1910. If the Liberals were to pass successfully from one Liberalism to another—assuming that a transition was both happening and necessary—it could only be with *that* electorate, one large enough to be responsive to particular legislative proposals, but not yet swamped by Bright's 'residuum'. The 1918 Act, however, did more than treble the electorate: it transformed its character by significantly lowering its

[97] See, e.g., Asquith's private view of Chamberlain in 1900, when publicly supporting the substance of this policy; Matthew, 192.
[98] H. Samuel, *Liberalism* (London, 1902), 242 n. 3.
[99] See above, pp. 93.
[100] Undated memorandum. (?), 1912, Gainford Papers 67.

political awareness. Not only was the new electorate divided by class in a way that increasingly excluded the Liberals, but it was less likely to respond to policies that demanded a comparatively high level of political intelligence. In these circumstances it was by no means clear that the new Liberalism would excite the electorate to enthusiasm any more than the old.[101] Thus, if the pre-war Liberal government instinctively or private feared the consequences of franchise changes, they probably had reason to do so, and this makes their nervousness more explicable. After 1918 the future lay between two distinctly popular parties; Labour increasingly competed for the new democracy, not with the Liberals, but with the Conservatives.

APPENDIX

Lancashire and the Franchise

Dr P. F. Clarke suggests that the Liberal performance is positively related to the level of enfranchisement. He very properly notes that this does not imply a causal relationship, so that it is not possible to draw the inference that those who were disfranchised were predominantly Liberal; he does, however, suggest that the evidence points in that direction.[102] The correlation certainly exists: we find that in seats with a high degree of enfranchisement,[103] the Liberals obtain 53.2 per cent of the total vote in January 1910, as against 50.6 per cent in seats with medium enfranchisement and 46.7 per cent where enfranchisement is low. This correlation is, however, quite spurious, and disappears when proper account is taken of the dominant religious influence on Lancashire politics.

Table 3.9 shows that a high degree of enfranchisement was associated

[101] Elibank, one of the Liberals most experienced in party organization, thought it would not, telling Maclean on 10 June 1919: 'Your Federations in the country should likewise be dissolved, and be revived as Free Trade organizations. Many a malcontent will join the Free Trade cause, but not the Old Liberal Party . . . The Free Trade Group should be made all powerful. Let the dividing line in future be Tariff. The old party cries [i.e., those of Edwardian Liberalism] are out-of-date and only confusing and embarrassing' (Maclean MSS, Bod. Lib. dep. c. 465, fo. 184).

[102] Clarke, *Lancashire and New Liberalism*, 112–13. 'High' enfranchisement implies more than 38% of all males on the register in 1911: medium 34–8%, low less than 34%.

[103] Catholic population categories are derived from Pelling, *Social Geography of British Elections*, pp. xxiii–xxiv.

TABLE 3.9. *Catholic population and enfranchisement, 1910*

Catholic population	No. of seats/Degree of enfranchisement		
	High	Medium	Low
High	0	2	4 (13)
Medium	1	7 (8)	8 (13)
Low	8	13	1

Note: Figures in brackets include seats in Liverpool and Manchester.

with a low Catholic population. (Figures in brackets include seats in Liverpool and Manchester, which Clarke excludes: we see little justification for this, but the results we give are not materially affected by their inclusion or exclusion.) Clearly there is no simple causal connection between these variables, but it seems likely that where there was high Catholic population there was usually also a mobile working-class element relatively unlikely to be enfranchised. The relationship between the size of the Catholic population and the political complexion of the constituency is even more marked: in December 1910 the Conservatives won 14 of the 15 seats in our 'high Catholic population' category (the other was Liverpool Scotland, held by an Irish Nationalist), 8 of those in the 'medium' group and only 2 of the 22 with few Catholics.[104] Thus Catholicism, low enfranchisement, and a poor Liberal vote are all closely associated, and we must consider whether the main causal link is from Catholicism to Conservative strength or from low enfranchisement to Liberal weakness. There are two tests we can apply. We can categorize Lancashire seats according to both enfranchisement and religious complexion. If enfranchisement is critical, we shall expect to see higher enfranchisement imply a higher Liberal vote in each category of Catholic affiliation, while if religion is the major determinant there will be an association between it and the Liberal vote in each category of enfranchisement. The evidence is displayed in Table 3.10 and it is clear that there is no indication of the first tendency and a very marked relationship of the second type. Once the influence of religion is noted, there is little association between the Liberal vote and enfranchisement: and any that exists is negative rather than positive.

The other test we can apply is to compare 1910 and 1922. The impact of differing degree of enfranchisement is removed by 1922: if categorization by religious characteristics continues to explain political behaviour it is

[104] Totals differ from those of P. F. Clarke because we have included only seats in Lancashire proper (see Clarke, 112–13).

TABLE 3.10. *Liberal share of two-party vote in Lancashire, January 1910*

Catholic population	Degree of enfranchisement/% of vote		
	High	Medium	Low
High	(no seats)	40.2 (1)	44.7 (8)
Medium	50.6 (1)	49.5 (7)	52.4 (10)
Low	54.8 (8)	56.9 (11)	(no seats)

Note: Figures in brackets give the number of seats on which proportions are based.

clear that it is a major determinant in its own right, and not merely a proxy for enfranchisement. We cannot compare the Liberal performances, since there are many seats they do not contest and others where strong Labour votes erode their support. But we can examine the Conservative vote, with the results shown in Table 3.11. The differentials are slightly reduced, which is hardly surprising given the facts of redistribution, the First World War, the rise of the Labour Party (to a position of strength in a number of the 'high Catholic population' areas), and the use of data on religious affiliation which is by then some forty years old: but they are still marked. There can be little doubt that religion was a dominant factor in Lancashire politics, before and after the First World War, and there is no evidence from Lancashire to support the view that high levels of enfranchisement conferred any benefit on the Liberals.

TABLE 3.11. *Conservative share of poll in Lancashire (%)*

Catholic population	Jan. 1910	1922	
		A	B
High	52.1	54.7	54.8
Medium	46.5	48.8	50.0
Low	41.9	47.0	47.0

Note: There were 6 unopposed returns in 1922, 5 of them Conservative: these seats are excluded in Column A, while Column B includes estimated results for them.

4

Working-class Gambling in Britain, 1880–1939

IF two of the main themes of this book are the internal culture of the British working classes and the way that culture was perceived by those who stood outside it hardly anything illustrates them better than the development of working-class gambling in the last quarter of the nineteenth century. As a mass phenomenon its existence cannot be doubted but nearly all we know about it is derived from people who did not practise it, who often disapproved of it, and whose observation of it was equally often a prioristic. The 'problem' of working-class gambling is thus a double one: we need to discover, in so far as we can, its 'actual' character but we have to do so via evidence which is, to a greater or lesser degree, ideologically hostile. In this chapter I would like to approach that double problem by examining the spread of gambling as a popular activity, the part it played in the economic and intellectual environment of the working class and by assessing it in the light of wider class relationships.[1]

[1] *Major sources*: There were no studies of gambling based upon organized surveys until those conducted after the Second World War: I have thus used the latter whenever I thought it appropriate. The first was the Social Survey publication by W. F. F. Kemsley and D. Ginsburg, *Betting in Britain* (Central Office of Information, NS 710/4; London, 1951). There have recently been two other important studies: O. Newman, *Gambling: Hazard and Reward*, (London, 1972) and D. M. Downes *et al.*, *Gambling, Work and Leisure: A Study across Three Areas* (London, 1976). On a conceptual level, R. Caillois, *Man, Play and Games* (London, 1962) is in a class of its own and supersedes J. Huizinga's rather naïve treatment of gambling in *Homo Ludens* (2nd English edn.; London, 1970). For gambling as a historical activity we are necessarily dependent upon evidence which is frequently tendentious and inaccurate. Nevertheless, if read with care, the reports of the four major inquiries into betting can be very fruitful. They are: Select Committee of the House of Lords on Betting, *Report*, PP (1901), v. 370 and PP (1902), v. 389; Select Committee on Betting Duty, *Draft Report*, PP (1923), v. 389; Royal Commission on Lotteries and Betting, 1932–3, *Interim Report*, PP (1932–3), xiv (Cmd. 4234) and *Final Report*, PP (1932–3), xiv (Cmd. 4341) and *Minutes of Evidence*; Royal Commission on Betting, Lotteries and Gaming, 1949–51, *Report*, PP (1950–1), viii (Cmd. 8190) and *Minutes of Evidence*. The law of gambling:

Throughout this period organized mass betting took three forms: betting on horses, on dogs, and on football. But they were not always synchronic activities. Before 1914 gambling was devoted almost exclusively to horses. There was, certainly, a good deal of betting on football by coupon, but it was decidedly regional—confined largely to the Lancashire towns from which it was to grow.[2] Similarly, dog-racing was unimportant until the mid-1920s, when the construction of large numbers of dog tracks made possible *legal* cash betting in earnest.[3] Gambling on football and on dogs as national occupations was effectively possible only after the First World War. However, when a study such as this should begin is less clear, though contemporary evidence suggests some moment in the 1880s. It is claimed that as early as 1851 £1m. changed hands on the Chester Cup,[4] though there is no reliable evidence that it did, and it is true that the 'classics'—the One Thousand Guineas, the Two Thousand Guineas, the Derby, the St Leger and the Oaks—together with the City and Suburban (the 'City and Sub'), the Lincolnshire, the Cambridgeshire, the Cesarewitch, and a couple of other flat races, had already established themselves as heavy betting events.[5] But it was not

Before 1960, when off-course cash betting was made legal, the law was confused and arbitrary. The 1853 Lotteries and Betting Act had, by intention at least, suppressed all forms of ready-money betting, except in specified clubs and enclosures. Credit betting, which was largely confined to the wealthier classes, remained permissible. However, cash betting on course (outside the enclosure) was not made illegal until 1897 (Hawke *v.* Dunne), but that decision was immediately overturned by the House of Lords in a collusive civil action (Powell *v.* Kempton Park) when Lord Chancellor Halsbury, well known as a sporting judge, delivered for the majority. This judgement made it difficult for the police to prosecute any form of cash betting. Until 1906 the characteristic mode of prosecution was under municipal by-laws, but these varied both in penalty and scope. Uniform legislation was introduced in 1906 (Street Betting Act) which made all off-course betting illegal. The effect of that was to make credit betting (upper-class) legal, but cash betting (working-class) a criminal offence. Although legal attempts were made on the football pools in the 1920s, they were able to get around the law. For details of the law on gambling, see Downes *et al.*, 35–41; W. Vamplew, *The Turf* (London, 1976), 199–212; J. A. Hawke, 'Existing Legislation', in B. S. Rowntree (ed.), *Betting and Gambling: A National Evil* (London, 1905).

[2] J. M. Hogge, *The Facts of Gambling* (London, 1907), 71–5.

[3] Since in the decision Powell *v.* Kempton Park, it had been established that cash betting on course could not be prosecuted; see n. 1 above.

[4] J. Ashton, *The History of Gambling in England* (London, 1898), 220. The Chester Cup was then the most important handicap of the year.

[5] T. H. S. Escott, *England: Its People, Polity and Pursuits* (London, 1885), 78. But steeplechasing was never heavily backed; only the Grand National had a following, and that grew slowly. See Kemsley and Ginsburg, *Betting in Britain*, 17.

until the electric telegraph system was completed and the press was thus able to publish almost immediately starting-price odds (the basis of all off-course betting) and results that mass gambling was made possible. It was in the early 1880s that the popular and 'sporting' press began to do this. In any case, it was probably not until the 1880s that a large enough part of the working classes had sufficient disposable income to bet even on the small scale that they did.[6]

Wagering in some form or other had been endemic among the lower classes since time immemorial,[7] but from the 1880s onwards witnesses had little doubt that older forms of gambling had been joined and largely replaced by an organized betting which had no precedent in its scope or character. A well-informed insider like J. G. Bertram ('L. H. Curzon') accepted the evidence of a London club steward who told him that: 'Here everyone bets . . . everyone from the City to the West End; the cabman who brought you from the railway station, the porter who took your hat, the man who sold you the copy of the special *Standard* [that is, the racing edition], all bet.'[8] One observer, who was no enemy of 'sport', noted in 1891 that 'until recently gambling in England was almost exclusively the sport of the wealthy, but now it has through the instrumentality of horseracing become a popular passion.'[9] In 1895 the *Westminster Review* concluded that the 'betting mania is all prevalent',[10] while at the same time Charles Booth's observer captured the furtive and hectic nature of street betting in his own staccato notes: 'All must bet. Women as well as men. Bookies stand about and meet men as they come to and from their work.'[11] Seebohm Rowntree, a puritan admittedly, argued a couple of years later that in 'recent years' betting had 'spread so widely . . . that those who know the facts name gambling and drinking as

The history of all major races can be followed in *Ruff's Guide to the Turf* which then, but not now, appeared twice annually. The best institutional history of horse-racing is Vamplew, *The Turf*.

[6] See below, pp. 110–12.

[7] See, for example, R. W. Malcolmson, *Popular Recreations in English Society, 1700–1850* (Cambridge, 1973), 15–31.

[8] L. H. Curzon, *A Mirror on the Turf* (London, 1892), 192.

[9] E. Bowden-Rowlands, 'A Glance at the History of Gambling', *Westminster Review*, 135 (1891), 659.

[10] W. J. K., 'Betting and Gambling', *Westminster Review*, 140 (1895), 146.

[11] C. Booth, *Life and Labour of the People in London*, rev. edn., 17 vols. (London, 1902–3), xvii. 57.

national evils of almost equal magnitude',[12] a conclusion supported by C. E. B. Russell and E. T. Campagnac, the well-known 'Christian' economists.[13]

In 1902 the House of Lords select committee on betting argued 'that betting is generally prevalent in the United Kingdom, and that the practice of betting has increased considerably of late years especially among the working classes'.[14] This conclusion is not surprising—indeed it would have been surprising had they reached any other—but it unquestionably cohered with the bulk of the evidence with which they were presented. The police and the magistracy were emphatic that street betting had reached an entirely new order of magnitude, and the following exchange was representative:

Lord Durham. Do you think [betting] has increased during the last few years?—Yes.
Very considerably?—Yes.
In what class?—Principally in street betting.
Amongst the artisan and working classes?—Yes.[15]

Police evidence, of course, should be treated with some caution, but licensed credit bookmakers, who had every reason to keep a close watch on illegal betting, were equally certain:

Lord Durham. But you said the increase in street betting has introduced (or do not say it if you cannot) a lower class of betting man?
F. W. Spruce, Leeds commission agent. No; well, of course, it places me in an invidious position to define street betting, you see, it has, at any rate, increased the number of men who bet in a smaller way and in smaller sums . . .
Bishop of Hereford. But the betting in small sums practically means the betting amongst the great mass of the working people?
Spruce. I presume such to be the case.[16]

It was thus widely assumed that gambling was more or less universal *before* 1914. But the two major inquiries into post-war gambling both asserted that it had 'increased' since the war, and did so in the most strident fashion. Sir Charles Cautley (chairman)

---

[12] Rowntree, *Betting and Gambling*, p. vii.
[13] C. E. B. Russell and E. T. Campagnac, 'Gambling and Aids to Gambling', *Economic Review*, 10 (1900), 482.
[14] House of Lords Select Committee on Betting, 1902, *Report*, p. v, para. 1.
[15] Ibid., QQ [Questions] 148–51, at p. 9; see also QQ 548, 1876–8, 2013–17, at pp. 27, 89, 94.   [16] Ibid., QQ 816, 1066–7, at pp. 40, 49.

wrote that the members of the 1923 select committee of the House of Commons

are amazed at the extent to which betting exists at the present time. The evidence of all the witnesses agrees that practically every class in the community now bet . . . Above all, the craze is most prevalent among clerks and the artizan class of our towns, urban and semi-rural districts. Many newspapers live entirely off this craze for betting . . .[17]

There is much unhistorical innocence here, some of it perhaps deliberate—many inquiries acted as if nothing had ever gone before them—but the 1932 royal commissioners attempted to meet just this objection. They noted that all their predecessors had expressed alarm at apparently unparalleled rates of betting, yet they still concluded:

that the total turnover on gambling to-day is probably at least as great as at any recent date and much greater than it was at the beginning of the century or earlier. Further, the amount of money so expended represents a considerable spread in the gambling habit, since a larger proportion of the turnover than at any previous time is represented by relatively small bets from the poorer classes of the community.[18]

Furthermore, the 1923 committee, which had been appointed to consider a betting duty and was anxious to calculate a putative return, was more careful than that of 1902, whose sessions were characterized by a high degree of obtuse comment. In addition both the Merseyside and New London surveys argued that betting had advanced since 1918, and offered suggestive explanations why it should have done so.[19] It can also be argued that the multiplied opportunities for betting inevitably implied more betting: not for nothing did John Hilton describe the football pools as 'one of the most momentous happenings of our time'.[20]

But what does it mean to say that betting 'increased'? Indeed, in what acceptable way can it be measured? How many people gambled and with what regularity? How much did they spend and

[17] Select Committee on Betting Duty, 1923, *Draft Report*, p. xli, para. 30. The report was not formally completed owing to the dissolution of parliament at the end of 1923.

[18] Royal Commission on Lotteries and Betting, 1932–3, *Final Report*, 54–6, with quotation in para. 203, at p. 58.

[19] H. Llewellyn Smith (ed.), *The New Survey of London Life and Labour*, 9 vols. (London, 1930–8), ix. 270–86; D. Caradog Jones (ed.), *The Social Survey of Merseyside*, 3 vols. (London, 1934), iii. 293–4.

[20] J. Hilton, *Rich Man, Poor Man* (London, 1944), 122–3.

how much did they lose? Did more people bet after 1918 than before? Most of these questions can be answered only with difficulty and some not at all. Two possible sources of evidence turn out to be quite useless: these are the police statistics on prosecutions and the early investigations into domestic budgeting. The police statistics are not dishonest (so far as I know); they are probably an accurate record of police activity. But police activity was dependent upon social pressures arbitrarily applied and upon individual whim. As an index of rising or falling levels of betting they are almost certainly unreliable.

The scanty yield from the private budget analyses is also not surprising. As Hilton pointed out, interrogators were unlikely to ask awkward questions and respondents were unlikely to give truthful replies.[21] The income surveys conducted before the Second World War tell us much about expenditure on housing, food, and clothing—and even on alcohol—but are coy about other 'pleasures'. This was realized at the time, but failure of nerve and technique stood in the way of any useful description of individual outlay on non-essential expenditure.[22]

Contemporaries were, therefore, reduced to three fairly crude numerical ways of 'measuring' betting: the computation of total turnover from a mass of discrete and sometimes conflicting information; an assessment of the numbers who gambled; and, thirdly, a guess at the size of individual bets. There are, as we shall see, problems with each of these, but they are at least a starting-point. As to total turnover, many estimates were merely shots in the dark, even that of J. L. Paton, whose view that 'little short of

[21] Ibid. 19.

[22] See the comments of the pioneer investigator Henry Higgs: 'If I go on to suggest [what] would promote family economy, I begin to tread on dangerous ground. News comes to me from an able economist and statistician . . . that his efforts to collect family budgets . . . gain ground very slowly. "Many people", he writes, "talk about it as being a stomach policy of the bourgeoisie, whereby the bad management of the working classes should be demonstrated".' H. H. Higgs, 'Workmen's Budgets', *Journal of the Royal Statistical Society*, 56 (1893), 268. Note the comments on Higgs's paper by the American publisher George Putnam, who said that Higgs 'made no reference to any allowance in such budgets for *amusement* expenditure. The budget of an American workman of the same class would assuredly include a regular weekly outlay for amusement' (ibid. 292–3). So, of course, would the budget of the British workman. How haphazard this type of investigation was may be seen by comparing Zweig's conclusions on gambling in the 1940s with Kemsley and Ginsburg's for the same period. See F. Zweig, *Labour, Life and Poverty* (London, 1948), 31–43; Kemsley and Ginsburg, *passim*.

£100,000,000 changed hands every year' was widely accepted.[23] The *Sportsman*, after guessing what might plausibly be the takings of an assumed number of (illegal) bookmakers, estimated the turnover on horse-racing to be £480m.[24] *The Times* hazarded £500m.,[25] which was John Hilton's figure for the 1930s.[26] *The Economist* suggested £381m. for 1938.[27] Sir Richard Hopkins, then chairman of the Board of Inland Revenue, advised the 1923 select committee, on the basis of the tax returns of credit bookmakers, that the figure could be anything between £84m. and £417m.[28] Judging by what the turnover seems to have been after the Second World War, a figure of £300–400m. is probably reasonable, and that level is likely to have been reached in the early rather than the late 1930s. Such a conclusion is, however, pretty much guesswork.

In any case, as a measurement of gambling, total turnover is confusing and probably useful only in assessing changes in the popularity of certain sports. For the total staked on gambling is not the same as the total spent on gambling. The total stake had, in fact, three components: the return on winnings, the expenses and profits of bookmakers, and the (small) part that went on taxation.[29] It is not possible to calculate the first; it is possible only to guess at the second; while the third, since it represented taxation on the profits of credit (legal) bookmakers, was a relatively insignificant portion of the whole. Furthermore, it does not, of course, distinguish the class character of betting and tells us nothing precise about working-class outlay.

Thus while the total turnover has some value in indicating the direction and spread of gambling, it can do little else. The same holds true of the Treasury technique—measurement of the gross

[23] J. L. Paton, 'Gambling', in *Encyclopaedia of Religion and Ethics*, 12 vols. (Edinburgh, 1913), vi. 164. Paton used takings on French race-courses (via the *pari-mutuel*) as the basis of his calculation. Sir Horace Hamilton, chairman of the Board of Customs and Excise, thought this estimate 'entirely guesswork'. Select Committee on Betting Duty, 1923, *Report*, 108.

[24] *Sportsman*, 16 Apr. 1923.

[25] *The Times*, 18 Apr. 1923.

[26] Hilton, *Rich Man, Poor Man*, 122–3.

[27] *The Economist*, 29 Mar. 1947.

[28] Select Committee on Betting Duty, 1923, *Report*, QQ 9366–9, at p. 534, and Appendix viii, p. 592.

[29] For the misleading use of total turnover as a reliable index of the extent of gambling, see B. S. Rowntree and G. R. Lavers, *English Life and Leisure* (London, 1951), 124.

profits of bookmakers.[30] The Treasury assumed that the *money* volume of betting in 1922–3 was double that of 1914; but this implied, because of inflation, that the *real* volume had very much less than doubled; indeed, had hardly increased at all. Nor does it establish whether the increased volume was due to increased money stake or to an increasing number of betters. It is clearly necessary to try to do this.

First, numbers: it was generally accepted that more people bet on horses in the early 1920s than had done so in 1914. The evidence suggests that this was probably so, but the increase could not have been very striking, and there seem to have been regional variations. Both the Mersey and New London surveys accepted a post-war rising in betting, though both were much influenced by the rapid growth in attendances at dog-racing.[31] There were also particular reasons for the apparent heavy betting in areas of high unemployment.[32] The 1923 committee's conclusion that gambling had much advanced was largely dependent upon a remarkable statement from a Glasgow street bookie, J. A. Croll, who was, it seems, given immunity from prosecution in order to make it. Although his evidence, in its detail and coherence, sounds too pat, it is certainly impressive:

What do you mean—there were two pitches in the five streets?

In the beginning of 1913, when this depot was no longer available to us . . . one other bookmaker and myself occupied this portion of the Plantation district.

Surrounded by four streets?—Yes.

Were you in partnership?—No, in competition.

What was your turnover then?

My average turnover then was £25 a day.

In 1920, after you came back from the War, did you bet in the same four streets?—Yes.

And in those four streets had the number of bookmakers, including yourself, increased to six?—Six or seven . . .

What do you say the average turnover had increased to at that time?

In the seven pitches to which I have referred, the average turnover then would be about £150 per day.

The £25 was your own takings?—The average combined takings have increased from £35 [in 1914] to £250 [in 1920].

---

[30] Their figures are used by Prest in his rather disappointing discussion of gambling; see A. R. Prest, *Consumers' Expenditure in the United Kingdom, 1900–1919* (Cambridge, 1954), 158–9.

[31] See below, p. 110.   [32] See below, pp. 123–4.

Now in this year there are still six bookmakers working in the same area? There are only about six bookmakers but there are twelve pitches. There are a number of bookmakers' agents who are working in the area. Does that mean twelve closes?—Yes. Would the turnover be £300 a day now?—Yes, it certainly is £300. Is this particular area the best area in Glasgow? No, it is just an average working class area, and the volume of betting that is done in this area is just the average that is done in all the working class areas of Glasgow.[33]

The committee took this evidence seriously; understandably, since it gave, or purported to give, the kind of information on gambling that was normally most difficult to uncover. Against it, however, need to be set the conclusions of the Revd E. G. Perkins's proto-social survey—perhaps the first on betting in this country—which suggested that the proportion of the working class gambling in 1927 was as it had been in 1914: about 80 per cent, more or less regularly.[34] Yet his figures, like Croll's are sensitive to probing. While there were probably no strict economic reasons why more people should gamble in the 1920s than before the war (though rising real incomes might have drawn increased numbers into betting),[35] there might have been other ones, psychological or social, for example. Moreover, Perkins made no attempt to assess new forms of gambling, particularly pools betting on football, which was highly developed in Sheffield. Probably the most reliable estimate of the number of regular betters in the 1920s is that of the National Sporting League, which put it at 4 million. This figure is given some real weight in that it is exactly the same as Kemsley and Ginsburg's in 1950.[36] In addition, of course, many more had a flutter on particular races—the Derby, which was a European as well as a British event,[37] the St Leger and the Grand

[33] Select Committee on Betting Duty, 1923, *Report*, QQ 4603–12, at pp. 273–4.
[34] Royal Commission on Lotteries and Betting, 1932–3, *Minutes of Evidence*, 275.   [35] See below, pp. 110–13.
[36] Kemsley and Ginsburg, 3.
[37] Arguably it was one of the few events that endeared foreigners to the English. Count Lagrange and Prince Batthyany were popular winners, as were even more alien creatures like the Chevalier Ginistrelli, whose filly, Signorinetta, was a sensational winner in 1908. See Roger Mortimer, *History of the Derby Stakes* (London, 1973). On the other side of the Channel the Derby had much cachet. The great classicist Wilamowitz even convinced himself that his uncle was the first German to win it. In fact his horse, Scherz, won the Cambridgeshire in 1854, the first foreign mount to win a major English race. He was apparently made a count on the strength of this. See Ulrich von Wilamowitz-Moellendorff, *Erinnerungen, 1848–1914* (Leipzig, 1928), 58.

National. It is, therefore, probably not unfair to conclude that about 4 million people bet regularly on horses; perhaps double that number less frequently. This was probably a larger figure than before 1914, but not much larger.

After 1920 horse-racing was joined by greyhound-racing and football pools as popular pastimes, and while it is true that many people bet on all or a combination of the three, their growth probably halted the expansion of horse-race betting. Of the first two, the pools were numerically much the more significant. Although the development of dog-racing was indeed spectacular— by 1931 there were 18 million attendances at licensed courses, and London alone had seventeen of them—attendance was confined to a very small part of the population. Even at the time, it was assumed that there was little off-course betting on dogs, since access was so easy, and that the huge attendances represented, so to speak, a stage army of proletarian betters.[38] This was confirmed by the post-Second World War surveys. Kemsley and Ginsburg, for instance, found that although 44 per cent of the adult population bet on horses, only 4.1 per cent bet on dogs.[39] That figure, furthermore, was obtained when dog-race attendances were at their highest. The number of *individuals*, therefore, attending dog-races before 1939 must have been no more than half a million, of whom presumably a fair proportion also bet on horses.

The football pools were quite different. By the late 1930s about 10 million people were on the promoters' books, and about one-third of the whole population at some time returned coupons. Since the majority of pools entrants also bet on something else the total number of working-class gamblers cannot be computed as the simple addition of horses plus pools plus dogs. But it is safe to assume that the numbers betting were between 10 and 15 million, and that the majority of working-class men at least bet fairly regularly, perhaps as much on horses on the pools.

Secondly, how much did they bet? Again, at least before the Kemsley and Ginsburg survey, it is not possible to answer this question with any certainty. For once, however, police evidence is both coherent and plausible, if not necessarily reliable.[40] It also

---

[38] Llewellyn Smith, *New Survey*, ix. 278. For a grim picture of dog-track life, see Zweig, 32–7.   [39] Kemsley and Ginsburg, 1.

[40] This evidence was provided by seizure of betting slips.

agrees with other such testimony as we have. Before 1914 the customary stake on a horse was sixpence or a shilling. It was sometimes as low as a couple of pence, but usually not more than a shilling. Bookies were surprised if it reached half a crown. Police seizures suggest that the average money stake rose only slightly after 1918. The chief constable of Liverpool told the 1923 committee that street bets ranged from 6*d*. to 2*s*. 6*d*.—'occasionally it goes higher'. Sums bet in factories were 'a little more than 6*d*. It might be 2s. to 2*s*. 6*d*. .'[41] The assistant commissioner of the Metropolitan Police deposed that the 'majority' of stakes ran from 2*s*. to 2*s*. 6*d*., 'but lately we have found much smaller stakes, as low as 2*d*. in the case of errand boys'.[42] J. A. Croll told the committee that the size of the stake had changed little: they were 'then [in 1914], even as now, . . . in sixpences, shillings, and 1*s*. 6*d*. and 2*s*.'.[43] Royal commissions, usually so eager to accept police evidence, were reluctant to do so when it seemed to show that the average stake was so low:

Generally speaking, among the workmen betting does not go beyond a moderate indulgence . . .?

Chief constable of Manchester. Yes, I think that. In my view the majority act very modestly indeed in betting transactions. You do get extreme cases. You cannot avoid it.

Is it only spasmodic . . .?

I should say it is a regular programme to have a bet on every week.

Is it a studied art?—Yes.

When you say 6*d*. or 1*s*. you do not surely mean only 6*d*. a week?

It will depend on the programmes that are being run. If there is any local or popular race during the week, it may happen two or three times during the week perhaps.

It seems to me unlikely that a man will have only 6*d*. bet?

Yes, during the racing season they probably bet more heavily than at ordinary times; but during the winter time the football betting is once a week . . .

Do you put it as 6*d*. or 1*s*. a week for the average better?

Yes, I should think it would be about that; 6*d*. up to 2*s*. a week.

It seems an extremely low figure, and totally against anything I have ever heard of?

Wages are so low.[44]

[41] Select Committee on Betting Duty, 1923, *Report*, QQ 768–71, at pp. 38–9.
[42] Ibid., Q 1369, at p. 67.   [43] Ibid., Q 4579, at p. 272.
[44] Royal Commission on Lotteries and Betting, 1923–3, *Minutes of Evidence*, QQ 801–9, at p. 61.

It is difficult to know what an average pools stake was at different income levels, but it seems inconceivable for most working-class families that it could have been much higher than a stake on horses. It appears from Kemsley and Ginsburg's figures that in 1949–50 it was, indeed, little more. (See Table 4.1.) The average stake on a greyhound race was almost certainly higher, as well as the number of bets. But this was, as we have seen, really serious wagering and occupied only a comparatively small part of the population.

TABLE 4.1. *Variation of pool stake with income group of better*

Income per week	Usual stake per week
Up to £3	2s. 1d.
£3 to £5	2s. 11d.
£5 to £7 10s.	2s. 11d.
£7 10s. to £10	3s. 7d.
£10 and over	4s. 6d.

Source: W. F. F. Kemsley and D. Ginsburg, *Betting in Britain* (Central Office of Information, NS 710/4, London, 1951), 11.

What cannot be discovered with any precision is the frequency with which people bet or who was most likely to bet. More recent evidence suggests that the very poorest bet least and the skilled working classes bet most.[45] Yet the variations do not appear to have been great. On the other hand, we have some evidence about individual types who gambled, and this, since it raises a number of important questions, will be discussed further on.[46]

Despite this particular uncertainty, however, it seems clear that gambling on this scale made few demands on the economy of those who practised it. Even at the time no significant material consequences were ever detected, and critics were driven either to untruths or simple ideological statements: 'Very likely his house is *not* broken up, his furniture is not sold, his wife and children never see the inside of the workhouse. He is degraded, that is all, and his

[45] See Downes *et al.*, 89–95.   [46] See below. pp. 124–6.

descent is progressive.'[47] Although it was not for want of trying, the various commissions could find no general relationship between gambling and poverty, or between gambling and crime, other than that most gambling was illegal to start with. Witnesses repeatedly confessed that they found poverty or crime unrelated to gambling,[48] and one actually admitted that 'there are cases where the prisoner alleges that his downfall is due to betting where the police, on making enquiry, can find no truth in his statement at all.'[49] John Martin, the author of the section on gambling in the New London Survey, concluded that in the Bermondsey, Southwark, and Lambeth area 'not more at the outside than 20% [bet] to the point of ruin'. Most, however, gambled for amusement and it involved no 'severe strain upon their resources'.[50]

Is it possible then to attempt a description of the betting cycle in this period? A tentative one would appear to be as follows: in volume it rose steadily from the 1880s until the mid-1930s, the increase being due both to the growing numbers betting as well as to the creation of new institutions for betting. It represented a small but regular charge on most working-class wages, but the proportion of that wage in real terms seems not to have increased much after the First World War, and probably declined gently until 1939. It rose again very sharply in the years after 1945, but for particular reasons, and it fell equally sharply from 1949.[51] It was a recurrent but strictly controlled element in such disposable income as the working class had.

Yet even if we admit that the sums bet were small and could easily be accommodated within a domestic budget it is reasonable to ask, as many did at the time, why they were not saved. The formal justification of gambling was, so often, that it was a way of

[47] D. C. Pedder, 'The Tipster and his Trade', *Monthly Review*, 12 (1903), 73–4.
[48] See, for example, Select Committee of the House of Lords on Betting, 1902, *Report*, QQ 1876–8, 2013–17, at pp. 89–94.
[49] Select Committee on Betting Duty, 1923, *Report*, QQ 673–8, at p. 34.
[50] Royal Commission on Lotteries and Betting, 1932–3, *Minutes of Evidence*, QQ 2017–123, at p. 141.
[51] All forms of gambling increased significantly after 1945 and none more so than dog-racing. Equally, attendances at the dogs dropped rapidly after 1948; others slid more gradually downwards throughout the 1950s. This remarkable 'kink' in the betting cycle was almost certainly due to an accumulation of wartime savings together with the continuance of rationing, as well as the enforced absence of alternative activities. The gradual restoration of a peacetime economy removed these conditions. See B. de Jouvenel, *Problems of Socialist England* (London, 1949), 108–9, 203–7.

acquiring material possessions.[52] At best, this is, in fact, only a partial explanation; anyway, at a time of highly stable money values the same result could (presumably) have been obtained by saving the amount gambled. Why was the money not saved?

To begin with, income was not necessarily too low. At the lowest, certainly, there was usually nothing left after essential expenditure, and often not enough even for that: provident 'putting by', in these circumstances, was almost impossible. (In any case, the very poorest were the least likely to gamble.) A more effective obstacle to saving was not low income, but intermittent income. Saving normally implies certainty and sureness, and implies an opportunity for calculation over the long term. Such opportunities were not normally given to the British working class before the Second World War. Even those who thought that the working classes mismanaged their finances at the best of times admitted the problem. Booth conceded that thrift 'needs the regular payment of weekly wages to take root freely',[53] while Mrs Bosanquet, than whom no one was more critical of working-class budgeting, allowed that 'the problem of equalising irregular income with regularly recurrent needs is one which only the most disciplined have solved.'[54] It was this irregularity of income which generated a rhythm of debt and credit of which gambling was to become an intrinsic part.[55]

The second impediment to anticipatory saving was the amount needed for a respectable funeral. There is no doubt that the great majority of working-class families invested in life (that is, death) insurance, and this was probably the case even before our period.[56] To that must be added the smaller sum placed for health insurance, old-age annuities and the still smaller, but increasing, amount paid in trade-union subscriptions. The whole edifice of working-class thrift was, in fact, built upon burial insurance. It can scarcely be regarded as money wasted given the intense emotional and social needs met by impressive obsequies, but as a rite of

[52] See below, pp. 116–17.

[53] C. Booth, *Conditions and Occupations of the People of the Tower Hamlets, 1886–97* (London, 1887), 18.

[54] H. Bosanquet, *Rich and Poor* (London, 1896), pp. 98–9. See also below, pp. 172–3.

[55] For a full discussion of this, see P. Johnson, *Saving and Spending* (Oxford, 1985).

[56] F. Le Play, *Le Ouvriers européens*, 6 vols. (Tours, 1878), iii. 276.

passage death had major significance: it demanded a 'negative' saving that consumed up to 10 per cent of a household budget. From this point of view, as Mrs Pember Reeves observed, it would have been better if the money had not been saved at all.[57] But it was, and income available for 'consumption' saving was that much smaller.

There is, furthermore, some evidence of psychological resistance to saving. The 'saver' as a type was disliked and too often associated with temperance: according to Booth's observer, 'those who yield to the seductions of temperance are too much bitten by the idea of saving.'[58] M. E. Loane, a devoted ally of temperance, nevertheless thought that the 'excessive thrift and prudence of many of the better-class poor weigh heavily on the children . . . the product of homes of this kind is not amiable.'[59] There was, anyway, much understandable scepticism about the virtues of saving. John Hilton recalled one popular story of a clerk who had retired, it was generally believed, with £5,000 put by. He told his fellow clerks that he owed it 'to my own abstemious and thrifty habits. Even more I owe it to the carefulness and good management of my dear wife. But still more I owe it to the fact that a month ago an aunt of mine died and left me £4,957.'[60]

The consequence of this irregular and often utterly unpredictable world was that saving or insuring became for most workers incompatible with their own culture. To the outsider, the intellectual life of the 'poor' seemed confined and narrow, without a past and a future, or of only short memory and immediate anticipation. Anything more than a few days ahead, or a few days before, was ignored or forgotten. And, indeed, this was in some sense due to training; working men and women 'learned'—more from the school of life than at their mothers' knees—that there was not much to prudence and the future would look after itself. The middle classes, on the whole, were taught the opposite. Thus the differences between the economic behaviour of the two classes were, broadly speaking, a result of different and somewhat paradoxical conceptions of time. Though the working-class attitude to time was probably fatalistic it was also optimistic; though the

[57] M. S. Pember Reeves, *Round about a Pound a Week* (London, 1913), 66.
[58] Booth, *Life and Labour*, xvii. 75.
[59] M. E. Loane, *The Next Street but One* (London, 1907), 80.
[60] Hilton, *Rich Man, Poor Man*, 47.

middle-class attitude was confident it was also pessimistic. Thus, for example, the middle-class propensity to insure is itself a gamble, but a pessimistic one—a gamble that property *will* be damaged or lost. This kind of gamble, however, comes from a culture where an acutely developed sense of time, of the past and the future, necessarily underpins most of life's decisions. The economic behaviour of the two classes was, therefore, in some ways intimately related. Both classes attempted to ameliorate insecurity, and Otto Newman has even argued that for the working classes, in certain economic circumstances, 'gambling makes sense'.[61] But over the long term gambling never makes sense for the individual gambler, and Newman's argument is acceptable only if the long-run net effect of gambling is ignored or deemed irrelevant; and only when the return on outlay is understood to be immediate, instead of being almost indefinitely postponed, can betting be regarded as a surrogate of saving.

But once this assumption is allowed then betting can be seen as 'rational'. It was fairly regular, and usually careful. Betters did not stake everything on one throw—though had they been behaving truly rationally they probably should have done so, placing short-odds winnings at long and hoping for the best. But that would have meant piling uncertainty on uncertainty—when the aim was to diminish it—and would have been psychologically intolerable.

Furthermore, any winnings could go towards increasing consumption by supplementing income, or simply towards tiding a family over in bad times. There is little evidence that the mass of betters imagined that their winnings would be spectacular, even in the 1930s, when the pools were paying out large sums. Lady Bell noted that the

systematic betting of women . . . is in many cases at first a quite deliberate effort . . . to add to the income. A man comes to the door of a woman who, either from her own thriftlessness, or from stern necessity, is hard pressed for money, and presents her with the possibility of spending a shilling and winning £5. How should she not listen to him?[62]

This does not suggest reckless abandon, and anyway M. E. Loane thought £5 the largest sum working-class women could actually comprehend.[63] The same attitudes held true after 1918, when the

[61] Newman, 227.
[62] Florence, Lady Bell, *At the Works* (London, 1911), 354–5.
[63] M. E. Loane, *The Queen's Poor* (London, 1905), 98.

level of expectation was certainly higher. John Martin, Llewellyn Smith's expert on gambling, argued that many bet 'because they want a specific object, to buy a gramophone, or to buy a wireless set, or to go for a holiday'.[64] John Hilton's published inquiry, *Why I go in for the Pools*, showed respondents more interested in household acquisitions than anything else. Even a 'big' win was narrowly conceived: ' "If I won bigger money, I should go in for a new house, which would be built to our own idea, so that we could get a bigger scullery . . . Why do they build such small sculleries which makes washday a dread?" '[65] The problem was that, while most people could 'afford' the goods they acquired or coveted, they could not guarantee regular repayment. Increasingly, therefore, the economic existence of most wage-earners was dependent upon access to credit, and individuals and institutions proliferated to meet this demand. This was why the smaller shops could not compete with the larger ones (or could only do so by extending credit, often fatally) and why the co-ops, which were supposed to be confined to cash transactions, were obliged to give credit.[66] Only credit-giving organizations could hope to survive in a low-wage, intermittent-wage economy, and where most people lived in an apparently unending cycle of debt and credit. By 1914 the characteristics of this cycle had become familiar, and wage-earners had habituated themselves to it by assimilating it to their own insecurity and uncertainty. As Mrs Bosanquet observed:

From this point of view the uncertainty of the future becomes a powerful argument against anticipatory provision and in favour of credit. There is no doubt that saving is often regarded, and perhaps justifiably regarded, as the sacrifice of present and certain advantages for the sake of meeting evils, which may, possibly, never occur, or which, if they do occur, may be met in some way not foreseen . . . And though I have never heard it openly argued that a burden may very like be escaped altogether by putting it into the future, yet no doubt the possibility is vaguely present to the minds of those who practise some form of indebtedness as their *modus operandi*.[67]

It is easy to see how betting fitted so neatly into this harum-

[64] Royal Commission on Lotteries and Betting, 1932–3, *Minutes of Evidence*, Q 2092, at p. 144.
[65] J. Hilton, *Why I go in for the Pools* (London, 1936), 26.
[66] Johnson, *Saving and Spending*, 133–41.
[67] H. Bosanquet, *The Standard of Life* (London, 1906), 68. See also p. 173 below.

scarum economy. The money goes round and round aspect—
'teeming and lading' it was called in Lancashire[68]—had immediate
appeal to people who believed that that was what money did
anyway. Any winning broke the debt-credit cycle, and however
temporarily, gave people relief from its demands. Since, with a
minimum of skill and luck, such winnings were from time to time
possible, the attractions of gambling are obvious. Lady Bell
recorded the experience of one do-gooder who tried to warn some
working-class wives of the dangers of gambling: 'The admonisher
was absolutely reduced to silence by one of the women saying, in a
tone of heartfelt conviction, "But that £5 we won at the new year,
it did fetch us up wonderful".' In the face of that marvellous
windfall it was, as Lady Bell commented, 'difficult to persuade the
winners that the chances were that it would not happen again'.[69]
Only winnings were recalled while losses were expunged from the
memory, and as long as the mental environment of the 'poor'
remained as it was, that would always happen.

Gambling was thus important to people because it played some
part in their economic lives. But it would not have spread as it did,
nor taken the form it did, had it been important only in their
economic lives. It was argued then—as it is now—that people
gambled because it produced thrills, risk, excitement, stimulation,
and they did so because their working lives were monotonous and
uncreative.[70] This might be true, but even if true, it conceals as
much as it explains. We still must ask what constituted this
stimulation and why gambling should have provided it.

To begin with, working-class gambling was generally neither
pathological nor compulsive: Dostoevsky's gambler was as like the
client of a street bookie as chalk is like cheese, and a pub parlour
was no Roulettenburg. The creation and release of physical

---

[68] Hilton, *Pools*, 10.   [69] Bell, 355.

[70] See, for example, the conclusions of the 1923 select committee: 'They believe
it [the increase in betting] to be probably due to the craving for some excitement
among the artizan and working classes, arising from the general monotony of their
daily work brought about by the intense specialisation of industry . . . Similarly,
they believe that the habit of betting has grown amongst clerks and other classes of
society as an escape from the monotony of their daily lives.' Select Committee on
Betting Duty, 1923, *Draft Report*, p. xli. See also Hobson's comment: the working
classes were driven to gambling because the 'dull, prolonged monotony of
uninteresting drudgery which constitutes the normal workaday life of large masses
of people drives them to sensational reactions which are crude and violent.' J. A.
Hobson, 'The Ethics of Gambling', in Rowntree, *Betting and Gambling*, 10.

tension was a very important part of gambling but there is little evidence that excitement was 'unnatural'—if only because so few betters saw the event on which they were betting. On the contrary, it seemed surprisingly controlled and workaday. Above all, the working-class better, unlike the primitive gambler of Veblen's type, did not believe in the primary importance of luck.[71] J. A. Hobson's definition of gambling—'it plunges the mind in a world of anarchy, where things come upon one and pass from one miraculously . . . The essence of gambling consists in an abandonment of reason'[72]—is an utterly misconceived view of popular betting, where the whole point was to *eliminate* chance from the bet. Men reckoned that the best way to win money was by skill, as they do today.[73] Typically, bingo (not then popular and today almost entirely a woman's game) and lotteries were 'despised and derided as mechanical and mindless',[74] since neither was the result of intellectual judgement.[75] Thus the growth of betting was both furthered and followed by the tipster and the sporting press.

Calculating form could be done indirectly by consulting a tipster, or directly by turning to the trade magazines. Tipsers were either local self-proclaimed experts operating under pseudonyms and with extravagant self-publicity, or superior establishments which, in order to avoid police interference, located themselves, like Webster and Topping, in Middelburg, Flushing, or Boulogne.[76] Most tipsters of pretension also published guides—*Hall's Tips* was the poor man's *Ruff's Guide*—and the emphasis was always upon method, system, and information. These titles (taken from the John Johnson collection in the Bodleian Library, Oxford) give the flavour of their appeal:

James Peddie	*Systems up to Date*
Anon.	*How to Make a Fortune on the Turf*
'Money Spinner'	*How I Made £1,000 out of 5/–*
'Metallic'	*The New System*
Capt. Crawley	*A Perfect System of Investment on the Turf*

[71] T. Veblen, *The Theory of the Leisure Class* (New York, 1899), 276–92.
[72] Hobson, 5.   [73] Downes *et al.*, 130.   [74] Newman, 221.
[75] Dr John Stevenson has pointed out to me that bingo was popular in the armed forces, particularly during the Second World War. (Letter to the author.) That is quite true; and hundreds of hours were whiled away, for example, on troop convoys. But it seems to me that these were exceptional circumstances and it is the case that after the war the popularity of bingo was confined largely to women.
[76] There is a huge collection of their catalogues, hand-outs, race-books, etc., in the John Johnson Collection, Bodleian Library, Oxford.

H. Bissell	*Racing for Riches*
Anon.	*Flashlight's Turf Method*
'H'	*The Law of Average v. the Law of Chance*
'Evox'	*The Daily Winner-Finder: Showing How the Stay-at-Home Punter Can Easily Make £1,000 a Year on the Turf*
F. L. Kelly	*'X' Rays on the Turf: A Backer's Vade Mecum*

The sporting press could be relied on to provide all the necessary facts. To make an intelligent bet, each better had to have a minimum of information: age of the horse, weight, sire, dam, dam's sire, owner, money won, previous form, jockey, handicap, position on the course, and the like. Thus the sporting press, which purveyed this information most accessibly, had a huge readership by the late 1880s. The *Sporting Life*, the *Sportsman* and the *Sporting Chronicle* each already had circulations exceeding 300,000,[77] and their inferior variants sold in untold numbers. James Haslam, author of the sentimental proletarian novel, *The Handloom Weaver's Daughter*, did a survey of the turn-of-the-century reading habits in the Manchester district of Ancoats, and recorded the following conversation with a newspaper seller:

'Why do these women show such eagerness to buy the noon edition?'
'Sporting', said the newsagent.
'How sporting? Do they bet?'
'Good heavens, man, it's all they live for.'
'And all newsagents in the neighbourhood do a good noon-edition trade?
'Yes', said the newsagent . . .
'That means that in half-a-dozen shops about one thousand sporting sheets a day are sold to poor people . . .'
'These people', I asked, 'do not read anything else, I suppose?'
'You bet', was the reply.[78]

It can hardly be true, as Robert Roberts suggests, that the need to read the sporting press almost alone made the working classes literate ('Many a man made the breakthrough to literacy by studying the pages of the *One O'Clock*'[79]) but it probably helped.

Discussion of form, both at work and during leisure hours, was also inexhaustible: to many it seemed as if workers talked about

[77] W. J. K., 'Betting and Gambling', 144.
[78] J. Haslam, *The Press and the People* (Manchester, 1906), 8.
[79] R. Roberts, *The Classic Slum* (Harmondsworth, 1974), 164.

nothing else. Robert Tressell's 'philanthropists' immediately got down to it during a tea-break,[80] and the possessor of information from the horse's mouth—as, for example, tipsters were supposed to be—was always closely examined:

'What are they going to do with the 'orse this autumn—did yer 'ear that?'

'I think I 'eard that he was entered for the Cambridgeshire, but if I remember rightly, Mr Leopold—that's the butler, not his real name, but what we call him—.'

'Ah yes; I know, after the baron [Baron de Rothschild, one of the greatest owners of the nineteenth century] . . . I should like to 've 'alf-an-hours' talk with your Mr Leopold . . .'

'. . . But what did he say about the Cambridgeshire?'

'. . . But there's no relying on what Mr Leopold says . . . But I 'eard William, that's the footman . . . [say that] he intends to have something on next spring.'

'Did he say any race? Did he say the City and Sub?'

'Yes that was the race he mentioned.'

'I thought that would be about the length and breadth of it,' Jim said.[81]

All this was, of course, a necessary part of the calculation of a 'rational' wager and it is entirely characteristic of Anglo-Saxon betting. I. K. Zola, in his study of betting in a working-class area of New England, has pointed out that all his subjects assumed 'an underlying order, a principle that can be figured out and mastered by a skilled observer'. He likens the ratiocination of a newspaper expert to the attitudes of the ordinary punter: the expert's is 'similar to the behaviour of the betters at Hoff's [a bar and grill], who consulted with the winners or joined in a general discussion to explain the results, to figure out why it happened or what factors had not sufficiently been considered'.[82] What was true of horse-race betting was almost certainly also true of the football pools. How far skill can in fact determine winnings on the pools—or even minimize losses—is conjectural;[83] nevertheless the amount of time

[80] R. Tressell, *The Ragged Trousered Philanthropists* (London, 1965), 17–18.

[81] G. Moore, *Esther Waters* (London, 1894), 97–8.

[82] I. K. Zola, 'Observations on Gambling in a Lower-Class Setting', in R. D. Herman (ed.), *Gambling* (New York, 1967), 26.

[83] The 1949–51 royal commission, which faced much conflicting evidence, was not prepared to accept that football pools had no elements of skill, though they conceded that it could not get you all that far (*Report*, 87). For a detailed discussion, see A. W. Peterson, 'The Statistics of Gambling', *Journal of the Royal Statistical Society*, 115 (1952).

in the 1930s (as today) spent poring over form and guides suggests that people brought to the pools exactly the same kind of intellectual and systematizing techniques that they used in horse-race betting.

Both betting on horses and via the pools demanded such techniques. Since most of the popular horse-races were handicaps, a decent return on outlay almost certainly depended on hedging and covering of bets—a difficult business that required concentration and mental agility. Pools coupons, then as now, allowed for a variety of bets, from the fairly primitive numbered draws to cross-systems of great complexity. Again, there was higher return on the latter, the pools' equivalents of hedged bets; and they too required concentration and mental agility. But in more traditional forms of wagering—match-making or dice, for example—such techniques were impossible and unnecessary.[84]

In these circumstances, therefore, it seems questionable how far terms such as 'pastime' or 'sport' can usefully be applied to popular gambling, except euphemistically. Betters hardly ever went to the races;[85] not all that many more went to football matches in 1930 than in 1901;[86] many even had little interest in teams or events as such. On the basis of his admittedly rather elementary researches John Hilton wrote that: 'I am told no, they have little interest in the game as a game or the teams as teams, they are only interested in the *results*, because the results may mean that they are one of the 67 who have won £124 each.'[87] As one Scottish housewife told him: 'My husband does not care a hoot one way or another—poor as he is—but he never gets off to *see* a game or get any other thrill from it other than by filling in a coupon.'[88]

Why did betting take on this 'intellectual' character? The conventional view is that it acted as an antidote to the tedium and intellectually undemanding nature of the division of labour in

[84] Although even here the tendency of the gambler to systematize and see regularities should not be discounted. I myself have been struck by how many players of poker [i.e. fruit] machines in Australian clubs will tell you that a win can be had by depressing and releasing the handle of a machine in a particular way or that there is nothing random in the way the machines operate. Certain punters are understood to possess this secret knowledge and their advice is discreetly sought.

[85] See, for example, Select Committee of the House of Lords on Betting, 1902, *Report*, QQ 211, 1939–40, at pp. 12, 92.

[86] Llewellyn Smith, *New Survey*, i. 297.   [87] Hilton, *Pools*, 12.

[88] Ibid. 33.

technologically and occupationally advanced societies: intellec-
tualized betting filled a mental vacuum. It would be unwise to
dismiss this view. At the same time it would be unwise to accept it.
It is, as I have suggested, not at all clear that individual working
men and women found their jobs as tedious as outsiders assumed
they must have done.[89] And even if they did it is still likely that the
workplace was central to their lives and social self-definition. The
relationship between gambling and work is thus likely to be more
complicated than the conventional view suggests. Certainly,
betting was related to the rhythms of work: men bet on the way to
work and on the way home; they bet in factories during breaks in
work and most workplaces had someone with whom men could
bet; they talked about betting at work. It was part of the business
of the working day. But betting was a 'hobby' and like hobbies its
function was not so much to provide 'excitement' to counter the
boredom of work as to endow working men and women with
intellectual initiative and spontaneity at a time when work
routines—which might or might not be tedious—were increasingly
being decided by others.[90] Betting, in addition, gave intellectual
structure to free time. By the end of the nineteenth century, the
development of the shift system and intervention by the state
forced on people substantial periods of non-work time, usually a
day and a half. 'Rational' betting requires time and concentration;
compulsory leisure permitted its existence—but it was not compulsory leisure alone which provided its temporal and social
environment.

This kind of betting also constituted a whole system of
knowledge, which, unlike bourgeois systems of knowledge was, at
least potentially, open to all working men. Thus men who excelled
in it attained the same kind of relative status as those who
excelled, for example, in the middle-class professions. If we see
betting in this light—as both work *and* a system of knowledge
which allowed men to prove themselves in an acceptable way—its
apparent fascination to the unemployed becomes explicable. In
1938 the Pilgrim Trust wrote:

The extent to which the interests and indeed the whole lives of so many of

[89] See above, pp. 152–7.
[90] For the view, which seems to me unacceptable, that gambling 'involves a set
of satisfactions in some respects alternative' to those of hobbies, see Downes *et al.*
203.

the Liverpool unemployed centre round the pools must be seen to be believed. The queues at Post Offices filling in coupons, the numbers of 'guaranteed systems' for correct forecast on sale in Liverpool's poorest districts, the periodicals containing nothing but pools analyses, the dirty and torn sports columns of the papers in Public Libraries with the rest of the paper untouched (apart from advertisements for vacant jobs), are some measure of the strength of this interest. It is not a direct interest in sport, but it derives from that and gives glamour to everything and everybody that has anything to do with sport.[91]

The Trust noted that a man 'who has been lucky enough to win money in the pool acquires thereby a definite social standing, and his views on very different matters are heard with respect'.[92] It stressed the intellectual importance of betting to men who *ipso facto* had no job satisfaction at all and whose days were otherwise empty. Betting offered to many unemployed 'the only possibility of making a decision, of a choice between alternatives, in a life otherwise prescribed in every detail by poverty and necessity'.[93] And it was more than just a pastime: it was 'a way of spending one's time in the discussion, analysis and decision with a seeming sense of purpose and ultimate achievement'.[94] The behaviour of the unemployed adds weight to R. D. Herman's argument that betting is work, but work of a more interesting kind than is normally available to the betters.[95] It was indeed, as the chief constable of Manchester agreed, a 'studied art'[96] and this evidence suggests that Caillois's conclusion—'whether it be a bet, lottery, roulette, or baccarat, it is clear the player's attitude is the same. He does nothing, he merely awaits the outcome'[97]—is in the case of this kind of betting almost certainly wrong.

That betting had these qualities was not unknown at the time. Although conventional opinion held almost unanimously that drinking and gambling were not only evils but evils which went hand in hand,[98] there were some who doubted it. The former Lib–

[91] Pilgrim Trust, *Men without Work* (Cambridge, 1938), 98–100.
[92] Ibid. 99–100.   [93] Ibid. 100.   [94] Ibid.
[95] R. D. Herman, 'Gambling as Work: A Sociological Study of the Race Track', in Herman *Gambling*, 91.   [96] See above, p. 111.
[97] Caillois, 12.
[98] For good examples, see Royal Commission on the Poor Laws and the Relief of Distress, *Report*, PP (1909), xli (Cmd. 4853), QQ 4194–5, 43889, 44618, 44750, 44807, at pp. 248, 352, 356, 389, 395, and ibid. PP (1909), xli (Cmd. 4888), Q 52169, at p. 147.

Lab trade-unionist A. G. Markham told the 1902 select committee that:

The ordinary domestic economy of a workman's household is this: You might put it roughly that the average earnings of a wage earner . . . [are] about 30s. a week; he would give the wife 20s. to 25s. out of that 30s.; the other 5s. he would use as his private spending money, and for his Oddfellows or other Friendly Society's subscription. Out of that money he will undoubtedly amuse himself as he thinks fit, and will not brook interference from any person . . . I should think there is a very small proportion of the tram and 'bus men [his union] who do not back horses; it is a topic of conversation right the way through, yet I guarantee you will find those men's homes generally tidy and comfortable. From what I have seen of bad homes, they are the homes of men who drink, and the man who backs horses as a rule is not a drunkard; the drunkard and the gambler do not go together. You will find a man who is a gambler is a sharper and keener man altogether . . . can you wonder that with the spread of education, if a man sees other men backing horses and winning money, he bets.[99]

Even Booth, not otherwise sensitive to social behaviour of this kind, observed this. Noting the decline of hooliganism, violence, and drunkenness, and the increasing social refinement that had occurred during the seventeen years his *Life and Labour* was being assembled, he concluded that there was 'greater intelligence, even though it be largely devoted to betting, and wider interests prevail.'[100]

Was Markham right in arguing that betters were 'sharper and keener men altogether'? Since their numbers were so large they could hardly represent a working-class élite. Yet it is clear what he meant. Betting and drinking were different kinds of activities; because betting frequently took place in pubs, critics drew the wrong conclusions. It was, furthermore, even at the time widely assumed that betting required sharp-wittedness and skill in the management of money. In 1908 Margaret Loane wrote:

I have scarcely ever seen an indoor game of any kind played in the houses of the poor. Cards, draughts, chess etc. are almost unknown. When they appear, they will be at once the sign and the cause of a great social and moral improvement. At present there is wonderfully little exertion of mind and body among the ordinary wage-earners.[101]

[99] Select Committee of the House of Lords on Betting, 1902, *Report*, Q 3196, at p. 147.　　[100] Booth, *Life and Labour*, xvii. 201.
[101] M. E. Loane, *From their Point of View* (London, 1908), 40–1.

But this quality—though she would have been the last to have admitted it—was exactly that demanded by betting, and the same quality—'exertion of mind'—Markham thought characteristic of the gambler. Evidence from the post-1945 period is perhaps here relevant. Newman has emphasized that betters show 'a greater pre-occupation with pay issues, with acquisition of consumer goods and furthermore, a budget awareness, a determination to make optimal use of one's financial resources'.[102] Downes argues that powerful competitive drives have been channelled into betting,[103] while Nechama Tec has suggested that Swedish gamblers are the most socially ambitious and competent element in the work-force.[104] Since so many men bet we can hardly go as far as Tec, and it is probably not possible to argue that gamblers were necessarily sharper and keener men, but it does not stretch the evidence too far to argue that gambling was a sharper and keener activity, sharper and keener than many of the 'recreations' the working classes had hitherto practised.

If it is the case that the working classes were not intellectually or financially degraded by betting—indeed, in some ways the reverse—why were such extravagant accusations advanced—families pauperized, industries ruined, a class corrupted? One reason, even to those without ideological preconceptions, was its physical character. The immediate result of making cash betting illegal was to make it public, and street betting gave town life in this country an aspect which has now disappeared. For many, the first and sharpest memories of city streets were those of bookies, touts, scouts,[105] and runners.[106] Street betting, necessarily hurried and agitated, made it seem as if gambling was becoming the principal business of the country:

One need only pass through the streets of a large town, especially when the evening papers are being published on the day of a race or football match, to see how all pervading is the gambling instinct among the working classes. Clerks, artisans, common labourers, railway employees,

---

[102] Newman, 223.   [103] Downes *et al.* 223.

[104] N. Tec, *Gambling in Sweden* (Totowa, NJ, 1964), 113–14.

[105] 'Scouts' or 'watchers' were employed to keep a look-out for the police. They were frequently paid actually to be arrested by the police in place of the bookmaker so that police who gave evidence in court could be identified and later avoided. In Australia a scout was felicitously known as a 'cockatoo'—after a species of parrot with an unnervingly raucous squawk.

[106] Runners carried betting slips from touts or other agents to the bookmaker.

all manifest the greatest eagerness to know the latest betting quotations or the result of the race. The cry of 'Winner', as the newsboys run along the street, causes as much excitement as a cry of 'Fire' or 'Stop Thief' might do.[107]

People waited at railway stations for passengers to shout the results from train windows. 'Over the long spider-legged bridge,' George Moore wrote in *Esther Waters*, 'trains had passed, scattering in their noisy passage the sensation of the news from Goodwood.'[108] Nor did the physiognomy of street betting ever change. In the late 1940s B. S. Rowntree wrote of a trip in a police car through a working-class district of London: 'As the police car came in sight, knots of men in street after street broke up and ran, like sparrows scattering at the approach of a cat. They were the street bookmakers.'[109]

Even when betting was not actually on the street it followed conventional and public routines. Pubs, barbers, newsagents, small general stores, could all be relied on to accept a bet. The elaborate innocence of a man in a pub parlour marked him immediately as a bookie:

In the corner of a smoking-room you may see a quiet impassive man sitting daily in a contemplative manner; he does not drink much, he smokes little, and he appears to have nothing in particular to worry him. If he knows you well, he will scarcely mind your presence; men (and boys) greet him, and little gentle colloquies take place from time to time.[110]

Equally, bookies' agents in factories and warehouses were easily recognized. They were also ubiquitous; hardly a factory gate or an unemployment exchange was without a 'pitch'. Large factories and shipyards were almost bureaucratically organized, with a whole hierarchy of touts and sub-touts.[111] It was all this which gave weight to the desolating description of gambling uttered by the 1923 select committee:

Work in our mills and factories is stopped and damaged by the amount of time given to the discussion and thought about betting . . . A class of persons of many thousands has grown up which lives entirely by giving tips

---

[107] S. Churchill, *Betting and Gambling* (London, 1894), 73.

[108] Moore, *Esther Waters*, 50.   [109] Rowntree and Lavers, 128.

[110] James Runciman, 'The Ethics of the Turf', *Contemporary Review*, 55 (1889), 607–8.

[111] Royal Commission on Lotteries and Betting, 1923–3, *Final Report*, 36–9.

and information . . . The streets of our towns are perambulated by bookmakers or their betting agents inviting persons to bet with them . . . Houses or shops exist in large numbers in all towns where . .. the real business is the receipt and collection of betting slips for some book-maker.'[112]

It is also true that actual ignorance played its part. There was at the time no reliable statistic information about gambling, and such as existed was treated clumsily. Invariably total turnover (itself largely guesswork) was presented as an accurate measure of the significance of gambling. This, however, as was noted earlier,[113] is quite misleading, but only in this way was it possible to equate gambling with drink as a proportion of total personal expenditure. Yet, when the appropriate adjustments are made for return on winnings and a redistributive effect, outflow on gambling is seen to be relatively unimportant alongside that on drink or tobacco. The 1949 royal commission calculated the comparative outflow as given in Table 4.2. Judging from these figures a little more statistical dexterity might have lightened some darkness.

Yet we should not overemphasize the extent to which the appearance of betting or plain ignorance determined the way others saw it. The fact that the 1949 royal commission reached such strikingly different conclusions from its predecessors was not

TABLE 4.2. *Personal expenditure on gambling, alcohol, tobacco, and entertainments, 1948–9 (United Kingdom)*

	£m. 1948	£m. 1949
Gambling	67.5	70.2
Alcohol	762	719
Tobacco	773	764
Entertainments	180	174

Note: Expenditure figures allow for return on winnings, licence duty, bookmakers' profits, and taxation.
Source: *Royal Commission on Betting, Lotteries and Gaming, 1919–51, Rept*, PP, 1950–1 [Cmnd. 8190], viii, p. 20.

[112] Select Committee on Betting Duty, 1923, *Draft Report*, p. xli.
[113] See above, p. 107.

due (or was only partly due) to the superiority of its evidence. Indeed, it is a fair assumption that these conclusions did not even come as a surprise to the commissioners. The actual evidence (as against the assertions) which was presented to the previous commissions and inquiries into gambling hardly ever supported the political and legislative conclusions they reached. Those conclusions were always ideologically a priori.

There were two reasons for this. The first was the part the Protestant clergy played in maintaining and encouraging the agitation against betting. The most violent critics of working-class gambling were clerics (Anglican and nonconformist) and their lay associates, who may themselves have been working-class, and they drew upon a powerful puritan tradition which had always loathed gambling. Then, as now, Protestant religious affiliation was the most perfect determinant of opposition to betting. On some occasions, clerical 'evidence' was tailored to suit an increasingly secular age: thus gambling was alleged to have extreme material consequences—ruined families etc. On others the 'evidence' consisted simply of extreme ideological statements which could even strain the credulity of otherwise sympathetic audiences, as the following exchange between Sir Charles Cautley, chairman of the 1923 select committee, and Canon Green, an ecclesiastical 'expert' on gambling, demonstrates:

Cautley. You have ventured to suggest that there are 100,000 cases of real demoralisation—robbing and dishonesty?

Green. Did I say 100,000 of demoralisation—I would like to say 1,000,000 cases of demoralisation. I said 100,000 cases of real moral loss.

Cautley. But you are giving evidence, you know. You say 1,000,000 cases. We must be the most immoral nation on the face of the earth. You are making us out to be most decadent; you do not suggest that?

Green. I expect we have different standards of morals, you know.

Cautley. I think we must have.[114]

The second reason to some extent related to the first. The hostile view of working-class gambling, which was the 'official'

---

[114] Select Committee on Betting Duty, 1923, *Draft Report*, QQ 6823–5, at p. 398. Green, canon of Manchester, royal chaplain and prolific moralist, though an ecclesiastical 'expert' on gambling and entirely representative of low church opinion, was known to be violent in his views. See, for example, P. Green, *Is Gambling Morally Wrong?* (London, 1926), 1. For a more moderate statement of the church's position, see R. C. Mortimer, *Gambling* (London, 1933).

view at least until the Second World War, was merely one of a number of negative stereotypes of working-class behaviour, ideologically determined and strongly held, which always existed—and exist—independently of what might or might not actually be happening. These stereotypes were probably accepted by much of the middle class and increasingly constituted a mobilizing agency for middle-class politics (as I shall argue).[115] As active stereotypes they were most strongly held by sections of the political and philanthropic middle classes and it was amongst them that the tendency to assume the worst, the conviction that the working class was incompetent in the management of its own interests, the obsession with a thrift and prudence often absent from their own lives, lasted longest. But this particular stereotype, that betting was a pathological feature of working-class life, was 'true' only so long as the official classes had an unquestioned position of authority over the working classes in the national hierarchy of esteem. The Second World War undoubtedly undermined this stereotype—almost fatally—by redistributing social esteem, by greatly weakening the political and ideological authority of the official classes.[116] Nothing illustrates this more than a comparison of the 'tone' of the 1949 royal commission with all its predecessors. Although that commission was unquestionably more technically sophisticated in its presentation and analysis of evidence than the others, that evidence, as I have suggested, did not point in an obviously different direction. But the conclusions were utterly different, and its Report, written by the same kind of people who wrote all the others, is undoubtedly a product of this wartime redistribution of esteem.[117]

It is clear, therefore, that the way betting was perceived was largely dependent upon class relationships. But that was merely one of the ways in which working-class betting was an aspect of class relations. There are several other questions we must ask. How far was betting peculiar to the working class? How far did it integrate classes? To what extent did it maintain authority—act as an agent, as it has been argued, of 'social control'?[118]

---

[115] See below, pp. 270–4.   [116] See below, pp. 290–3.

[117] Though it should be noted that it took parliament another ten years to legislate for its main recommendation, the legalization of off-course betting.

[118] See the discussion of this in 'Conference Report. The Working Class and Leisure: Class Expression and/or Social Control', *Society for the Study of Labour History, Bulletin*, 32 (1976), 10–14.

First, how far was the organization of betting itself class-integrative? Mass betting was the most successful example of working-class self-help in the modern era. It was at every stage a proletarian institution and bore all the characteristics of the British working class. Although illegal it was almost entirely honest;[119] its corruption was confined to corrupting the police and it provided few opportunities for petty or large-scale crime. To some working-class families like the Stoddarts, it brought great wealth, to others a little money to throw around and a certain style: 'They have now a bank account and enjoy the luxury of clean linen and water-tight boots.'[120] To the unemployed it sometimes meant a temporary job, and young boys were able to scrape a bit extra by operating on its margins.[121] It is very difficult to say how many were employed in any capacity at all by gambling: the whole of the full- and part-time fraternity at most numbered 100,000, and probably considerably less. In absolute terms this appears rather large, but as a proportion of the total work-force it is almost insignificant—less than 1 per cent.[122] As an institution for economic and social mobility, therefore, it recruited only few.

In any case it seems unlikely that those who carved more than a living out of it were liberated from their class. Bookmakers then, particularly street bookmakers, had little more respectability than do pornographers today. The Stoddarts were driven from the country, and the leviathan bookmakers of the nineteenth century—Gully, Davis, and Fry, for example—inhabited a *louche* sporting milieu, independent of all classes, except perhaps the *demi-monde*. Moreover nearly all bookies and their employees were at some time subject to police harassment, and this certainly reinforced class ties. As John Martin wrote: 'the bookies' tout who had long been one of the most interesting became after the War indubitably one of the most popular figures of poorer London. For one thing a halo of romance enveloped him. Here was one who was engaged in a perpetual and stimulating warfare with authority.'[123] Bookmaking as a vocation led nowhere but to modest

---

[119] Even so ferocious an opponent as J. A. Hawke admitted this. See Select Committee of the House of Lords on Betting, 1902, *Report*, QQ 357–9, 1793–4, 2844–5, 2904, at pp. 16–17, 83, 131, 134.
[120] Curzon, 200.
[121] Llewellyn Smith, *New Survey of London Life and Labour*, ix. 270–86.
[122] Royal Commission on Betting, Lotteries and Gambling, 1949–51, *Report*, 20.
[123] Llewellyn Smith, *New Survey*, 275.

wealth, while its social unacceptability inevitably impelled its practitioners back to the class from which they came.

Even so, however, it can be argued that betting, racing, and indeed the whole 'sporting' environment, necessarily perpetuated the subordination of the working classes to their social superiors. Of Edwardian gambling Ramsay MacDonald wrote:

> Gambling is a disease which spreads downwards to the industrious poor from the idle rich. In its most common form, betting on horse-racing, it is the only way in which the outcast plebeians can be joined with their betters in a bond of freemasonry. An elevating knowledge of distinguished jockeys and an exhilerating acquaintance with the pedigree of horses raise the poor parasite to the level of the rich one and make them both men and brothers.[124]

Robert Roberts, recollecting an Edwardian boyhood, agreed: 'Racing held the rabid interest of millions. It bound the labourer with a cap-touching loyalty to the aristocrat. There were those who would back only King Edward's, Lord Derby's or Lord Rosebery's horses. Winning, they felt for a brief moment a glow of unity with the greatest in the land.'[125]

Nevertheless, this interpretation, though certainly plausible, can be sustained only with difficulty. While it might be true that gambling percolated from top to bottom, in practice working-class betting was quite unlike the betting of the social classes from whom it was supposed to be derived. It was widely noticed that as the 'leviathan' betting of the early and mid-nineteenth century— stand-up, man-to-man wagering, 'match-making' as it was called, often for huge sums—declined in the upper classes, popular betting rose. No less a sportsman than Mr Speaker Lowther attested it:

> I should say there is less sensational betting amongst the upper classes. The sums are much smaller; you rarely, if ever, hear of any what are called leviathan bets amongst leading racing people, such as certainly existed in former days. I do not know the extent to which the example of one class may react upon another, but if the relative diminution of betting had occurred amongst what might be called the lower classes that certainly has occurred . . . amongst the upper, I should say, the example had been good.[126]

---

[124] J. R. MacDonald, 'Gambling and Citizenship', in Rowntree, *Betting and Gambling*, 120.   [125] Roberts, 123.

[126] Select Committee of the House of Lords on Betting, 1902, *Report*, Q 2436, at p. 110.

This abandonment of 'sensational' betting was due partly to the growing decorum of upper-class life, partly to the increasing prize money of major races which meant that owners could finance their stables without recourse to betting, partly to a desire to discourage the corruption of the sport so characteristic of it in the 1840s and 1850s. This decorum, however, as it affected gambling did not seem to be transmitting itself to the working classes: in face of unanimous testimony the 1902 select committee could only conclude that: 'the practice of betting has increased considerably of late years especially amongst the working classes, whilst, on the other hand, the habit of making large bets, which used at one time to be the fashion amongst owners and breeders of horses has greatly diminished.'[127]

It has also been argued that racing was itself a conservative social adhesive. MacDonald makes something of this—'an elevating knowledge of distinguished jockeys' united poor with rich—and it is true that the 'apotheosis of the jockey'[128] was one of the most remarkable public phenomena of the period. Jockeys were mobbed wherever they appeared, and a sensational win, like Robinson's in the St Legers of 1887 and 1888, made a boy a national hero. 'So it comes about,' James Runciman wrote with distaste:

that we have amidst us a school of skinny dwarfs whose leaders are better paid than the greatest statesmen in Europe . . .

If General Gordon had returned and visited such a place as Liverpool or Doncaster during a race meeting, he would not have been noticed by the discriminating crowd if Archer had passed along the street . . . I do not know how many times the Vanity Fair cartoon of Archer has been reprinted.[129]

There is little doubt that Barrett, Fordham, Wood, Donoghue (after 1918), and above all the incomparable Fred Archer were national figures whose only rivals, if even they, were the queen and Mr Gladstone. Archer's suicide in November 1886 led to demonstrations of mass feeling unprecedented in Victorian Britain.[130] 'Hardly anything', *The Times* wrote editorially:

[127] Ibid., *Final Report*, v. 184, para. 1.
[128] R. Black, *Horse-Racing in England* (London, 1893), 237.
[129] Runciman, 613–14.
[130] It is alleged that suburban trains leaving central London were stopped to allow boys to sell the afternoon papers containing the news of Archer's death.

that could befall an individual would cause a more widespread and painful sensation than the news which came from Newmarket yesterday afternoon. A great soldier, a great statesman, a great poet, even a Royal Prince, might die suddenly without giving so general a shock as has been given by the news of the tragical death of Fred Archer . . . Archer was known and admired by all that large proportion of the upper class that cares for racing; and to the populace, his skill, his daring and his prodigious good fortune had endeared him . . . Consequently the news of his death has come with a sense of shock and almost personal loss literally to millions.[131]

Yet it is hard to see exactly what was the social significance of jockey worship. Adulation of jockeys was an inevitable part of the professionalization of sport in society and such adulation accompanies successful sportsman in all social systems. Furthermore, jockeys were not of working-class origin. As Wray Vamplew has shown, most jockeys were country boys and usually raised around racing-stables and stud-farms;[132] and though it is quite true that a large, but declining, part of the working class still had links with the countryside, the rest grew up in utter ignorance of it. In any case the real pampering of jockeys came from the owners. This was partly because owners were now financially dependent on skilful jockeys, partly because the aristocracy had always permitted a social rapport with successful sportsmen, as with successful actors and actresses. This patronage was often of the most extreme kind:

The chief jockey is petted like a prima donna, and made a companion by sporting lords. His movements are chronicled as carefully as those of a Prince of the Royal Blood. His cartes-de-visite are in constant demand. He is surrounded by a host of parasites; his 'mounts' are backed till they are quoted at the shortest odds; his opinion of the animal he rides is anxiously asked for by owner and trainer . . . his bon-mots are circulated as good things, and his clothes are imitated by the vulgar.[133]

Intercourse was often more than social and horses were not the only things chief jockeys mounted. Elizabeth, Lady Hastings, on whose horse, Melton, Archer won both the Derby and the St Leger, told E. M. Humphris that nearly

---

[131] *The Times*, 9 Nov. 1886.
[132] Vamplew, 145–77.
[133] Curzon, 342.

all Archer's acquaintances were, to put it vulgarly, titled people and he practically spent his life among them. The way in which some women ran after Archer was amazing. They would not let him alone. People in society went simply mad about him and hunted after him. It was their fault more than his: they would not let him alone.[134]

This, as a particular phenomenon, is of real interest—in Archer's case of macabre interest[135]—but it is doubtful whether it has any broad social significance. Jockeys were not symbolic representatives of a working-class pseudo-mobility or of the amiability of the British class-system: the relationship between owner and jockey was of a narrow and specific kind.

Finally, it must be said that the working classes had a perfectly obvious reason for backing the leading owners and jockeys: their horses were more likely to win. This was, after all, the great age of systems and, as L. H. Curzon wrote, 'many people's "system" was to simply back those horses ridden by the leading jockeys.'[136] A man who backed only the King's, Lord Derby's or Lord Rosebery's mounts may perhaps have been reinforcing his inferior position in the social hierarchy, but he was also more likely to make money.

The relationship between class and popular gambling is thus ambiguous. Attitudes to gambling were by no means independent of class, but in certain circumstances they could be—as a result of religious affiliation, for example. Broadly speaking, active opposition to popular betting came from three areas: from the Protestant churches, from certain sections of the professional upper middle classes, and from the political leadership of the labour movement. On the whole, the non-Catholic churches were united in their hostility—though the bishops tended to be more cautious in their behaviour. While there probably was a uniformity of view within the middle classes there was no uniformity of practice. It was the spokesmen of the administrative–professional middle classes, what I have called the official classes, who were most ready to assert that betting would ruin industry and pauperize the working classes. But industrial employers, while they might well have 'believed' these assertions, were inclined to

---

[134] E. M. Humphris, *The Life of Fred Archer* (London, 1923), 245.

[135] Archer committed suicide during a fever he caught while trying to reduce his weight for the Cambridgeshire, the only major handicap he had never won.

[136] Curzon, 216.

the view that the cure was probably worse than the disease. They disliked shop-floor betting because it wasted time, but even then most turned a blind eye.[137] In practice they tended to favour legalization since that would clear betting out of the factories, and most were familiar enough with their work-force to know that the claims made about workshop betting could be absurdly exaggerated.

The third source of opposition to betting—the leadership of the labour movement—in part drew its inspiration from the other two. Many labour leaders (and, of course, many rank and file) were nonconformist and shared the views of their co-religionists of whatever class; others agreed with the official middle-class view that gambling depressed the educational and cultural levels of the working class.[138] There was, however, a specifically socialist critique which did much to determine the attitudes of the labour movement to popular betting. In the first place, it was argued, in the event of a win, particularly on the pools, the disproportion between the effort required and the reward obtained was so gross that no socialist could defend it. In the second, that, as MacDonald suggested, betting really did encourage a spurious democracy: the democracy of good fortune. Men and women were encouraged to believe that life could be transformed not by social change but by luck; the fraternity of 'sport' was no true fraternity at all, merely the fraternity of those who lived by chance. Most labour leaders tended in practice to hold, at least in part, both the official and the socialist views, and the holding of them created a cross-class alliance which did much to strengthen the case against popular betting and diminish hostility to anti-betting pressure groups which were, in fact, drawn very largely from the official classes.[139]

Even more ambiguous was the attitude of the state. Legislative attempts were repeatedly made to suppress working-class gambling, but the execution of this legislation was usually half-hearted. Again, as with employers, it is likely that many of those involved in the drafting and policing of this legislation 'believed' that betting was harmful, but, also like employers, were inclined to

[137] Royal Commission on Betting, Lotteries and Gaming, 1949–51, *Report*, 47–8.

[138] For a discussion of this, see above pp. 118–26. See also the comic and revealing exchange between David Grenfell, MP, and a police officer in Select Committee on Betting Duty, 1923, *Draft Report*, QQ 5279–450, at pp. 305–13.

[139] See MacDonald, 'Gambling and Citizenship'.

think that the harm done by suppressing it almost certainly outweighed the harm done by tolerating it. The tension created by these contrary beliefs is most obvious in the police. Police activity was characterized by long periods of inertia interrupted by frenetic bouts of activity—as it has always been in the case of these sorts of 'crime'—and triggered usually by complaints from interested pressure groups that 'nothing was being done'. The police openly confessed that they were reluctant to do their duty in the face of so much hostility and were, in particular, unwilling to implement legislation that appeared to favour one class against another—as the betting laws unquestionably did. It was not until after the Second World War, however, that they formally asked to be relieved of their burden.[140] For nearly a century, therefore, the police were obliged to implement legislation which they knew to be futile but which they none the less thought morally defensible. But the charge of class-bias and of interfering with the pleasures of the people was one to which the state was extremely sensitive. Thus Lord Salisbury repeatedly refused the Bishop of Hereford's demand that there should be a House of Lords select committee into betting on the grounds that these things were best left alone and, when he did capitulate, appointed a committee on which the racing peers were, to say the least, well represented. In turn, this sensitivity to class-bias was relentlessly exploited by the 'sporting' lobby, and the argument from class-equity was the most powerful, if also the most disingenuous, in the armoury of those who wished to legalize cash betting.[141] The argument from common sense— that popular gambling was not immoral and ruinous—was much feebler since it was contested by representatives of all social classes. In the end it was fear of violating the apparently supra-class character of the legal system that made penal legislation against betting so ineffective, even though the individuals responsible for the flaccid administration of the law continued to believe that gambling was immoral and ruinous.

The role of gambling in the class system was a neutral one:

[140] Royal Commission on Betting, Lotteries and Gaming, 1949–51, *Minutes of Evidence*, Memorandum submitted by the Chief Constables of England and Wales, 373–4.

[141] See, for example, the interrogation of the chief constable of Manchester by Lord Durham, a great owner and leading light of the Jockey Club, in Select Committee of the House of Lords on Betting, 1902, *Report*, QQ 440–6, at pp. 20–1.

contradictory tendencies eliminated each other. In itself betting did nothing to preserve or undermine the social system. It is true that the predominant classes were more likely to want to suppress than to encourage it, but they made few serious attempts to do so. While this kind of betting emerged from a specifically proletarian culture, such a culture is likely in any system of production based upon an extreme division of labour and of authority within the workplace. Who owns the system is to that extent irrelevant.

Nor should we exaggerate the degree to which working-class betting was a reaction to the 'boredom' of work; rather it was a reaction to the loss of autonomy at work and thus of a certain spontaneity. Furthermore, there is no reason to accept the contemporary view that the discharge of physical tension which could accompany betting—its 'thrill' and 'sensation'—was necessarily mindless or uncreative. On the contrary, working-class betting provided the opportunity for both intellectual activity and the acquisition of intellectual status to a class which was excluded by others and excluded itself from an officially defined national culture.

5

Work and Hobbies in Britain, 1880–1950

IN 1856 R. W. Emerson concluded that while an Englishman might eat and drink 'not much more than another man' he laboured three times as much: everything in England 'is at a quick pace. They have reinforced their own productivity, by the creation of that marvellous machinery which differences this age from every other age.'[1] Fifty years later such a view was not the predominant one. If anything, conventional opinion held the reverse to be true: Englishmen laboured less hard than others; they were ill-adapted to even more marvellous machinery; their work irritated them; ingenious Americans and docile Germans passed them on all sides. The argument that industrial life and division of labour had become intolerably monotonous to many workers was, of course, a commonplace of the nineteenth century. When Marx wrote that the 'the worker feels himself at home outside his work and feels absent from himself in his work' there were few who would not have conceded that he was at least partly right. By the end of the nineteenth century, when the British economy appeared to flag, it came to be argued not only that boredom demoralized the worker but that it also damaged the economy by undermining his efficiency. Thereafter it was implied in the reports of royal commissions, departmental committees of inquiry and delegations of concerned persons. It was, of course, argued explicitly as well, both by employers and by workers themselves. The London engineering employer A. Bergtheil told the Tariff Commission that not only was 'the foreign workman—I speak more particularly of the German and the Belgian—a more intelligent and better class of labourer . . . but he takes more actual interest in his work'.[2] At the same time, W. J. Davis of the

---

[1] R. W. Emerson, *English Traits* (London, 1856), 89.
[2] *Report of the Tariff Commission*, iv. *The Engineering Industries* (London, 1909), para. 403.

Brassworkers' Union could write that Berlin brassworkers 'appear to enjoy their work more, and to be able to work more easily, and with more satisfaction, and also to have a better time than our brassworkers in Birmingham'.[3] Boredom had allegedly gruesome consequences: a decline in craft-skills and inattention to detail and design,[4] irregular attendance at work, and dogged resistance to technological changes that would further accelerate and decompose labour.

The doctrine that boredom makes men inefficient is a pretty simple one. It had, however, a more subtle variation whose proponents shifted the emphasis from work to leisure. In brief, they argued that the mental energies necessary for effective industrial work were being diverted to, and absorbed by, substitute work: by sport and by hobbies. This variant was a considerable advance on the argument from which it was derived. It accepted that the British working class was in fact more disciplined, more sober, more regular at attending work than it had been. Non-vocational interests rescued workers from the inanition of factory labour and from its usual antidote: the bottle. 'It would be pretty hard', C. B. Hawkins wrote, 'to show that the increasing sobriety of Norwich . . . does not owe something, at any rate, to this new habit of watching football matches.'[5] Proponents of this view even accepted that men were not always bored by formal work; they just did not care one way or the other. The Englishman, Margaret Loane thus wrote, liked work, as long as it was someone else's work he was doing.[6] In the Edwardian period it was Shadwell who argued the case most strongly, and although he was catholic enough to attack all classes, the weight of his assault fell heavily on the working class. Britain was, he argued, 'a nation at play'; Englishmen were still interested in beating records, but only sporting records; their competitive drives and ambitions now centred not on the workplace and its product but on cricket and football and their product, betting.[7] The case was even more violently urged at the end of our period. Writing

[3] R. H. Best, W. J. Davis, and C. Perks, *Brassworkers of Berlin and Birmingham: A Comparison* (London, 1910), 23.

[4] See Royal Commission on Technical Instruction, *Report*, PP (1884), xxix (C. 3981), 519.

[5] C. B. Hawkins, *Norwich: A Social Study* (London, 1910), 311–12.

[6] M. E. Loane, *An Englishman's Castle* (London, 1909), 35.

[7] A. Shadwell, *Industrial Efficiency*, 2 vols. (London, 1906), i. 29; ii. 252–306.

with the admittedly grim post-war years still clearly in mind, and anxious to assert that the desire to work is culturally and not biologically determined, the industrial psychologist J. Cohen wrote that in Britain there was 'a universal spivery, with its major industry in gambling, horse-racing, dog-tracks, football pools, etc. If half the working population spends a goodly proportion of leisure completing coupons for football pools, this can only mean that large numbers of workers are moved by the desire not to have work.'[8] Even at first sight both Shadwell and Cohen over-argued their case,[9] but since it appeared to fit in with much other evidence it is a hypothesis worth examining. In this chapter I would like to test it by trying to answer three questions. What is the evidence that hobbies began to occupy more and more of the British working men's waking time? Is there any evidence that interest in hobbies led to a deterioration in formal work? What satisfactions did hobbies provide in their relation to formal work?

At the outset we need to be clear as to what can legitimately be called a hobby. Until recently no distinction was commonly drawn between 'craft' hobbies and sporting interests: it was assumed that both demanded the same kind of energy and skill, or at least were the same kind of activity. How eclectic these activities were can be seen from the contents of the inaugural number of *Hobbies* magazine (October 1895): fretwork and inlaying in wood (its celebratory project was a fretwork model of St Paul's Cathedral), photography for amateurs, stamps and stamp collecting, magic lanterns, bazaars and how to decorate them, cycling, football, athletics, bent iron work, and so on.[10] C. E. B. Russell wrote of working-class 'pals' that 'they invariably spend the evening together and usually share the same hobby',[11] and in context it is clear that he meant the same interest. C. B. Hawkins put the cinema and music-hall on one side as 'amusements', and football, angling, and hobbies (including in Norwich, of course, canary breeding) on the other as 'interests'.[12] As late as 1922, Margaret Phillips could make a similar distinction: between 'personal' interests, of which the basic was sex, but which also included the

[8] J. Cohen, 'The Ideas of Work and Play', *British Journal of Sociology*, 5 (1953), 318–21.
[9] See particularly Shadwell, *Industrial Efficiency*, ii. 455–63.
[10] *Hobbies*, 1 (Oct. 1895).
[11] C. E. B. Russell, *Manchester Boys* (Manchester, 1913), 4.
[12] Hawkins, *Norwich*, 310–15.

cinema (or both, presumably, at the same time) and 'objective' interests which in the case of young men 'may be an interest in sport, or in engineering and mechanical inventions connected with their work: in the case of girls an interest in housecraft or clothes'.[13] J. G. Leigh thought that most working men's hobby was sport and he conceded that it had all the satisfactions normally associated with a hobby.[14] What, then, were the satisfactions normally associated with a hobby? First, it was an activity freely chosen, though not exclusively practised in free time; it might, for example, be talked about at work. Second, it was neither random nor disorganized, but required regularity and physical and/or intellectual discipline. Third, it demanded knowledge and sustained interest. Finally, it was usually accompanied by the creation and discharge of some kind of mental or physical tension. All the activities I will discuss in this chapter have these qualities, and if we argue that the following of a sport and the practising of a 'craft' hobby should both be classified in the same way, as hobbies, we are accepting a tradition that only the most up-to-date sociology has broken.[15]

It would be difficult to say exactly when hobbies as a significant activity outside formal work became widespread; contemporaries usually only notice these things after they have become frequently adopted; commercial institutions as often reflect as create a market: the publication of *Hobbies* magazine in 1895, for example, though indeed indicative, clearly post-dates the growth of organized hobbies. *The New English Dictionary* gives 1816 as the first year for which there is literary evidence of the word being used in its modern sense (Scott, *The Antiquary*: 'I quarrel with no man's hobby'). But there is a certain 'Englishness' about hobbies which suggests pre-nineteenth-century antecedents. In every European language the phrase for 'killing time' is the same—*tuer le temps, die Zeit totschlagen*, etc.—but only English has the word 'hobby', which all others have eventually borrowed, even when, as in French, there were already antique words of some charm. Domestic gardening was always popular in the industrial towns wherever it was physically possible, and that popularity came from

---

[13] M. Phillips, *The Young Industrial Worker* (London, 1922), 18–19.
[14] J. G. Leigh, 'What do the Masses Read?', *Economic Review*, 14. 2 (1904), 171–2.
[15] See above, pp. 122–3.

a long tradition of a competitive and refined artisanal horticulture.[16] Emerson noted in the early 1850s how passionately the English of all classes decorated their homes and how fond they were of improving them.[17] The habit of 'pottering around the house', for which Dumazedier suggests there is no real European equivalent,[18] is clearly one of immense age. All forms of animal husbandry were ebullient English activities long before dog and pigeon breeding became working-class pastimes. Games and sports, of course, were endemic to English life. We must assume that the nineteenth century probably drew upon pre-industrial traditions which were only reshaped, not made, in the last quarter of the century. What characterizes hobbies thereafter is their intellectual systematization, physical organization, and commercial exploitation. To an extent they also became vicarious. With some the emphasis was increasingly upon individual effort and skill, for example with carpentry, gardening, and dog-running. In others, most obviously sport, it was upon information and knowledge, and the individual was not so much a participant as an informed observer. The reshaping of these traditions seems to have taken place in the 1870s and 1880s. By 1885, T. H. S. Escott could write that there was no better way of measuring the advance in 'popular amusement' than by comparing the newspapers of 'to-day' with those of less than fifty years before.

One would look in vain now for the announcements of pugilistic encounters between bruisers of established and growing reputation, cock-fights, dog-fights, and performances of terrier dogs . . . One would have looked in vain then for the accounts of cricket-matches . . . which now occupy entire pages of sporting journals; for the notices to excursionists that are a regular feature in every newspaper during the summer season; for the miscellaneous programmes of picture exhibitions, lectures, theatres, music-halls . . . Within the last five-and-twenty years cricket and

[16] For details, see J. C. Loudon, *An Encyclopaedia of Gardening* (London, 1934), 350, 353, 1036, 1227. The weavers of Lancaster, Spitalfields, and the west of Scotland were famous florists and they were largely responsible for the development of auriculas. It is said that Gertrude Jekyll, wife of the great gardener William Robinson, designed her first garden for a factory operative in Rochdale 'who wanted his plot to contain as many varieties of plants as could be contained within its confines'. M. Hadfield, *A History of British Gardening* (1979), 353–4. See also S. Constantine, 'Amateur Gardening and Popular Recreation in 19th and 20th Centuries', *Journal of Social History* (Spring 1981), 387–401.

[17] Emerson, *English Traits*, 61.

[18] J. Dumazedier, *Sociology of Leisure* (Amsterdam/New York, 1974), 57.

football clubs have been formed in all the towns and most of the villages of England.[19]

He pointed to the proliferation of reading-rooms, clubs, lecture-halls in the north and the popularity of athletic sports of all kinds. In the Potteries and around Manchester, 'rabbit-coursing, with a peculiar breed of little greyhound, is much in vogue'.[20] By the 1890s it was assumed that a man would as like as not spend his leisure time on a hobby. To the members of the Royal Commission on Labour it went without saying that a man would dig in his lot, and they were surprised when this often turned out not to be true:

Then in your experience the workpeople have not ill-used the greater leisure they have had?

No, I do not think they have. There is no greater leisure now except the two hours . . .

The men, then, in your experience have no more time to attend to their plots of land now than they had when you commenced operations?

There are not many plots in our district.[21]

Hobbies magazine was always insinuating that no fully equipped human being could be without a hobby. 'The chief object of these articles on Pigeons', it wrote in January 1896, 'is to induce those readers who have no favourite hobby to try their hands at Pigeons.'[22]

There can be little doubt that from the 1880s onwards, substantial and almost certainly increasing amounts of time were given to hobbies. In those industries where legislation or trade-union pressure had significantly reduced working hours, make-work activities were often simply forced upon workmen. As Ernst Dückershoff noted of the Northumberland miners: 'Their spare time impels them to contrive things to smarten their homes.'[23] For children of skilled artisans (particularly) adoption of craft-hobbies was partly a result of parental training and partly the result of possession of a back garden. R. A. Bray wrote of artisanal gardens:

[19] T. H. S. Escott. *England: Its People, Polity and Pursuits*, 2 vols., (London, 1885), ii. 417–18.

[20] Escott. *England*, ii. 423–4.

[21] Royal Commission on Labour (1891–94), *Minutes of Evidence* PP (1892), xxxv (C. 6795), QQ 7880–1 at p. 1032.

[22] *Hobbies* (Jan. 1896), 2.

[23] E. Dückershoff ('A German Coal Miner'), *How the English Workman Lives* (London, 1899), 33.

This useful appendage to the dwelling even though shared by more than one family, opens out a rich field for the development of new interests. Rabbits are often kept in a hutch . . .; pigeons are hung in a cage just outside the back door; fowls are encouraged and even ducks may flourish with an occasional swim in a tub of water. A few flowers are grown in the garden, which in addition affords room for a mild game of cricket or football. All this may seem very trivial to the general reader, but as a matter of fact this small outgrowth of the dwellings possesses a significance not easily overestimated. The boys are indeed crushed out of the house, but can overflow into the yard, where various hobbies occupy their attention and invest the dwellings with a new colouring and a new importance.[24]

But for most working men and boys an overflow into the yard was not a possibility. As late as 1944, with the exception of Wales, in not one British industrial region was there a majority of households with a back garden.[25] This put allotments even more at a premium. From 1892, when Collings' Small Holdings Bill was finally enacted, there was a large and unsatisfied demand for urban allotments.[26] As with back yards, so with allotments: their ubiquity was exaggerated and their provision inequitable. The 1892 Act and the subsequent legislation of 1907–8 were not fully implemented until the First World War and local authorities were often less willing than private companies to provide plots: the railwaymen, and to a lesser extent the miners, became famous gardeners, because their employers were fairly ready to rent out company land cheaply.[27] But employers had no doubt that allotments were popular and that men spent much time in them. C. J. Wilson, president of the South of Scotland Chamber of Commerce, argued the case for co-operative housing before the Royal Commission on Labour precisely because the houses had garden plots. 'Do they use their time in these plots?—Yes, greatly.'[28] The First and Second World Wars occasioned an increase in the number of allotments and there is no evidence that

[24] R. A. Bray, 'The Boy and the Family', in E. J. Urwick (ed.), *Studies of Boy Life in our Cities* (London, 1904), 72–3.

[25] E. Hyams and E. Smith, *English Cottage Gardens* (London, 1970), 163.

[26] *The Land: The Report of the Land Enquiry Committee*, 2 vols. (London, 1914), ii. 131–3.

[27] F. A. Talbot, 'Those Amazing Allotments', *The World's Work*, 33 (1919), 130–3.

[28] Royal Commission on Labour, *Minutes of Evidence*, PP (1892), xxxv (C. 6795), QQ 7580–3 at pp. 305–8.

time occupied in their cultivation was in any way reduced. The post-war Departmental Committee of Inquiry into Allotments found that lot-holders spent around an hour and a half per day on allotments in summer and almost as much in spring.[29] What other spare-time activity, the committee chirpily asked, 'receives so much attention from its adherents?'[30] In their study of the mining town 'Ashton' (Featherstone), Dennis and his colleagues found (in 1953) that some allotment-holders, though a minority, 'spend so much time there as to separate themselves from their families for considerable periods',[31] which is presumably one reason why they did it, and one reason why so many working-class wives were suspicious of their husbands' hobbies. A student of working-class life in Oxford in the 1950s described the allotments as a kind of married men's club to which husbands went as soon and as often as they could. 'It's what a lot of people quarrel over, isn't it?' he was told.[32]

How much time was spent on 'home-hobbies', repairing, making, decorating, tinkering, is not known—at least for the period before the 1950s—except that it was extensive.[33] 'Private' hobbies were most resistant to amateur survey, particularly the most private of them all, betting.[34] This, however, is not true of animal raising: dog breeding, canary breeding and the prime 'fancy' itself, pigeon breeding, were necessarily active consumers of time, particularly if individuals were breeding for profit. Canary breeding, always satisfying and sometimes profitable, but also very difficult and chancy, could easily upset the domestic economy and force men to dodge formal work.[35] We have similar evidence about sporting hobbies. This was so partly because the late nineteenth-century absorption in sport was obvious to anyone with eyes to see, and partly because casual or 'boy' labourers, the most passionate followers of organized sport, were deemed to be an Edwardian social 'problem' and thus fit for study. To a foreigner like Dückershoff there was almost nothing to be said: 'all is sport

---

[29] Department Committee on Inquiry into Allotments, *Report*, PP (1968–9) xxxiii (Cmd. 4166), 178.   [30] Ibid. 178.

[31] N. Dennis, F. Henriques, and C. Slaughter, *Coal is our Life* (London, 1956), 167.

[32] Quoted in J. Klein, *Samples from English Cultures*, 2 vols. (London, 1965), i. 171. See also M. E. Loane, *From Their Point of View* (London, 1908), 39.

[33] See below, p. 160.   [34] See above, pp. 110–12.

[35] Hawkins, *Norwich*, 313–16.

in England. It is sucked in with the mother's milk.'[36] C. E. B. Russell noted that to most Manchester 'lads' outdoor games meant only one thing, football. 'Football is as popular in summer as in winter, and were it not for the fact that the rules governing the game prohibit the playing of games during the summer months, doubtless it would be played from one year's end to the other.'[37] Freeman wrote (in 1914) that 'football is the greatest single interest in the life of the ordinary working boy' and his printed diaries of working life emphatically support that judgement.[38] Paterson argued that London working adolescents had three real interests: smoking, clothing, and conversation. But in a boy's 'click' conversation, in effect, meant sport talk.

For the greater part of the year football holds the stage. Cricket is never quite such an engrossing topic, though the fortunes of the Surrey county team are followed with that breathless and extravagant interest which demands a copy of every edition of the 'Star'. A most amazing knowledge is betrayed of the personal appearance, character, and moral weakness of each individual player . . . None of the Heads [his 'click'] are [*sic*] without a cricket or football guide in the inside pocket of his coat . . .

This genius for hero-worship is not confined to the cricket or football fields. Boxers or wrestlers, runners and cyclists, weight-putters, and dog-fanciers . . . are in the sweetstuff shop assumed to be national celebrities, their times, weights and records stored away in minds that seem capable of containing little else.[39]

Freeman, like Paterson, noted that attention was not confined to sports that could actually be played. For industrial workers before 1914, cricket for example, was not a game that most knew. Many young workers could hardly tell one end of a bat from the other; yet, Freeman wrote,

it is strange that in the face of this, and the comparatively small extent to which boys play the game, they nearly all take a great interest in County Cricket. The evening papers are eagerly read each night, and scores of boys who never play themselves are able to name at any time the runs made by prominent cricketers . . . and in seasons like the present, discuss

[36] Dückershoff, 67.
[37] Russell, *Manchester Boys*, 56. For the only published scholarly study of the social development of football, see Tony Mason, *Association Football and English Society 1863–1915* (Brighton, 1980), 222–42 particularly.
[38] A. Freeman, *Boy Life and Labour* (London, 1914), 151–2.
[39] A. Paterson, *Across the Bridges* (London, 1911), 144–5.

readily and ably the claims of the individual members of the Australian cricket team to be considered really worthy exponents of the game.[40]

Alfred Williams was not the first, but was among the best placed, to assert that sport drives out politics. 'Politics, religion, the fates of empires and governments, the interest of life and death itself must all yield to the supreme fascination and excitement of football.'[41] There is no reason to believe that any of this changed before 1950; even by then Ferdynand Zweig could write that 'sport has an indescribable fascination for the British worker . . . It may sound absurd, but one could say that sport has bewitched [him].'[42]

It seems indisputable, therefore, that the British worker spent a considerable part of his non-working life either on craft-hobbies or on sporting interests which had the same characteristics and provided the same satisfactions as craft-hobbies. But is there any evidence that such hobbies encroached upon formal work by diminishing the interest and energy that men might otherwise have devoted to it? It would be wrong to pretend that the question can easily be answered; we know little enough of people's attitudes to work at the best of times and have almost no accurate knowledge for the period before the 1930s. As for how people see the relation between work and leisure, or, in this case, between one form of work and another, we can only proceed by delicate inference. The real obstacle is the absence of a corpus of reliable autobiographical or biographical information. Of that which survives, little suggests that hobbies significantly changed attitudes to paid work, though it strongly suggests that for many, hobbies alone made work bearable, and for some, absorption in hobbies precluded interest in work altogether.

The sample of adolescent labourers whose diaries Freeman published certainly points to the dreariness of work and the attraction of hobbies, but not much more:

I do hinge making and grinding on Emery wheel.
It requires no intelligence it can be picked up in a few minutes.
Not so hard but very monot.

For this boy waking life had value only when he played his banjo, to which he was addicted.[43] Both Durant in the 1930s and Zweig in

[40] Freeman, *Boy Life and Labour*, 60–1.
[41] A. Williams, *Life in a Railway Factory* (London, 1915), 287.
[42] F. Zweig, *The British Worker* (Harmondsworth, 1952), 124.
[43] Freeman, *Boy Life and Labour*, 112.

the 1940s found it common for men to be so absorbed in their hobbies that working life became almost intolerable. Durant, the pioneer of the Gallup Polls in England, carried out a survey of young East London working men one of whose published diaries demonstrates the tension between the hatefulness of work and the compulsion of hobbies in its most extreme and poignant form.

On the Sabath day, I am unlike most animals, I do not lay in bed from noon till night, semiquaver! I take my parents a cup of tea, and take my fellow animal, the dog, for a stroll and a swim in the balmy waters of Wanstead Flats pond. I then have breakfast and traverse to church. After dinner, I sleep till tea-time, then I practise on my viola with piano-forte accompaniment.

On Monday I get up at seven o'clock and tone up my muscles for work with aid of chest-expanders, springs. I then breakfast and go to hell—in other words—to work. I work in that hatred, a wretched debt [i.e. department]—the Grocery. Monday night's I go to night school.

On Tuesday night's I go to Band Practise, because I am in the [YMCA] intermediate string orchestra. On Wednesday night's I go to Gymnasium to learn gymnastics and acrobatics. Thursdays I go swimming with the swimming club.

Friday night I do my night-school homework, which takes me about three hours instead of 1 hr, because as far as *arithmetic* is concerned my name is, (*dense*).

Saturday night I go to music lessons, unless I have a (date) with my viola or violin.

My favourite hobbies are music, which I spend all my money on, and put my heart and sole to.

Also gymnasium, swimming and reading English Litterature. Altogether my full repertwar of hobbies is:—football . . . Also Boxing and Acrobatics arts and crafts and reading, music and gymnastics, are my hobbies.

Semibreve—
full stop.[44]

Ferdynand Zweig, who wrote more extensively than anyone on working-class attitudes to both work and hobbies, was convinced that 'for a man who takes a passionate interest in dog-racing or football or making models, the job becomes of secondary interest. Sometimes the hobby can be so absorbing that it takes his mind off his work and lowers his efficiency.' Whereas most men were never entirely certain whether they worked simply in order to live or

[44] H. Durant, *The Problem of Leisure* (London, 1938), 84–5 fn.

because it also gave some creative satisfaction, 'men with absorbing hobbies had no doubt at all'.[45]

There is, therefore, some evidence that the Shadwell–Cohen 'thesis' has weight; nevertheless, few, of whom Zeig is the most plausible, were prepared to argue it explicitly. Its major premiss is both inarticulate and unproven. It presupposes that pre-industrial work was in some way expressive and purposive; that before labour became divided, *en miettes* in Georges Friedmann's phrase, work and leisure were integrated, part of a unified mental and material world and mutually enriching. Although this assumption is fundamental to many critiques of industrial capitalism, not least that of Marx,[46] there seems very little to suggest that it is true; more likely, as Anderson has observed, it is simply 'romantic and wishful thinking'.[47] To argue successfully that hobbies emerged as therapy for the pathological symptoms of extreme division of labour (as Friedmann does to the point of bone-headedness[48]), for a labour force in some sense 'denatured', it would be necessary to demonstrate that industrial work was unquestionably more monotonous and less autonomous than the kind of work which preceded it. This has not been done and I would be surprised if it could be. It would also be necessary to show that *within* the workplace itself there were no means by which boredom could be tempered. In fact, it can be argued that in some trades workmen actually paid more 'attention to work' as the factory system developed, and in other trades the patterns of industrial life were so disjointed as to lessen the tedium of factory work significantly.

Employers who gave evidence before the Royal Commission on Labour were nearly unanimous in believing that increasing leisure made their men 'steadier' at work and happier in their lives, even if they also believed, rightly in my view, that in an important sense those same men remained wilful and ill disciplined.[49] W. A. Valon, president of the Incorporated Gas Institute (which represented engineers, managers, and secretaries of the gas

---

[45] Zweig, 97–8.

[46] For the most comprehensive, though not always the most comprehensible, account of Marx's attitudes, see P. Naville, *De l'aliénation à la jouissance* (Paris, 1957), 130–60.

[47] N. Anderson, *Man's Work and Leisure* (Leiden, 1974), 11.

[48] G. Friedmann, *The Anatomy of Work* (London, 1961), 110 particularly, and below, pp. 159–61. [49] See below, pp. 164–6.

companies) was questioned by the commissioners as to the changed character of the gas workers.

What do you say as to the general character and conduct of the gas
  workers in your experience? Have the men improved in this respect and
  become more temperate?—Yes.
More orderly?
Yes. Thirty years ago it was sometimes painful to go into our retort-
  houses. At that time we had to employ . . . a special class of men for
  lifting the very heavy scoops. Every chance they got they drank a large
  quantity of beer, and the result was that we had a great deal of trouble
  with them from time to time. Since then the managers and engineers of
  companies have laid themselves out to have reading-rooms on the
  works, to supply the men with tea and coffee etc.[50]

The commissioners, not unnaturally, were anxious to establish this
point and pushed and coaxed employers hard.

And it is according to your experience that increased wages and greater
  leisure tend to produce more attention to the work and greater
  constancy to the work?
It depends entirely upon the use that is made of the leisure. I think our
  population has been improving. It has been improving during the time
  they have had more leisure. Therefore I should say that on the whole
  they have been spending their leisure wisely. A wise and better
  educated man would probably give better attention to his work than an
  unwise man; so that I think I may answer your question by saying, yes.
You find in your experience the greater wage and reduced hours have
  been the means of causing your workman to pay more attention to work
  than otherwise would be the case?
That is true with limitations—distinct limitations. The factory system in
  Scotland is not an old one, and the factory system has been growing up
  by degrees, and it simply means this, that where improved machinery
  costing a large sum of money, is employed, that machinery must be
  carefully and effectively worked; and that, of course, tends to the
  improvement of the workman as well as to the improvement of the
  work. I think that is the answer.
But has [sic] increased wages and more leisure interfered with them in any
  way, or has it increased the tendency to fire attention among the
  working men?
I cannot speak very decidedly on that point . . .

[50] Royal Commission on Labour, *Minutes of Evidence*, PP (1893–4), xxxiv
(C. 6894), QQ 25751–3 at p. 188.

Since reaping these advantages have the workmen become more attentive
to their work or less so?
I think rather more so.[51]

One might argue that this was evidence painfully extracted and
ambiguous in its implications; since, however, the whole point of
employers' evidence before the commission was to show how
badly done by they were, any admission that the work-force was
more placid and docile than it had once been has to be treated with
respect.

More characteristic than apathy was simple ambivalence:
workers were often bored, but sometimes (or even often)
interested. Craft-pride was continued in factory life; men prided
themselves on their strength; work routines were easily disrupted
by non-attendance or strikes; the workplace became an important
social institution. Craft-skill, and satisfaction in it, did much to
mitigate the effects of increasing simplification of industrial
routines. Alfred Williams noted the élan and craft-sense of the
carriage finishers at the GWR's Swindon works. Of their
meticulousness and style, he wrote:

The carriage finishers and upholsterers are a class in themselves, differing
by the very nature of their craft, from all others in the factory. As great
care and cleanliness are required for their work, they are expected to be
spruce and clean in their dress and appearance. This, together with the
fact that the finisher may have served an apprenticeship in a high-class
establishment and one far more genteel than a railway department can
hope to be, tends to create in him a sense of refinement higher than is
usually found in those who follow rougher and more laborious occupations.[52]

Even in trades where there was little craft-skill or where it no
longer existed, men could endow their work with intense craft-
pride.

The bricklayers are nevertheless very jealous of their craft, such as it
is . . . occasionally it happens that a bricklayer's labourer, who has been
for many years in attendance on his mate, shows an aptitude for the work,
so that the foreman, in a busy period, is induced to equip him with the
trowel. In that case he at once becomes the subject of sneering criticism:

---

[51] Royal Commission on Labour, *Minutes of Evidence*, PP (1892), xxxv
(C. 6708), QQ 7682–4 at pp. 305–8.
[52] Williams, 38–9.

whatever work he does is condemned, and he is hated and shunned by his old mates and companions.[53]

These techniques, though infuriating for management (and perhaps bad for efficiency), helped to give work a value it might not otherwise have possessed. This was also true of pride in strength, a pride particularly important in heavy labouring where it was probably the only 'skill' the job possessed. Dennis *et al.*, whose book is partly a chronicle of work-shirking, nevertheless stress that 'pride of work' was a 'very important' part of the miner's life.

Old men delight in stories of their strength and skill in youth. A publican or a bookmaker will often joke about the number of tons 'filled off' each day in his establishment by the old men. Older men in the pit who go on to light work will confide that they can still 'go as well as the young 'uns' but they think they deserve a rest.[54]

Occasionally such pride took on menacing proportions. Williams tells the sad tale of 'Herbert' who achieved prodigies of physical labour, but whose appetite, alas, grew in the eating. 'In reality, such a man as Herbert is a danger and an enemy of his kind, though he is quite unconscious of his conduct and does it all with the best intentions, he must be forgiven,' Williams comments unforgivingly.[55]

We can see the same ambivalence in attitudes to machinery. There was, in fact, very little Luddism in British factory work: machinery as such was rarely at issue, though levels of manning often were,[56] and there is little evidence that workmen were able to resist the introduction of new machinery where management was determined on it. But this was so partly because workmen themselves were often keenly interested in machinery and took pleasure in examining and discussing it. Gerhard von Schulze-Gaevernitz, who believed (like his compatriot Dückershoff),[57] contrary to received wisdom, that the British worker was better educated and technically more acute than the German, noted that 'technical problems awaken [the] most lively interest' in the British factory worker. Salutary for the continental observer, he wrote,

[53] Ibid., 49.
[54] Dennis, *et al.*, 73.
[55] Williams, *Railway Factory*, 52.
[56] Dückershoff, 60.
[57] G. von Schulze-Gaevernitz, *The Cotton Trade in England and on the Continent* (London, 1895), 138–9.

was 'a visit to some machinery exhibitions in the industrial districts. The operatives here crowd around the exhibited objects and discuss their advantages and failings.'[58] Even Shadwell conceded that the British workman, though perhaps less quick and inventive than the American, was much sharper than the German.[59] Machine-tool operators delighted in comparing American and British machines (American light, speedy but rackety; British heavier, slower, but more reliable) and their views usually corresponded with those of their employers. Fifty years later Zweig still thought many British workers took pleasure in machines and in the handling of them.[60] In any case, we might doubt whether all workers found repetitive work boring; some, as Viteles argues, clearly got 'satisfaction not observed by the spectator: at the successful working of complex machinery', for example.[61]

Men could even develop covetous attitudes to new machinery. Williams (again) tells an extraordinary story of a frame-shed foreman, 'an inventor himself', who could not keep his hands off other people's machinery.

More than once he was known actually to purloin a machine from the neighbour foreman's shop in the night and transfer it to his own premises. Once a very large drilling machine, new from the maker, and labelled to another department at the works, came into the yard by mistake, but it never reached its proper destination. Calling a gang of men, he removed the drill from the truck, caused a foundation to be made for it, fixed it up in a corner half out of sight, and had it working the next day.

Successful in this, he failed in his greatest coup, the attempted theft of three large drop hammers.[62] As for men like carpenters, in journeymen trades where machinery was slow to intrude, it is doubtful if the factory system made much difference at all. 'Not for

[58] See here the interesting observations in O. Banks, *The Attitudes of Steelworkers to Technical Change* (Liverpool, 1960), 124–5: 'It should be emphasized, however, that although our hypothetical situation specified that 500 men would be out of a job as a result of the new machinery, most of the men rejected the idea that this was necessarily a corollary of technical change. It was the firm conviction of the majority that displaced workers could always be found something to do in the firm.'
[59] Shadwell, *Industrial Efficiency*, ii. 73–5.
[60] Zweig, 111.
[61] M. Viteles, *The Science of Work* (London, 1934), 322–9.
[62] Williams, *Railway Factory*, 79–81.

us the years and years in the same factory, the same office, the regular routine,' Max Cohen wrote.[63]

Even if attitudes to machinery were simply hostile or work generally just got too much, there were ways in which routines could be made bearable. One was plain non-attendance. 'St Monday' was common in most industries, not just mining. In mining itself 'Mabon's Day', the first Monday of each month (an agreed holiday) was capable of almost indefinite extension, and managers were fatalistic about it. The exchange between George Caldwell, the former president of the South Lancashire and Cheshire Coal Association, and James Mawdsley is not atypical, even if Caldwell laid it on pretty thick. Caldwell doubted if an eight-hour day would make much difference:

My experience of colliers is that they like a day or two a week under any circumstances . . .
What do they do on that day that they lose . . .?
Dog running, pigeon-shooting, and things of that kind, any kind of enjoyment . . .
What do the employers do with these men?
Nothing, they let them go their own way; we cannot control them; we have no power to control them.
Have you taken into consideration the advisability of insisting upon more regular attention to work?
We have thought about it many times, but it is no use; we cannot help ourselves; we are entirely in the hands of the Miners' Union; we have no control whatever.[64]

This is admittedly lachrymose evidence; but sixty years later Dennis *et al.* came to the same conclusion. It was, they argued, 'generally assumed that a man who has won the weekly draw in "Ashton" or a dividend on the pools will not turn up for work on Monday'.[65] Foreigners were startled at the irregularity of work in England. De Rousiers, observing Birmingham smithies, thought that few worked their nominal week. 'One, for instance never arrives before nine o'clock; others occasionally extend the Sunday holiday until Tuesday or Wednesday, if last week's pay is not exhausted. [The employer] complains greatly of these irregularities but bears them in silence in order to keep his men.'[66] Dückershoff,

[63] M. Cohen, *What Nobody Told the Foreman* (London, 1953), 3.
[64] Royal Commission on Labour, *Minutes of Evidence*, PP (1892), xxxiv (C. 6708), QQ 5904, 6061–73 at pp. 324–30.   [65] Dennis, *et al.*, 30.
[66] P. de Rousiers, *The Labour Question in Britain* (London, 1896), 6.

refugee from a country where they did things differently, was less surprised at the casual attendance than at the fact that so little was done about it.[67] Before 1914, only in the textile industry were serious attempts made to enforce strict attendance, but with limited success even there. In casual trades like building or the docks 'come-day, go-day' was elevated to an art-form.

In the 'newer' industries, particularly those based upon high-speed production lines, this kind of slap-happiness was harder to accomplish. Yet even here it would be difficult to argue that tedium was entirely unmitigated. For those workers who did not take pleasure in machinery there were a number of routine-breaking techniques. Where permitted, the most basic was conversation; and the most basic conversation was about how slow, or how fast, time was passing. Mass-Observation recorded the following dialogue between two girls in a wartime machine-tool factory.

It [time] went quick this morning, didn't it?
Yes, it went lovely and quick between eleven and twelve, but it dragged after that I thought.
Yes, just after the twelve o'clock buzzer. It started to drag then.
Funny, wasn't it? It usually goes so quick after the twelve o'clock buzzer. I hope it will go as quick this afternoon.
Hope so. You can always tell, can't you? If it goes quick up to half-past two, then its going to go quick all the afternoon.
It's funny that.[68]

Girls seemed to derive considerable pleasure from this sort of nattering and, as Mass-Observation suggested, it substituted interest in time for non-interest in work.

The opportunities for men to vary routines were probably greater than for girls. Horseplay and practical jokes were common and popular,[69] just as they were for the machine-tool workers of Saxony studied by the evangelical pastor Paul Göhre.[70] Further-more, for men, more than for women, the workplace was an important social institution. Men did not just *work* there, it was in the factory more than anywhere else that they had their social being. Brown *et al.*, in their study of the 'occupational culture' of

[67] Dückershoff, 19.
[68] Mass-Observation, *War Factory: A Report* (London, 1943), 78–9.
[69] Williams, *Railway Factory*, 267.
[70] P. Göhre, *Three Months in a Workshop* (London, 1895), 78–9.

shipyard workers, argue that 'this sociability is an important intrinsic work satisfaction', and that it partly explains the otherwise inexplicably large number of men who had their lunch in the yards.[71] Williams reported that smithies were often 'in love' with their forges and he was incredulous that 'men cling to the shed as long as they possibly can; they have an unnatural fondness for the stench and smoke!'[72] Thus it was the loss of the social relationships implied by work as much as the loss of the work itself that made long-term unemployment so alarming for many men in the inter-war years.[73] One final activity almost certainly ameliorated monotony: the creation of tension via strikes, unofficial stoppages, and workshop disputes. While it might be the case that the majority of strikes in Britain are economic in origin, though I think the case by no means unarguable, their rituals are not necessarily so: they are one way of raising interest in the workplace, if not in work, and the number of unofficial stoppages in highly automated industries is presumably not accidental. Men when bored will create tension. De Grazia even claims that there is a Mediterranean game, *passatella*, which was so successful in creating tension it had to be suppressed by law,[74] and it would have required instruments of coercion available to neither the state nor management to prevent its creation in British industry.

In the late 1940s, Zweig concluded that, at most, only about one-third of the British working class were affected by 'dull, repetitive and uninteresting jobs', but he doubted whether even this one-third were actually bored with their work.[75] Zweig underrated, I would guess, the degree of technical change in British industry. He was over-familiar with the mining and textile industries and underfamiliar with the rest, but it would be hard to quarrel with his conclusion. It is, furthermore, easy to underestimate British labour productivity before 1940. Writing in the 1880s, when clouds no bigger than men's hands were being detected on every horizon, the Scottish industrialist Alexander Wylie was urging workers to go easy: the 'tide of over-labour' had

[71] R. Brown, P. Brannen, J. Cousins, and M. Samphier, 'Leisure in Work', in M. A. Smith, S. Parker, and C. S. Smith (eds.), *Leisure and Society in Britain* (London, 1973), 107.   [72] Williams, *Railway Factory*, 292–3.
[73] See the sensitive discussion of this in Durant, *Problem of Leisure*, 4–5.
[74] S. de Grazia, *Of Time, Work and Leisure* (New York, 1962), 425.
[75] Zweig, 113.

inundated the country 'with desolating effects' on the hard-wrought workman.[76] Although the casual attitude of British working men worried him, de Rousiers was astonished at their capacity for work:

Everybody works very quickly here . . . There is no effort wasted and no talking. French workmen, so energetic by starts, would find it difficult to equal the rate of production . . . [A] merchant of precious stones told me he had often tried to introduce French workmen . . . The experiment had never succeeded: the masters found that the work was not turned out fast enough.[77]

The 'pace' of British industry did not slow down before 1914 (except perhaps in mining); the evidence suggests the contrary and Britain's was the only European economy where 'Taylorism' had been adopted on any significant scale.[78] Although the relative rate of its growth was probably decelerating, labour productivity was considerably higher than in (say) Germany and although that gap continued to narrow in the 1920s it continued throughout the 1930s. The apparent débâcle of British productivity since the Second World War, while almost certainly a continuation of longer-term trends, is much more remarkable than those trends actually imply.

Nor is there any evidence that the British factory proletariat was more alienated from its work than the continental work-force: it can be argued, indeed, that the reverse was true.[79] Similarly, it is hard to see that the work-experience of continental workmen differed much from that of the British. To read Paul Göhre's famous *Three Months in a Workshop* after reading Alfred Williams's *Life in a Railway Factory* is like seeing the replay of a silent film with German instead of English subtitles. What is clear, however, is that British management permitted, or was compelled to permit, techniques for ameliorating boredom and stress that were not permitted by European or American management, or only in a much-attenuated form. The conclusion from that is plain: those sectors of British industrial life in which monotony or work was most tormenting were in the minor clerical, distributive, and packing trades where such ameliorating techniques were hardly

---

[76] A. Wylie, *Labour, Leisure, and Luxury* (London, 1884), 19.

[77] De Rousiers, 5.

[78] For an assessment of the evidence see P. Stearns, *Lives of Labour* (London, 1975) 219–35.   [79] Ibid. 233.

possible. Not only was the work itself intrinsically hopeless but the 'occupational culture' was equally impoverished. Evidence to the Royal Commission on Labour on the condition of shop assistants, warehousemen and packers is among the most dispiriting of all. We have seen W. Johnson's evidence to the commission but it is worth repeating:

The average warehouse clerk and assistant goes into the business at an early age. Indeed, from the time he goes in as a rule he is shut from all communication with the world and he does not know really the changes that are taking place around him. He does not read the daily papers . . . and knows nothing of the outside world.

[Mundella] But how is it that intelligent men cannot combine as well as working-men who have less education and less intelligence?

Because working-men have the opportunity for social intercourse with each other and for discussing these matters, which shop assistants have not.[80]

This is the world of Durant's hobby-obsessed London grocery assistant[81] or the minor clerks of the 1960s who found their work almost unrelievedly repellent.[82] It is, to some extent, also the world of casual and boy labourers, amongst whom work was not discussed, and whose 'restlessness' and 'excitability' convinced the Edwardians that the 'nerviness' of the town was characteristic of industrial life generally. But these men, since they did not work directly in production, should probably be excluded from the original Shadwell–Cohen 'thesis', though it might be true they more neatly fit it than most. There is even evidence that individual workers were as often interested in their work as bored by it, and little evidence that their work suffered even if they were bored. If we can argue both that industrial division of labour did not necessarily lead to monotony and that, anyway, it is unlikely to have been much more monotonous than the work which preceded it, then the simple antithesis between work and leisure (or work and not-work) proposed by the Friedmann–Dumazedier school hardly stands. By this proposition, industrial work, synonymous with highly divided labour, is almost always deleterious and its consequences sometimes pathological. Leisure is 'time liberated'

[80] Royal Commission on Labour, *Minutes of Evidence*, PP (1893–4), xxxiv (C. 6894), QQ 31120–2, and above, p. 5.

[81] See above, p. 149.

[82] S. Parker, *The Future of Work and Leisure* (London, 1972), 47–9.

during which men can recover from one day's tedium in order to arm themselves against the next day's.[83] This is close to Shadwell's argument and not far from that of Zweig, who argued that men always chose hobbies unrelated to their work: clerks preferred manual work and railwaymen gardening, but labourers would avoid heavy work.[84] But there is, so to speak, no such unilinear relation. For one thing, too many hobbies were simple extensions of work itself. The hobby of many carpenters or painters was carpentry or painting. Most artisans liked 'pottering' and pottering could mean building all the furniture in a house or even rebuilding the house itself. 'In the evening he prosecutes his craft at home and manufactures furniture and decorations for himself and family . . . Very often the whole contents of his parlour and kitchen—with the exception of iron and other ware—were made by his hands.'[85] Not only did carpenters prefer carpentry, but manual labourers were energetic gardeners. Lady Bell, in her survey of the reading habits of Middlesbrough iron workers, noted how often men borrowed books on subjects 'connected with their work'.[86] After 1918 many men in automobile factories found their hobby in the product of their work—in making racing or rally cars, repairing, tinkering, reading auto magazines. Here again work routines defined the hobby.[87] Indeed, the most notorious case of men refusing to entwine work with leisure was not that of industrial workers but that of agricultural labourers whose allotments were, and still are, much less cherished than town lots.[88] Even if men selected hobbies unrelated to their work the hobbies had all the characteristics of work: indeed that is their fundamental quality.[89]

In any case, the relation between work and hobbies is as likely to be 'organic' as 'dialectic'. We have already seen that for skilled craftsmen the hobby was often simply an extension of ordinary work routines with the crucial modification that routine was replaced by autonomy and choice. Furthermore, before 1914,

[83] For the best statement of this position, see Friedman, *Anatomy of Work*, 110 ff.   [84] Zweig, 153.

[85] Williams, *Railway Factory*, 38–9.

[86] Florence, Lady Bell, *At the Works* (London, 1911), 209–29.

[87] See also M. Young and P. Willmott; 'The hobby of a sound engineer of Islington, hi-fi, was evident from the speakers we heard in every room.' *The Symmetrical Family* (Harmondsworth, 1980), 219–20.

[88] F. E. Green, 'The Allotment Movement', *Contemporary Review*, 114 (1918), 90.   [89] A. Tilgher, *Work* (London, 1931), 184–5.

when tools of the trade were normally the personal possession of the craftsman (and expensive) it is improbable that many unskilled men would buy tools in order to practise a craft hobby. Despite Zweig's assertion that men choose hobbies unrelated to their work, the direction of the evidence, so far as the historian is able to tell, points the other way. Men with the most complicated or 'leisure-enriching' hobbies appear more likely to be those whose work is itself 'enriched'. Caradog Jones and his colleagues found that hobbies 'are less common . . . among male manual workers than in other social classes'.[90] Young and Willmott comment, with obvious surprise, that they 'did not find in the working classes as many men who were enthusiasts for a sport or hobby, in compensation for the relatively greater dreariness of their work, as we did amongst other classes who (one would think) needed the compensation less'.[91] It seems fair to suggest (as a rule of thumb) that craft 'make-work' as a hobby was confined chiefly to the skilled working class while the principal hobby of the unskilled labourer was certainly sport. But this must be a rough rule: it is by no means clear whether (say) pigeon-fancying is a sport or a craft, nor is it clear that the miners who were its most enthusiastic adepts can be classified as skilled or unskilled workers. A more reasonable statement, therefore, of the Dumazedier–Friedmann–Zweig position is a simple functional one. In other words, hobbies helped to make work acceptable ('without a hobby you might as well be dead', Zweig was told[92]) rather than that hobbies made men inefficient workers. Yet even that is not proved. It is equally arguable that for many men there is *no* relation between work and leisure, work time and free time, and that preferences between the two are as much temperamental as occupational; or, indeed, that the *only* relation is a negative one: a dreary job means a dreary hobby.

This can, however, only be a partial conclusion. Hobbies had two other characteristics which were almost certainly connected with working habits. The first is that they gave an autonomy to working-class working life, even skilled working life, that was denied by the industrial division of labour and no doubt by pre-

[90] D. Caradog Jones (ed.), *The Social Survey of Merseyside*, 3 vols. (London, 1934), ii. 276.

[91] Young and Willmott, *Symmetrical Family*, 223.

[92] Zweig, p. 150; Banks, *Attitudes of Steelworkers*, 32–3. See also F. Zweig, *Men in the Pits* (London, 1948), 104.

industrial labour as well. This was true even of activities such as football which eventually became mere simulacra of commercial capitalism. The free nature of hobbies is obvious. They were as complicated and as prolonged as the individual decided: only self-satisfaction determined whether the model was finished, the garden dug or whether the canary was a good singer or not. Though there were some constraints, seasonal for example, individual control of time was perhaps the main difference between formal work and hobby work. This freedom could also be collective. The co-operative organization of hobbies provided rare opportunities for working-class collective activity without managerial and middle-class intervention. Pigeon, dog and canary breeders met frequently and eventually developed national organizations for the control and growth of the hobby. The tendency for publicans to provide premises and act as officials of such organizations perhaps gave them a new function when the old one of simply pouring alcohol down thirsty throats was declining.[93] Spontaneous organization was also true for football. C. E. B. Russell was startled at the 'businesslike methods' adopted by working-class youths in establishing football clubs. They were 'in some cases surprisingly well managed and controlled, and it is, in every way, a good thing that young lads should learn to organise and work for their fellows'.[94]

The second of these characteristics is that most hobbies were intensely competitive. Even when men banded together to promote them, the implied objective of their co-operation was individual competition. In many hobbies this is self-evident: the whole point of the elaborate breeding of pigeons and dogs was to win races; of canaries to produce new colours and a better song. In these cases a man's success at his hobby was measured by public competition. It is self-evident also of gardening. Flower and vegetable shows were always competitive. When asked in 1892 by the Royal Commissioners on Labour whether there had been 'an increasing tendency' to cultivate allotments, C. J. Wilson replied: 'Oh increased . . . because the advantages of them have been seen, and because interest has been taken in them, and [there is] a certain amount of vieing with one another as to whether they shall

[93] J. Mott, 'Miners, Weavers and Pigeon Racing' in Smith *et al.*, *Leisure and Society in Britain*, 93–4; Hawkins, *Norwich*, 314–15.
[94] Russell, *Manchester Boys*, 63–4.

have better vegetables, fruits, and gardens than their neighbours, and that is how it has come about.'[95] It was a competitive spirit cunningly and profitably encouraged by the government in both world wars. Competition even came to dominate the brass bands and their 'idealist' origins were almost entirely lost. 'Contesting', Brian Jackson commented, 'has altered the whole movement, quite as radically as the introduction of beer has altered the working men's clubs.'[96] Sport was, of course, intrinsically competitive. Moreover, when hobbies were not directly competitive their individualism could imply competition. Most hobbies, however private, usually involved some public display and this was unquestionably exploited by the commercial salesmen of hobby perquisites.

The individualism of hobbies was, and is, in clear contrast to the work experience of most of their practitioners. The gradual elimination of competitive stress from working life by technological change and (to some extent) by the work-force itself helped to make that life more tolerable for those who led it; but it conceivably diminished it as well. Stress and tension are disagreeable yet necessary. It was one of the functions of hobbies, therefore, to provide an acceptable competitiveness to lives otherwise circumscribed both by the requirements of increasingly mechanized work routines and (probably, but less certainly) by the demands of group loyalties. That is why for so many men some kinds of betting (though not, for example, betting on dogs) were ideal hobbies. They created and released physical tension and intellectual energy while, in effect, being as competitive as other organized hobbies where the competition, the winner, and the prize were more obvious. It is a mistake, and a serious one, to assume that all manifestations of working-class life were, or should be, collective; or to conclude that leisure activities 'set within definite limits, the most fundamental of which was the acceptance of the individualistic value of hegemonic ideology' were typically those of the middle and lower middle classes because of the absence of those 'substainable alternatives' found in working-class culture.[97] Working-class hobbies certainly had their collective

[95] Royal Commission on Labour, *Minutes of Evidence*, PP (1892), xxxv (C. 6795), Q 7686 at p. 308.

[96] Jackson, *Working-Class Community* (Harmondsworth, 1972), 31.

[97] R. Q. Gray, 'Religion, Culture and Social Class in Late Nineteenth and Early Twentieth Century Edinburgh', in G. Crossick (ed.), *The Lower Middle Class in Britain, 1870–1914* (London, 1977), 149.

organizations but it is hard to see how they differed from the associative bodies that absolutely underpin middle-class leisure. In any case their competitive nature was quite as characteristic and this, arguably, was part of their attraction. When other sides of life, working and domestic, were all too collective, the pleasure of an activity that emphasized privacy and solitude seems explicable on grounds other than those of imposed ideologies.

Hobbies had one more function: they permitted a socially acceptable level of intellectual activity. The degree to which the British working class rejected that we might call an official culture must not be exaggerated, but it is true that attempts to impose such a culture on it very largely failed. There was, however, no difference in the kind of intellectual activity that each class devoted to its own pursuits. The mastery of a craft-hobby or a sport demanded accuracy, knowledge, discipline and skill: all the qualities that the elementary educational system attempted to promote with such little obvious success. Hobbies, however, were socially permissible outlets for these qualities. It was for this reason that Paterson, having spent several years teaching in a Southwark board school, concluded that twenty years of compulsory education (he was writing at the turn of the century) had done little in a formal sense, but that 'in the organization of games as a definite and regular part of the schoolwork lies the hope of the future.'[98]

We can accept, therefore, that hobbies met a number of individual and collective needs; that they stood in a complicated, but very ambiguous, relation to work. Nevertheless, the 'thesis' that hobbies were undermining the British workman's interest in vocational work must fall. The evidence that there was a kind of 'work fund', a given sum of intellectual and emotional energy being drained by hobbies, though it exists, is not convincing. Yet if that is so, why should the thesis ever have been proposed? The most obvious reason is that hobbies (or at least one of their variants, mass sport) were by the turn of the century extremely conspicuous. Employers had learned to live with large-scale absenteeism during 'big' mid-week football fixtures, however much they disliked it. But that worried them less than what appeared to be happening in the workplace. One does not need to look far for evidence that management felt it was losing control,

[98] Paterson, *Across the Bridges*, 97–8.

that in some sense the rate of production was being determined by others, that its continental and American competitors were unfairly favoured. Much of this was, of course, pure fantasy. Managers always fear they are losing control; German and American employers almost certainly felt the same thing. Furthermore, there is little evidence that the labour force was working less hard, was effectively opposed to technological change when management was determined on it, or was much more irritated by labour than one would expect given the nature of the work. Yet it appeared to management that workers, if just by dead weight, were devising only half-resistable techniques to defeat measures that would individuate the work-force and make it internally competitive. The extent to which these techniques were successfully used is debatable; that they were used and had some success is not.

What explains even this partial success? One answer may be found in the social traditions of British life; the emphasis upon group loyalties and corporate affiliations which both worked against individualist practices. The physical representation of this was the trade union, which the employers could not wish away and against which they were feebly armed. A second, and most likely explanation, is to be found in the 'collective' nature of so much British factory work, usually undertaken either by gangs or by an artisan with one or more assistants, and the whole edifice propped up by the continuing vigour, or at least the continuation, of the apprenticeship system.[99] Both traditions reinforced each other, and the attitudes they produced ('dead-levelism' the mid-Victorians called them[100]) were something that management disliked but knew it could not overcome. It was for this reason that attempts to introduce bonus payments were so often resisted in England and it was this that Zweig meant when he described the British work force as 'defeatist' and 'without ambition'.[101]

In these circumstances it is not hard to see why so many should claim that work *itself* was the problem. Both sides had an interest in perpetuating this view. Management, apparently incapable of

[99] See Stearns, *Lives of Labour*, 216–17; for the apprenticeship system see the excellent discussion in C. More, *Skill and the English Working Class, 1870–1914* (London, 1980), 41–93, 215–20.

[100] See the use of the word and its context in W. G. Ward, *Seven Night's Discussion, Capital and Labour* (Nottingham, 1872), 33.

[101] Zweig, *British Worker*, 93.

managing as it believed it should, and conscious of competitive weakness, was happy enough to blame anything that would excuse it. The political left was attracted by an argument which suggested that divided labour was intrinsically pointless and that organized leisure alone liberated a man under capitalism. As a slogan, 'the right to useful labour' had a doubly pleasing resonance: work could provide both utility *and* self-satisfaction. In fact, neither work nor hobbies was the 'problem'. The 'problem', in so far as there was one, was in social codes. As we have seen, the casualness of British discipline always surprised foreigners; whether or not they approved of it depended on the political point they wished to make. The real difference between Britain and its competitors was not in attitudes to work but in factory discipline and the ability of management to enforce the order of production. The British ideology, for in effect that is what it was, ensured a high degree of social cohesion but not social integration. Associations, groups, and classes lived and let live; they knew there were certain boundaries that could not be crossed and rights that could not be infringed. This had its inevitable effects in the factory: within certain broadly accepted limitations the British workman went his own way.

6

Class and Poverty in Edwardian England

IN 1887 Charles Booth addressed the Royal Statistical Society on the condition and occupations of the inhabitants of the Tower Hamlets, and this was to be the pilot study for the great *Life and Labour*. After he had spoken the statistician Leone Levi asked the question:

Who was a poor man? . . . The author [Andrew Mearns, writer of *The Bitter Cry of Outcast London*] had not mentioned the causes of poverty . . . His own impression was that poverty proper in the district which had been described was more frequently produced by vice, extravagance and waste, or by unfitness for work, the result in many cases of immoral habits, than by real want of employment or low wages.[1]

It was, as Peter Hennock points out, this question and not Hyndman's famous challenge that moved Booth to the inquiry into London.[2] Levi's question had both ideological and methodological implications. Ideologically, it suggested that the poverty of the Tower Hamlets was a result of the lifestyle of the people who lived there—and thus could not be 'structural'; methodologically, that Booth was unable to demonstrate a structural or any other cause of poverty. In *The Life and Labour* Booth attempted to answer Levi. The result was a hybrid of the new and the old sociology. On the one hand, Booth tried to construct a generally acceptable 'poverty line' below which poverty could only be structural; on the other, he still relied on external (but not participant) observation to describe the cultural and 'spiritual' condition of the poor. There was thus a clear methodological tension in Booth's survey. This tension was also political: each technique seemed to point in a different direction. The 'quantitative' suggested that there were 'causes' of poverty which no poor man, however

---

[1] C. Booth, 'The Inhabitants of Tower Hamlets (School Board Division), their Condition and Occupations', *Journal of the Royal Statistical Society*, 1. 2 (1887), 394.

[2] E. P. Hennock, 'Poverty and Social Theory in England: the Experience of the 1880s', *Social History*, 1 (1976), 83.

heroically provident he was, could expect to overcome. The 'qualitative', however, equally suggested that a feckless and relentlessly short-sighted way of life, which mere numbers could never expose, was indeed one of the reasons why the poor were poor.

The ambiguous conclusions of Booth's methodology were central to and partly determined the ambiguity of Edwardian sociology. If the best way to 'know' the poor was by establishing numerical data, then the political implication of knowing the poor was a collectivist one. If the best way to 'know' them was via a kind of cultural archaeology dependent upon imaginative and apparently informed observation, then the political implication was individualist. Like the contemporary German *Methodenstreit* this tension was as much political as methodological.

Since, of course, this *was* an ambiguity most sociologists and social theorists tended to do a bit of both. Sensational revelations, from which the reader could derive widely divergent conclusions, continued to come out thick and fast.[3] Rowntree in the York study argued for the existence of structural poverty ('primary poverty') in a much more sophisticated way than Booth but at the same time insisted on a category of culturally determined poverty ('secondary poverty') which was inferred from more or less casual observation and impression.[4] To some extent the same was true of C. F. G. Masterman and even the more obviously distributional studies of Money and Mrs Pember Reeves.[5] Yet it was clear which way things were going. The Bowley and Burnett-Hurst five towns survey eschewed all cultural observation and seemed to ensure that in future surveys of working-class social conditions would be based upon sampling techniques where the only room for human imagination was what set of questions the surveyors chose to ask.[6] However, not only did these apparently neutral techniques suggest non-neutral political action, they seemed to narrow severely the ways in which one could 'know' the working class. Much of what

[3] See, for example, Rachel Vorspan, 'Vagrancy and the New Poor Law in late-Victorian and Edwardian England', *English Historical Review*, 92 (1977).

[4] B. S. Rowntree, *Poverty: A Study of Town Life* (London, 1901).

[5] C. F. G. Masterman, *The Condition of England* (London, 1909); L. C. Money, *Riches and Poverty*, (London, 1905); M. S. Pember Reeves, *Round about a Pound a Week* (London, 1913).

[6] A. L. Bowley and A. R. Burnett-Hurst, *Livelihood and Poverty* (London, 1915).

we understand by social and mental life cannot be examined by sampling techniques. Thus in 1914 Victor Branford wrote:

While the Booth type of survey is admirable in giving a picture of the economic and material conditions of the family it remains deficient . . . in the difficult task of describing the family's life of leisure, its spiritual condition . . . Here the problem is to discover some method of observing and recording . . . the thoughts and emotions, the habit of mind and life, of persons in their interior relations with one another and with their surroundings. The sort of question that this more intensive survey has to put before itself is—How can we decipher and record people's ideals, their characteristic ideas and culture, and the images and symbols which habitually occupy their minds?[7]

The subject of this chapter is three women—Mrs Helen Bosanquet, Miss Margaret Loane and Florence, Lady Bell—who in their writings on social class attempted to meet the conditions for Branford's 'more intensive survey'. Their preoccupation was essentially cultural; not in how society could be apportioned statistically but in how social classes could be understood ('known') through their codes, conventions, habits, and mental horizons. They were all three probably the most accomplished Edwardian practitioners of a cultural sociology; but they were also all three hostile to structural explanations of poverty and collective solutions to it. They thus embody two questions intrinsic to Edwardian social theory. Were the social data gathered by Booth, Rowntree, and their even more numerical successors too slight and jejune to bear the weight of the political conclusions apparently to be drawn from them? And did a cultural sociology of their kind necessarily produce an alternative political outcome?

First, who were they? Mrs Bosanquet (1860–1925) was born into the well-known Manchester unitarian family of Dendy (her sister, Mary, was also active in social work), took a first in the moral sciences tripos in Cambridge, and began her vocational life as a social worker with the Charity Organisation Society (COS) in London. There she met and married the philosopher Bernard Bosanquet, whose half-brother C. B. P. Bosanquet had been Charles Loch's predecessor as secretary of the COS. She was one of the society's most powerful intellectual and political influences before the First World War, if an increasingly isolated one.[8]

[7] V. Branford, *Interpretations and Forecasts* (London, 1914).
[8] For some details of her early life, see A. M. McBriar, *An Edwardian Mixed Doubles* (Oxford, 1987), 10–14.

Of Miss Loane (18?–1922) we know very little. She was born in Portsmouth, the daughter of a captain in the Royal Navy, trained as a nurse in the Charing Cross Hospital and then worked as a district nurse in both urban and rural England, before ending her active life where she had begun it—in Portsmouth—as super-intendent of district nurses.

Mrs Bosanquet and Miss Loane were professionals and, being childless, full-timers. Lady Bell (1851–1930) was neither—and nothing in her early life suggests the author of a minor classic of industrial sociology, *At the Works*. She was the daughter of Sir Joseph Oliffe, a fashionable physician in both Paris and London, and in 1876 she became the second wife of one of the great iron and steel magnates of the North-East, H. L. Bell—and thus, incidentally, the stepmother of Gertrude Bell. She was related by her own and her sister's marriage to a surprisingly large section of the Liberal aristocratic intelligentsia, including Bertrand Russell. Her husband's immense industrial interests took her to Middles-borough where she was (somewhat mysteriously) drawn into the life of that town's working class. She had a copious pen and devised a large number of plays, playlets, novels, games for children, and foreign language texts—on the way to writing one classic she wrote another, *French without Tears*.

They were all formidable women and by their own standards emancipated. But the way they observed the world had much to do with a conventional gender role allocation. The emphasis upon cooking, marketing, child-rearing, dress, fashion, cleanliness, dirt, and above all the housekeeping money—that is to say, upon those things most women then would have regarded as of singular importance—was partly a result of their sex. It was inevitable, furthermore, that their view of the working class would be haphazard and domestic, dependent upon observation and insight. This is most obvious in Miss Loane's case. The district nurse had access to working-class home-life in a way no other member of the middle class did; and the access was necessarily intimate and repeated. It was also access to the working class at its most vulnerable, when the defences it normally erected against outside intrusion were at their weakest. Equally, the techniques of the COS were always personal and demanded 'complete' knowledge of a family over the long term. Mrs Bosanquet not only inherited this tradition; she transformed it into the diagnostic case-study system now the basis of most modern social work.[9] As with the district nurse, this demanded home-visiting and individual attention. Again, like the district nurse, the COS social worker could develop a sharp eye for the texture of private life. Lady Bell, it is true, was less committed to the private and domestic. *At the Works* was partly a team effort and it involved some interesting surveys into reading habits and family budgets.[10] But the latter were very narrowly based, rather like those conducted by the 'Economic Club' in the 1890s,[11] and Lady Bell was at her most confident when expounding 'moral and temperamental' problems on the basis largely of ancedotal evidence.

Although nearly all their writing was drawn from this kind of evidence, as observers they had no doubt that British society revolved around one central fact—social class—of which all its conventions and habits were mere epiphenomena. In turn, they argued, the sociologist should ask himself three questions about this central fact: what were the typical and identifying characteristics of the British working class? how could the members of one social class ever understand those of another? and, finally, how were the cultural values of one social class transmitted to another, and how far should they be transmitted?

In their discussion of the working class two themes are insistently repeated, often in tandem: incompetence at cooking and incompetence in the management of money. Mrs Bosanquet wrote:

The poor are incapable of cooking, they have no ranges and no places to store anything. But even when the means are there the time and skill necessary to the art are often wanting, and a ready-cooked dinner from the fried fish shop, the eel-pie shop, or the tripe shop is too apt to prove less troublesome and more tempting.

Besides her ignorance, the London housewife often has to contend with a hopeless incapacity to spend her money properly. It is not that she cannot make good bargains . . . But her money when it all comes in on Saturday, is irresistible to her; she cannot remember that it has to last seven days, and spends as if Sunday were the one day of the week.[12]

---

[9] R. G. Walton, *Women in Social Work* (London, 1975), 113.

[10] Florence, Lady Bell, *At the Works* (London, 1911), 80–128.

[11] 'Economic Club', *Family Budgets: Being the Income and Expenses of Twenty-eight British Households, 1891–94* (London, 1894).

[12] H. Bosanquet, *Rich and Poor* (London, 1896), 89–90.

But of the two, it was money-management which most preoccupied them: as evidence illuminating in itself and since, unlike cooking, it was not an activity largely exclusive to one sex, as the most sensitive indicator of what they thought to be the characteristic working-class view of the world.

All three wrote extensively on the domestic economy of the working class. And if some of this had a strictly educational purpose—how to teach thrift—it also contained much descriptive detail. Even Miss Loane, whose main interest was in codes of personal behaviour, was capable of a sustained exposition of working-class expenditure. Of its nature she had no doubt:

> Few people try to realise the practical bearings of the fact that the self-taxation of the poor, the amount wasted by recklessness, ignorance, credulity and misplaced suspicion, by lack of temperance, foresight and self-discipline would satisfy an oriental despot . . . or supply even a progressive government with a temporary surplus.[13]

Neither Mrs Bosanquet nor Lady Bell (a less harsh judge) dissented. Lady Bell, confessing the unrepresentative nature of her budget analyses, which all described the thrifty management of economy added: 'I fear it would be idle to pretend that this description can be applied to most of the houses at the works. The all-devouring tendencies to drink, betting and gambling, the main channels of the waste and leakage, will be discussed in another chapter'.[14] And a very long chapter it is.[15] But it was inevitably Mrs Bosanquet who wrote most elaborately on personal expenditure: COS workers were taught that economic foresight was the greatest boon they could give the poor while budgetary fecklessness was the real generator of poverty. Thus her own instructional essays proceeded from a premiss which Booth and Rowntree had dismissed as (at least in part) untrue:

> we also maintain that the more flagrant cases of poverty which are generally supposed to be evidence of insufficient income are, on the contrary, comparatively seldom due to insufficient earnings. In the great majority of cases a wise economy is all that is needed to remedy the poverty. That this is so seldom realised is due to imperfect observation; it

[13] M. E. Loane, *Neighbours and Friends* (London, 1910), 278.
[14] Bell, *At the Works*, 117.
[15] Ibid. 341–76.

needs the skilled observer to distinguish between the poverty due to insufficient income and that due to unwise economy.[16]

This is, of course, a highly questionable assertion. Yet it is the case that while Booth had almost nothing to say about the debt–credit cycle in which most working people actually led their lives,[17] it was a subject to which Mrs Bosanquet repeatedly returned, both as student and as critic. Her essay 'The Burden of Small Debts' is a *tour de force* which encapsulates the cycle with elegance and succinctness. What are its characteristics?

Of course the old-fashioned morality goes in favour of thrift as opposed to credit, but I am interested to find out to what a large extent the advantages of credit are now being preached as well as practised. The pawnbroker especially is extolled as 'the poor man's friend', and the system of credit at the general shop . . . is regarded as the one salvation of the wage-earner in bad times . . . Thus the prestige which attaches to credit in the commercial world is fast being transferred to the region of private indebtedness, and as we turn to the poorer classes we find ourselves regarding it as tinged with a curious kind of semi-professional, semi-sentimental benevolence.

From this point of view the uncertainty of the future becomes a powerful argument against anticipatory provision and in favour of credit. There is no doubt that saving is regarded, and perhaps justifiably regarded, as the sacrifice of present and certain advantages for the meeting of evils which may, possibly, never occur, or which, if they do occur, may be met in some way not yet foreseen . . . And though I have never heard it openly argued that a burden may very likely be escaped altogether by putting it into the future, yet no doubt the possibility is vaguely in the minds of those who practise some form of indebtedness as their *modus operandi*.[18]

This is a neat formulation. She does not approve of the system, but she does see how it works and why it was plausible to argue that it should. Furthermore, by concentrating on the relationship between present and future, security and insecurity, she gave a rationale to working-class economic behaviour she was often not otherwise prepared to admit.[19] Nevertheless, she argued that the cycle was

[16] H. Bosanquet, 'Wages and Housekeeping' in C. S. Loch (ed.), *Methods of Social Advance* (London, 1904), 133.

[17] Booth's comments were relegated to appendices in the last volume of his *Life and Labour of the People in London* (rev. edn.; London, 1902–8), xvii.

[18] H. Bosanquet, *The Standard of Life* (London, 1906), 68.

[19] See below, pp. 176–7.

very leaky and the poor lost more than they gained. The money went on 'boozing' (her word) and gambling, on endless knick-knacks, pianos and gramophones, looking-classes, etc.—and it went not through direct expenditure, but through instalment buying and the gimcrack credit systems that had countless variants throughout the country. Thus the two institutions most loathed by all three were the 'tallymen'—the itinerant hawkers who went through the streets selling absolutely anything on tick ('even *toys* can be bought in this way'[20])—and the general stores, local shops which invariably sold on credit.

To Miss Loane the tallyman was 'morally tainted';[21] to Lady Bell the working-class housewife was a simple pushover for him.

If she has a penny in her pocket, she will be quite ready to spend it on the first thing that comes within her ken, as she stands at her door. It may be a 'tallyman' who comes along with something to sell on the hire system—a worsted shawl, perhaps, a workbox, or even a gramophone, but whatever it is the woman buys it simply because it is suggested for her—after which she ends in having to pawn some of her belongings to pay for what she has hired.[22]

Mrs Bosanquet thought he was 'the most insidious exponent of credit' whose 'success depends upon the skill with which he can magnify the delights of immediate acquisition and minimise the pains of future payment.'[23]

Like the tallyman, the general store exploited the present at the expense of the future. They had little sympathy for the general shopkeeper and looked to his supersession by the high-street department stores, where goods were cheaper and where credit was stringently controlled or, even better, by the co-operatives where all transactions were thought to be ready-money. Mrs Bosanquet, whose experience was confined largely to London, actually believed that the co-ops had poor prospects there, and argued that an infallible sign of the superiority of northern man over southern was his readiness to go to a co-op.[24] In fact, as we shall see, there is little doubt they seriously underestimated the need for credit in a low-wage economy—largely because they would not admit that low wages as such were a problem. From the

[20] Loane, *Neighbours and Friends*, 278–9.   [21] Ibid. 280.
[22] Florence, Lady Bell, *Landmarks*, (London, 1929), 24–5.
[23] Bosanquet, *Standard of Life*, 80.
[24] H. Bosanquet, 'Wages and Housekeeping', 143.

point of view of a ruined shopkeeper like Frank Bullen the picture seems very different.[25]

Nevertheless, their account has considerable explanatory power. Why were the poor so improvident in their management of money? To uncover the answer to this question was also to uncover the most significant characteristic of the working class. And that was absence of memory and anticipation: a mental view confined to the instant and momentary. In a manual for COS workers Mrs Bosanquet conceded that the 'mental horizon' of the poor might be seven days,[26] but elsewhere she suggested that it was narrower even than that. 'Surely', she wrote in 1896, 'the people of London are like none other in their intense devotion to the present moment, and their blind forgetfulness of past and future.'[27] At its most extreme, life had lost all organized meaning:

The true type of this class lives in the present moment only; not only is he without foresight—he is almost without memory, in the sense that his past is so completely past that he has no more organized experience to refer to than a child. Hence his life is one incoherent jumble from beginning to end; it would be impossible to make even a connected story out of it . . . all is aimless and shifting.[28]

They thus carried the argument beyond the mere philistine assertion that the first thing the poor do with their money is to spend it. On the whole, of course, they did believe that is what the poor did with their money, but only because the poor were trapped in a mental culture which they did not create and over which they had little control.[29] Miss Loane carried the argument furthest of all. She agreed that people suffered much more from refusal to remember the past or to resist immediate temptation than by 'any "iron law" or "incalculable vicissitudes of trade" '.[30] But she did not regard that as the main feature of this mental culture; the attitude of the poor to memory and causation was much more fundamental. Because the world of the poor was immediate they could not remember effectively; because they could not do that, they could not develop a proper sense of causation. Facts

[25] F. T. Bullen, *Confessions of a Tradesman* (London, 1908).
[26] Bosanquet, 'Wages and Housekeeping', 136.
[27] Bosanquet, *Rich and Poor*, 40.
[28] Bosanquet, *Standard of Life*, 168–9.
[29] Bosanquet, *The Strength of the People*, (London, 1903), 51; Bell, *At the Works*, 196; M. E. Loane, *From Their Point of View* (London, 1908), 104–5.
[30] M. E. Loane, *The Common Growth*, (London, 1911), 116.

became muddled and misplaced, and while people told the truth, it was the truth only as they could recollect it; that is to say, not the truth at all. Working-class women were as incapable of keeping all facts steadily in view, she wrote, as we would be of all the facts 'marshalled by a parliamentary commission'. Only in a police-court was it reasonable to suppose that working-class witnesses were lying: outside that 'one only needs to doubt [their] completeness, and beware of their conclusions', and she contrived the following as an example of the 'contradictoriness and apparently wilful falsity of the evidence given from day to day . . . [by] the relative weakness of the power of seeing things as a whole':

One day the general consensus of opinion in an entire village, or in a couple of streets in a working-class quarter, will be that Mrs Purkiss is an excellent wife, and if the faintest chip or flaw can be found in her character it is entirely due to her husband; and a large amount of evidence, all substantially true, is brought forward to prove the case. Mr Purkiss' character in no way changes, but he breaks his neck, has a bad attack of pneumonia, or develops consumption. Instantly opinion veers around: every scrap of evidence in favour of Purkiss and against his wife rushes hurriedly to the neighbours' minds and tongues, and Mrs Purkiss' virtues sink out of sight with equal completeness and rapidity.[31]

Furthermore, they argued that this confined sense of time influenced all aspects of working-class behaviour: the urge for sensation, excitement, rapid change of interest together with quick loss of concentration. They even suggested that it showed itself in physical taste: liquids had to be very sweet or very sharp; medicines strong and instant in effect.[32] In the mental culture of the poor, therefore, they did not regard money-management as the only significant theme. But it was the main one: not simply because money does make the world go round, but because it was the surest way of measuring how men controlled their lives: if a man was far-sighted in his own economy, he was likely to be able to control and understand other spheres of his life. They believed that the middle classes were, on the whole, able to impose order on the chaos of information and evidence about them because they

---

[31] Loane, *From Their Point of View*, 67–8.
[32] Bosanquet, *Rich and Poor*, 92; Bell, *At the Works*, 135; M. E. Loane, *An Englishman's Castle* (London, 1909), 32–3.

had been taught to; the poor were unable to because they had not been. Similarly, just as the short time-scale was the overriding characteristic of the working class, the long time-scale was the overriding one of the middle classes. This, Mrs Bosanquet argued, had clear political consequences: it was one reason why there could be no revolution in Britain. In an essay (entitled 'Klassenkampf') she noted that the labour movement was led, and necessarily led, by middle-class or would-be middle-class individuals, who, though sympathetic to the proletariat, were busy running the non-ideological element of their lives in an entirely bourgeois style—buying railway stock, coddling bank accounts, fussing about insurance. In brief, constantly thinking about the future.[33] And it was this which mattered. They thus concluded that memory, anticipation, and the ability to attribute rational causality were determined by social class. Although they believed that classes differed in numberless ways, the primary difference, the one that lay behind all the others, was in attitudes to time.

They had no doubt that the poor, by which they almost certainly meant the majority of wage-earners, had a defective sense of time; but they did not believe the poor were congenitally incompetent. They had been taught foolish habits and, since that was so, they could be untaught them. Yet this demanded the projection of new habits and values across formidable obstacles of class ignorance and suspicion and it suggested the second question which should engage the sociologist: how could these obstacles be overcome? Whereas the 'quantitative' school had tended to duck this question—or not even consider it—it was both ideologically and vocationally impossible for them to do so. For example, the function of the first generation of district nurses, of whom Miss Loane was one, was never really to bring the wonders of modern medicine into the slums of Britain but to stop people behaving (as they believed) stupidly.[34] The same was obviously true of a COS worker or even of a casually benevolent force like Lady Bell. But to make people behave sensibly you had to understand them, to win their respect and trust; and at every point their writings suggest that this was a difficult if not impossible task. Even if the classes could communicate it was communication of the crudest

[33] Bosanquet, *Standard of Life*, 152–6.
[34] As an illustration of this, see Miss Loane's own manual, *Simple Sanitation: The Practical Application of the Laws of Health to Small Dwellings* (London, n.d.).

kind, each being insensitive to the nuances and peculiarities of the others.

At the beginning of her first published guide for social workers, *Rich and Poor*, Mrs Bosanquet wrote:

The artisan will speak of trades people and small shopkeepers as 'middle class' meaning 'not ladies and gentlemen'; while, I suppose, the aristocracy would speak of professional people in the same way . . . And within the large class massed together by the outsider as 'working people' there is the same manifold gradation in the social scale as that which exists at the other end; there is the same sensitiveness to class distinctions which are invisible to all but themselves, and the same resentment felt at any intrusion of one grade into another.

It was this tendency 'to mass together' which made it impossible for 'us' to understand 'them'. Stereotypes of rich and poor were, however, accepted by both 'and are very detrimental to sympathetic intercourse between people who have much to learn from each other'.[35] This mutual incomprehension had clear political implications which Mrs Bosanquet announced with her customary bluntness. 'The industrial class will work out its own future,' she wrote,

but whether it does so with revolt or suffering, through much failure or delay or by steady progress and with the co-operation and sympathy of the rest of the community will depend mainly upon the attitude taken by the community. At present it is somewhat in the position of the spectators at a melodrama: it varies between the wildest sympathy with wrongs which are largely imaginary and righteous indignation against sins which are hardly less so. Of real understanding and co-operation there is little; for understanding involves insight and patient study, both of which are very difficult to bestow beyond one's own familiar circle of interests.[36]

In her revisions of COS syllabuses she attempted to teach social workers 'communications',[37] with what success we do not know but she could hardly have had much confidence in the outcome.

The same is true of Lady Bell. In *At the Works* she notes how administratively difficult and circumscribed a workman's life could become by mistrust of those outside his own class—either

[35] Bosanquet, *Rich and Poor*, 4–5.
[36] Bosanquet, *Strength of the People*, 313.
[37] M. Rooff, *A Hundred Years of Family Welfare* (London, 1972); also M. J. Moore, 'Social Work and Social Welfare: The Organization of Philanthropic Resources in Britain, 1900–1914', *Journal of British Studies*, 16 (1977).

employers or 'officials'. It isolated him from the technology of modern life and perpetuated a vagueness about 'how to get things done', since all instruction about how it might be done, how, for example, sick-clubs might be founded, how money might be saved, was not so much resented as suspected and ignored.[38] But she had little idea how this could be corrected. Of the ignorance of working-class mothers she wrote:

How are we going to attack all the ramparts that stand between us and the possibility of enlightening the mothers? We have to reckon with their incapacity in most cases to learn; and perhaps with a still more serious obstacles, the uncertainty of the teachers as to what should be taught, in what way, and at what age.[39]

Mrs Bosanquet and Lady Bell were primarily concerned with the consequences of this for social policy, but a district nurse like Miss Loane, if she were to function at all as she was supposed to, had to get around it, and quickly. She agreed that it was not easy. Class-barriers, she wrote, 'are firmly erected and closely guarded by the poor. Any working man's wife would more readily confine her private affairs to the neighbour with whom she has had bitter, year-long quarrels, than she would to the kindest and most discreet of nurses or district visitors.'[40] Elsewhere she stated flatly that it 'would be a mistake to imagine that class feeling and class consciousness are generally accompanied by active dislike; they are chiefly important because they so heavily discount the values of all benevolent effort working from above.'[41] Yet since she also argued that social life was regulated by a series of codes and etiquettes, which differed from class to class, it was possible, she suggested, to penetrate the working class, not by accepting or understanding its codes—which was not possible—but by counter-feiting them. Thus the first quality a nurse had to learn was self-effacement. There was no surer way of improving what she called 'interclassic sincerity' than by never asking 'unneccesary questions and [accepting] without the smallest visible hesitation any and every statement that is voluntarily made'.[42] The chapter 'A First Visit' in her nursing manual *Outlines of Routine in District Nursing* is worth quoting, as an example of what she believed to be

[38] Bell, *At the Works*, 175–6.   [39] Ibid. 289.
[40] M. E. Loane, *The Next Street But One* (London, 1907), 79.
[41] Loane, *From Their Point of View*, 64.
[42] Loane, *The Common Growth*, 144.

necessary on the part of the official classes and the social expectations of working-class women.

The first thing to be remembered in knockerless, bell-less regions is that a never-to-be-departed from etiquette demands that only the hand should be used; and it is desirable that the neighbours should be able to testify that the first two or three taps, at any rate, have been soft and low.

Before going to the house the nurse should, if possible, have learnt the family name, and in order to avoid an alarming number of direct questions, it is desirable to know something of the patient's circumstances. But the name is the principal thing; among the poorer classes it is clung to with extraordinary persistency. To call a person 'out of her name' is unpardonable, not to call her by it early and often is scarcely less wounding to her feelings . . .

In all the preliminary conversation the voice should be carefully lowered. Although the poor commonly speak to one another with what might be considered unnecessary loudness, they resent this tone in their social superiors, not only because it enables inquisitive neighbours to hear too much, but because they know that is not how a lady speaks to a friend . . . The manner to be cultivated is simple and unaffected but qualified by extreme gentleness.[43]

Everything was painfully slow, but that was unavoidable.

Confidence grows slowly and can never be forced . . . but surely slow and real progress is preferable to forcing her will upon the friends at the first visit, being plainly shown at the second that she is unwelcome, and at the third being plainly told so? The poor will always be grateful for a courtesy that constantly keeps in rememberance the facts that they are in their own house, that they have a 'right' to do almost exactly as they choose, and that the district nurse is merely an adviser and cannot immediately be expected to be a trusted one.[44]

She noted that working men and women were amazingly quick to pick up solecisms. She recalled one old man who told of his policeman son's amusement at upper-class electioneering:

Oh, he did crack his sides of laughing when he told us how on polling-day the wife of one of them men that wants our votes shook hands—yes, *shook hands* with 'em all, and tried to split jokes. 'Taint becoming these fine folks do or try to do, as they think we does; but there's a big path between us, and they'll never understand our ways. Let them keep to their'n and us to our'n. Let's all act straight and becoming.[45]

[43] M. E. Loane, *Outlines of Routine in District Nursing* (London, 1905), 141.
[44] Ibid. 145.   [45] Loane, *The Common Growth*, 271.

As an example of the crucial way in which the British class-system operated this story is more revealing than even Miss Loane realized; nevertheless, she has characteristically appended to it an important social precept:

Feminine 'fine folk' would do well to remember that, although it is usually 'becoming' for them to shake hands with any working women they meet indoors, it is seldom 'becoming' to shake hands with a working man, even in his own house and after an acquaintance of some years standing, and that it is far safer to err on the side of omission.

Violation of etiquette could even be a danger to the person. She recalled one occasion when she was required to show, without introductions, a local notable around the tiny 'house' of one tough old widow. When she later encountered her, the widow bawled at Miss Loane: 'The nex' time ya forgets yer manners and don't present ladies prop'ly when ya brings 'em to MY HOUSE, I'll knock 'ee down with a poker!'[46]

In the end, like Mrs Bosanquet and Lady Bell, she concluded that acquiescence in the codes made possible administrative and medical contact, but not much more. Although she was unclear exactly what part speech played in class-relationship,[47] her last word was decidedly pessimistic:

I doubt if any real conversation between members of two classes is possible. All my conversations with my patients and their friends have been of an exceedingly one-sided character . . . in some cases I talked, and in some they did, but we never took anything like equal parts. A question, a shade of surprise, the faintest dissent . . . the lack of instant approbation, would generally be enough to silence them and in many instances to cause them to veer round suddenly, and bring forward opinions in direct opposition to those they had already expressed.[48]

On one side, therefore, they described social classes not mutually hostile, but mutually ignorant, and between whom no communication, except of the most elementary kind, was possible. On the other, however, they saw evidence everywhere that the cultural values of the upper and middle classes did indeed become those of the working class as well—most spectacularly in dress and fashion. Mrs Bosanquet wrote:

---

[46] Ibid. 5.   [47] See below, pp. 182–3.
[48] Loane, *From Their Point of View*, 231.

In a town where there are both rich and poor the dress of the latter will invariably follow that of their well-to-do neighbours; the fashions spread like an epidemic from high to low, repeating themselves in poor materials with all extravagance of cut and colour accentuated.[49]

Miss Loane thought the poor were 'martyrs to fashion',[50] and nominated dress as the most unfailing way of categorizing her patients.[51] Lady Bell claimed that the first thing women munition workers did in 1915 was to devote their new earnings to gaudy and apparently smart clothing.[52] But if dress-fashion spread from one class to another like cholera, other changes spread like rabies— more slowly, but still irresistible. They noted, as did most of their contemporaries, the increasing refinement of working-class life: the rapid disappearance of physical brawling and the growing approximation of working-class family life to that of the middle class. Miss Loane adduced it a good sign that working families had begun to keep anniversaries and to exchange gifts on festive days.[53] It was an even better sign that the district nurse observed in working-class eating habits the same regularity as in those of their social superiors.

Orderly serving of meals is less exceptional than it was a few years ago. In a considerable number of working-class homes the district nurse, passing through the kitchen during the evening meal, catches the thousand-times-repeated warnings of the nurseries and schoolrooms of the well-to-do: 'Sit up straight in your chair'; 'Don't eat so fast'; . . . Your Mother's speaking, don't interrupt her'.[54]

Only in speech was Miss Loane unsure which way the movement went. She sometimes argued that speech was just another unfathomable class code which, like all class codes, was incomprehensible to those who lived outside it, and where stereotypical assumptions governed the behaviour of outsiders. Thus the middle classes had always talked to the working classes loudly, slowly, and in words of one syllable, while the lower now talked to the middle loudly, slowly, and in words of many syllables. The poor, she suggested, when speaking to the not-poor chose their words with care, particularly on subjects normally beyond their range: as

[49] Bosanquet, *Rich and Poor*, 150–1.
[50] M. E. Loane, *The Queen's Poor* (London, 1905), 120.
[51] Loane, *The Common Growth*, 233.
[52] Bell, *Landmarks*, 68.
[53] Loane, *The Next Street But One*, 46.
[54] Loane, *The Common Growth*, 221–2.

with the patient who, after talking to her in an entirely unforced way, suddenly said in a tone of excruciating gentility: 'Our monarch would appear to be upon amicable terms with the majority of the foreign royalties.'[55] On occasion she comes close to arguing that people speak without affectation only to members of their own class; that language obstructs as well as facilitates communication. On balance, however, she seems to have concluded that changes in speech patterns were of the same kind as other changes in social behaviour. Although she conceded that differences in intonation, pronunciation, and grammar were still great, she thought those in vocabulary were rapidly diminishing. The periphrasis of much working-class speech was actually a result of developing literacy and a slow familiarization with a more sophisticated vocabulary:

A rich and picturesque vocabulary is a real pleasure to the working-class. 'Not to have no language' is about the most damning criticism of any preacher or teacher . . . and for polite use they greatly delight in the capture of general utility phrases, such as 'The happy medium'.[56]

There was, also, a new emphasis upon politeness and correctness in speech; she quotes tellingly one 'favourite expression' which had recently become popular: ' "Ah, that made him put in his aitches", used in the sense of "That brought him to his bearings".'[57]

What was the speed of this cultural transmission? Clearly, they regarded fashion changes as unique in their pace, though they did not say why. For the rest they thought that change tended to be generational. This was particularly so of refinement of manners. Miss Loane quotes two examples:

When forms of courtesy are taught [by the working classes], one can frequently recognise them as those current at an earlier day among the upper classes. For instance, a poor woman will say at parting to a lady who has been calling on her, 'Thank you for your visit'—the very words that I have heard used by old ladies in the provinces to their equals.[58]

The second is more evocative; she pointed out that the new gentility of the poor led to stories of the kind that used to be told of their social superiors a generation or so earlier.

A women with half a dozen children asked a friend to tea, and for the first

[55] Loane, *From Their Point of View*, 83.   [56] Ibid. 82.
[57] Ibid. 85.   [58] Loane, *An Englishman's Castle*, 201–2.

time placed a complete set of china on the table, including a slop-basin. The children stared to see the use to which it was put, and presently one of them so thirsted for information that she was obliged to ask: 'Mammy, why don't you throw the grouts in the grate, same as you always does?'[59]

Acceptance of protective legislation or new working techniques was equally generational. Thus the working class accepted the enforcement of anti-fever legislation, but regarded more recent water-purification and sanitary statutes as a well-meant but foolish interference in their lives.[60] She thought the process best illustrated by the propensity of road-menders to wear eye-protectors: of three, the oldest probably would not, the middle-aged one might, the youngest almost certainly would. Similarly, the kind of medical acuity commonplace in the middle classes was almost impossible to inculcate in the oldest generation of the working class. This again was a genuine problem for the district nurse. In a piece entitled 'Teaching the Patient's Friends' she wrote:

A considerable number of the generation who will bear sway in the sickroom for many years to come, especially among the extremely poor or in very backward districts, are fatalists, nay more, convinced that to alter the course of a serious illness is not only useless but impious . . . Unless the nurse can undermine these superstitions by argument, example, persuasion, mild bribery, or fear of the law . . . she will have to visit these cases with a frequency which would otherwise not be needed.[61]

How then do cultural values move from one class to another? This is for them an important methodological question, not only because of its intrinsic difficulty, but because they argued emphatically that social classes lived in tight, private worlds between which there was little contact. In practice, they concluded that there were two processes; the first, entirely impersonal and unforced; the second, the result of direct pressure on the working classes from above.

The first of these processes, they argued, determined the behaviour of *all* classes, but not synchronically. For example, coarseness of behaviour, which they saw disappearing from the working class of their own time, was equally characteristic of the middle and upper classes a generation or so earlier. Every class, they believed, was being disciplined by economic and social forces

[59] Loane, *The Queen's Poor*, 63.
[60] Loane, *An Englishman's Castle*, 121.
[61] Loane, *Outlines of Routine in District Nursing*, 146.

which operated almost independently of each of them. There was, therefore, an already existing shared culture which differed from class to class only in detail and chronology. So in her analysis of working-class reading Lady Bell could argue that the content of the papers, novels, novelettes, etc. read by the poor were analogous to the reading of the educated, only more simple, more direct, less subtle, and more immediate in its stimulation: romance was more romantic, tragedy more tragic, melodrama more melodramatic, happy endings even happier.[62] As for the much-read *Illustrated Police Budget* and other violent rags, they were merely 'the counterpart, in cruder form, of the detective stories revelled in by readers of more education and a wider field of choice, such stories as "Monsieur Lecoq" and "Sherlock Holmes" '.[63] (Indeed, the point she was now making had been made a century before by Jane Austen in *Northanger Abbey*.) Mrs Bosanquet, as we have seen, suggested that what was true of literature was also true of dress: the forms were the same but the style was gaudier and more crude. Even here middle-class taste was being adopted. Miss Loane noted how much *less* bombastic working-class dress was in 1900 than it had been twenty years earlier.[64] The district nurse could even turn this kind of thing to advantage. Why, she asked, did the middle classes now look after their teeth—not because teeth were found actually to be useful, but because the sight of poor or rotting teeth had become repulsive.[65] Once the poor shared that repulsion the battle for teeth was won.

They were not entirely consistent here. In fact, they gave a higher place to exemplary behaviour and social mimicry than was probably compatible with an explanation based upon a form of pre-existing 'common culture'. Mrs Bosanquet, for example, sometimes argued that the poor always copied the rich, and the more ostentatiously the rich behaved, the sooner they were copied. She was, therefore, bitterly opposed to upper-class gambling on these grounds. In that she was probably wrong,[66] but in fashion and dress it may be difficult to find any other explanation. Furthermore, they were agreed that social imitation was encouraged by the fact that the poor did not resent the rich.

[62] Bell, *Landmarks*, 30–1.   [63] Bell, *At the Works*, 205–8.
[64] Loane, *The Next Street But One*, 37–8.
[65] Loane, *The Common Growth*, 151–2.   [66] See above, pp. 132–3.

They noted, on the contrary, that the poor rather admired upper-class extravagance and were quick to ape it. Nevertheless, the argument by mimicry caused them problems, as it has (we shall see) their intellectual successors.[67] Lady Bell and Mrs Bosanquet thus tended to disapprove of the voracious working-class consumption of 'luxury goods'—ornaments, pianos, etc.—while Miss Loane was true to what we might call the argument by all-round uplift: a parlour permanently closed and stuffed with unused goods was no doubt a waste of space but it was also an important symbol of the absorption of the working classes into a more controlled and decorous world.[68]

The second process—the imposition of 'proper' values on the working classes from above—was one of which they were an intrinsic part and they were quick to notice the institutions which embodied it. The first was domestic service and there seems little reason to quarrel with them here. There is abundant evidence that as a result of service the poor knew much about the lives of the rich,[69] and both Mrs Bosanquet and Miss Loane were probably stating no more than truisms when they argued that service was one of the most effective ways of transferring the values of one class to another. They also believed that girls who had been in service were more competent wives and mothers, more able to cope with the rigours of working-class life. It was, they argued, thus the duty of a mistress to teach her servants economic and orderly household management. Whether service had the long-term consequences they clearly assumed it would have is hard to say but it is reasonable to argue that it did.

The second of these institutions was compulsory education. Again, this seems a truism, but one must note in what sense they thought it important. As a way of inculcating the three Rs they dismissed it as time-wasting; the content of syllabuses trivial and deadening.[70] Miss Loane did not even believe that it was yet necessary to be literate in Britain.[71] Compulsory education was desirable for its extra-curricular effects, on deportment, demeanour, and regularity of habits. It enforced punctuality and self-

---

[67] See below, pp. 190–3.   [68] Loane, *From Their Point of View*, 240.
[69] See P. Horn, *The Rise and Fall of the Victorian Servant* (Dublin, 1975), esp. pp. 109–32; Flora Thompson, *Lark Rise to Candleford* (World's Classics edn.; London, 1954), 180–2.   [70] Loane, *An Englishman's Castle*, 142–3.
[71] Loane, *The Next Street But One*, 11. But she thought literacy would soon be 'indispensable'.

control: it compelled children to be physically examined and to learn elementary hygiene. It prolonged childhood and thus postponed a premature entry into adulthood. Miss Loane regretted (revealingly) that board school teachers were not permitted greater access to their pupils' homes.[72] Mrs Bosanquet wrote that the

greatest influence in our parish outside the home is beyond doubt the school . . . For good and evil the rising generation is there receiving instruction and discipline . . . in face of all criticism our children are being firmly and gently brought into line, and helped up the first steep steps of order and knowledge. I do not think we attach nearly sufficient weight to this fact in estimating the advance that has been made towards reclaiming the 'submerged' classes of the communtiy.[73]

They would certainly have agreed with George Sims that the crucial social division in London was now between those who had been to board school and those who had not.[74]

The third institution was the improving classes (typified by themselves) whose authority they were happy to have reinforced by state coercion. While they were uniformly hostile to state intervention in the form of, say, non-contributory old age pensions—interventions which only encouraged, as they thought, dependence—they had no doubt that the didactic powers of the state could and should be mobilized by 'improving' agencies or by the state itself so long as their aims were disciplinary. Miss Loane's technical manuals, for example, make it clear she believed that eventually the poor would have to behave in the way the outside world she represented thought rational. The district nurse—to whom the other two paid eloquent tribute[75]—was only one of a number of improving agencies—often medical—which actively intervened in working-class life. So these three individualists were ardent for the rigid application of housing and sanitary legislation, even though that was often a risky and sometimes impossible thing for the poor to do.[76] In supporting compulsory education at a time when there were plausible reasons for doubting its necessity they

[72] Loane, *The Common Growth*, 250–1.
[73] Bosanquet, *Rich and Poor*, 50.
[74] G. Sims, *How the Poor Live and Horrible London* (London, 1889), 116–17.
[75] Bosanquet, *Rich and Poor*, 37; Bell, *At the Works*, 319.
[76] Bosanquet, *Standard of Life*, 240; Loane, *Simple Sanitation*, 16–20. For the difficulty of enforcing the legislation, see J. Burnett, *Plenty and Want* (London, 1966), 137–66.

were, of course, supporting the most direct intrusion into working-class privacy it was possible to make.

Finally, but in no organized way, they looked to improvements in 'labour conditions', by which they usually meant regularity of work and increased labour productivity—that is, higher wages. Both Mrs Bosanquet and Miss Loane argued that high wages encouraged foresight and the long view, if only because those who worry most about the future are those who have the least to fear from it.[77] As a psychological assumption—that concern for the future encourages pessimism which encourages concern for the future—that is characteristically suggestive and perhaps even true: we know, for example, that the poor gamble but the rich insure. Nevertheless, the process by which new patterns of work and payment influence social behaviour is certainly less mechanistic and more subtle than they supposed. What they had to say here was interesting but lacked support, partly because they had, with the partial exception of Lady Bell, so little to say about the organization of work itself; but that in turn was probably inherent in the way they looked at the world.

What then are we to conclude about their work? The first thing is self-evident. It is clear—despite the fact that *At the Works* was dedicated to Charles Booth—that their approach to the study of the working class was radically different from the kind of sociology whose Edwardian exemplar was A. L. Bowley, but which, in a more or less tentative manner, had been anticipated by Booth and Rowntree. In meeting the conditions which Victor Branford had demanded of the sociologist in 1914 they had actually embarked upon an unselfconscious cultural anthropology. They had little of the intellectual reticence of the modern anthropologist but their preoccupations were the same—the reader is sometimes surprised that the apathetic, death-obsessed natives they describe inhabit the banks of the Thames and not the Limpopo—and to that extent are in many ways more interesting to the historian than the work of, say, Bowley. Furthermore, if for the moment we ignore the all too obvious ideological mould in which their observation was cast, if we assume that the class system they described was autonomous of other social forces—things are as they are—then they provide a remarkable mass of evidence central to the life of

[77] Loane, *An Englishman's Castle*, 262–3; also Bosanquet, *Rich and Poor*, 46–54.

any people; and they do it with intellectual power and insight. The themes they thought not simply important but culturally decisive—debt, credit, time, etiquette, speech, dress, hygiene, affection—were treated by none of their contemporaries in such detail and by hardly anyone else until John Hilton took them up in the 1930s.[78] And their observation was neither sentimental nor condescending. Precisely because they had a 'total' and, indeed, rather tough-minded view of social classes, their work is not marked by the single-issue moralizing which to some degree disfigures the work of Booth and Masterman (Christianity), Rowntree (gambling), or Sherwell (drink).[79] (Lady Bell, though a devout Anglican, did not waste her time, as Booth did, in bothering about the religious life of the poor; Helen Bosanquet was actually hostile to the Christian churches; and Margaret Loane was principally concerned to show that the poor, in so far as they had them at all, were entirely eclectic in their religious allegiances.)

Finally, their observation was anchored to a central organizing theme—social class—which gives unity to material which would otherwise appear antiquarian and discrete. The things they thought worth observing—emotions and attitudes—cannot, of course, be studied outside the structures that created them, and they may not have been necessarily right in thinking that the structure which does create them is class, but it is a principle that has great explanatory force. Thus Miss Loane could argue that happiness varies not from temperament to temperament but from class to class or that patterns of sleep are entirely conditioned by social class—no working man or woman will ever know a 'good night's sleep'. Given certain assumptions, therefore, this is 'neutral' evidence, a description of what is the case.

But, of course, their observation was by no means neutral; it was heavily laden with ideological cargo and partisan politics. We might argue that the ideology was a priori; they argued that their prescriptions were, on the contrary, the result of the patient study, the keen insight, which, as Mrs Bosanquet wrote, only long experience of social work amongst the working classes could

---

[78] See, for example, John Hilton, *Rich Man, Poor Man* (London, 1944).

[79] For an example of Sherwell's work, see A. Sherwell, *Life in West London* (London, 1897) and J. Rowntree and A. Sherwell, *The Temperance Problem and Social Reform* (London, 1889). These represent only a fraction of his writing—usually with Joseph Rowntree—on temperance and social policy.

allow. If they concluded that the poor were poor because of improvidence or fecklessness, if it were money-management and not low wages which was responsible for poverty, this was not an a priori conclusion, but the *only* conclusion which could be drawn from their observation. The content of their sociology was thus not only different from Rowntree's or Bowley's, so was the social policy which might be derived from it. If poverty were dynamically reproduced by the culture that created it in the first place—which is on the whole what they argued—then a collectivist or interventionist solution suggested by the distributional studies of Rowntree or Bowley was not only useless, it was conceivably worse than useless.

Edwardian Britain was not particularly sympathetic to their conclusions and it moved in directions which they greatly disliked, even if, like Mrs Bosanquet, they had to accommodate themselves to this movement.[80] In fact, however, they were participating in a more timeless debate which culminated intellectually not in Britain but in the United States. To give us, therefore, some sense of the historicity of their work we should for the moment turn to the American literature. As J. T. Patterson has pointed out, the United States itself has had a long tradition of 'cultural' sociology not unlike that of Edwardian Britain, though rarely argued with the same force and confidence,[81] but it has had an ethnic (and thus crucial) significance which it has not had in Britain. More particularly, the relationship of the black community, and its apparently deviant value system, to society and its value system in the 1950s and 1960s raised the question again in terms which Mrs Bosanquet and Miss Loane would instantly have recognized. In 1954 H. H. Hyman delivered the classic American exposition of the Bosanquet–Loane view. 'It is our assumption', he argued,

that an intervening variable mediating the relationship between low position and lack of upward mobility is a system of beliefs and values within the lower classes which in turn reduces the very *voluntary* actions which would ameliorate their low position . . .

The components of this value system, in our judgement, involve less

---

[80] Thus in the Majority Report of the Royal Commission on the Poor Law she was prepared to recommend a form of state-supported unemployment insurance, something it is improbable she would have supported a decade earlier.

[81] J. T. Patterson, *America's Struggle Against Poverty* (Cambridge, Mass., 1981), 3–19.

emphasis upon the traditional high success goals, increased awareness of the lack of opportunity to achieve success, and less emphasis upon the achievement of goals which in turn would be instrumental for success.[82]

Ten years later, we find Nathan Glazer and D. P. Moynihan, in their widely read *Beyond the Melting Pot*, saying:

And what after all are we to do with the large numbers of people emerging in modern society who are irresponsible and depraved? The worthy poor create no serious problem—nothing that money cannot solve. But what of the unworthy poor? No man has come up with the answers.[83]

In the decade which separated these two contentions the view that the 'poor', or at least large numbers of them, are outside the predominant value system and see the world in different ways, received immensely influential support from the work of the cultural anthropologist Oscar Lewis. Lewis adopted techniques which were, in effect, almost identical to those of Miss Loane and Mrs Bosanquet (though less similar to Lady Bell's), give or take a tape recorder. His books consist very largely of edited conversations with women in their homes, and if with men also at home. The structure of these conversations and the manner of editing is unclear, while the role of Lewis in prompting the conversation, in determining what his subjects report to be true, is never really disclosed. In the Introduction to *Five Families* he said that he had attempted 'to give the reader an intimate and objective picture of daily life in five Mexican families, four of which are in the lower income group'.[84]

Lewis himself believed that his findings were almost universal over time and place. In the same Introduction, he said:

I am impressed by the remarkable similarities in family structure, the nature of kinship ties, the quality of husband–wife and parent–child relations, time orientation, spending patterns, value systems and the sense of the community found in lower-class settlements in London . . . in Puerto Rico . . . in Mexico City slums and Mexican villages . . . and among lower class negroes in the United States.[85]

[82] H. H. Hyman, 'The Value Systems of Different Classes: A Social Psychological Contribution to the Analysis of Stratification', in R. Bendix and S. M. Lipset (eds.), *Class, Status and Power* (London, 1954), 426–7.

[83] N. Glazer and D. P. Moynihan, *Beyond the Melting Pot* (New York, 1963), 63–4.

[84] O. Lewis, *Five Families* (New York, 1962), 1.   [85] Ibid. 2.

The 'culture of poverty', of whose existence Lewis was probably the most formidable proponent, was thus not confined to the United States. Its characteristics, as Lewis described them in *La Vida*, are worth repeating:

Low wages, chronic unemployment and underemployment lead to low income, lack of property ownership, absence of savings, absence of food reserves in the home, and a chronic shortage of cash. These conditions reduce the possibility of effective participation in the larger economic system. And as a response to these conditions we find in the culture of poverty a high incidence of pawning of personal goods, borrowing from local moneylenders at usurious rates of interest, spontaneous informal credit devices organized by neighbors, the use of second-hand clothing and furniture, and the pattern of frequent buying of small quantities of food many times a day as the need arises.

People with a culture of poverty produce very little wealth and receive very little in return. They have a low level of literacy and education, usually do not belong to labor unions, are not members of political parties, generally do not participate in the national welfare agencies, and make very little use of banks, hospitals, department stores, museums and art galleries. They have a critical attitude towards some of the basic institutions of the dominant classes, hatred of the police, mistrust of the government and those in high position, and a cynicism which extends even to the church.[86]

In *A Study of Slum Culture* he noted that we would also expect to find in a poverty culture 'lack of impulse control; strong present-time orientation, with relatively little ability to defer gratification and to plan for the future; sense of resignation and fatalism'.[87]

On any reading, Lewis's conclusions are startlingly similar to those of all three of our Edwardian observers; we hardly even need to allow for the passing of time. What he describes as the culture of poverty, and the characteristics he imputes to it, are undoubtedly what they were describing. At first sight that would appear to strengthen their case, and to some extent it probably does. But it also opens it to scrutiny. Precisely because Lewis was so self-conscious in what he was doing, so anxious to make his methodology public, and the political implications of his work were so obvious, he attracted the kind of directly critical response that they hardly ever did.

It is, in the first place, unquestionaly a priori. Lewis himself

[86] O. Lewis, *La Vida* (London, 1967), p. xiii.
[87] O. Lewis, *A Study of Slum Culture* (New York, 1968), 10–11.

explicitly admits that the aim of his work was to illustrate a culture of poverty whose existence was already assumed. This culture was not constructed from the data, therefore; rather, the data were deployed to 'contribute to our understanding of the culture of poverty'.[88] Furthermore, much of his material does not actually support the conclusions. Many of his subjects turn out to have strong and informed views on politics; have a perfectly reasonable view of society, the way it works and their place in it; to be much more *au fait* with the medical and financial systems than Lewis insists they could be; and to have a scepticism about the predominant value system which seems entirely appropriate to their circumstances. And what Lewis is observing is curiously unidimensional. Men play a disproportionately small role in his work; and young men a very small role indeed. Work and the workplace occupy little of his time or interest—except in the case of several of his women who are full- or part-time prostitutes, and they talk entertainingly and often shrewdly about their work. The setting is domestic and familial, the sample skewed by age and sex. As Charles Valentine commented:

the focus is so restricted to the family that the social system as a whole and its culture patterns become little more than a shadowy background for personal and household intimacies. There is no doubt that this orientation is perfectly legitimate for some kinds of research. What the approach cannot adequately support, however, is the portrayal of a culture, a whole way of life.[89]

Finally, and it follows from Lewis's methodology, there is almost nothing about the economic and occupational structure of people's lives. Actual earnings, actual outgoings, actual interest payments are hardly ever mentioned; what he says about this might, in fact, be right; it is just that there is little evidence to support it.

It also follows that most of these criticisms of Lewis apply almost *ex hypothesi* to Mrs Bosanquet, Miss Loane, and Lady Bell. Anecdotal and domestic evidence inevitably leads to a looseness of definition. Thus they use the words 'poor' and 'working classes' almost interchangeably, but it is clear that most of the evidence they adduce comes from the lower strata of the working class: in Mrs Bosanquet's case, usually Booth's classes A and B. Again, as with Lewis, household evidence immediately biases the sample.

[88] Lewis, *Five Families*, 1.
[89] C. A. Valentine, *Culture and Poverty* (Chicago, 1968), 64.

The greater part of their observation is of married women at home, or of elderly men and women, often ill. The attitudes of the working male population are not well represented, and in so far as they are, often indirectly. Lady Bell, it is true, tried conscientiously to describe life at work and did her best to assimilate the masculine world of pubs and clubs; but the real location of her book is not at the works, it is at home, a point made by the *Times Literary Supplement* reviewer.[90] Given the real difficulty of engaging the working classes in their own homes, a problem freely admitted by the three of them, what they inevitably saw was those classes apparently at their worst: obstinate and credulous. The young working men whose mechanical inventiveness and mental flexibility surprised Schulze-Gaervernitz do not appear in their pages.[91] And, like Lewis, they much too quickly discounted simple poverty as a restraint upon working-class efficiency. While they acknowledged the force of environment in people's lives they rarely gave it much weight, and they never asked the economist's question: was the 'long view' a good the poor could not afford? Despite the real brilliance of Helen Bosanquet's analysis of working-class debt and credit, it is doubtful, as Paul Johnson has pointed out, whether she ever understood it.[92] Nor could she ever understand it, given her determination to deny that structural poverty, except in limited circumstances, could ever exist. Hence the feebleness of her contribution to the debate with Seebohm Rowntree as to what constituted the 'poverty line'.[93]

[90] *Times Literary Supplement*, 9 Apr. 1907.   [91] See above, p. 154.

[92] P. Johnson, *Saving and Spending* (Oxford, 1985), 219 and *passim*.

[93] Mrs Bosanquet denied the truth of Rowntree's argument that there was structural poverty, the result of low wages alone. She contended (*The Poverty Line* (London, 1903) and letters to *The Times*, 16 Sept. and 4 Oct. 1902) that all poverty was 'preventable', and that, in any case, it was impossible, given the nature of the working-class family and economy, to calculate wage-rates the way Rowntree had done. She also asserted that York was not a representative town since it contained large numbers of ecclesiastical charities 'with all the endowments and abuses incidental to cathedral cities'. She so overargued her case that Rowntree had little trouble in disposing of her objections. (B. S. Rowntree, *The 'Poverty Line': A Reply* (London, 1903), 13, 20–8; also A. Briggs, *Seebohm Rowntree* (London, 1957), 21, 34–5). There were, however, a number of problems in Rowntree's use of evidence and Mrs Bosanquet's recklessness deprived her criticisms of some force. She argued her case better in the *Contemporary Review*, 85 (1904). More recent work gives her limited support: see D. J. Oddy, 'Working Class Budgets in Late Nineteenth Century England', *Economic History Review* (1970), 322; Elizabeth Roberts, 'Working Class Standards of Living in Barrow and Lancaster, 1890–1914', *Economic History Review* (1977), 319.

We should not, of course, force the analogy with Lewis too far. They were much less consistent in their argument than he at least thought he was. For example, while they would certainly have agreed that the poor behaved as he said they did, and while they agreed that the culture of poverty was self-reproducing, they also argued that the non-poor once behaved very much as the poor now did. Thus social fashion, together with a certain state coercion and the general development of capitalist society, would sweep the poor up as it had all the rest. It is not clear how they could have resolved this inconsistency, except in some such way as Hyman Rodman has done—to suggest that all members of society share the same values, but the poor 'stretch' theirs to suit circumstances.[94] As material circumstances change so the values of the poor narrow to fit those of the rest of society. Mrs Bosanquet, for example, clearly thought this would be the effect of both increasing wages and lengthening the time between which they were paid.

We should now return to the questions posed at the beginning of the chapter. Was a cultural sociology a better way of 'knowing' the working classes than the sociology begun by Booth and apparently completed by Bowley? And did it necessarily produce an alternative and superior political conclusion?

The first question is difficult to answer. A cultural sociology, as I have suggested, obviously does produce the kind of evidence that no distributional study could do, and the evidence itself is probably not 'untrue': that is to say, it is what the observers saw when they saw it. There are, however, three reasons for doubting, not so much the authenticity of the evidence, as its reliability. The first is its static nature. It consists of a series of social snapshots; people's attitudes and their mental life are indeed captured but in a frozen posture. The observation can never be dynamic, and it can incorporate social change (at best) only by reference to inter-generational development or to social imitation. The tendency to inertia is further exaggerated by the age bias of those being observed. The second comes from the act of observing. Mrs Bosanquet, Miss Loane, and Lady Bell (in so far as Lady Bell observed *in propria persona*) were not participant observers as a modern sociologist might be; they were external observers and represented authority. It is very doubtful, therefore, whether they

[94] H. Rodman, 'The Lower Class Value Stretch', *Social Forces* (Dec. 1963), 209–10.

could ever see in the mental life of the poor anything else than a jumble of time and memory; if it had an internal coherence, which it almost certainly had to the poor, it is unlikely they would have noticed it. The third follows inevitably from the second. If, as they argued, social classes inhabit closed mental universes, if they all operate via codes, and if, as Miss Loane argued with great power, no person from one class can talk 'naturally' to a person from another, then it would seem, on their own grounds, methodologically almost impossible for any observer to 'know' the working classes in the way they thought they did. The more limited quasi-statistical studies of Booth and Rowntree and the more directly statistical work of Bowley are unquestionably less open to this criticism.

Does a cultural sociology produce a different political answer? If we assume no a priori judgements (which in the case of Mrs Bosanquet we cannot) it is fair to suppose that it could. Observers of this type, confronted with an apparently unchanging and incompetent culture, unsurprisingly concluded that the way out was by moral and behavioural changes. But even here there were difficulties from which none of them could escape. The moral changes they looked to were, in practice, largely coercive, with the state as coercer of last resort. It is not clear, if this is so, why state intervention of this kind should be superior to or more effective than any other kind of state intervention—non-contributory old-age pensions, for example. And the behavioural changes they did suggest were not convincing; in a way anticlimatic. Although Lady Bell was generous and sympathetic in her attitude to working-class life, fully aware of the burdens most working men and women carried from the cradle to the grave, given the way she structured her observation, the relentless emphasis upon domesticity, the most she could advise was that young girls should be taught proper cooking. Above all, they could not escape from the effects of partial observation, from which only partial conclusions could be drawn.

7

The Economic Policy of the Second Labour Government, 1929–1931

THE second Labour government was once conventionally seen in terms of its fall. It came to office in 1929 after an election which gave no party a majority, and which left it dependent upon the support of the Liberals.[1] It fell in August 1931 when its members were unable to agree upon a programme of budgetary economies that would satisfy both the Conservative and the Liberal Parties. The prime minister, Ramsay MacDonald, thereupon formed a 'National' government with representatives of the former opposition parties and three of his colleagues from the previous Labour ministry; the great bulk of the Labour Party opposed this new government. The 'desertion' of MacDonald caused great bitterness and generated a partisan history usually designed to justify the behaviour of one side or the other in the débâcle.[2] The level of strictly economic content was usually not high.[3] But with the release of public and private records on the one hand, and with the general acceptance of a developed Keynesianism on the other, historians have increasingly sought only to explain why the Labour government did not adopt economic policies which might appear to have been obviously the right ones. Why did it not, for example, attempt to reverse economic contraction by a programme of public works financed by budget deficits, or by tax-cuts, or—a policy less untypical of a socialist party—by a redistribution of income that might have raised demand? Why was the government apparently so inflexibly attached to existing monetary policies? Politically, the real contribution of Keynes was to suggest that governments did not have to stand helpless in the face of cyclical movements in a

---

[1] The election result was: Labour 288, Conservative 260, Liberal 59.
[2] The best example of this, both as history and bibliography, is R. Bassett, *1931: Political Crisis* (London, 1958).
[3] See Sidney Webb's account: 'meanwhile the Government finances were seen to be getting into a bad way', in S. Webb, *What Happened in 1931: A Record* (London, 1932), 5.

capitalist economy: thus the Labour government did not have to wait for 'socialism'—effective counter-cyclical techniques were available to them within the system.[4]

The most sustained and stimulating 'neo-Keynesian' analysis of the second MacDonald ministry is Robert Skidelsky's *Politicians and the Slump*.[5] This book is chiefly interesting as an explanation of the Labour Party's apparent economic conservatism, but he does not doubt that an alternative was readily at hand. 'The absence of developed Keynesian theory', he writes

was not a decisive barrier to the adoption of what might loosely be termed Keynesian economics, as is proved by the experience of the United States, Germany, France and Sweden which in the 1930s all attempted, with varying success, to promote economic recovery through deficit budgeting. In Sweden this was done especially effectively by a democratic Labour Government operating a normal parliamentary system.[6]

Sir Oswald Mosley's achievement was 'to see that in a capitalist economy the only way for a socialist party to get action was by adopting the interventionist policies of capitalism's own spokesmen'.[7]

Skidelsky implies here two propositions: that alternative policies towards the economic depression were wilfully ignored by the Labour government, and that international comparison shows that these policies were more or less effective ones. Though Skidelsky's thesis is heavily dependent upon both these being true, curiously he makes no attempt actually to test them. In this chapter I would like to do this.

Nearly every country affected by depression in 1929 took refuge in deflationary policies, many of them of a very rigorous kind. It would be tedious to catalogue them all,[8] but two—Australia and

---

[4] For the development of Keynesian economics in Britain and the United States respectively, see Donald Winch, *Economics and Policy* (London, 1972), and Herbert Stein, *Fiscal Revolution in America* (Chicago, 1969).

[5] R. Skidelsky, *Politicians and the Slump: The Labour Government of 1929–1931* (London, 1967).

[6] Ibid. (Pelican edn.; Harmondsworth, 1970), 426.

[7] Ibid. 425. See also the discussion reported in *Society for the Study of Labour History Bulletin*, 21 (1970), 6–7.

[8] For good general accounts, see C. P. Kindleberger, *The World in Depression* (London 1973), R. Nurske, *International Currency Experience* (Geneva, 1944). It seems only reasonable to exclude Germany from any discussion since the economic policies followed by both the Hitler and pre-Hitler governments were determined

the United States—are perhaps of more special relevance. In the political complexion of its government Australia is the most comparable case. Throughout the worst years of the depression (1929–31) Australia had a Labour government with traditions and expectations very much like those of Britain's. Scullin's government was no more prepared for the collapse of the financial system than MacDonald's. Though possessing an instinctive feeling that the standard of living ought to be protected, his ministry tried to avoid the consequences of deflationary policies while conceding in principle that they should be followed. Furthermore, as in Britain, all the weight of 'expert' opinion—central bankers[9] and economists[10]—was on the side of deflation. Within the labour movement opposition to this policy was quick to develop, but it was grouped around an essentially negative feeling that wage-cutting and expenditure-reduction were probably foolish and certainly unfair.

Without the pressure of this opposition, it seems unlikely that the Scullin government would have tried to find alternatives to orthodox opinion, but in the first half of 1931 E. G. Theodore, the federal treasurer (finance minister), introduced legislation that moved towards such alternatives. He proposed to expand credit by the issue of 'fiduciary notes', to suspend legal requirements governing the gold reserve, to reorganize the banking system, and to allow the exchange rate to fall to its 'natural' level.[11] In the face of violent opposition from a conservative-controlled upper house and from well-entrenched banking and business circles, the 'Theodore Plan' came to nothing. Thus in the second half of the

largely by political objectives. Nevertheless, it ought to be noted that the Brüning cabinet practised ruthlessly deflationary policies, and that these policies were not modified until the second half of 1932.

[9] Sir Robert Gibson, the governor of the Commonwealth Bank, played a role almost analogous to that of Sir Montagu Norman. See L. F. Giblin, *The Growth of a Central Bank* (Melbourne, 1951). Sometimes it was the same bankers. Sir Otto Niemeyer, the genius of the gold standard, shipped out to Australia to advise her governments, devised the deflationary premier's plan. See E. O. G. Shann and D. B. Copland, *The Crisis in Australian Finance* (Sydney, 1931), 18–29. The Federal Labour government under J. H. Scullin took office in Oct. 1929 and resigned, after electoral defeat, in Jan. 1932. Though it had a large absolute majority in the lower house of parliament, the upper house remained in the hands of the Conservative opposition.

[10] This was true even of L. F. Giblin, who had conceived a theory of the multiplier as early as 1928–9. See L. F. Giblin, 'Australia in the Shadows', *Australian Quarterly*, Dec. 1933.

[11] E. O. G. Shann and D. B. Copland, *Battle of the Plans* (Sydney, 1932); D. B. Copland, *Australia in the World Crisis* (Cambridge, 1934), 50–71.

year the government returned to conventional remedies[12]—essentially those deflationary policies that the National government in Britain was created to implement.

There are four noteworthy features of Scullin's government, the only wholly social democratic government, other than Britain's, actually in office when the slide began.[13] First, the government was incapable of assembling its own policies until it had lost the ideological battle in any case. Secondly, even had it done so, it was unable to console the people it needed to—the bankers and businessmen. When Theodore said, 'the demand for money is greater than the supply. Very well, let us increase the supply',[14] he was no doubt on the right track, but such remarks lacked the dexterity to convince even the economists that this was not dangerous inflationism. Thirdly, it seems fairly clear that the 'Theodore Plan', adventurous as it then appeared, was in fact too modest to be other than a palliative: at best it could have nudged on economic recovery, at worst retarded it by lowering business confidence. Finally, it is probably true that the 'solutions' devised by the Australian labour movement were never seen as cures for the depression; rather they were designed to redistribute sacrifice and to protect what the working class already had.[15] In this they failed: a Labour government which, on whatever index one chooses, 'pure' socialism or interventionist capitalism, was more radical than MacDonald's had to accept deflationary policies that the British Labour Party never accepted. But, like MacDonald's it had the ill-luck to take office on the downturn.

If Australia had an ideologically similar regime, the United States was a country whose experience was very much before British eyes. The British and the American governments worked

[12] F. A. Bland and R. C. Mills, 'Financial Reconstruction', *Economic Record*, Nov. 1931; D. B. Copland, 'Readjustment in Australia', *Economic Journal*, 41 (1931), 534–49.

[13] The German government of June 1928–March 1930 (second Müller), had a Social Democratic chancellor, but only 4 of its 11 ministers were Social Democrats, and in no real sense can it be regarded as a Social Democratic government. In the same year a coalition Social Democratic–Radical Government was formed in Denmark. This was more obviously Social Democratic, but still a coalition.

[14] Quoted in Shann and Copland, *Crisis in Australian Finance*, p. x n. The authors, both later converts to a milk-and-water Keynesianism, cite this as an example of Theodore's financial irresponsibility.

[15] W. Denning, *Caucus Crisis* (Sydney, 1937); C. B. Schedvin, 'The Long and the Short of Depression Origins', *Labour History*, 17 (1969).

within the same traditions of economic thought and financial practice. When the economically orthodox pointed to helpful international comparison, they pointed to Hoover; the activists later pointed to the New Deal. However inspiriting continental experiments might have been, most people recognized that in practice they could not be repeated in Britain. What, then, did happen to the American economy in this period?

The American economy suffered more devastation than the British, and its recovery was slower and more fitful.[16] A variety of experiments were practised upon it, and none seems to have made much difference. Until the second half of 1931, the Hoover administration followed a modestly vigorous policy towards the contraction of economic activity: taxes were reduced in 1930, public expenditure was held at pre-1929 levels, and government construction programmes were accelerated. At the same time, however, Hoover turned his face against large-scale public works or any sort of federal unemployment insurance. Such a policy did little, if anything, to reverse economic decline, so in the second half of 1931 he decided to take more positive steps to generate new investment by restoring 'confidence'—that is, to further deflate the economy along orthodox lines. The budget was to be balanced by reducing government expenditure and raising taxes. What effect this had on confidence is problematical: it did result in the near-destruction of American private savings as the unemployed tried to keep alive without assistance, and may have hastened the collapse of the American banking system, quite apart from its effects on the economy generally. Hoover's policies were conventional, and not particularly ruthless; how different they were from those of the British Labour government will be discussed later.

The New Deal stood as an alternative to Hoover, and it is reasonable to ask how far it did bring about economic recovery; reasonable, at least, if one assumes that there was within the capitalist system a workable alternative to the policies of the MacDonald government.

A straightforward answer to this question is, of course, difficult. It is a commonplace that there was no single New Deal; rather,

---

[16] There is an immense literature on this. The best general analysis is L. V. Chandler, *America's Greatest Depression, 1929–1941* (New York, 1970). For Hoover, see Stein, *Fiscal Revolution*, 6–38.

there was a series of improvised responses to individual problems. Public works projects, let alone counter-cyclical budgets, were never conceived as part of a coherent economic programme; in fact, the New Deal was deflationary and reflationary by turns.[17] Yet it is possible to calculate with some precision the impact of New Deal policies. E. Carey Brown has devised a way of measuring the direct effects on aggregate full-employment demand of United States fiscal policy in the thirties.[18] He concludes that these effects were, in relation to 1929, clearly stronger only in 1931 and 1936 with, sadly, '1931 markedly higher than in 1936'. These two years were strong because in both veterans' bonuses were dispersed. If the bonuses are excluded from the calculation then only 1931 would stand above 1929. If the measure is *expansionary* effect alone, then 1930, 1932, and 1939 stand 'somewhat higher' than 1929; in 1934 and 1935 it was virtually the same, but in 1933 and 1937 it was markedly less expansionary.

Why were New Deal measures so disappointing? The explanation lies partly in the nature of all heterodox policies. It could not be known at the outset that the agencies of the National Recovery Act would encourage oligopolistic tendencies whose general effect was certainly deflationary.[19] It lies also in the vagueness with which policy was put together. Thus the public work schemes were conceived as (primarily) employment-creating activities and as (secondarily) pump-priming, but within a budgetary framework that was intended to be in balance in a short term.[20] The expansionary effects of fiscal policy were almost certainly undone by a steady increase of taxation at all levels, much of which was punitive. On the other hand, despite Schumpeter's strictures,[21] some of the new taxation—that to finance social security in particular—was a political and humanitarian necessity. But the collection of that taxation was further to deflate the economy at a time when an accumulation of both inventories and savings was

[17] A. Smithies, 'The American Economy in the Thirties', *American Economic Review*, supplement, Proceedings of the American Economic Society May 1946, 13.

[18] E. C. Brown, 'Fiscal Policy in the Thirties: A Reapprasial', *American Economic Review*, 46 (1956), 857–79.

[19] L. S. Lyon *et al.*, *The National Recovery Administration* (Washington, 1935), 743–8, 871–7.

[20] Smithies, 14.

[21] Joseph Schumpeter, *Business Cycles*, 2 vols. (New York, 1939), ii. 982–1043.

already depressing it, and this conjunction led to the 'Roosevelt recession' of 1937.[22]

These were probably idiosyncrasies inherent in the Roosevelt administration and perhaps not of a sort from which one can generalize; but there were other difficulties that one cannot imagine any British government overcoming. In the first place, the scale of the national budget was too small in relation to the economy as a whole to have much impact even when there was a rapid acceleration in expenditure. In the second place, policy was undermined by a real ignorance about the workings of the economy.[23] No one, therefore, ever had any real idea of how large spending programmes should be; and there was further confusion about where the money should be spent. It seems likely that a good deal of it was squandered on projects whose 'multiplier-effect' was strictly limited.[24] It is more than possible that a 'British New Deal' would have replicated all these errors, and in an economy much less resilient than the American, which could at least bear the strains of trial and error.

On the other hand, it can reasonably be objected that the New Deal was merely one case; that what was true of the United States was not true of (say) Sweden, and the Swedish experience has indeed led to much debate. Under a social democratic government, which took office in the autumn of 1932, and which practised carefully prepared counter-cyclical budgeting, Sweden had a rapid recovery and then steady growth throughout the 1930s. Such budgetary techniques may well have been responsible for this, yet

[22] See K. Roose, 'The Recession of 1937–38', *Journal of Political Economy*, 56 (1948); M. Friedman and A. J. Schwartz, *A Monetary History of the United States, 1857–1960* (Princeton, 1971), 520–31.

[23] And confusion began at the top. See Roosevelt's comments on the gold standard at his first press conference: '*The President*. That includes, for example, the question of the control of gold. That is obvious. As long as nobody asks me whether we are off the gold standard . . . that is all right, because nobody knows what the gold standard or gold basis really is. If you want a definition . . . read my friend Robey's story in the *New York Evening Post* of last night. I think it is about as good a definition as there is. It is quite short and if you would like to hear it I will read it to you. It is a pretty good document. *Audience*. If it really tells us what the gold standard is—. *The President*. It is pretty good, it doesn't say whether we are on it or off it.' *Public Papers and Addresses of Franklin D. Roosevelt*, 13 vols. (New York, 1938), ii. 33–4. Much of this, of course, was characteristic Rooseveltian hocus-pocus, but it did point to a genuine frailty of economic grasp.

[24] J. K. Galbraith and G. G. Johnson, *The Economic Effects of the Federal Public Works Expenditures, 1933–1938* (National Resources Planning Board, n.p., 1940), 108–9.

there is sufficient doubt about it to make us treat the (largely contemporary) claims about their success with some scepticism. What is striking about Sweden (as it appears to me) is the similarity with British recovery: both devalued decisively in 1931— Sweden even more decisively than Britain; both saw a strong recovery of home demand, and in the same areas of the economy. Sweden's growth rate was faster, though not markedly. Only in one respect did she differ significantly—and that was in the remarkable growth of her exports. This had two components. The first was a response to the boom in British residential construction (timber); the second was to the demands of German (and principally German, but later British) rearmament. By the late 1930s Sweden was to a considerable degree an adjunct of the German war economy. Thus even Heinz Arndt, who believed that Swedish budgeting was largely successful, is forced to conclude that 'owing to the peculiarly favourable circumstances in which Sweden found herself, Swedish experience supplies no answer to the question whether monetary measures of this type [fiscal measures] constitute by themselves an adequate remedy to the problem of the trade cycle.'[25]

The purpose of this necessarily brief excursus into foreign example has not been to excuse the British performance by inculpating others in Britain's guilt. It is to show how shaky are any assumptions that there were easy and workable solutions that Britain might have borrowed. While Labour was in office there were, in fact, no such solutions abroad: 'active' policies of the later thirties, as in the United States, actually failed, or, as in Sweden, were hedged with ambiguity and doubt.

But the British economy itself had very particular characteristics, and two of the assumptions which all British governments worked were true enough to inhibit innovation even more than in the United States or Sweden. The 1929 Labour government assumed,

[25] H. Arndt, *Economic Lessons of the Nineteen Thirties* (London, 1944), 220. I freely admit that I know a great deal less about Sweden than I do about Australia, the United States, or Britain; much, therefore, I have had to accept on trust. Arndt has a chapter on Swedish recovery (ibid. 205–20), and there is a brief discussion in Kindleberger, *The World in Depression*, esp. 182–3. For more detail, see Brinley Thomas, *Monetary Policy and Crises: A Study in Swedish Experience* (London, 1936); M. Cole and C. Smith (eds.), *Democratic Sweden* (London, 1938). There is an interesting discussion of a paper by Professor Donald Winch in *Society for the Study of Labour History Bulletin*, 21 (1970), 8–10.

first, that the problems of the British economy were partly structural; and secondly, that Britain's place in the international economy almost uniquely influenced her monetary policies. These assumptions were related: structural weakness (so the argument went) led to falling exports and payments difficulties, which in turn exacerbated Britain's 'international' problems. On the other hand, the requirements of the City led to monetary policies that made internal reconstruction difficult.

Both these propositions were powerful impediments to economic orthodoxy. It was unquestionable that British industry had failed in the post-war world, partly because it was concentrated in staples—textiles, shipping and heavy engineering, coal-mining—producing goods that people did not want or at prices they could not afford. Thus, notoriously, Britain did not really benefit from the international prosperity of the mid-twenties. Its structural distortions became a stock criticism of the economy in this period. Everyone was aware of them—hence the craze of rationalization and industrial efficiency;[26] hence also the importance to industry of the great amalgamations of the same time.[27] But once it was conceded that structural problems were important difficulties in the way of recovery, then financial problems came to appear less relevant. Henry Clay went so far as to tell the Macmillan Committee that the real cause of unemployment was 'the mal-adjustment of our industry to the demand for commodities of all sorts in the world as a whole, and we are so much a part of the world that the mal-adjustment, was bound to cause unemployment *whatever the financial policy pursued*.'[28] Clay was certainly not right. Restrictive credit policies and an overvalued pound did affect employment; since, however, the structural weaknesses were obviously there, it was not so difficult to come to this conclusion. But no one was sure how reconstruction was to be financed; by the standards of an earlier generation both the government and the Bank of England were active supporters of reconstruction,[29] though all too often government policy tended

[26] A. J. Youngson, *Britain's Economic Growth* (London, 1967), 35–50.

[27] See the illuminating paper by L. Hannah and J. A. Kay, 'Concentration and Merger in the United Kingdom, 1919–1969' (mimeo,; May 1974).

[28] Committee on Finance and Industry [Macmillan Committee], *Minutes of Evidence*, PP (1931), i (Cmd. 3897), Q 8523. (Italics mine.)

[29] For a reminder of this, see Sir Henry Clay, *Lord Norman* (London, 1957), 318–59.

either to be exhortatory, or one that only mitigated the consequences of industrial decline.

Likewise the MacDonald government shared the view of its predecessor that Britain was inextricably entangled in the world economy, and that this entanglement imposed its own restrictions on British economic policies. In the late thirties the belief that this was a mistaken view came to have a certain vogue. But it was never unreasonable to suppose that the more or less orderly working of the international trading and financial system was of singular importance to Britain. Certainly, the unprecedented prosperity of Western Europe since the Second World War that accompanied an equally unprecedented expansion of international trade has lent some *ex post facto* plausibility to the argument that the 'closed' economics of the thirties would have had only short-term benefits.

But domestic and international reconstruction were obviously long-term projects, if not actually impossible. In the short run there were four conceivable policies open to MacDonald's government when it took office: a programme of public works financed by budgetary deficits; simple monetary measures (devaluation, for example) to restore international competitiveness; a more rigorous deflation (to do the same); or a policy that avoided doing any of these things. In the end, the first three policies eliminated themselves. Why was this so?

In practice, deficit budgeting was probably never a serious possibility. There was no reason to expect that the same kinds of physical restraints upon an effective reflationary policy apparent in the United States, Australia, and elsewhere, were not also restraints in Britain. The small scale of British budgetary operations almost certainly stood in the way of rapid and government-induced expansion. The direction and control of investment which would have been a corollary was probably a political and bureaucratic impossibility, even if anyone assumed it ought to be attempted. Both would have required the growth of public expenditure and state intervention that was only achieved in the Second World War. So far as the United States was concerned, it was indeed this colossal expenditure that finally lifted the economy out of depression; but what was acceptable later for defence was neither acceptable nor imaginable in the twenties and early thirties.

Yet why was the government not able to mobilize the state against depression as it could against the Germans? In the first place there was a widespread view that the depression in Britain was comparatively gentle, and by international standards it was. Unemployment never reached the levels of the United States, Germany, Australia, Sweden, or Canada; the contraction of economic activity was less sharp; distress was cushioned by a high level of public expenditure; above all, perhaps, the banking system remained stable and savings always recoverable.[30]

Socially there were a number of restraints to treating depression as war. At all levels there was—as after the Second World War—a traditional reluctance to accept rigorous state intervention during peacetime and at no time in this period was there any political agreement about what should be done. In the Second World War all classes were more or less agreed about the immediate future, and all, to a surprising degree, accepted, or were forced to accept, 'equality of sacrifice' and social change.[31] Before the war, however, no such change was possible since too many people had, or thought they had, an interest in preserving the status quo against any redistribution of wealth or political power. Nor, even, was equality of sacrifice likely, since the economically and politically preponderant classes showed no signs of wanting to make any sacrifice at all.

But the location of political power introduced problems other than merely distributive ones—who was to sacrifice what. It stood as a central obstacle to unorthodox policies. For it seems certain that any seriously intended counter-cyclical budgeting (for example) would have led to capital flight—and that, after all, was what the 1931 crisis was largely about—and it would, therefore, as Arndt has pointed out, have presupposed the imposition of exchange control of capital transactions.[32] Further, rapid economic expansion would have presumably led to increasing deficits on payments. This could have been met by internal deflation (self-defeating in the circumstances) or by currency depreciation (which would have worsened the terms of trade) and, consequently, by extensive import controls and restrictions. In Britain, at least,

---

[30] For a comparative discussion, see W. Woytinsky, *Social Consequences of the Economic Depression* (Geneva, 1936). Indeed, Schumpeter was able to write that 'the outstanding fact about the English depression is its mildness which makes it doubtful whether that term is applicable at all': *Business Cycles*, ii. 917.

[31] See below, pp. 286–92.   [32] Arndt, 133.

reflationary policies would probably have meant effective state direction of the economy, if only to stop serious payments deficits driving the country back to deflation. But such direction would have interfered not only with the normal course of British economic life, it would have upset the structure of British political power. It is difficult to conceive of the then British ruling classes, however broadly or narrowly that term is interpreted, consenting to state direction of the economy, since it is difficult to see how much direction would have stopped at exchange control, itself probably repugnant enough. It was argued in the United States at the time that the compelling beauty of a 'spending policy' was that it bypassed structural or political questions; and it was pushed most strongly in 1938 when it was clear that the New Deal had lost the structural battle anyway. Neo-Keynesians in Britain essentially argue the same way when they suggest that 'socialism' was irrelevant to Britain's particular economic problems. But in Britain, if only because of the nature of her economy, the problem of who had *political* control of the economy had to be solved before reflationary policies could be followed. The real barrier to such reflation was thus always a political one.

Similarly, while the existing form of the British state remained intact, theoretical constrictions on economic policy were tight, and their effect easily underestimated. Reflationary economics was not simply spending money; while there was in Britain, as in the United States, no acceptable theory of income determination and no way of assessing aggregate demand, there was small chance that aggregate demand could be raised by the conscious effort of the state. Furthermore, until there was a broad agreement upon what did constitute such an acceptable theory, it was hard to justify large-scale public expenditure, since (apparently) such intervention could have little utility. Contemporaries judged public works on their direct effects, and projects without obvious utility were dismissed as 'wasteful'. By contrast, a high social service expenditure (like the dole) could be, and was, justified on grounds of *social and political* utility.[33]

In fact, nobody at the time doubted that public works *might* be a helpful instrument of economic policy. In Britain there had been various, if limited, essays at public works throughout the twenties,

---

[33] For a discussion of this, see below, pp. 244–53.

primarily to provide work, and usually on 'useful' projects.[34] In the United States the demand for public works became more urgent; but largely because there was no dole, and the unemployed had to be kept alive somehow. Yet American economists, both amateur and professional, calculated putative public works expenditure with extraordinary haphazardness—apparently on a number-you-first-thought-of basis.[35]

In Britain there was similar confusion, though with the added complication that she already had, by international standards, an extremely expensive system of unemployment benefits, which diminished the need for a charitable public works programme. Nevertheless, there were still many to argue for works; what they could not do was judge with any accuracy the necessary size of a public works programme, nor could they refute with any real confidence the view (which became associated with the Treasury) that such a programme would 'distort' the course of investment.[36]

In the end, large-scale public works were only justifiable if it could be shown that they had a greater utility than that of parochial unemployment-relief. The concept of the 'multiplier', which suggested that public works expenditure had effects in the economy greater than the expenditure itself, was to provide this justification. But before the mid-thirties, if even then, no such theoretical underpinning was available, and it is idle to imagine that one could, or should, have been intuitively grasped by a lay public. The pamphlet *Can Lloyd George Do It?* (1929), written by Keynes and Henderson, implied a multiplier effect, but the argument of the *Liberal Yellow Book (Britain's Industrial Future)* that public works were better than the dole because they were cheaper as well as more useful, though fair at one level, shows at another that the multiplier was hardly understood at all by those who were propounding a 'radical' alternative.[37] In Australia, L. F.

[34] K. J. Hancock, 'The Reduction of Unemployment as a Problem of Public Policy', *Economic History Review*, 15 (1962–3).

[35] Stein, *Fiscal Revolution*, 23.

[36] For the 'Treasury view', see Youngson, 295–6.

[37] J. M. Keynes and H. D. Henderson, *Can Lloyd George Do It?* (London, 1929); Liberal Party, *Britain's Industrial Future* (London, 1928), 267–317. See also S. Pollard, 'Trade Union Reactions to the Economic Crisis', in S. Pollard, *The Gold Standard and Employment Policies between the Wars* (London, 1970), 149. It is worth noting that there were significant theoretical differences between Keynes and Henderson, and that these differences were to grow wider. See H. D. Henderson, *The Inter-War Years and Other Papers*, ed. Henry Clay (Oxford, 1955), 151–77.

Giblin adumbrated a theory of the multiplier in 1928–9, but his work in 1930 and 1931 was unexpectedly coventional.[38] A number of younger Cambridge economists had been sketching a multiplier theory at the same time, but it was not until June 1931 that R. F. Kahn's seminal article 'The Relation of Home Investment to Unemployment' was published. Kahn's was indeed a 'classic' statement, but he did not pretend to do more than suggest a new approach to fiscal policy. Thus his modest introduction: 'The case for "public works" has often been discussed', he began,

and there is a final plea that the advocate almost invariably appends to his argument. It is important, we are told, not to overlook the beneficial repercussions that will result from the expenditure of the newly-employed men's wages. But little is done to evaluate these repercussions in concrete terms. The main purpose of this article is to outline the means by which this gap could be filled, and incidentally to suggest that the case for 'public works' may be stronger than is always recognized.[39]

The chronology of his work is important, even if one accepts, which is unlikely, that political organizations immediately respond to intellectual trends. It appeared on the eve of the European liquidity crisis, when it was too late and probably irrelevant to adopt great public works programmes. In any case, he by no means settled the issues. It was open to objection on three grounds. First, as Kahn himself recognized, it proved to be difficult to calculate specifically the employment ratio, and the experience of the United States, and the work of later economists, suggests that he was over-optimistic in his predictions.[40] Second, it

[38] P. H. Karmer, 'Giblin and the Multiplier', in D. B. Copland (ed.), *Giblin* (Melbourne, 1960). His work was known in Britain. See his correspondence with Keynes in *The Collected Writings of John Maynard Keynes*, ed. D. E. Moggridge (London, 1973), xiii. 414–17.

[39] R. F. Kahn, 'The Relation of Home Investment to Unemployment', *Economic Journal*, 41 (1931), 174. Kahn had actually presented a draft of this article to the Committee of Economists of the Economic Advisory Council in Sept. 1930, but its implications do not seem to have been realized: D. E. Moggridge, 'From the *Treaties* to the *General Theory*: An Exercise in Chronology', *History of Political Economy*, 5 (1973), 74.

[40] The employment ratio was the ratio of secondary employment (employment created by the spending of the wages earned by those employed on public works) to primary employment (the number of men actually employed on the works). The ratio was dependent upon the relationship between the wages of the unemployed (in Britain, the dole) to the wages of the fully employed. Thus in Britain the ratio would be lower than in the United States where there was no dole; in America it could be expected that the rate of secondary employment would be higher than in Britain.

could be argued that he underplayed the importance of confidence and expectation in investment.[41] Finally, it could also be argued that he depreciated the effects of reflationary expenditure on the balance of payments.[42] The consequence was that the theoretical and empirical problems of the multiplier were a lively controversy in the thirties, and attempts to measure a multiplier-effect, to devise fiscal imperatives that finance ministers could actually obey, such as those of Colin Clark or R. and W. M. Stone, frequently came to grief.[43]

Addendum I to the Report of the Macmillan Committee (written largely by Keynes) went to some lengths, in a guarded way, to argue the case for 'Capital Development'.[44] It disputed the idea (again associated with the Treasury) that there was a fixed 'loan fund',[45] and denied that 'state-aided' schemes were likely to distort investment, or raise interest rates. But it hedged on two important questions: on the size of the budget, and on the speed with which the general level of economic activity could be raised. Furthermore, it seems to have reckoned that capital schemes would be financed within the *existing* budgetary structure; it doubted whether they would 'put some burden on the budget and therefore lead to the evils of increased taxation'.[46] As to the actual practicability of development schemes, the Addendum said that the

main obstacle in the way of remedying unemployment by means of organized schemes of investment is probably to be found, not so much in any of these arguments as in the practical difficulties of initiative and organization. It is not easy to devise well-conceived plans on a large scale.[47]

No doubt the slightly reticent tone was deliberate and designed to seduce unsympathetic readers. Even so, these conclusions were plainly unhelpful to any government, particularly one faced by an

[41] See below, n. 49.

[42] He did not ignore this. He merely said it was a question of whether the present was to be sacrificed to the future. Kahn, 194.

[43] There is a detailed discussion in H. H. Villard, *Deficit Spending and the National Income* (New York, 1941), 123–202.

[44] *Committee on Finance and Industry, Report*, Addendum I (III), 'Schemes of National Development'.

[45] The Doctrine that the fund for capital investment was given, and that an increase in state investment must lead to a proportionate decline in capital available for private investment.

[46] Committee on Finance and Industry, *Report*, 205.   [47] Ibid. 206.

alarmingly rapid contraction of economic activity. Previous policies had certainly been mistaken in many areas, but the Macmillan Committee only indicated long-term changes. There was little in its Report to show how the economy might be immediately bludgeoned into activity. Sir Josiah Stamp, by no means a reactionary economist, wrote that

the worst that can be said about the Macmillan Report is that in the face of our present and urgent problems, its recommendations for immediate relief seem feeble and nerveless; but no one ought to make this criticism unless he is prepared to assert that there actually exists a field of active possibility which has been unexplored.[48]

Though not lacking in goodwill, but being unconvinced of the utilty of half-hearted policies, and also (fairly) worried about 'confidence',[49] the Labour cabinet repeatedly rejected large-scale capital projects as likely to be money ill-spent.[50]

The second possibility open to the Labour government was a monetary one: to devalue, or to use interest rates more positively, or to do both. Being essentially technical operations they would have been administratively simple and in that way easier than budgetary experiments. Some indeed, like R. G. Hawtrey, an enthusiast for cheap money (though an early advocate of a return to gold), thought that monetary maladjustment was more or less the sole cause of the economy's difficulties:

[48] Josiah Stamp, 'The Report of the Macmillan Committee', *Economic Journal*, 41 (1931), 431.

[49] The reflationists were less help here than they might have been. In 'Relation of Home Investment to Unemployment', 197, Kahn wrote: 'if there were no opposing forces in operation . . . the ordinary processes of home investment would be promoted rather than retarded by a policy of public works. This supposes that the state of general confidence is not affected. There is strong justification for concluding on *a priori* grounds that the inauguration of an active economic policy would promote confidence rather than upset it. But this is not a valid reason for disbelieving the warning, so frequently put forward at the present time, that an extensive policy of public works would promote a feeling of distrust.' He thought that these dangers were overrated, but confidence was incalculable, and he gave it 3 paragraphs in 24 pages. But see also the mature Keynes in the *General Theory*: 'There is, however, not much to be said about the state of business confidence a priori. Our conclusions must mainly depend upon the actual observations of markets and business psychology. That is why the ensuing disgression [ch. 12, 'Long-term Expectations'] is on a different level of abstraction from most of this book.' *Collected Writings of J. M. Keynes*, vii. *The General Theory of Employment, Interest, and Money*, 149.

[50] Skidelsky, *Politicians and the Slump*, 107–89.

[Keynes] Coming back to the main argument, as I understand you, you regard the history of events from 1924 to 1930, and their effect on unemployment, as the tragedy of a series of avoidable errors in monetary policy.

[Hawtrey] Well, yes.[51]

But in the way of monetary correction, which in practice meant devaluation of the pound, lay the decision to restore its pre-1914 rate of exchange, and its gold convertibility. There was probably nothing wrong in principle in returning to gold payment, but returning at par ($4.86) almost certainly overvalued the pound in relation to other currencies.[52]

The Labour Party had been unenthusiastic about returning to gold payment in 1925, but as Sayers points out, like most other institutions, accepted return as inevitable in due course.[53] On the other hand, there was less intellectual, as opposed to emotional, support for the 'gold standard' than may be supposed. Even Oliver Sprague, economic adviser to the Bank of England, admitted to the Macmillan Committee that it was no longer working satisfactorily.[54]

By 1931 it was, in fact, hardly novel to question the wisdom of returning to gold at pre-war parity. Yet not many people, and virtually none of the 'experts', believed that it was right to abandon it. The full Macmillan Committee, though it 'conceded that return to gold at par may well have been mistaken', had 'no hesitation in rejecting' devaluation.[55] This was plainly *bien-pensant* opinion, but the authors of Addendum I to the Report (Keynes *et al.*) also concluded that the 'disadvantages would greatly outweigh the advantages', and so rejected it.[56] The

[51] Committee on Finance and Industry, *Minutes of Evidence*, i. Q 4816. See also R. G. Hawtrey, *Trade Depression and the Way Out* (London, 1933); *The Gold Standard in Theory and Practice* (London, 1933).

[52] But the statutory minimum gold reserve of £150m.—two-thirds of which had to secure the note issue—was certainly too small.

[53] R. S. Sayers, 'The Return to Gold, 1925', in L. S. Pressnell (ed.), *Studies in the Industrial Revolution* (London, 1960), 315.

[54] Committee on Finance and Industry, *Minutes of Evidence*, ii. QQ 9250–3.

[55] Id., *Report*, 109–10.

[56] Ibid. 199. Moggridge is a little easy on Keynes. He writes that 'although Keynes preferred to try other means than devaluation of removing Britain's competitive disadvantage, and solving her balance of payments in the first instance, he ultimately advised devaluation. Similarly, R. G. Hawtrey, by the early spring of 1931, was so convinced that devaluation or depreciation was the only available alternative that he refused to present memoranda justifying the maintenance of

reservation to Addendum I, signed by Ernest Bevin and Sir Thomas Allen of the Co-operative Wholesale Society, was more reluctant to abandon devaluation, but agreed that there were great obstacles.[57]

The Labour government's adhesion to parity, despite Snowden's later behaviour, was as reluctant as the Macmillan Committee's. The president of the Board of Trade, William Graham, speaking during the national economy debate (February 1931), admitted that by returning at par the British people 'had made an utterly disproportionate sacrifice'. He agreed that return might have been 'precipitous'. But he did not 'believe it is possible to go back upon that decision to-day'.[58] The government was thus influenced by the same pressures that forced its advisers to the same conclusions: a belief (uppermost probably in Keynes's case) that one ought to make the best of the situation until the situation itself became intolerable; by the real English disease—the idea that, in the end, all the best economic measures are unpleasant ones; above all, by a determination to save the disintegrating international finance system from collapse. Devaluation was not avoided by stupidity or malice: 'Nobody told us we could do that [go off gold],' Sidney

$4.86.' D. E. Moggridge, *British Monetary Policy* (Cambridge, 1972), 228 n. But it was not until 5 Aug. 1931 that Keynes wrote to MacDonald that 'it is now *nearly* certain that we shall go off the existing gold parity at no distant date. Whatever may have been the case some time ago, it is too late to avoid this.' He suggested that MacDonald should consult a 'Comee. consisting of all living Chancellors of the Exchequer' to see whether 'they believe that deflation *à outrance* is possible and are in favour of attempting it, or whether we should not at once suspend gold convertibility and then take collective thought as to the next step.' Keynes, it ought to be said, always believed that a once-for-all deflation might have worked, though the idea of a committee of ex-chancellors was one that MacDonald could hardly have taken seriously. Keynes, however, preferred a new currency unit (which 'might be a gold unit') to be created by devaluing 'existing units by not less than 25%'. All 'Empire countries' together with 'all South America, Asia, Central Europe, Italy and Spain' should adhere with Britain to the new unit. This was indeed adventurous, and perhaps anticipated the currency arrangements of the later thirties, but was not in the short term any more practicable than a conclave of ex-chancellors. Keynes to MacDonald, 5 Aug. 1931: MacDonald MSS, PRO. 'Ultimately' everyone favoured devaluation in 1931, and Keynes evidently not much earlier than most. See also R. F. Harrod, *Life of J. M. Keynes* (London, 1951), 438; there is tacit recognition of this in D. E. Moggridge and Susan Howson, 'Keynes on Monetary Policy, 1910–1946', *Oxford Economic Papers*, 26 (1974), 235–6. As for Hawtrey, he had been all for returning to gold in the twenties, and his conversion to devaluation was very recent: K. J. Hancock, 'Unemployment and Economists in the 1920s', *Economics*, 37 (1960), 309–11.

[57] Committee on Finance and Industry, *Report*, 209–10.
[58] *HC Deb.* 5th ser. 248 535–8 (11 Feb. 1931).

Webb is supposed to have said, and that was a perfectly good reason for not doing it.[59]

There was a third possibility open to the British government: that was to follow international fashion, and deflate energetically. The tendency of British policy since 1920 had been gently deflationary. The measures of 1920, which sharply raised interest rates, began it,[60] and the return at par presumably accelerated it. But this was, as Donald Moggridge points out, a policy that appeared more deflationary than it actually was.[61] Before July 1931 the Labour government made no serious attempt either to reduce government expenditure or to enforce wage-cuts and so on. On the contrary, the National Insurance Act of 1930 liberalized what to many contemporaries was a lavishly expensive scheme, and abandoned all attempts to 'balance' the Unemployment Insurance Fund. British unemployment insurance was amongst the most comprehensive in the world, and its social and political consequences were profound, but it involved the government in the kind of expenditure which, in a deflationary epoch, was regarded in orthodox circles as profligate and dangerous.

The cost to the Exchequer of unemployment benefits had risen from £12m. in 1928 to about £125m. in 1931. In January 1930 benefit payments had been increased and access to benefit widened—a piece of 'wilful optimism', as Sir Ronald Davidson called it.[62] The Fund itself might have carried the increased expenditure, but it was 'bankrupted' by the rapid rise in unemployment. The government resorted to borrowing from the Treasury and then made no attempt to balance the Fund or to reduce borrowing. In 1930 the Fund's deficit was £75m.; in 1931 it was expected to be £100m.[63] Since the government neither reduced general expenditure nor increased taxes (except marginally in 1930) the national budget itself was forced into deficit.[64]

The actuarial chaos of the Fund and the 'extravagance' of

[59] A. J. P. Taylor, *English History, 1914–1945* (Oxford, 1965), 297.
[60] Susan Howson, 'The Origins of Dear Money, 1919–1920', *Economic History Review*, 27, (1974), 88–107.
[61] Moggridge, *British Monetary Policy*, 237. See also below, pp. 217–18.
[62] R. C. Davison, *British Unemployment Policy* (London, 1938), 6.
[63] Royal Commission on Unemployent Insurance, PP (1931), ii (Cmd. 3872), 381.
[64] U. K. Hicks, *The Finance of British Government* (London, 1938), 11–14, 193–205.

benefit payment became the symbols of the Labour government's financial unsoundness,[65] and it is no accident that the course of the 1931 crisis centred so much upon unemployment insurance. 'Official' opinion had for some time regarded its affairs with dismay. The alarmist evidence which Sir Richard Hopkins was allowed to present to the Royal Commission on Unemployment Insurance set the tone. In any circumstances, he said, a deficit on the Fund would overstrain the budget:

In the present conditions it would, taken in conjunction with the continuing liabilities . . . not merely disturb, but entirely upset the equilibrium of the Budget on the basis of existing taxation. The 1931 revenue must be expected to fall: the extent of the fall cannot yet be estimated: the fall requires to be balanced, if equilibrium is to be preserved by reduced expenditure. The large debt charges, however, representing this year 41% of the Budget, is fixed and savings in other branches of expenditure, such as would balance a great increase in one item, cannot be obtained except by wide alterations of policies approved by parliament . . .

. . . continued state borrowing on the present vast scale without adequate provision for repayment by the Fund would quickly call in question the stability of the British financial system . . .

It has sometimes been suggested that the existing debt should be 'written off'. There can be no question of writing it off. The money which has been borrowed must be repaid.[66]

This remorseless and highly political statement could be construed in only one way: as demanding a general subordination of social policy to budgetary orthodoxy. Now Snowden had read, and apparently approved, the memorandum before public submission; he even hoped that it might stir the pot a little. Yet it was precisely the kind of advice the government did not want and was not prepared to accept. The royal commission itself had been appointed as a delaying tactic and as a way of getting more money for the Fund.[67] The reductions in benefit approved by the cabinet in 1931 were trivial;[68] the budget in April surprised contemporaries by doing nothing,[69] and in June it was decided to 'postpone serious

---

[65] See, for example, *HC Deb.* 5th ser. 248 427–542 (11 Feb. 1931).

[66] Royal Commission on Unemployment Insurance, *Minutes of Evidence*, ii. p. 381, paras. 2–6; see also QQ 3264–71. Hopkins was controller of finance at the Treasury, 1927–32.   [67] Skidelsky, *Politicians and the Slump*, 293–5.

[68] PRO, Cab. 42/222, CP 153, 16 June 1931.

[69] Winch, *Economics and Policy*, 136.

action' when the interim report of the Royal Commission on Un-employment was published.[70] Whatever they might have thought privately, both MacDonald and Snowden knew that any real attack on 'profligate' expenditure was politically impossible.

By the standards of the time, the Labour government was not particularly orthodox: as Schumpeter commented—all 'this was not "pump priming". But neither was it "deflation".'[71] In a way, therefore, the Labour government was rightly regarded as financially untrustworthy. The majority report of the May Committee went out of its way to make this point. 'The electoral programme of each successive Party in power, particularly when it was formerly in opposition, has usually been prepared with more regard to attracting electoral support than to a careful balancing of national interests.'[72] Such spurious even-handedness did not conceal which party the majority, in fact, meant. *The Economist* put it less delicately: 'was sound finance to be shipwrecked on the hard rock of democracy?'[73]

The practicable alternatives open to the Labour government were not drift or reflation, but drift or deflation. Until the crisis of July–August 1931, Britain alone of the major countries seriously affected by depression refused to follow deflationary policies. Her relatively generous social services were not only maintained but somewhat increased in scope; despite the shrinking of the tax-base, government expenditure continued to rise; no serious attempt was made to balance the budget. The government might have attempted a reflation generated by capital expenditure, but that was probably never physically possible, and in any case the results were indeterminate. Moggridge, unsurprisingly,[74] sees the real mistake of the Labour government, and that of its predecessor, as not taking the appropriate monetary action. That is a better-founded criticism, but since even the most avant-garde of the Cambridge school, led by Keynes himself, shrank from this action, it is probably hard on the Labour ministers to push the point too far. Finally, they might, by rigid deflation, have indulged in a

---

[70] Clay, *Lord Norman*, 389.   [71] Schumpeter, *Business Cycles*, ii. 920.
[72] Committee on National Expenditure, *Report*, PP (1931) (Cmd. 3920), p. 223, para. 574. See the specific reply of the minority, p. 228, para. 5. This committee is generally known as the May Committee, after its chairman, Sir George May.
[73] *The Economist*, 15 Aug. 1931.
[74] Dr Moggridge, in addition to his detailed work on the period, is, of course, editor of the Royal Economic Society's edition of Keynes's *Collected Writings*.

desperate cost-cutting exercise to restore competitiveness and confidence. For both political and humane reasons they would not do this.

The second Labour government collapsed in August 1931 when the pressure to abandon drift and adopt deflation became too strong. Two movements came together: the pressure to solve Britain's internal budgetary problems by deflation reached its peak when the May Report was published on 31 July[75]—at the same time as the European liquidity crisis reached London and immediately called into question the exchange rate of the pound.[76] The budgetary crisis and the exchange crisis were originally distinct phenomena, but throughout August 1931 they played upon each other.[77] Both, however, intensified demands for the same kind of deflationary policies: 'confidence' could be restored at home by budgetary balance alone, while foreign credits— needed to stop the haemorrhage of gold from London—could only be obtained by heavy reductions in government expenditure, particularly in unemployment insurance.

The government had been facing these demands for over a year, but a positive reaction one way or the other was forced upon it unexpectedly. After a fruitless three weeks bargaining with the banks and the opposition parties, during which time ministers went a long way towards meeting their requirements, the government resigned. It resigned because its members could not agree among themselves; it would, however, have been forced out anyway once the Liberals deserted—as they did desert—to the Conservatives.

On 24 August the National government was formed to solve the budgetary crisis and to protect the dollar parity of the pound. It attempted to do this by the Economy Act of September 1931, which, together with the extraordinary budget of the same month,

[75] For the conclusions of the May Report, see Skidelsky, *Politicians and the Slump*, 379–81.

[76] For the liquidity crisis, see David Williams, 'London and the 1931 Financial Crisis', *Economic History Review*, 15 (1962–3), 513–28; there is a slightly different interpretation in D. E. Moggridge, 'The 1931 Financial Crisis—A New View', *The Banker*, 120 (1970), 832–9.

[77] B. B. Gilbert, *British Social Policy* (London, 1973), 162–75. Clay, who knew this world well, says that the Labour government's internal policies 'excited' the same fears as had the Nazi successes in the 1930 German elections: Clay, *Lord Norman*, 373.

forced the budget into equilibrium by reducing government expenditure, cutting categories of salaries, together with, of course, unemployment benefits, and raising direct and indirect taxes. The pound was not saved: the gold and currency loss continued at eventually torrential proportions, and by 21 September gold payment was suspended.[78] The exchange rate fell from $4.86 to around $3.40 at the end of the year—a devaluation of about one-third.

The role of the bankers in all this seems indisputable. They were clear that their conditions were to be accepted, and accepted by all three parties. Whether they framed them with an eye to bringing the government down is less clear. More disputable is the action of a number of ministers who, at the last minute, jibbed at budgetary cuts they had, until a few days before the end, accepted. Why did they do this? For one thing they had resisted uncompromising deflation in the past, and to surrender to it in August 1931 was to desert long-held positions. But that alone does not explain it. Labour ministers are as inclined to put country before party as anyone else: in the terms the crisis of 1931 was presented to them they might have done so again.

It was only the trade unions which could, within the labour movement, decisively influence the cabinet. Between the formation of the government in June 1929 and its end in August 1931 the unions had interfered little. While the National Insurance Fund was nourished and protected, and further deflation resisted, the unions, if not content, were at least acquiescent. However, while there was no collective trade-union view of the depression, the unions tended to know what they did not like. In their submission to the Macmillan Committee, the Trades Union Congress commented:

Since the fall in wholesale prices beginning in 1920 was due to the policy of deflation deliberately pursued, it is small wonder that the industrialists generally have complained bitterly that monetary policy is decided without adequate considerations to the effects on industry. The inevitable result to industry of the further deflation carried out on the return to the Gold Standard in 1925 has similarly been commented on in trenchant terms by Mr Keynes.[79]

[78] By mid-September gold reserves were £20m. below the minimum statutory level specified by the 1925 Act which restored gold payment.

[79] Committee on Finance and Industry, *Minutes of Evidence*, i. 311.

There was certainly a good deal of hindsight here, but it constituted, if anything did, an official trade-union version. Thus in their minority report of the May Committee, the two TUC representatives, Charles Latham and Arthur Pugh, took the position 'that the present financial difficulties of the country and of industry do not arise from . . . wasteful public expenditure . . . but are much more closely related to the policy of deflation followed since the war and confirmed by the return to the gold standard.'[80]

Yet no coherent reflationary policy emerged from this. Until August 1931 the unions were primarily interested in maintaining unemployment benefits, and ensuring that if there had to be sacrifices, they must be distributed evenly. Nor were the unions in principle opposed to budget-balancing or 'reasonable' economies. Latham and Pugh conceded the need for 'wise economy' but insisted on equality of sacrifice.[81]

Arguably, the lines of union policy ran at least parallel to those of the government until the end of July 1931. While Snowden continued to do nothing, and while experience suggested no easy way out, the unions saw no need to intervene.

Though there were all the signs of a real financial crisis, the TUC appears to have seen no real threat to existing policies until about 10 August. After all, despite Snowden's tragic tones on 30 July, and the publication of the May Report on 31 July, the cabinet's 'economy committee'[82] moved pretty sedately. Mac-Donald's sudden return from Scotland on 11 August, together with press sensations and the now well-publicized gold losses, made it clear that the policy of drift was likely to be overtaken by deflation, and the kind of deflation that the government had for so long avoided. From 10 August onwards, Skidelsky writes, 'the hidden hand of the trade unions becomes increasingly discernible', and he notices the relentlessly tendentious reporting of the *Daily Herald*.[83]

[80] Committee on National Expenditure, *Report*, 270.

[81] Ibid. As late as Apr. 1931 the general council of the TUC concluded that Britain's problems were due to the world trade depression and could only be overcome by international co-operation: TUC Archives, Congress House, 'Minutes of the General Council', 19 Apr. 1931.

[82] A sub-committee of the cabinet appointed to consider economies in government expenditure. Its members were MacDonald, Snowden, Henderson, J. H. Thomas, and William Graham. It met first on 12 Aug.

[83] Skidelsky, *Politicians and the Slump*, 405–6.

The TUC then began to take more active steps. Citrine, secretary of the TUC, contacted Arthur Henderson, and insisted upon a meeting of the Labour Party and the general council of the TUC before anything was agreed upon. 'I found Citrine somewhat difficult,' Henderson wrote, but a joint meeting of the national executive of the Labour Party and of the general council was agreed for 20 August.[84]

On 19 August the cabinet met to consider the report of the 'economy committee'.[85] The May Committee had recommended total savings of £66.5m. in unemployment insurance; the economy committee could come up with just a little over £48m., of which, as Bentley B. Gilbert points out, only £28.5m. 'represented genuine reductions'.[86] But the cabinet was plainly uneasy about even this: 'the Cabinet were not prepared to entertain the main recommendation of the May Committee in regard to Unemployment Insurance.'[87] Yet it is equally clear that many ministers had geared themselves for bigger cuts in unemployment insurance. At the cabinet of 19 August, Lord Sankey tells us, '15 members . . . supported a revenue tariff. Eleven wanted a 10% reduction on dole, 7 a 5% and the others wouldn't vote. I tried to get agreement for one penny in the 1/– i.e. 8½% and I rather thought the compromise would be agreed to.'[88] Thus, if Sankey is right, a majority of the cabinet had already committed themselves to a cut in benefit equal to the amounts demanded a few days later by the bankers and the opposition, a demand that led to the resignation of the government on 24 August. Furthermore, on his reckoning, the great majority of ministers were prepared to countenance at least some reduction in payment. But the cabinet resigned because nearly half, and the weightier half of its members, those led by the party secretary, Arthur Henderson, refused to accept any cut.

What had supervened? On 20 August leading ministers met the TUC twice. In the afternoon there was a joint sitting of the general council and the national executive. It was a rather tense and belligerent session. MacDonald began badly, and, as Citrine truly said, told them only 'what had already appeared in the leading

[84] Labour Party Archives, LPLF 'Misc. Uncat.', Henderson to J. S. Middleton, 14 Aug. 1931.
[85] This report is filed as PRO., Cab. 24/222, CP 203.
[86] Gilbert, *British Social Policy*, 166.
[87] PRO, Cab. 23/67 (Cab. 41), 19 Aug. 1931.
[88] Bodleian Library, Oxford, Sankey MSS, 'Diaries', 20 Aug. 1931.

articles of many papers'. Citrine, on the other hand did not beat about the bush: 'The Council had no knowledge whatever of any line the Government might propose to take or of any other reason, other than that which had been stated publicly, as to *why at that stage it felt it necessary to do anything*.'[89] The same point—that really there was no crisis—was made by Bevin. He said that 'if anyone had dramatised this position, the Prime Minister had. He had given interviews of the most dramatic character to the *Daily Mail*, and if ever a Government had dramatised a crisis in the press he thought this Government had done it.'

The TUC met the cabinet (the 'economy committee') for a second time the same night. The unions now presented 'concrete' proposals of their own, the closest they came to an alternative policy throughout these years. They proposed the replacement of unemployment insurance by a graduated levy; the suspension of the sinking fund; taxation of all fixed-interest bearing securities; possibly a revenue tariff. MacDonald claimed that 'nothing the General Council representatives had put forward touched the actual problem that faced the Government.'[90]

It is hard to know whether the general council expected McDonald to treat these proposals seriously. To the problem as he understood it, there were now only two solutions. The first was to make the budgetary cuts demanded by the bankers and the opposition, and in this direction the cabinet was moving. The second was to suspend gold payment and allow the pound to find its 'natural' level; but this, it was agreed, was apparently impossible. He wanted the unions to accept policies that now were alone acceptable to predominant opinion. In practice, all the unions could do was to deny the existence of the liquidity crisis— or to assert, that, if it did exist, it was someone else's crisis. Thus after 24 August, they opposed *all* cuts in expenditure (except, as Snowden grimly told the cabinet, salary cuts for judges and ministers), and took the view that since the crisis was caused by the Bank of England, it was up to the Bank to find a way out.

There was a certain polemical plausibility to this position. It can

[89] Labour Party Archives, 'Minutes of the National Executive Committee', 20 Aug. 1931, Addendum I. (Italics mine.) MacDonald was at his very worst. He 'wanted to give them a general idea of the situation . . . The situation was this. If the banking situation was allowed to go on it was going to become a matter for the working classes unless they could stop the movements that were going on.'

[90] A. Bullock, *Ernest Bevin*, 2vols. (London, 1960), i. 483–5.

be argued that the financial crisis was distinct from Britain's own budgetary problems and was the result of the heavy short-term indebtedness of the City—fundamentally, of unwise lending policies.[91] But there *was* a crisis, and, if suspension of gold payment were excluded, the solution had to be deflation. Yet the disagreement between the government and the unions was not, as Gilbert has suggested, merely a symbolic one, a quibble over £12m.[92] There were now broad differences between the two, just as there were broad differences between the policies of the Labour government and those which the National government was created to introduce. The Economy Act of September 1931 was intended as a serious deflationary stroke; Citrine even suggested that the whole crisis had been engineered to balance the National Insurance Fund—a revealing example of how important the unions considered a high level of benefit payment.[93] Opposition to the cuts was not about symbols but about the standard of living of the working class, and substantial sections of the middle class as well. In opposing cuts, the cuts of Cabinet Paper 203 (those suggested by the Labour cabinet's 'economy committee') as much as those of the Economy Act, the unions were merely trying to defend a policy they did not find imaginative but which was better than the likely alternative. To do this they were forced to drive the Labour Party into opposition.[94] The ministers who approved the economies of Cabinet Paper 203, and who were probably prepared to go further, could now only dissociate themselves from policies they were well known to have once supported. It was this that lent weight to the charge—used so successfully against them at the 1931 election—that they 'ran away', for clearly they had run away.

The end of the government on the evening of 23 August was by no means inevitable: left to themselves ministers might well have come to an agreement with the opposition. But the actions of the unions, and the Parliamentary Labour Party acting under union pressure,[95] made the government's end more likely. Sankey,

[91] See Williams, 'London and 1931 Crisis', 526; but also Moggridge, '1931 Financial Crisis', *passim*.   [92] Gilbert, *British Social Policy*, 173.
[93] *Report of Proceedings of the Sixty-Third Annual Trades Union Congress, 1931* (London, 1932), 457–8.
[94] A point neatly taken by Keynes in an otherwise hectic article: 'Notes on the Situation', *New Statesman*, 29 Aug. 1931.
[95] Labour Party Archives, 'Minutes of the National Executive Committee', 20 Aug. 1931, 'Interview between the Consultative Committee of the Parliamentary Labour Party and the Secretary'.

lugubrious narrator of the fall, had no doubt where blame lay. In a last lapidary entry, he wrote:

24 Aug. 1931. PM to take resignations to King. The result due to Henderson changing his mind. At Llandrindod he and I agree to equality of sacrifice and cut in the dole and a revenue tariff. The TUC won't agree so Henderson gave way.[96]

Defending the unions from the charge of 'dictation', Donald Winch concludes that 'when the bankers offered advice (which it was), it was called simply advice; when the General Council of the TUC offered advice (which it was), it was called dictation.'[97] But both sides *were* dictating; the question was whose dictatorship the government was prepared to accept. Until the intervention of the unions, it was moving in the direction of deflation, because that was the only practicable alternative at a moment when an alternative to drift was demanded. By reversing the movement, the TUC could claim to have brought the government down.

At the beginning of this chapter it was suggested that a neo-Keynesian critique of the policies of the second Labour government has to depend on the truth of two conjectures: that international experience pointed to alternative reflationary policies, and that the Labour cabinet was free to choose this alternative. But neither of these conjectures can easily be sustained. Even a casual examination of international experience shows that if there were a reflationary alternative it was being practised in hardly any Western country between 1929 and 1931. On the contrary, deflation was almost universal. British policy, in relation to this, appears generous and almost unorthodox.

Within Britain, it is too easy to underrate the barriers to fiscal or merely financial manipulations. The structural problems of the economy, though by no means intractable, required large-scale shifts in investment patterns, and the way in which the government could force such shifts was highly problematical. They did take place in the later thirties, but the part the government played in this is unclear.[98] From another direction, there were real obstacles

---

[96] Bodl. Lib., Sankey MSS, 'Diaries', 24 Aug. 1931.

[97] Winch, *Economics and Policy*, 154.

[98] It is conventionally argued that the devaluation of 1931 and 'cheap money' (the bank rate was 2% for most of the period) were the government's contribution

to an apparently simple measure like devaluation. So far as Britain was concerned, at least in the short term, the devaluation of 1931 was unquestionably right, but it is important to remember what it began: the destruction of the European financial and trading system and the retreat into competitive devaluations and a scarcity economics with profound social and political consequences—nearly all of them disagreeable.

It can be argued that a developed multiplier theory would have provided the necessary intellectual support for some kind of counter-cyclical capital expenditure. In fact, no such theory existed and it may not have been the answer even if it had.

The absence of a mature reflationary economics was matched by the physical incapacity of the state. Budgets were too small and administrative traditions not flexible enough. Even today, despite an immense multiplication in the sum of economic knowledge, it can hardly be argued that the modern capitalist state has developed a comprehensive means of economic management. It must be concluded that the ability of the state before the Second World War to do more than marginally influence the economy was limited. Above all, the state had no way then, and scarcely has today, of determining investment rates. Recovery in the United States, for example, was interrupted by a persistent tendency to transfer income from current to capital balances before full recovery was achieved.

Nor, in this respect, is it really possible to argue from post-war experience. If Britain's full employment after 1945 had been the result of a Keynesian 'demand-management' consciously practised by the state, then it would indeed, as R. C. O. Matthews has written, 'be a most striking vindication of Keynes' celebrated dictum about the ultimate primacy of abstract thought in the world of affairs'.[99] But the relative success of the British economy in the twenty-five years after the war was due largely—though not entirely—to a rapid expansion of exports and to a sharp increase in

to these changes and the subsequent boom in private housing and consumer industries. Yet even this must be open to doubt. The main achievement of the government, as Pollard argues, was to 'channel additional demand into home-produced goods and services rather than imports'. S. Pollard, *The Development of the British Economy, 1914–1967* (London, 1969), 240; for more detail, see H. W. Richardson, *Economic Recovery in Britain, 1932–1939* (London, 1967).

[99] R. C. O. Matthews, 'Why has Britain had Full Employment since the War?', *Economic Journal*, 78 (1968), 556.

investment rates.[100] It seems unlikely that the state has had much to do with either.[101]

The behaviour of the Western economies after the autumn of 1932 lent as much weight to cyclical theory as it did to anything else. All of them began to recover then, and, with one exception, that recovery was sustained throughout the decade *regardless* of the regimes they possessed. The exception was the United States, one of the few countries practising 'active' policies. It appears, therefore, that so long as fiscal policy respected the traditional structure of the capitalist state contingent factors were likely to be more important than government intervention.

This points to other conclusions. The claim made by neo-Keynesians that 'socialism', if by that is meant some level of state control or ownership of the economy's functions, was more or less irrelevant, must be treated with caution. To begin with, a successful reflation in Britain would probably have required as a preliminary, or at least as a corollary, very wide state supervision of the economy. Thus the economic success of such policies was dependent upon an essentially political act.

The political consequences of reflationary politics, however, were more far-reaching even than that. There is little evidence to suggest that Keynesian policies could ever be apolitical, that a parliamentary or popular majority could have been mobilized to support them. While the existing structure of power remained intact it is scarcely conceivable that a Labour government would have been permitted to introduce such policies. The bureaucracy, the Bank of England and most of the commercial banks, the great financial institutions, the dead weight of conventional wisdom, were thrown against innovation. Though industry had its dissidents, it too, in the end, preferred an orthodox Conservative government to any kind of Labour one. But the opposition to a 'Keynesian' reflation was not simply institutional. What had been created after the First World War was, as I shall argue,[102] an 'anti-Labour' majority which could *only* be held together by the adoption of a deflationary ideology. That majority was not, it is true, monolithic

---

[100] Ibid., passim. See also Axel Leijonhufvud, *Keynes and the Classics* (London, 1969), 10–11, 30–42; and the interesting comments of Sir John Hicks in J. R. Hicks, *The Crisis of Keynesian Economics* (Oxford, 1974), 3–4.

[101] Matthews somewhat alarmingly suggests that had 1964 budgetary policies been followed in 1937, national income would then have been 1% less than it actually was: Matthews, 557.   [102] See below, pp. 267–75.

in all circumstances; but it was monolithically anti-inflationary. Thus the Liberal Party immediately began to fall apart as soon as Britain was affected by the international depression. The bulk both of its MPs and voters committed themselves to sound finance and their recruitment by the National government was an essential element in the establishment of the Conservative Party's hegemony over that anti-Labour majority. 'Socialism' could not have been avoided simply by government spending; on the contrary spending would have made 'socialism' a central problem. The second Labour government's failure to adopt reflationary policies, therefore, was structural and not intellectual; and it did about as well as a 'progressive' party could do in an advanced capitalist economy which was showing few signs of cyclical recovery.

8

The 'Social Psychology' of Unemployment in Inter-war Britain

IN 1938 P. Eisenberg and P. F. Lazarsfeld published a 'final' statement of the social-psychological theory of unemployment and so completed the only systematic analysis of the effects of unemployment on the individual and the family.[1] The theory suggested that men and women went through 'stages' in their reaction to unemployment—from optimism to resignation and despair—and these stages were accompanied by a progressive deterioration in the individual's social and intellectual capacities. Social engagement was succeeded by social withdrawal; political activity by apathy; and mental interests by inertia. Differences of personality and temperament influenced only the timing, not the progression of the stages. Here I shall examine how far the literature available to Lazarsfeld supports such a theory. I have used only that material cited by Eisenberg and Lazarsfeld in their 1938 article or which was otherwise accessible to them, together with some more recent work when that does not seem anachronistic; and I have ignored the problem of physical deterioration with which the psychological literature was only obliquely concerned.[2]

The theory was elaborated in three remarkable publications of which the most celebrated was the first, *Die Arbeitslosen von Marienthal* (1933), written by Marie Jahoda, Paul Lazarsfeld, and

---

[1] P. Eisenberg and P. F. Lazarsfeld, 'The Psychological Effects of Unemployment', *Psychological Bulletin*, 35, 6 (June 1938).

[2] Nor have I raised the possibly analogous question of retirement. First, 'retirement' as we understand it was very unusual in working-class life before the Second World War and Lazarsfeld *et al.* could rightly argue that it is an unhistorical comparison. Second, it is questionable whether it is analogous. Modern retirement is, in fact, part of the structure of employment: all of us know we must plan for it. But inter-war unemployment, particularly, was often unexpected and random. It could not be planned for.

Hans Zeisel.[3] Marienthal was a small industrial village about 30 km. from Vienna whose work-force, entirely dependent on a textile mill which closed in 1929, was almost completely un-employed by 1930. The team, all social psychologists from the University of Vienna, attempted a 'total' study of the lives of the unemployed and this they did by an imaginative and eclectic technique of personal observation, sample budgets and diets, autobiographies, essay competitions for schoolchildren, and questionnaires. It was the single most influential study of the unemployed of the inter-war years.

The second, by Zawardski and Lazarsfeld, is the most striking, if also the most eccentric.[4] In 1930–1 the Institute of Social Economy in Warsaw published fifty-seven autobiographies of unemployed men. The autobiographies, of which there were many hundreds, had been elicited by competition. The contributors were asked to record the course of their daily lives; the management of the household budget; the diet of the family; the effect of unemployment on health. The most vivid autobiographies alone were accepted; 'colourless' ones were excluded.[5]

The third was the Eisenberg–Lazarsfeld article of 1938, a bibliographical piece which attempted to collect and make sense of the international literature on unemployment. These two concluded that

all writers . . . seem to agree on the following points. First there is shock, which is followed by an active hunt for a job, during which the individual is still optimistic and unresigned . . . Second, when all efforts fail, the individual becomes pessimistic, anxious and suffers active distress; this is the most crucial state of all. And third, the individual becomes fatalistic and adapts himself to his new state but with a narrower scope. He now has a broken attitude.[6]

Lazarsfeld was part author of all three publications and it was thus not accidental that 'all writers' conformed almost exactly to the findings of *Marienthal* and Zawardski–Lazarsfeld.[7] Thus

[3] M. Jahoda, P. F. Lazarsfeld, and H. Zeisel, *Die Arbeitslosen von Marienthal* (Leipzig, 1933), and English edn., *Marienthal: The Sociography of an Unemployed Community* (London, 1972). All references here are to the English edition.
[4] B. Zawardski and P. F. Lazarsfeld, 'The Psychological Consequences of Unemployment', *Journal of Social Psychology*, 6, 2 (May, 1935).
[5] Zawardski and Lazarsfeld, 224–5.   [6] Eisenberg and Lazarsfeld, 378.
[7] P. Kelvin and J. Jarrett, *Unemployment* (Cambridge, 1985), 19.

Jahoda *et al.* divided their families into four categories: 'unbroken', 'resigned', 'in despair', and 'apathetic'.[8] The great majority (70 per cent) were 'resigned'. Families did not react in different ways; rather, they progressed from hope to despair and these were 'stages' through which all, or nearly all, must go. Zawardski–Lazarsfeld detected six stages:

(1) As a reaction to dismissal, there comes generally a feeling of injury; sometimes strong fear and distress; sometimes an impulse towards revenge; hatred, indignation; fury. (2) Thereafter comes a stage of numbness and apathy which is gradually (3) replaced by calming down and an increase in steadiness, bringing one again to a relative mental balance. This mental stage is characterized by a resumption of activity; the unemployed become calm as they see that things go along somehow and adapt themselves to circumstances; they trust in God, fate, or in their own ability, and try to believe that the situation will improve very soon. (4) But this hope becomes constantly weaker, when they see the futility of effort. (5) When the situation becomes harder, the old savings and new sources exhausted, then comes the hopelessness which expresses itself at first in attacks of fear . . . (6) After these outbreaks comes either sober acquiescence or dumb apathy and then alternation between hope and hopelessness, activity and passivity, according to the momentary changes in the material situation.[9]

These conclusions anticipated those of Eisenberg–Lazarsfeld in 1938. 'From our biographies', Zawardski and Lazarsfeld argued in 1935, 'it appears that the basic attitudes stated in . . . *Die Arbeitslosen von Marienthal* namely: the *unbroken*, the *resigned*, the *distressed*, and the *apathetic*, can be seen clearly in our material, a fact indicating that these basic conceptions are sound.'[10] That a 'stage'-theory of unemployment should have emerged fully formed in 1938 was, therefore, not surprising. Although Lazarsfeld later had some doubts about its conceptual sophistication,[11] Jahoda has not,[12] and, as Kelvin and Jarrett comment, 'a notion which was little more than an afterthought in *Marienthal* has since become a basic concept in accounts of the psychological effects of unemployment.'[13]

---

[8] Jahoda *et al.*, 56.   [9] Zawardski and Lazarsfeld, 235.   [10] Ibid.
[11] In the introduction to the English edition of *Marienthal*, Lazarsfeld wrote that he had for a long time been reluctant to consent to a translation because 'certain aspects of our approach were very naïve' (*Marienthal*, p. xi).
[12] M. Jahoda, *Employment and Unemployment* (Cambridge, 1982).
[13] Kelvin and Jarrett, 113.

This theory argues one other proposition: that is, the fundamental importance to people's lives of formal work. Not only does worklessness lead to intellectual and social disintegration, but, by abolishing a sense of time, it makes life aimless, particularly for men, and 'demoralizes' the unemployed individual. Furthermore, demoralization undermines the capacity or the desire to seek work and renders the unemployed helpless to devise alternative structures. Apathetic men and women cannot generate new routines because these demand personal autonomy and self-dependence. The theory thus describes an emotional progression through which the unemployed seem fated to go: a social fact—unemployment—becomes transformed into a universally observable series of mental states.

The stage-theory, partly because it is the only psychological theory of unemployment, has been very influential,[14] perhaps more in the United States—the Lynds' *Middletown in Transition* was clearly affected by it[15]—than in Britain.[16] But even in Britain it directly stimulated one of the most important studies of inter-war unemployment, Beales and Lambert's *Memoirs of the Unemployed*. 'The idea of collecting the present volume of *Memoirs*', they wrote in its Introduction, 'arose as a result of the experiments which certain continental countries have begun to make in the investigation of the psychological effects of unemployment.' Specifically, they note the Polish autobiographies and the work of 'a group of Viennese psychologists'. The evidence thus collected 'at these two different sources bears sufficient marks of similarity to show that the subject is worth pursuing in our own country'.[17] In the event, the memoirs were decidely ambiguous in their implications, and the authors made no real attempt to impose a pattern on them; it would, none the less, not have been difficult

---

[14] For a general discussion of the literature, see Royal Institute of International Affairs, *Unemployment: An International Problem* (London, 1935), 14–15; J. A. Garraty, *Unemployment in History* (New York, 1978), 178–87.

[15] R. S. Lynd and H. M. Lynd, *Middletown in Transition* (London, 1937), 254–6 partic. The Lynds' conclusions, however, were significantly different from those of *Marienthal*.

[16] Though in America it became hopelessly confused with the debate on the 'culture of poverty' and lost much of its force. For an excellent discussion of this, particularly of Oscar Lewis's work, see C. A. Valentine, *Culture and Poverty* (Chicago, 1968).

[17] L. Beales and R. S. Lambert (eds.), *Memoirs of the Unemployed* (London, 1934), 9–10.

to have extracted a stage-theory from the material. If true, the theory could explain much of the apparent behaviour of the unemployed in inter-war Britain: political quiescence, geographical immobility, and a widely observed languor in personal and collective life; very indirectly, if true, it might even support the more extreme neo-classical interpretations of unemployment. How far does the evidence support such a theory?

To begin with, there was nothing particularly startling in this description of unemployment: it was the plain man's view and seemed to cohere with experience. In 1911 Rowntree and Lasker recorded that

even men of strong character tell us how exceedingly difficult it is to resist this demoralisation . . . [The unemployed] suffer psychically because of the depression amounting to acute despair, which comes after days and weeks spent in tramping the streets and meeting with nothing but disappointments and refusals.[18]

It was what many unemployed felt. 'A young casual labourer in London' told Beales and Lambert that he and his unemployed 'chums' 'usually play draughts or dominoes. We are just about able to play games like those, which don't require much thought. You stop and talk in the middle, and in any case the games never last very long. Card games want too much patience and attention.' He was interested in football when in work but 'I have not been to a match for years and don't feel much interested in reading up the sports news . . . Besides the results seem to matter so little to me.'[19] Max Cohen felt the same inertia. His brother-in-law kept urging him to join organizations: but in his 'unhealthy state of mind' he felt unable to.[20] Even when some sort of routine was established people were conscious of a slippery slope. 'I was one of a gang,' a young unemployed man from Lancashire wrote:

We used to stay in bed late in the mornings so as not to need breakfast. I used to have a cup of tea, and then we would all go down to the library and read the papers. Then we went home for a bit of lunch, and then we met again at the billiard hall where you could watch the play for nothing. Then back for tea and to watch the billiards again. In the evening we all

---

[18] B. S. Rowntree and B. Lasker, *Unemployment: A Social Study* (London, 1911), 242.

[19] Beales and Lambert, 227.

[20] M. Cohen, *I Was One of the Unemployed* (London, 1945), 91.

used to go to the pictures. That was how we spent the dole money. In the end I thought I'd go mad if I went on like that.[21]

Furthermore, it is the view of unemployment which many of the then-unemployed hold today: 'That's the queer part of unemployment. I didn't want to do anything . . . the fact of being unemployed seemed to take away any desire to do sort of unpaid jobs out of my mind.'[22]

'Deterioration' or 'demoralization' was nearly always noted by outsiders, however amateur or professional was their acquaintance with the unemployed. Ruth Durant, in her study of the new LCC estate at Watling, thought that the 'depression of 1929' more or less finished off what little communal life there was, just as it was most needed: 'People were too worried to develop social interests, and often too tired to seek entertainment.'[23] The well-known Save the Children Fund study argued that parental neglect of children—late waking, sending children to school without breakfast—'may be symptomatic of a gradual change of character. Inertia and lack of vitality among some of the unemployed are a common story among the answers to the questionnaire.'[24] The London social worker S. F. Hatton described the phenomenon in terms an Edwardian would have recognized: 'Three or four months on the streets, and what a difference there is in the appearance and the general attitude of the lad. From the bright, keen youngster eager to work and make his way in the world, he rapidly declines into a lazy, livery street lounger.'[25] Even so pragmatic a sociologist as A. D. K. Owen saw 'stages'. After a man's repeated failure to find a job 'a fatalistic stage appears to be reached during which many men are ready to turn to some new interest sometimes with great enthusiasm. But often as not apathy and listlessness have by this time obtained a stronghold.'[26]

If the professionals thought this it was almost inevitable that even the interested observer should have done so as well. Everyman's view was well represented by Beveridge's evidence to the 1930 Royal Commission on Unemployment Insurance.

[21] Pilgrim Trust, *Men without Work* (Cambridge, 1938), 149.
[22] K. Nicholas, *The Social Effects of Unemployment on Teesside, 1919–1939* (Manchester, 1986), 103.
[23] R. Durant, *Watling: A Social Survey* (London, 1939), 46.
[24] Save the Children Fund, *Unemployment and the Child* (London, 1933), 23.
[25] S. F. Hatton, *London's Bad Boys* (London, 1931), 72.
[26] A. D. K. Owen, 'A Report on Unemployment in Sheffield', *Sheffield Social Survey Pamphlet No. 4* (Sheffield, 1932), 64.

I think [he was asked] you have frequently in your Memorandum used the word 'demoralisation'?—yes.

Do you think that it is an inevitable sort of cause and effect—so many months unemployment, so much demoralisation?

No, I do not think there is any mathematical relation; obviously there is not. But I should think that it was absolutely inevitable that you cannot go on being idle indefinitely without becoming less fit for work—beyond a certain point that is clear . . . I am not blaming the men, but we all know you cannot be idle for two or three years without losing some of your taste for work, or without losing interest in life—none of us can be.[27]

It must be said that Everywoman was not far behind. 'Personally, I would prefer to write a book than to be absolutely unemployed and I should be very disconcerted if I had not a book to write,' Mrs Sidney Webb said;

But directly you get to the young person in whom you have actually encouraged the habit of not working, of course he prefers not to work. Most people at some time, and some people at all times, prefer to lounge rather than to work . . . I know nothing more melancholy, than the sight of idle young men in the mining villages of South Wales and Durham, with their listless unoccupied look. You can see that many of them will obviously take to bad practices . . . It is a terrible, an awful tragedy.[28]

As evidence this tells us as much about the progressive classes as about the unemployed but it also demonstrates how well entrenched a stereotype of unemployment was.

Like all stereotypes, it was as much ideologically determined as based upon observation, though at one level it was a not unreasonable description. It was the nature of worklessness to drive unemployed men (but not unemployed women) out of doors and this was as true of an area of high casual but low long-term unemployment like Greenwich as one of very high long-term unemployment like South Wales. E. Wight Bakke thought that the streets, even more than the cinemas, were where the unemployed spent their spare time. And the streets meant 'loafing', or such was the impression which outsiders formed of what the unemployed actually did. Furthermore, the men did not seem to talk together. An 'outstanding feature' of loafing in Greenwich was the silence.

[27] Royal Commission on Unemployment Insurance, *Minutes of Evidence* (London, 1933), QQ 6033–44.   [28] Ibid., QQ 10, 514–18.

Men stood alone more often than in groups. The young men were more sociable; so were the older men who, I suppose, were pensioners. The middle-aged men were perfectly willing to talk, when I approached them, but more often than not I found them alone.[29]

It seemed the same in Wales. When not visiting the Labour Exchange, Hilda Jennings wrote, 'some men stand aimlessly on the Market Square or the street corners content apparently with a passive animal existence, or with the hour-long observation of passers-by, varied by an occasional whiff at a cigarette.'[30] The unemployed juveniles Meara studied 'congregate on corners, near the unemployment exchanges or on level ash-tips, where somebody might come along with a football or a bat. Conversation is desultory and usually is concerned with local events or with racing and football news.'[31]

This was the public face of unemployment, either in Greenwich and Brynmawr or in Marienthal, where observers concealed themselves behind curtained windows so as to measure the pace at which the unemployed idled up the street.[32] As much as bookies or dockers the unemployed had their stands. They gathered in public libraries, labour exchanges, outside football matches, lolled on street corners, and leant against lampposts. Lampposts, indeed, because one of the folk-myths of unemployment; even absorbed into the gallows humour of the unemployed themselves. Thus one workless rural carpenter thought the lot of the town unemployed almost enviable: they 'have at least got lamp-posts . . . to loll up against'.[33] To some the unemployed simply resembled old cars: J. A. Newrick of the Iron and Steel Trades Confederation commended trades-based labour exchanges on the grounds that their use stopped the unemployed 'standing at the streets and deteriorating'.[34] The view that the unemployed lounged about looking aimless, that they seemed 'listless' and 'apathetic', and that this was a 'demoralized' condition, was, therefore, to some extent factually grounded. That is what unemployment must have looked like to those who were not unemployed. The *Marienthal* conclusions were in part a systematic account of what was

[29] E. W. Bakke, *The Unemployed Man* (London, 1933), 183–9.
[30] H. Jennings, *Brynmawr: A Study of a Depressed Area* (London, 1934), 138–41.
[31] G. Meara, *Juvenile Unemployment in Wales* (Cardiff, 1936), 99.
[32] *Marienthal*, 66–7.   [33] Beales and Lambert, 191.
[34] Unemployment Insurance Committee [Blanesburgh] *Minutes of Evidence*, PP (1927), ix. Q 647.

apparent. In fact, it was a misleading view and once known to be so. In 1909 Chapman and Hallsworth, describing Edwardian loafers, had concluded that 'they flock to the towns where relief funds are being dispersed, hang on to street processions, and being always in evidence . . . *confound public opinion about the nature of the problem of unemployment.*'[35] Since the stereotype was also an ideological one, that was one of the lessons of history people rarely learned.

But the unemployed were not lounging twenty-four hours a day, and when they were lounging, they did not all lounge at once. Much of the life of the workless was concealed from the public and the evidence which supports 'demoralization' is actually very intractable. Lazarsfeld and his colleagues, however, did try to go beyond appearances. 'Demoralization', they argued, showed itself in four ways: in the disintegration of daily routines, in an inability to devise alternative 'work', in the progressive collapse of intellectual interests, and in the abandonment of direct political activity. Let us examine these.

First: routines. It seems obvious that unemployment will disrupt routines established in work; in practice, it is not so obvious. For casual labourers whose work was intermittent anyway, it was likely that routines were always flexible. For skilled workers, experiencing both first-time and long-term unemployment, the *initial* effects could have been disorienting. Sinfield found that men never before workless 'will often be very eager to talk about the injustice and outrage'; in contrast 'the unskilled man in his forties, now in his second or third spell out of work this year, may be laconic to the extent of disconcerting the most experienced interviewers.'[36] In fact, after the first shock when men might show signs of going to pieces, routines of a sort were re-established. 'Signing-on' at the labour exchange twice a week was obligatory and changeless; then, even in areas where it was usually pointless, there was the business of trying to find a job. As Bakke noted, 'hunting a job is the "job" of the unemployed worker.'[37] He calculated that the average Greenwich man spent 4–5 hours a day

[35] S. J. Chapman and H. M. Hallsworth, *Unemployment: The Results of an Investigation Made in Lancashire and an Examination of the Poor Law Commission* (Manchester, 1909), 69. (Italics mine.)
[36] A. Sinfield, *What Unemployment Means* (Oxford, 1981), 37–8.
[37] Bakke, 129.

looking for one. The Carnegie researchers often had difficulty in locating their sample because their men were out looking for jobs.[38] This was a fairly inflexible procedure; skilled men went as far afield as the cheap tram would take them; unskilled men as far as they could walk. Much of the apparent aimlessness of unemployed life was due to the fact that unskilled men often looked for jobs in an aimless way. Skilled men had better contacts and pen and paper.[39] In the 1970s Sinfield found that amongst the unemployed he interviewed it was 'very evident that there is no single "right away" to look for work and what is seen as luck has often tended to dominate the job-search . . . This helps to account for the fatalistic attitude expressed by many men without skills.'[40] But that they were fatalistic did not stop them seeking work; they merely looked purposeless while doing it. Furthermore, this kind of unrewarding 'job' made men very tired and tiredness was easily mistaken for apathy.[41]

If anything, such new routines were too inflexible. Max Cohen remembered the week being divided into 'more or less rigid periods';[42] a 'longing for something diverting, exciting and stimulating, constantly torments the one unemployed.'[43] In some cases the frantic anxiety to find a job could disrupt routines established after the loss of work. Marsden cites the example of 'Mr Vickers', whose 'work' in his garden-shed, which was very important to him, fell apart as his 'obsession' about joblessness became more severe.[44] Max Cohen, though he found life on the dole 'unendurable',

had at any rate settled into a sort of routine. I had become established in a definite lodging. I had become acquainted with different people, had even begun to strike up friendship here and there. And then I had shattered all the slowly built up edifice and cast the pieces away, in order to migrate to Newslum to get a job.[45]

Many women simply continued old routines or had new routines imposed on them. If they were married domestic duties expanded to fill the day; if unmarried and living at home much the same

---

[38] Carnegie U.K. Trust, *Disinherited Youth: A Survey, 1936–1939* (Edinburgh, 1943), 67.   [39] Bakke, 128–9.   [40] Sinfield, 44–5; also Bakke, 14.
[41] Bakke, 71.   [42] Cohen, 12.   [43] Ibid. 134.
[44] D. Marsden, *Workless* (London, 1982), 147.
[45] Cohen, 181–2. 'Newslum' was an outer London suburb.

happened. Single women living away from home, about whom we know little, may have been more disorientated than anybody.[46]

'Hunting a job' became a routine because there was no diminution of the desire for work. The stage-theory is ambiguous here; Lazarsfeld appears to have believed that demoralization on the one hand and the dole on the other inhibited job-search. Many classical and neo-classical economists, of course, have argued that the dole almost infinitely prolonged job-search.[47] None, however, of the contemporary 'sociological' evidence to which either Lazarsfeld or the economists might have had recourse supported this. Every Ministry of Labour study of the period denied it.[48] Neither the Blanesburgh Committee (1925–7) nor the Holman Gregory Commission (1930–2) received any convincing evidence that it was so and much positive evidence that it was not. R. C. Davison, who knew the unemployed well, thought the danger was not that men would not seek work but that they would too readily degrade skill—the real point at issue: 'unemployed men are themselves really eager to work, at wages even below their own usual standards.'[49] J. J. Astor's committee went out of its way to dismiss the notion that job-search was either prolonged or non-existent:

The anxiety of the individual to get back to work, attested by employers, Employment Exchange officials, trade union secretaries, and the individual workmen whom our investigators interviewed, that flocking after the bare report of a job of which they discovered many instances, the application of the men on relief work to which they were unaccustomed . . . are all evidence to the contrary.[50]

What was probably true was that men became reluctant to do small jobs for fear that they would be reported to the exchanges;

[46] This was the Pilgrim Trust view. Pilgrim Trust, 251.

[47] For a rather tidied up account of contemporary 'classical' views of job search, see M. Casson, *Economics of Unemployment* (Oxford, 1983), 37–61; 84–100. For the debate on the extreme neo-classical position, see D. K. Benjamin and L. A. Kochin, 'Searching for an Explanation of Unemployment in Interwar Britain', *Journal of Political Economy*, 87, 3 (June 1979), and replies in the same journal, 90, 2 (April 1982). It is worth noting that only one of the contributions, P. A. Ormerod and G. D. N. Worswick, makes any reference to the sociological material—the Pilgrim Trust survey. No one refers to Bakke.

[48] R. C. Davison, *The Unemployed* (London, 1929), 170; J. Jewkes and A. Winterbottom, *Juvenile Unemployment* (London, 1933), 24.

[49] Davison, 192–3.

[50] J. J. Astor, *et al.*, *The Third Winter of Unemployment* (London, 1922), 73.

but that is because the dole was too mean, not too generous.[51] Bakke thought the dole, by keeping body and soul together, actually facilitated job-search, and he concluded that without it men and women would have starved in exactly the same places where they just scraped by with it.[52] Thus, even in areas where looking for a job was often futile new routines were apparent. This is not to suggest they were satisfactory substitutes for work; simply that there *were* new routines and that people retained a surprising hold over life.

Second: were the unemployed willing to find substitutes for ordinary work? The stage-theory suggests not; it does so not on grounds of poverty—that the unemployed were simply too poor to afford alternative work, which might be a fair proposition—but on grounds of 'demoralization'. After a certain point people did not *want* alternative work. *Marienthal* noted as an example of this the unemployed's loss of interest in allotments and in rabbit breeding, both once enthusiastically followed.[53] But the evidence from Britain cannot support this.

To start, for most unemployed women finding alternatives was not a problem. They either had to or were expected to continue household work; how they reacted depended partly on temperament and on the demands of the home. For some, unemployment could be liberating while for others a disaster. A conventional division of labour often doubled the miseries; men would not do housework and had to find other ways to kill time, while women could not, therefore, get relief from domestic duties which unemployment might otherwise have procured them.[54] The position of single women living away from home is unclear. Caradog Jones concluded that 'hobbies seem . . . to be unknown among women and artistic pursuits are rarely followed by female manual workers.'[55] They were, however, according to the Pilgrim Trust, more gregarious than unemployed men and this may have

[51] Though in certain areas, according to the Carnegie Trust, 'side-lines' were so common 'that betrayal by the neighbours to the Unemployment Assistance officer would have involved every other household. It seemed that the more widespread the subterfuges, the more they were accepted as normal means of augmenting unemployment allowances.' Carnegie Trust, 70–1.

[52] Bakke, 133–4.

[53] *Marienthal*, 70–4.

[54] Three times a problem if the woman also gave up paid work because she 'could not bear to be the breadwinner'. (Pilgrim Trust, 147.)

[55] D. Caradog Jones *et al.*, *The Social Survey of Merseyside* (London, 1934), ii. 276.

mitigated the isolating effects of unemployment. The remarkable success of (say) the 'keep fit' movement among women had no male equivalent. But for many single women manual workers unemployment could have been desolating, not because of 'demoralization' but because of the material and cultural impoverishment of their ordinary life.

As to men, where alternative work was available they did it. This had probably always been so. The Rowntree and Lasker diaries suggest that for unemployed skilled workers hobbies and home repair could be therapeutic. One of their sample wrote that when he returned home at night 'foot-sore with tramping about all day' he often found that

some little item wanted attention, one in particular being the chimney, which was causing us annoyance with smoking very badly. So, on making a careful inspection, I found a soot-door in the attic which no doubt was for cleaning purposes, and naturally I grasped the idea at once; and after carefully covering the fireplace I took some water and poured it through the soot-door, which I am proud to say had the desired effect.[56]

A 'skilled millwright' told Beales and Lambert that 'though there is nothing I can do to keep myself efficient', he liked to do 'odd jobs, like mending boots, chopping up boxes for firewood and repairing things'.[57] Even in down-at-heel Brynmawr men worked where they could; they 'work on allotment or garden, tend fowls or pigs, or do carpentry in their backyard or kitchen, make sideboards out of orange boxes.'[58]

For many men gardens and allotments were obviously a godsend; how far they created an 'alternative life' out of them partly depended on how far they had previously been absorbed in their work. Of the saving value of gardens to those who had them there seems little doubt. Walter Brierley's unemployed miner 'Jack' hated winter and even spring since he could do

nothing but walk around the garden; everything was in but nothing yet ready for coming out . . . He would be glad when the early potatoes were ready so that he could stay in the garden for whole mornings or whole afternoons . . . When he worked at the pit he could finish the garden in a month and only work in it in the evenings and on the occasional holidays . . . gardening had then had never been a delight in itself . . . But for the last two springs he had almost been too slow, too careful.[59]

[56] Rowntree and Lasker, 242.   [57] Beales and Lambert, 104.
[58] Jennings, 138–41.   [59] W. Brierley, *Means Test Man* (London, 1935), 11.

Terence Young noted the popularity of allotments amongst the unemployed on the LCC estate at Becontree.[60] Sir Francis Dyke Acland, an enthusiastic but tasteful observer, wrote that the unemployed in the north of England 'use the hideous huts they put up almost as country cottages'.[61] The Pilgrim Trust believed that the unemployed Durham miner 'had not a perpetual sense of grievance, but . . . rather a determination to make the best of things; to make his allotment or his poultry holding a life for himself'.[62] In the Special Areas 'they are to a large extent providing a fairly full "alternative life" for younger men.'[63]

It is unlikely that for many men make-work adequately stood in for ordinary work, though it might for some.[64] For older men, particularly those who had a long history of continuous skilled or semi-skilled work, an intensification of hobbies was probably never adequate. One unemployed man, who had a wide range of hobby interests, wrote that 'sports and pastimes banish depression whilst they are taking place but when I get to bed at night, I lay and imagine every silly possible thing that may happen.'[65] The problem was that make-work activities usually lacked association; very few, as Kelvin notes, 'demand the interdependence, on a continuing basis, which is of the essence of most work relationships'.[66] None the less, where circumstances made access to alternative work possible, the unemployed took the chance and were anxious to do so.

If this is right, it seems likely that *Marienthal*'s conclusions about the intellectual interests of the unemployed are, as a rule, equally

[60] T. Young, *Becontree and Dagenham* (London, 1934), 162.
[61] Quoted in S. P. B. Mais, *S.O.S. Talks on Unemployment* (London/New York), 87–8.   [62] Pilgrim Trust, 75.
[63] Ibid. 216. Though not always. One of Beales and Lambert's memoirists, an engineer's turner, regarded allotment digging as only an unsatisfactory alternative to an alternative. One of the economic consequences of unemployment, he said, 'includes the abandonment of hobbies'—in his case photography, an expensive one. 'Mending boots or digging allotments is by no means a substitute for those normal satisfactions of interests and hobbies which are the necessary antidotes to the debilitating effects of modern industrial life' (Beales and Lambert, 244–5). This is a very sophisticated analysis which defies conventional categories.
[64] The Pilgrim Trust recorded the case of one Blackburn weaver in his 30s who refused to learn fancy weaving since that might have meant getting work. 'His interest was in the construction of models which he did skilfully and the member of his family who alone took his situation seriously was his wife' (Pilgrim Trust, 86).
[65] Beales and Lambert, 201 ('A Carpenter's Younger Son').
[66] P. Kelvin, 'Work as a Source of Identity: the Implications of Unemployment', *British Journal of Guidance and Counselling*, 9, 1 (Jan. 1981), 8.

suspect. Jahoda *et al.* used as their principal index the increasing reluctance of the unemployed to read newspapers and books, even when public library charges were either abolished or reduced, and a growing readiness to occupy themselves with passive pastimes, like going to the cinema: 'one can mention in this connection the well-known fact that people unsuccessful in their search for a job usually end by going to a movie,' Eisenberg and Lazarsfeld wrote.[67] It would be surprising if some of this were not true and evidence can be mobilized to support it. The Marienthal data on newspaper and book reading have to be accepted, and the objection that poverty alone might explain them can probably be discounted.[68] Indeed, the cinema, like the lamppost, was part of folk-wisdom. The cinema, Bakke thought, was the 'most prominent feature of the spare time activity of the employed and unemployed alike';[69] of Brynmawr Hilda Jennings wrote: 'at nights, there are the pictures, and the long queues outside the "Picture House" probably account for more of the "pocket-money" of the unemployed than do the public houses.'[70]

In fact, again, much British evidence did not support *Marienthal*. It did not suggest that the unemployed 'read' less than they did previously; if anything they read more. A Welsh miner thought the one thing that kept him 'from doing something desperate' was that he now read a lot.[71] Another of the Beales and Lambert autobiographers, a millwright, wrote: 'I read a lot more and enjoy it; I buy the *Daily Herald* and borrow as many other papers and magazines as I can, and I am able to borrow books from the county library.'[72] Bakke argued that unemployed workers read at least as much as they previously had and that newspaper reading had probably risen.[73] On Merseyside at the height of unemployment 'it has been usual to find the reading-rooms full all day of unemployed men.'[74] The rooms were warm, free, they possessed the newspapers, and the newspapers contained positions vacant columns

[67] Eisenberg and Lazarsfeld, 365.

[68] Because library charges were effectly abolished in Marienthal.

[69] Bakke, 178.

[70] Jennings, 138–41. See also A. D. Lindsay, 'Unemployment: the "Meanwhile" Problem', *Contemporary Review* (June 1933), 687–95.

[71] Beales and Lambert, 70.   [72] Ibid. 105.

[73] Bakke, 194. His diarists read on averge 10.7 hours a week. Eisenberg and Lazarsfeld concede that Bakke's evidence ran counter to their own (Eisenberg and Lazarsfeld, 364).   [74] Caradog Jones *et al.*, ii. 300.

and (where interfering librarians had not excised them) the racing results. The scene in a principal Liverpool library was typical of much of urban Britain:

Some [unemployed men] come to look for vacancies in the newspapers; others read trade and technical papers, detective stories or magazines. Three of those reading rooms have a special arrangement by which urgent vacancies for workers are reported to them by telephone from the Employment Exchange and are posted up.[75]

Like the labour exchanges they were markets of gossip but since they were also where books reposed, books were often read. They were ideal places for someone like this embittered engineer who thought only of 'warm sheltered places like the public library, where I like to read revolutionary novels'.[76] For both cultural and economic reasons the library in Marienthal did not perform these functions with, presumably, the consequences Jahoda *et al.* record.

As to the cinema, it is unlikely that the unemployed went to it any more than they did when in work. The Pilgrim Trust's survey, indeed, seemed to show that unemployed men in the large towns went to the pictures less than they used to;[77] and Bakke, though he admitted that skilled workmen were very reluctant to abandon the cinema, thought they would do so if they had to. Like Jennings he believed the unemployed were more likely to desert the pub than the picture palace.[78] The important point, however, is simply that cinema-attending was a very popular working-class pastime; that the unemployed continued going showed nothing except that they wanted to do what they had always done.[79]

Equally, what constitutes intellectual interests depends partly upon cultural definitions. The pervasiveness of racing-talk and betting amongst the unemployed was noticed by everybody but whether it was regretted or not depended on a priori assumptions. One assumption, argued specifically by Zawardski and Lazarsfeld, was that the passion for betting was a 'pathological' consequence of unemployment.[80] To the unemployed the future was dominated by fortune; the best a man could hope for was good luck. Bakke also thought this: 'The worker sees all about him experienced and skilled men with no work to do. If he is in work, he feels lucky. If

[75] Ibid.   [76] Beales and Lambert, 75.   [77] See below p. 257.
[78] Bakke, 263.   [79] Kelvin and Jarrett, 69.
[80] Zawardski and Lazarsfeld, 248.

he is out of work he is the victim of hard luck.'[81] It is not surprising if the unemployed thought good luck as likely to find a man a job as anything else, since in many places clearly it was. It is doubtful, however, if betting can be explained in the same way. I have already argued that betting, both for the employed and the unemployed, *was* an intellectual activity where the minimizing of luck was part of the satisfaction.[82] Furthermore, if, as to many unemployed they were, the operations of the labour exchange appeared random and vindictive, it was not 'irrational' to trust in fortune's smiles. One unemployed man 'actually drew a contrast between the fairness of the pools and the alleged favouritism of the Exchange'.[83]

Betting had another obvious function. It allowed physical and emotional excitement when comparative poverty deprived people of other 'stimulation'. Max Cohen thought that people's 'stamina' was 'undermined' when they were denied stimulants, tea and cigarettes in his case: 'Anyone who is deprived of a stimulant to which he has become accustomed suffers, in the early stages, at any rate, from a weakening of the faculties.'[84] Betting might also have helped to compensate for the loss of what was politely called 'romantic' interests, something the unemployed felt keenly but about which it was still thought not nice to enquire.[85] In fact, the appeal of betting to the unemployed was straightforward: it was culturally sanctioned, it permitted a genuine intellectual activity, and it induced physical excitement.

The last and most important of the stage-theory's conclusions

---

[81] Bakke, 14.   [82] See above, pp. 118–24.   [83] Pilgrim Trust, 99.

[84] Cohen, 41. Beales and Lambert's 'skilled millwright' told them that 'perhaps I miss cigarettes most' (Beales and Lambert, 105).

[85] Cohen, who was a little less reticent about these things, wrote that 'young people need that interchange of experience between the sexes known as "romance". Too often unemployment makes a romantic social life impossible' (Cohen, 159). Although this is exactly the area where the social psychologist might have enquired, Lazarsfeld *et al.* do not appear to have done so. Zawardski–Lazarsfeld say that only two of their autobiographies mention sex, though one of those is pretty febrile (Zawardski and Lazarsfeld, 234 n.). There is an appendix to the Beales and Lambert volume by Morris Robb on the medical consequences of unemployment. He concluded that for married men and women 'sexual congress' first increases and then decreases with unemployment. 'Additional nervous strain' is imposed on the individual by *coitus interruptus*, the cheapest form of contraception. (Beales and Lambert, pp. 277–8.) Perhaps this is proof of A. J. P. Taylor's famous assertion that withdrawal rendered the British a repressed nation, with all its awful consequences (A. J. P. Taylor, *English History, 1914–1945* (London, 1965), 166).

concern the political activities and associationalism of the un-employed. The authors of *Marienthal* measured the unemployed's growing disinclination to retain, let alone seek, membership of clubs and organizations, and a dimunition of both political activity and partisanship.[86] They concluded that this was accompanied by a disintegration of ideological solidarity. Zawardski and Lazarsfeld wrote:

This fact of the disassociation of feelings of solidarity among the proletarians, the shift in class consciousness, the split in the masses, *explains the weakness of the unemployed as a mass: the masses cease to exist as such when the social bond—the consciousness of belonging together—does not hold any longer.* There remains only scattered, loose, perplexed, and hopeless individuals. *The unemployed are a mass only numerically, not socially.*[87]

The unemployed's explanation for their plight is thus individualistic and not structural. Their anger was directed not against capitalism or 'the system' but against the lucky, those in work.[88]

As a description, much of this was true. Not only did trade-union membership decline (which could, however, be explained on a number of grounds) but there appears to have been considerable hostility to the unions among the unemployed: largely because they seemed helpful only to those in work. The Beales and Lambert autobiographies are eloquent here. A South Wales miner, asking himself what effect unemployment had on him, replied:

It has definitely lessened my interest in politics, because it has led me to believe that politics is a game of bluff and that these people do not care a brass farthing for the bottom dog . . . The same applies to the trade unions; when it comes to a real test they are hopeless.[89]

A 'skilled millwright' said he 'had no wish to attend political meetings',[90] an unskilled labourer was simply 'not interested in politics'.[91] Newsom noted how cynical about the Labour Party and the trade unions many unemployed miners were.[92] Further-more, some unemployed or their families might well have directed their bitterness against the employed, as did the wife of Walter Brierley's hero.[93]

[86] *Marienthal*, 38–41.   [87] Zawardski and Lazarsfeld, 245.
[88] Ibid. 242.   [89] Beales and Lambert, 69.   [90] Ibid. 105.
[91] J. Newsom, *Out of the Pit* (Oxford, 1936), 21–2.   [92] Ibid. 127–8.
[93] Brierley, 66–7.

The stage-theory argues, in effect, that the unemployed have no politics. The elimination of political interests is no doubt gradual but it is inexorable: the last stage of unemployment extinguishes the last flickerings of political enthusiasm. This is the conventional wisdom and a good deal of the literature has attempted to explain why the unemployed were so apolitical. But *everyone* has a politics. The question is not why the unemployed were apolitical but whether their politics was appropriate to their circumstances.

In brief, beyond wanting employment, the political aims of the unemployed in Britain were twofold: to defend personal privacy and to maintain unemployment benefit. The theatre of their politics was the labour exchange and its actors were the claimaints, the clerks, the supervisors, the interviewing officers, the court of referees, and the 'means test man'. The exchanges themselves were politically contentious; however benignly they behaved they were regarded by the unemployed as enemy territory. The first reason for that was material; being underfinanced, the exchanges were grim and shabby. To the unemployed these impressions were powerful and unforgettable. 'The inside of the Exchange was dingy and repellent to the eye,' Max Cohen remembered. 'There appeared to be a large number of notices forbidding one to do this and warning one of the penalties of doing that.'[94] The Ministry of Labour was aware of this. 'We are not at all proud of the premises we are in,' J. F. G. Price told Margaret Bondfield, 'and we are always doing our best, without being extravagant, to get more suitable accommodation for our work. Some of our premises are certainly not a credit to us.'[95] On the whole, they remained not a credit to them for another forty years. Though men and women, despite their fears, usually adjusted to the dole queue and real or imagined stigmas, to the horrors of the exchanges themselves they hardly ever adjusted:

Well, it's the way they treat you, somehow. It's the way the chairs are arranged. You go in and you sit down on a chair and you find it's bolted down to the floor and you can't move it. And when you come up to the counter, if you want to speak to the guy you've got to sit forward on the edge of your chair, and he's behind a little window, and he says 'Speak Up' . . . I don't mind them messing me about, but the trouble is there are some genu-ine claimants up there, and they get messed about as well.[96]

[94] Cohen, 3; see also 6–7.
[95] Unemployment Insurance Committee [Blanesburgh], *Minutes of Evidence*, Q 270.
[96] Marsden, 88.

The second reason was the individuals they had to deal with. The clerks at the exchanges were in an impossible position. They were under constant pressure from on-high (as they are still) to detect abuse and this became almost obsessional.[97] Before the abolition of the 'genuinely seeking work' clause in 1930 the unemployed were subject to 'a futile and sometimes brutal ritual' in which few believed.[98] After 1931 new discriminations were introduced, *inter alia* the means test, even more resented. The result was that however helpful or willing were the overworked clerks, however well-intentioned the supervisors and means test officers, however fair the courts of referees, they all were servants of 'them', all trying to do down the unemployed. Unemployed men, particularly, were disposed to regard the exchanges as hostile from the outset, even if for the great majority most of the time the collection of benefit was automatic. Jennings wrote:

If he has been out of work for some time, each Friday he will have a short period of sickening anxiety lest the clerk should single him out and tell him he is to be sent to the 'Court of Referees'; then will follow a few days' consequent dread lest his benefit should be stopped and he be cast on to the Poor Law, have to do 'task work' for his maintenance, and take home less to his family in return for it.[99]

The clerks themselves did not help—'pleasantness soon wears off when forty to fifty men step up to [his] box every fifteen minutes.'[100] Their permanently interrogatory air acounted for their unpopularity. Bakke records one man saying

And the bloody blokes wouldn't have their jobs if it wasn't for us men out of a job either. That's what gets me about them holding their noses up.
     They treat you like a lump of dirt they do. I see a navvy reach across the counter and shake one of them by the collar the other day. The rest of us felt like cheering.[101]

The dislike of the unemployed for the interviewing officers (who investigated claims of dubious eligibility) and the courts of referees was probably more justified. The interviewing officers, even more than the clerks, were on the hunt for scroungers; success on the job was measured by disallowed claims. Bakke noted of the officers:

[97] Kelvin and Jarrett, 88.
[98] A. Deacon, *In Search of the Scrounger* (London, 1976), 61.
[99] Jennings, 138.   [100] Bakke, 79.   [101] Ibid. 80.

There is an altogether disproportionate sense, on the part of the men connected with the interviewing with whom I came to touch, of their ability to 'size up' their man by a sort of intuition. It was a significant fact to me that the source of satisfaction which seemed to me most prominent was the ability to detect the 'non-genuine' cases rather than the ability to be really helpful to a man in his search for work.[102]

The result was that the unemployed person was ready for war if summoned before the officer. 'He goes in a defensive state of mind prepared to engage in a battle of wits.'[103] The unemployed responded with considerable ingenuity. What a particular officer wanted to hear was quickly transmitted down the line and successive 'candidates' met him with increasing confidence.

The unemployed were most likely to come before the court of referees when they went on to transitional benefit. For the state this marked an important boundary; for the men and women it signified only that all insurance contributions had been exhausted. The court was supposed to discover whether the claimant was in practice seeking work. Neither court nor claimant actually knew what was meant by that, whether (say) a skilled worker *should* accept unskilled labour. Furthermore, the courts were over-burdened, ill-informed about the applicant, and composed of people whose acquaintance with the life of the unemployed was, to say the least, second-hand.[104] The unemployed approached the court as '*an individual* who during the last quarter was the same man with the same qualifications and the same worth, save for the very important fact that at the moment he is not able to show thirty stamps on his cards during the last two years.'[105] He thus bore the courts the same hostility he bore the interviewing officers and adopted the same tactics. As to the means test officers, little needs saying. However helpful and pleasant individual officers were found, as representatives of a system which intruded humiliatingly into working-class privacy they were hated.

The third reason for the dislike of the exchanges was their failure as exchanges. Throughout the 1930s only about one-fifth of adult vacancies were filled through them. There seems little doubt that the unemployed lacked faith in the exchanges as places to find work; a scepticism shared by those many employers who made no

[102] Ibid. 98.   [103] Ibid. 97.   [104] Deacon, 57.
[105] Bakke, 106–7.

attempt to use them. The result was, as Llewellyn Smith observed, that the

unemployed worker who relies on the Exchange became disheartened . . . Sometimes even the Exchange appears to him as an obstruction standing between him and a job.

> 'The Labour Exchange is closing down to-day
> And father's going to work to-morrow'

is the refrain of a popular East End song.[106]

The exchanges became simply instruments for state hand-outs; normally given but (it appeared) grudgingly, and by hostile officials searching for any excuse to withdraw them. The Carnegie team (which used the exchanges as places for interview) indeed commented on the difficulties this caused them:

In the minds of many unemployed men all statements made within the Exchange buildings are liable to investigation or a measure of correction on the spot . . . They tend to regard all interviews as things to be avoided or, at least, opportunities for revealing as little as possible, in case any statement made should subsequently work out to their detriment.[107]

The attitude of the unemployed to the exchanges was, therefore, almost wholly negative; *pro tanto* so was their attitude to similar government agencies and to philanthropic bodies such as the National Council for Social Service. The Pilgrim Trust study, written under the influence of the National Council, admitted that the 'queue' created an unemployed 'community' and generated a powerful 'opinion':

Evidently the unemployed clubs are in many places the subject of unemployed gossip in the queue, and the frequency with which the laconic criticism 'dope' is made against them, suggested that it was also an idea originating in this way. It looks as if many of the unjustified views of the Unemployment Assistance Board regulations are derived from the same source. Many unemployed men, for instance, conceal small occasional earnings for which no deductions would be made from their allowances. The printed leaflet stands little chance against this strong public opinion.[108]

---

[106] H. Llewellyn Smith (ed.) *The New Survey of London Life and Labour* (London, 1932), iii. 175.   [107] Carnegie Trust, 4.

[108] Pilgrim Trust, 161; for examples of this hostility to the clubs, see E. Wilkinson, *The Town that was Murdered* (London, 1939), 233–4; A. Hutt, *The Condition of the Working Class in Britain* (London, 1933), 45–6.

All this was certainly an introverted and local politics but it bears little resemblance to Lazarsfeld's account of the political apathy of the unemployed. It was actively hostile not so much to the general policies of the state—though they also were disliked—as to its agents. Jennings, who thoroughly disapproved of this sectarianism, none the less admitted that it was effective politics:

For the mass of the unemployed, local politics in South Wales only concentrate their thoughts more firmly on the material problems of their existence. 'Vote Labour, and put an end to poverty, misery, and Courts of Referees' is the popular slogan, not 'Stand together and assert the value of man and his right and duty to express himself by work.'[109]

Its governing dictum was 'always believe the worst' and it was assumed, rightly or wrongly, that the unemployed were engaged in a perpetual struggle to win their due. Four years after writing *The Unemployed Man* Bakke concluded that 'workers who have been without jobs for long periods in all parts of the country begin to look upon the protection of their benefit at a maximum rate as their main object.'[110]

It is, of course, possible to argue that though this might indeed be a 'politics', it was a mutilated one. Above all, it failed to achieve, and did not even try to achieve, the first hope of the unemployed, employment. This is, in effect, what W. G. Runciman has argued. Since, he suggests, the unemployed's range of reference was so limited, they were incapable of making political judgements except in relation to their own kind. Politics was not an activity concerned with the state but with maintaining comparabilities with other unemployed. It is this, he believes, which gives the 'uprising' of the unemployed in 1935 its significance.[111] Justifying his fairly lengthy account of the reaction of the unemployed to the 1934 Unemployment Insurance Act, he writes:

The episode is worth narrating in some detail because it provides a striking illustration of the extent to which the frustration of modest expectation led not only to a more intense and widespread sense of

[109] Jennings, 141.
[110] E. W. Bakke, *Insurance or Dole* (New Haven, 1935), 198.
[111] Under the 1934 Unemployment Insurance Act the government imposed centrally determined benefit rates. When they were introduced in 1935 it was found that in some parts of the country this meant an actual reduction in benefit. Widespread demonstrations by the unemployed and much public opposition forced the government to introduce a series of 'standstill' orders suspending the changes.

relative deprivation than, for instance, the cuts of 1931 but also earned the victims of the new dispensation more outspoken and influential support than they would have been accorded if their hardship had not been compounded by the Government's fallacious predictions of improvement.[112]

Lazarsfeld's description of the political inertia of the unemployed might, therefore, still be right, even though his explanation for it might be wrong.

It would be surprising if there were not at least something to Runciman's view; but, none the less, it almost fundamentally misunderstands what were the political possibilities open to the unemployed. In the first place, the different behaviour of the unemployed in 1931 and 1935 is largely to be explained by different historical circumstances. In 1931 the *whole* country was supposed to be making a sacrifice; in 1935 the sacrifice was visited gratuitously upon the unemployed alone. That the 'sacrifices' made by the rest of the country in 1931 were largely spurious does not alter the fact that the way the crisis was presented made it very difficult for the unemployed to claim an exemption. This was not true of 1935.

In the second, Runciman's argument implies political alternatives for the unemployed which simply were not there. It was not possible (as I have argued)[113] to include the unemployed in a kind of Keynesian majority because it was not possible to create such a majority anyway. The unemployed were socially and geographically isolated; they were poor or very poor; they were largely excluded from conventional political life, and they were a minority. Nothing they said or did was likely to change overall government policies and if much of their anger was directed at those in work this was not an unreasonable response to a government one of whose implied strategies after 1931 was the attempted mobilization of those in work against those out of it. Although many of the unemployed may well have regarded unemployment as a misfortune, as Runciman suggests, there were also many who thought it was the fault of the state. The Carnegie survey noted that when

a young man finds that his own community has no use for the services he has to offer, there is a natural tendency for him to look to the super-

---

[112] W. G. Runciman, *Relative Deprivation and Social Justice* (Harmondsworth, 1972), 78–80.   [113] See below, pp. 259–86.

community, the State to set the crooked straight. The attitude was the more noticeable as unemployment increased. Failure to find work became less a matter of personal reproach and more a cause for criticism of the Government.[114]

They could, however, contrive no way of inducing the state to change its practices. Cynicism or indifference was a fair response.

But the unemployed were not indifferent to *dole* politics. This was so partly because other people's guilt was one of the few political weapons the unemployed possessed. Society might not have been ready to create jobs for them but it did not deny all responsibility: the dole was the ransom property was prepared to pay. But it was also partly due to the fact that the state chose to fight the battle on the ground of the dole. The attitude of successive Conservative governments was necessarily ambiguous here: indefinite dole payment was 'safe' because it obviated other more politically unacceptable forms of coping with unemployment and it created a huge client population which might be rendered docile by the threat of withdrawal of payment. But equally the government could not appear to be soft-hearted or weak or to be publicly sanctioning a way of life (unemployment) in which, in fact, it undoubtedly connived. Thus one of the purposes, and certainly one of the consequences, of unemployment insurance legislation was to marginalize the unemployed, to divide them by newer and ever more refined discriminations, and, by a public pursuit of the scrounger, to confirm politically necessary stereotypes. Thus it was that the exchanges themselves, the size of the dole, and the manner of its payment became, as we have seen, the appropriate focus of politics. Furthermore, by localizing politics, by confining it to the exchanges and their personnel, the unemployed maintained some command over the political structure of their lives and ensured that psychological tension which is an essential part of successful political action. A more 'revolutionary' politics almost certainly would have failed, and by failing have discredited politics altogether. Even Hannington tacitly recognized this and 'unemployed struggles' became increasingly a struggle to maintain benefit 'at its maximum rate'.[115] As Eveline Burns pointed out, what was remarkable after the 'standstill' crisis was the extreme nervousness of the Unemployment Assistance Board

[114] Carnegie Trust, 68.
[115] W. Hannington, *Unemployed Struggles* (London, 1936), 298–313.

about deploying the elaborate apparatus of coercion or discipline which the 1934 Act created and the obvious reluctance of the government to put pressure on it to do so.[116] The success of the 'uprising' in 1935 shows, indeed, how correctly the unemployed had judged what was politically available to them. Runciman's argument must, therefore, be treated with considerable caution; as must Lazarsfeld's.

What then remains of the stage-theory? Not much. And what can be rescued is largely truistic. There was never any reason to doubt that the lives of most men and women were in some sense work-centred. Nor is it surprising, therefore, that the loss of work could cause dismay and even despair. But it is hard to go beyond that. We cannot convincingly argue that the unemployed disintegrated, that their mental faculties withered, that they lost interest in work, that they became apolitical, or that there was some sort of progressive decline. What is surprising, rather, is how little any of these things happened. We are left with a thesis which is at best descriptive, at worst misleading and with almost no explanatory power.

What went wrong? The empirical basis upon which the thesis was built was much too slight. It was difficult to generalize from Marienthal itself. The town had 77 per cent unemployment, high even by depressed area standards, and was small, smaller than Brynmawr. It was unusual in having extremely high rates of both male and female long-term unemployment. In addition, the study was of the residential population. There was no attempt to look at those who had gone to find work in Czechoslovakia or other parts of Austria; nor did the authors make much allowance for the fact that it was a residual survey. *Marienthal* is, therefore, a rather hit-or-miss *description* of a single-industry village of exceptionally high long-term unemployment from which limited conclusions can be drawn.

The Polish autobiographies, though they make compelling reading, have negligible value as historical evidence. Their commissioning was itself a dubious enterprise. The sample was not established with any rigour; indeed, almost the reverse is true. The main criterion for selection was the writer's ability to 'express

---

[116] E. M. Burns, *British Unemployment Programs, 1920–1938* (Washington, DC, 1941), 295.

himself'. Although Zawardski and Lazarsfeld admitted their contributors were of the 'higher' strata of the unemployed and perhaps not statistically representative, they contented themselves with the alarming observation that the writers were 'phenomeno-logically representative': their 'utterances give a vivid picture of the experiences of those who are less able to express themselves'.[117] The result is a collection of autobiographies embodying the more deeply felt existential experiences of those who wrote them and little else.

Further, Lazarsfeld and his colleagues had no clear idea of what questions should be asked. Lazarsfeld originally wanted to look at working-class leisure; it was Otto Bauer who put him on to unemployment.[118] But the study was never put in a cultural context; at no point did they ask what the *employed* life of Marienthal had been like. An unemployed community was abstracted from its history and a series of secondary effects described. In part, this was due to the then nature of social psychology. In 1934, the American social psychologist Harvey Cantril, in a famous article, suggested that the questions the social psychologist should ask of unemployment included: to what extent did it affect the unemployed man's sense of time, personal appearance, attitude to shaving—women did not become un-employed in 1934, it seems—washing, sexual behaviour, reading, etc. These questions, though interesting, all concerned secondary effects.[119] Only an inquiry into the cultural and social circum-stances in which the unemployed lived prior to unemployment could make these secondary effects intelligible.

What should the prior questions have been? Bakke suggested that the way a man reacted to unemployment was influenced by eleven variables,[120] but we probably need to look only at five, recognizing that in practice all overlap; income, length of unemployment, degree of skill, the sex of the unemployed person, and (above all) the occupational and associational culture from which the unemployed came.

[117] Zawardski and Lazarsfeld, 224–6.

[118] D. L. Sills, 'Paul Lazarsfeld', in *International Encyclopaedia of the Social Sciences*, 18 (1968), 411–13.

[119] H. Cantril, 'The Social Psychology of Everyday Life', *The Psychological Bulletin* 31. 5 (May 1934), 317–18.

[120] Bakke, 257–8; see also A. Sinfield, 'Unemployment in an Unequal Society', B. Showler and A. Sinfield (eds.), *The Workless State* (Oxford, 1981), 153.

The first, degree of poverty, was largely overlooked by Lazarsfeld and his colleagues. This was important since the economic conditions of the unemployed differed widely. The workless of Marienthal were paid a dole even after their insurance contribution had been exhausted; the Polish received nothing after thirteen weeks. The British unemployed lived under yet a different economic regime, a bit more above the margin, and their preoccupations were thus somewhat different. The ability to cope with unemployment is in part dependent upon existing financial resources; a hungry man, for example, is less fitted to find a job. Even so, as Kelvin and Jarrett point out, it is almost impossible to make 'the crucially important distinction between the effects of unemployment and the effects of the poverty which almost invariably goes with it'.[121] Nowhere was this distinction made adequately and often not at all in the psychological literature of the 1930s.

The second thing we would need to know was a man's experience and expectations. For an unskilled worker whose life was always one job after another even a prolonged period out of work might not seem very unusual; and we should remember that, even at the bottom of the depression, most unemployed were not long-term but typically came on and off the unemployment register. A skilled worker might be buoyed up by the hope that skills gave him a premium in the market. However, he could also find unemployment more difficult than that same unskilled worker for whom it was a recurrent fact of life. In Liverpool, the Pilgrim Trust wrote, 'the importance of this must be clear to anyone who knows the sordid but easygoing and social atmosphere of the old districts'—

where the unemployed man has his corner, his friends, his library, and his bookmaker, where he speaks freely when you call on him, where he calls his friends in to tell you all about it, where not much is spent on rent and next to nothing on upkeep. Such an atmosphere is utterly different from that in the housing estates, where the unemployed man takes an anxious look round when you mention unemployment to him and rapidly tells you to come in.[122]

For some, usually called 'work-shy' in the literature, the distinction between employment and unemployment hardly even mattered.

[121] Kelvin and Jarrett, 127–8.   [122] Pilgrim Trust, 92.

The chances are that he is mixed up with some betting concern, or that he keeps greyhounds, or picks up something here and there in addition to his Unemployment Assistance by hawking or street singing . . . He may be dressed rather flashily and the chances are that he will complain of those men who won't work, contrasting them with hard triers like himself.[123]

They were like the hard trier interviewed by the Trust, despite a warning that he 'throws culinary articles at his parents, habitually uses filthy language, frequents gambling clubs, and is a book-maker's tout'. ' "A real clever boy", his mother . . . described him.'[124]

Experience was also affected by skill. The skilled worker was more likely to know the ropes than the unskilled; he was probably more competent at finding a job—by writing letters, for example—and was more likely to have a union to fall back on. Since skilled men were better paid he usually had greater resources at the outset and probably more domestic comfort. He was also in a better position to devise alternative routines; more likely to have a garden or an allotment and his own tools and skills which could be converted. Kelvin and Jarrett's 1981 observation that 'we have . . . occasional fleeting glimpses of unemployed skilled men pursuing skilled activities in garden sheds, of salesmen setting out to sell themselves, or managers making an office of their dining room to manage their search for work and so on'[125] should in principle be true of the inter-war years, and much of the evidence suggests that it was. (But we should not exaggerate distinctions between skilled and unskilled; 'unskilled' men could be very flexible and, in certain circumstances, might have been able to cope better than that comparatively small part of the work-force we can properly call 'skilled'.)

Although the psychological literature (and not just the psychological) made little of sex differences, it is clear that women's experience of unemployment could differ widely from that of men. This had little to do with unemployment as such. How women reacted to unemployment was largely dependent upon cultural conventions, of which family status was the most important. For an unemployed woman spinner with an unemployed husband (quite common in Lancashire) and several children receiving perhaps for the first time a comparatively secure needs-related

[123] Pilgrim Trust, 173.   [124] Ibid. 174–5.
[125] Kelvin and Jarrett, 56.

income, unemployment could be a blessing; on the other hand, for a not-very-sociable single woman living in lodgings, a misery.

Finally, the way people managed unemployment was very largely determined by the life they led before they became unemployed. Lazarsfeld *et al.* were impressed by the rapid decline in the associational *capacity* of the unemployed. But in Britain there is little evidence of this. If men dropped out of clubs, or organizations dissolved, this was due largely either to poverty or to the migration of those normally most active in clubs and societies.[126] If unemployed people were aimless or isolated this was often because their non-working lives had always been aimless or isolated. The Pilgrim Trust was struck by this: a place like Rhondda ('a hotbed of associations') gave great associational support for the unemployed because it had always led an intense collective life. Liverpool was exactly the reverse. The trust comments:

In the case of unemployed men . . . the sample visit suggests strongly that it is not because they spend time going to the cinema or taking part in other commercialised pleasures that in large towns it is so difficult to run effective clubs for them; but rather that in the large towns they live very much emptier lives and that they probably go less often, and not more often to the cinema . . . the real obstacle in the way of building up a good club in a large city is not the competition of commercialised amusements but the lack of any social foundations on which to begin.[127]

This was by no means the only obstacle in the way of an 'effective club'—though the Trust would not admit that—but the general point is almost certainly right. What and how much unemployed people read, went to the pictures, were politically active, or joined clubs largely depended on how far they did those things when they were in work. 'Pathological' characteristics of unemployment, the passion for betting, for example, were simply 'pathological' characteristics of working-class life. Furthermore, the dole was a kind of wage and it permitted a good deal of social continuity. Consequently, as Bakke pointed out, the unemployed did not think of themselves as a class *qua* unemployed. 'The comparative security provided by the social services . . . has served well to

[126] A. D. K. Owen, 'The Social Consequences of Industrial Transference', *The Sociological Review*, 39 (1937), 343–4.
[127] Pilgrim Trust, 275–6; see particularly, Table LIX, 274.

keep them from being conscious that they have interests as a group of *unemployed* apart from their interests as *workers*.'[128] Even if not working they remained tied to many aspects of working-class life, to old habits and expectations, which they tried to preserve.[129] That people were not wrenched from their class and community, and that family life remained largely intact, explains why the unemployed were so resilient and, in the circumstances, so unscathed.

[128] Bakke, 236.

[129] The curious lack of an imaginative sympathy for the unemployed which Lazarsfeld *et al.* possess is almost crassly displayed here. Noting the tendency of the unemployed to indulge in 'irrational spending', they write: 'For example, it is reported that in a small group of partially unemployed Flemish workers just outside of Brussels pigeons are bought and kept at great expense because of the owner's hope that some day his pigeon will win a worthless trinket in a race. These same workers spend a good part of their annual income so that their children will have the proper outfit for communion' (Eisenberg and Lazarsfeld, 360). See also S. Constantine, *Unemployment in Britain between the Wars* (London, 1980), 17–44.

9

Class and Conventional Wisdom:
The Conservative Party and the 'Public' in
Inter-war Britain

IN a previous chapter I argued that the British constitutional and political system promoted its legitimacy in two ways: by excluding the relationship of the organized working class to civil society from the sphere of 'politics' and by discreetly undermining the authority of the employing class.[1] This strategy was pursued with considerable success until the outbreak of the First World War. Yet it was also faltering. The argument that the claims of the industrial working class on society could indefinitely be confined to the margins was by 1914 increasingly unconvincing. Equally, it is doubtful that the employing class would accept for long a situation in which it seemed more and more disadvantaged, or would refrain from seeking allies amongst social groups who also felt themselves oppressed by the weight of the organized working class. By 1918, it was clear that the strategy had not simply faltered, it had failed: society's relations with the working class had at last become the central political problem, while the 'middle classes' had made it clear that they were not prepared to play a subordinate role in the new order. It is the purpose of this chapter to examine one of the most significant consequences of that transformation: the Conservative Party's electoral domination of inter-war Britain.

The electoral success of the Conservative Party between the wars is something we almost take for granted, yet we have hardly any adequate explanation for it. While folk-wisdom, for example, has it that the Conservatives are always in office (and thus there is nothing to explain) folk-wisdom is actually wrong: there has in most of recent British history been close two-party competition. In the period 1886–1915, from the Home Rule crisis to the formation of the Asquith–Bonar Law coalition, the Conservatives were in office 16½ years and the Liberals 12½. In the period 1940 to 1979,

[1] See above, pp. 26–32.

from the formation of Churchill's coalition to the defeat of the Callaghan government, the Conservatives were in office 17 years, Labour 17 years, and they shared power in the Second World War. In the inter-war period, however, the Conservatives, either independently or in governments they dominated, were in office for 17 of the 20 years. For all these 17 years, as is well known, they had huge parliamentary majorities. Furthermore, while it is true that the British electoral system absurdly favours a party with a plurality of the votes, we should not depreciate the Conservative Party's popular success, which is actually concealed by the raw votes (see Table 9.1.)[2]

TABLE 9.1. *Conservative Party performance in general elections (% of vote)*

	1923	1924	1929	1931	1935
Votes actually cast	38.0	46.8	38.1	60.7	53.3
'Two-party preferred' vote estimate	58.0	58.0	55.0	67.0	59.0

Note: In calculating the Conservative Party's preferred vote in 1923 and 1924, the Liberal vote has been allocated as it seems to have split in 1924—3: 2. In 1929 it is assumed that the split was more likely to favour the Conservatives—3: 1. For the 1930s calculations the Opposition Liberal vote is more evenly split, though still favouring the Conservatives; this may underestimate the preferred Conservative vote, but not significantly.

But if we adopt a two-party preferred analysis—that is, if we suppose that at each general election all voters who did not vote for either of the two largest parties (Conservative and Labour) were required to choose between them[3]—it is likely that the Conservatives would have got a majority of the preferred vote at every general election, including those two, 1923 and 1929, which they 'lost'. Why should we think this? The 'old' Liberal vote, which the Liberals lost more or less permanently after 1918, divided almost equally between the Conservatives and Labour Parties. After 1923, however, the Liberal vote was, I shall argue, or was becoming, a quasi-Conservative vote, a protest vote by

[2] Percentages are of the vote for the United Kingdom.
[3] This is a technique devised by Mr Malcolm Mackerras to analyse voting figures for Australian general elections where preferential voting is compulsory.

social groups who would in future normally vote Conservative.[4] If this is so, Liberal voters would not give their second preferences more or less equally to the two major parties. Nor did they: in 1924 the ex-Liberal vote went to the Conservatives by about three to two; in 1931 it did so almost unanimously. It is true that in 1931 circumstances were uniquely favourable to the Conservatives, but it is less true of 1924 when in many ways the rhetorical victory was Labour's. It is thus likely that in those two inter-war elections, 1923 and 1929, in which the Conservatives were apparently defeated,[5] they still had the first or second preferences of the majority of voters—a majority of the 'preferred vote'. Although the 1929 elections indicated the later pattern of the Labour vote, they almost certainly exaggerated Labour's preferred support. What exactly that preferred vote was in the 1920s we can only guess. In the 1930s, however, we can estimate the two major parties' preferred vote more accurately, since in much of the country a two-party system was by then operating.

There are undoubtedly problems with calculating a preferred vote in a country where preferential voting is not required; we must inevitably try to guess what people might have done in circumstances where they are not expected to give a preferred vote. Many, probably, would not have voted at all. But it is, none the less, useful in several ways. By overriding (so to speak) the vagaries of the electoral system it establishes a certain continuity between the Conservative Party's actual vote in the 1920s and its actual vote in the 1930s. If our calculation of the preferred vote is roughly correct, for example, then the Tory preferred vote in 1923 was only slightly lower than in 1935, yet in 1923 the Conservative Party won 258 seats and in 1935 (with its allies) 429. It also has a negative utility. It suggests that overall the Labour Party made no two-party gains between 1923 and 1935; that while its actual vote in 1935 was a little higher than in 1929, its preferred vote was still substantially lower;[6] and that there was throughout the period a

[4] See below, pp. 276–82.

[5] That is, Labour governments dependent upon Liberal support took office on both occasions. In 1923 the Conservative Party was still the largest party.

[6] Dr Butler has pointed out that the percentage of the vote obtained by each Labour candidate at elections between 1922 and 1935 also remained constant, at 40% (D. E. Butler, *The Electoral System in Britain since 1918* (Oxford, 1963), p. 177). This, however, is slightly misleading as the total number of Labour candidates rose from 414 to 552, nearly all of the increase being in seats which were hopeless for Labour.

large anti-Labour majority in the country, with the Conservative Party struggling to mobilize it. This it did more successfully in the 1930s than in the 1920s. The difference is the degree of partisan support: as the electorate was polarized the Conservative Party's actual vote approached its preferred vote and that accounts for its gargantuan parliamentary majorities. This was, however, exceptional. We can see how exceptional by comparing it with the Conservative Party's preferred vote in the two elections on either side of the inter-war period—the two 1910 elections and those of 1945 and 1950 (see Table 9.2.).

TABLE 9.2. *Conservative Party share of estimated two-party preferred vote (%)*

Jan. 1910	Dec. 191	1945	1950
47.0	47.0	45.5	49.0

There is no comprehensive historical explanation for this success. We could begin, for example, by concluding that to vote Conservative is the 'natural' thing to do: to do anything else, as Frank Parkin argues, is simply deviant.[7] The Conservative Party is associated with the predominant value order and only those outside that order, those who for some reason or other feel themselves excluded from it (and who are, almost *ex hypothesi*, a minority), will support other political parties. This rather universal explanation has a narrower variant: the Conservative Party is the English nationalist party and while this diminishes its appeal in Scotland and Wales it gives the Conservatives an immense cross-class appeal in England itself.

We could add to this a couple of more historically specific explanations. First, as John Ramsden points out, the post-1918 electoral redistribution was particularly favourable to the Conservative Pary. The new boundaries had given the Conservatives a net gain of about 30 seats, while the withdrawal of the Irish from Westminster had deprived the 'progressive' parties of the support

[7] F. Parkin, 'Working-class Conservatives: a Theory of Political Deviance', *British Journal of Sociology* 18 (1967), 278–89.

of anything from 70 to 80 MPs.[8] And this was a greater gain than Ramsden suggests. The Irish settlement left Northern Ireland with representation in the House of Commons (12 seats of whom at least 10 were Unionists); since the other 2, Irish Nationalists of various sorts, hardly ever took their seats the settlement was pure loss for the non-Conservative parties. Contrary to what is often thought, the pre-1914 Liberal governments did not 'need' the Irish—in the elections of December 1910 the Labour and Liberal parties had a majority of 57 in England, Scotland, and Wales. They 'needed' the Irish only in so far as the Irish were represented at all at Westminster, as they had been since 1800. What they did not need was a settlement which eliminated all southern Irish representation but guaranteed the Unionists 10–12 seats from the North.[9] Furthermore, the universities retained their separate representation in the House and the Conservatives never won fewer than 8 of their 12 seats but Labour never won any. The City of London continued to elect two members—always Conservatives—although the vast majority of the electors did not live in the constituency. And a modified plural vote, the 'business vote', gave the Tories half a dozen or so seats which they otherwise would have lost. Northern Ireland and anachronisms thus inflated the Parliamentary Conservative Party by anything up to 30 seats.[10]

Second, and perhaps the most compelling of these contingent explanations, was the Conservatives' defeat at the 1929 elections. They had, so the argument runs, the extraordinary good fortune to be in opposition at the bottom of the depression. In addition, the Labour Party could scarcely have contrived a more disastrous exit from government than it did in 1931.[11] There must, at least, be some truth in this. In no other English-speaking country did a party ruling in 1930 or 1931 survive for long and it is certainly arguable that a Conservative Party which won the election of 1929 would have been swept away like all the others.

---

[8] J. Ramsden, *The Age of Balfour and Baldwin, 1902–1940* (London, 1978), 122–3.

[9] The 1950 Labour government, for example, was deprived of a good majority in the House of Commons as much by the 10 Unionists as by the workings of the electoral system.

[10] Had these anachronisms been abolished and the Irish Unionists excluded Labour would probably have won an absolute majority in the 1929 elections, a result which almost certainly did not represent opinion in the country.

[11] See above. pp. 218–24.

It might be that these explanations either alone or in combination tell us everything we need to know. All of them are in some sense 'true'; but it is doubtful if they are true enough. The argument that a Conservative vote is a 'normal' vote—as we have seen—runs against the pre-1914 and post-1945 voting patterns when a Conservative vote was often not the 'normal' vote. Furthermore, it exaggerates the extent to which the Liberal and Labour Parties actually disputed the predominant value system or the degree to which their followers felt outside it. Historically, as I have suggested, the area of contention hardly concerned predominant values at all, even if market conflict was acquiring an increasing political centrality.[12]

Equally, the argument that the Conservative Party achieved a unique success by promoting itself as the English National Party is only partly sustainable. It is the case that in every inter-war election the Conservatives polled better in England than in Scotland and Wales. It is also the case that even in 1931 the opposition parties won a majority of the votes and seats in Wales, and Labour probably had a majority of the preferred vote. But while it might indeed be right that 'Englishness' succeeds in England and not in Wales, 'Englishness' cannot explain the Tory Party's electoral triumphs in Scotland. The 1931 general election began a thirty-year cycle in which in Scotland the Conservatives usually had a majority of the preferred vote (64.5 per cent in 1931, 54 per cent in 1935) twice had a majority of the actual votes cast (1931 and 1955) and in 1945, 1951, and 1955 had as high a preferred vote as in England. Nor is it clear why 'Englishness' should be so much more powerful in the inter-war years than before or after.

Finally, we cannot be certain that the depression would have done for the Conservatives as it did for the second Labour government. It is almost inconceivable that they would have surrendered power the way Labour did; it is unlikely that they would have *appeared* as helpless as Labour, even if they were; and they were in a much better position (as I will argue) to exploit the depression as a means of ideological entrenchment than the other British parties or traditional conservative parties elsewhere.

It is clear, however we measure it, that between the wars the

---

[12] See above, pp. 1–41.

Conservatives assembled as formidable and unprecedented coalition of social groups. But they could not and did not (at least objectively) govern in all their interests. In whose interest did they govern, and in whose interest should they govern? At the outset they were not certain, and even after an effectively binding decision had been made in 1920–1 it was some time before the leadership realized how binding it was. Bonar Law and Baldwin, for example, both offered the chancellorship to the former Liberal chancellor, Reginald McKenna (now chairman of the Midland Bank), even though he was consistently critical of the monetary policy the Conservative Party was actually following.[13] In 1922 Sir Robert Horne, Conservative chancellor in the coalition government, overruled the Treasury and risked an 'inflationary' budget (that is, one with a small deficit), while Churchill as chancellor (1924–9) was instinctively sceptical of the policies—particularly the return to the gold standard at parity—which he was compelled to administer. Furthermore, much of industry remained unconvinced about deflationary policies and several of its most powerful representatives, like Sir Alfred Mond, were openly hostile. Nor were Conservative ministers necessarily admirers of the City. In 1931 many of them were dismayed at the performance of the bankers when they actually had to deal with them in government.[14] High interest rates, the gold standard, an overvalued pound, even 'economies' in government expenditure, all had their critics within the Conservative Party. Yet, from 1920 on, when 'dear money' was enthroned,[15] the Party became committed to a 'deflationary' political economy and remained committed to it until the rearmament programmes of the late 1930s made it almost impossible to uphold.[16]

But there was always an 'inflationary' alternative which in an extreme form much of continental Europe experienced and in a

[13] See, for example, his speech to the annual meeting of the Midland Bank, Jan. 1921, reprinted in R. McKenna, *Post-War Banking Policy* (London, 1928), 30–1 partic.

[14] D. Kunz, 'The Battle for Britain's Gold Standard in 1931', M. Litt. thesis (Oxford, 1985), 149.

[15] S. Howson, *Domestic Monetary Management in Britain, 1919–1938* (Cambridge, 1975), 23–4.

[16] I have used 'inflationary' and 'deflationary' here in the way contemporaries used the words, both as technical expressions and as a shorthand to describe tendencies rather than consistent policies. The second, more lax definition is the one which best describes inter-war policies.

modified form the Lloyd George coalition in 1919 felt obliged to adopt. It did this because its main political preoccupation was the need to absorb ex-soldiers rapidly into the civilian labour force. The post-war boom did not simply happen, it was deliberately encouraged by government policy. The boom, even if in a modified way, could amost certainly have continued. It would have meant, for a time anyway, much higher price-inflation than anyone was used to in peacetime, the elimination of considerable private and government debt, high levels of industrial investment and employment, and (necessarily) a depreciating pound. Many would have suffered: those on fixed incomes or on pensions, holders of the national debt and lenders of all sorts, those merchant bankers who lived off foreign issues—since it is unlikely London would have remained for long the major international financial centre, and the non-unionized. Many others would have prospered: industrialists (Keynes believed the inflation was caused by the 'megalomania of Lord Leverhulme' and other industrialists seeking superprofits[17]), the hated 'profiteers', borrowers and heavily indebted sections of the economy, and, of course, the unionized working class. An inflationary regime would have redistributed wealth, and perhaps political power, while establishing a status-order unacceptable to much of the country. It also had real political dangers; it risked almost perpetual industrial strife, the stability of financial institutions, international 'complications', and a reaction from the losers which the political system might not have survived.

In practice, we might expect neither of these rather starkly opposed alternatives to be adopted: however, one was, even if it was not as rigorous as it could have been. From the first half of 1920 onwards, from the raising of bank-rate in April 1920, Britain lived under a 'deflationary' regime which put the safety of the financial institutions ahead of the interests of manufacturing industry, which did not seek large-scale unemployment but was happy to live with it as part of a long-term 'adjustment', which pursued persistently deflationary budgets,[18] determined a fixed exchange rate that, when abandoned in 1931, more or less

[17] Private Sessions of the Macmillan Committee, Transcript, 31 Oct. 1930, 8, Brand Papers, Bodleian Library, Oxford.

[18] R. Middleton, 'The Constant Employment Budget Balance and British Budgetary Policy, 1929–1939', *Economic History Review*, 34 (1981), 281.

everyone said was indefensible, and, though it was not seen as such, plainly put the anxieties of one social class over those of all the others. From 1920 onwards, therefore, the country was governed *essentially* in the perceived interests of those who felt themselves most likely to benefit from deflation, the professional and commercial suburban middle classes and the holders of the government debt (often the same people), the servicing of which, at least until 1931, was regarded as first charge on the budget. It was, certainly, not governed exclusively in their interest but they were the first to be considered and the last to be sacrificed. The earliest casualty of deflation was much of the industrial working class; the next was Lloyd George. A coalition led by him was justifiable only so long as it was an 'inflationary' one; immediately it adopted deflation it had no *raison d'être*. Its last two and a half years, though not without achievement, were demeaning; not because Lloyd George, like much of the Conservative leadership, had capitulated, but because he had capitulated to policies and a social class he instinctively despised.

There is an abundant literature on the adoption of this regime. Yet, even though Moggridge, for example, concedes that many of its policies were adopted for 'moral' reasons, it is still easy to exaggerate the role of formal economic argument.[19] Such explanations underrate what was almost certainly more important— the intense political and ideological pressures put upon Conservative MPs, particularly those from the south of England. Such pressures were most intense throughout 1920 and the first half of 1921, when the cost of living index reached its inter-war peak: 269 in November 1920 (July 1914 = 100).

There were two reasons why the Conservative Party should have been so susceptible to these pressures. The first was the huge increase in its membership in the early 1920s, an increase confined almost exclusively to middle-class suburbs and constituencies. By the mid-twenties the party had about 700,000 members—at least twice the membership of the Labour Party—who gave it a remarkably homogeneous tone. It is true, as R. T. McKenzie pointed out, that 'only a tiny fraction of this paper membership

[19] D. E. Moggridge, *British Monetary Policy, 1924–1931* (Cambridge, 1972). Prof. Moggridge writes: 'The "Norman Conquest of $4.86" was ultimately an act of faith in an incompletely understood adjustment mechanism undertaken for largely moral reasons' (p. 228).

plays any regular part in the affairs of the party.'[20] But that is accidental. Because its membership *was* now so homogeneous its 'opinion' was easily articulated and organized, not least by the *Daily Express* and the *Daily Mail*. The second was the character of the Parliamentary Party itself. It is a truism that the inter-war Conservative Party was a business party. But this view, argued most forcefully by 'Simon Haxey' in 1939, is not easy to confirm, largely because our categories must overlap: barristers can also be company directors, for example, but whether an MP regards himself more of a barrister than a company director is hard to measure. Even so, and allowing for overlap, we find that in 1939 the majority of Conservative MPs (245, about 57 per cent) were not businessmen, but had been in the armed forces, the civil service, or the professions.[21] Nor was there anything new in this: in July 1914 almost exactly the same number (58 per cent) of Conservative MPs came within that definition.[22] That such people were instinctively sympathetic to the ambitions and worries of people whose life experience was similar to their own is not surprising: indeed, it is possible that a real businessman's party would have been considerably less sympathetic. In any case, the views of the local Conservative associations were soon known. The success of the Anti-Waste and other independent candidates at by-elections in the early 1920s, at the Wrekin (November 1920), Dover (January 1921), Hertford and Westminster St George's (both June 1921), indicated the drift of Conservative opinion. Although the Anti-Waste League, founded by Lord Rothermere, officially stood outside the Conservative Party, most Conservative associations were overtly or discreetly anti-waste and Tory MPs took their cue from them. Furthermore, anti-waste, which purported to be an attack on wasteful government expenditure, was a codeword universally understood: it represented a general assault on 'inflationary' government policies which were, so it was believed, designed to buy off the working classes at the expense of everyone else. After the fall of the coalition (1922) the leadership of the Conservative Party quickly adjusted itself to these pressures. Thus in October 1923 Baldwin told his listeners: 'You will no doubt have seen, as I have, suggestions for creating out of nothing

[20] R. T. McKenzie, *British Political Parties* (second edn.; London, 1964), 187 n; see also Ramsden, 254–5.

[21] S. Haxey, *Tory M.P.* (London, 1939), 185–8.   [22] Ramsden, 98.

artificial money to finance this, that, and the other. It is not in that way that the problem of unemployment is to be tackled.' While he denied that the government was following a policy of 'active deflation', he emphasized that 'we certainly do not propose to proceed in the direction of inflation. No such project has ever been considered.'[23] Within a few years his style had become almost formulaic:

The creation of new money for that purpose [employment] is inflation. We saw the result of that in the war, when everything was paid for by borrowing. Every housewife knows what inflation means in prices; every wage-earner knows what inflation means when his wages lag six months behind the inflated cost of goods. No one in the country wants this . . . Therefore we will rule it out.

Borrowing is like drink. You cannot go on for ever, and the headache is inevitable sooner or later. We are too busy repaying the loans to-day which we raised in the war to consider creating any new ones for a bit.[24]

All MPs think there is a class which cannot be deserted without dishonour or whose interests are in some fundamental sense inseparable from those of their party: in 1846 the Tories thought that class was the tenant farmer; in 1920 the man on £500 a year.

Whom the economic policies of inter-war Conservative governments 'objectively' favoured is almost impossible to identify; whether in the long term they served anyone's particular interests is open to doubt. In the short term the man on £500 a year, even more the man on £1,000, did pretty well. Stable money incomes, steadily falling prices, consistently low levels of middle-class unemployment,[25] utterly safe deposit banks, were all real gains. As was a personal taxation system, which, except possibly for the years 1931–4, was designed to favour the middle middle and lower upper middle classes: in 1929 a married man with two children on £400 a year paid no tax and a man on £500 a year paid only £8. Even in 1931, when Snowden raised taxes to cover the deficit, the changes were 'comparatively trivial'. As Glynn and Oxborrow point out, despite talk in 1931 of 'sharing burdens' tax rates were

---

[23] S. Baldwin, *Employment, Trade and Empire Development* (London, 1923), 1–2.

[24] S. Baldwin, *Liberal Unemployment Plans Exposed* (London, 1929), 8.

[25] The very low levels of white-collar unemployment as a politically stabilizing factor are often overlooked. See Colin Clark, *National Income and Outlay* (London, 1938), 45–6.

not at levels which really hurt the majority of the middle classes, and Chamberlain abolished the increases in 1934 and 1935 anyway.[26]

Nevertheless, whatever happened to personal living standards in the period, many people who usually supported the Conservative Party did not do as well as the men on £500 a year. For one, the interests of manufacturing industry, particularly in the 1920s, were subordinated to the short-term need to mollify the middle classes. The stabilization of the pound at par (which, it is true, industry did not seriously oppose), the abandonment by all political parties of a capital levy, and the shift of taxation on to limited liability companies (which industry very much opposed) are good examples of this.[27] Nor was agriculture, despite the propping up begun by the second Labour government and continued by the National Government, given first claim on the Conservative Party's sympathies. Indeed, here the gap between Baldwin's bucolic imagery and active policy was almost embarrassingly wide. Furthermore, the number of people for whom successive Conservative governments showed such solitude was comparatively small. The proportion of pre-tax incomes over £250 was never more than 13 per cent of all incomes and as late as 1938 only 14.3 per cent of the population were salary earners while another 6 per cent were self-employed.[28] Evidently, the colossal Tory majorities could not be based on them alone. We must ask ourselves how a deflationary political economy could be universalized, made acceptable to social groups other than those for whom it was designed. But if we look simply at 'objective' self-interest we get more or less nowhere. On the contrary, we must look at 'subjective' and often inarticulate attitudes, for the Conservative predominance was, in reality, based not on economic self-interest but on ideologically determined class stereotypes and conventional wisdoms which mobilized, first, nearly all those who were not working-class and then much of the working class as well.

Those outside the working classes have always seen them in

[26] S. Glynn and J. Oxborrow, *Interwar Britain: A Social and Economic History* (London, 1976), 48.

[27] For personal taxation, see M. Short, 'The Politics of Personal Taxation' unpublished Ph.D. thesis, (Cambridge, 1985); for the capital levy, Short, 34–91, R. C. Whiting, 'The Labour Party, Capitalism and the National Debt', in P. J. Waller (ed.), *Politics and Social Change in Britain* (Brighton, 1987), 140–55.

[28] Glynn and Oxborrow, 47.

stereotypes and their behaviour towards them has been instinctively shaped by varieties of folklore. In the inter-war years, more perhaps than in most, these stereotypes were constantly hostile; and even when so hostile as to be parodied—as with the most famous of the inter-war inventions, 'the coals in the bath'—parody merely suggests how strong and not how foolish they were. Before 1914, stereotypes, though also tending to be hostile or contemptuous, were (as I have argued) usually, though after 1900 not always, social or cultural: the working class behaved in this or that way.[29] It was not until the First World War and the years immediately after that a more specifically *political* conception became predominant. To the middle classes after 1918, as Bonham wrote, 'the political characteristic of the working man is that he is in a constant state of bargaining with his employer, with the strike weapon as the final argument.' Thus when people spoke of the 'working class' they came to think first of manual workers in well-organized trades with aggressive unions.[30] It is, of course, essential to the power of any stereotype that it should in part be true; to a casual observer who was not working-class (or even was) the working classes in the three or four years after the war must have looked rather like that: constantly disputing with their employers. And to people who had no trade union of their own, would not have wished to join one, and felt themselves struggling against life, it must have seemed inevitable that all trade-union action would in the end be at their expense. And not simply at their economic expense; at the expense of their social dignity and standing. It was this which made the developing political stereotype of the working class so negative.

Even if Conservative MPs had not been made aware of this electorally, there was plenty of evidence about the mood of the middle classes in the 1920s. C. F. G. Masterman's description of it in 1922 was unsympathetic but certainly memorable. His London middle-class suburb 'Richford'

hates and despises the working classes as all Richfords hate and despise the working classes. Richford hates and despises them partly because it has contempt for them, and partly because it has fear of them. It has established its standard of civilisation, modest in demand, indeed, in face of life's possibilities, but very tenacious in its maintenance of its home and

[29] See above, pp. 167–96.
[30] J. Bonham, *The Middle Class Vote* (London, 1954), 54.

garden . . . and agreeable manners and ways. Just on its borders, and always prepared seemingly to engulf it, are those great masses of humanity which accept none of its standards, and maintain life on a totally different plain.[31]

What the middle classes chose to read also tells us something. It is, of course, difficult to find a 'representative' text: everything is to some extent idiosyncratic. But if there is one for the 1920s it is certainly Warwick Deeping's *Sorrell and Son*. This extraordinary bestseller, with its forty-one editions and innumerable impressions, came straight from the heart of bourgeois England, a grim pot-pourri of middle-class grievances and fantasies. The hero, an ex-officer of virtuous background (though probably only a temporary gentleman) has fallen on hard times. His wife, a bolter with an eye for the high life, has abandoned him and his son, Kit. In the early days, therefore, the 'boy had to go to a Council school. He had hated it . . . He had all the fastidious nausea of a boy who has learnt to wash and to use a handkerchief, and not yet yell "cheat" at everybody in the heat of a game.' But Sorrell, despite his vicissitudes, was unattracted by socialism.

He had seen too much of human nature. Labour, becoming sectionalised, would split into groups, and group would grab from group, massing for the struggle instead of fighting a lone fight. Only the indispensable and individual few, would be able to rise above this scramble of the industrial masses.

The working classes are full of malevolence. Sorrell 'had seen that these sons of working men hated the son of the ex-officer. They hated his face, his voice, his pride, his very good temper. They hated him for his differences, his innocent superiorities.' The novel is also replete with Richford's resentment at those other beneficiaries of economic wantonness—the 'profiteers' and the new-rich, a resentment endlessly worked on by the middle-class press. By a complicated route Sorrell ends up employed in a country hotel which promptly heads for bankruptcy because it will not cater for the ill-bred post-war plutocracy. Despite all this the book ends triumphantly. Sorrell becomes rich; Kit, after various crises, becomes a famous surgeon, rejects his opulent mother, marries. His father, fulfilled, discloses a terminal illness on Kit's

[31] C. F. G. Masterman, *England After War* (London, 1922), 54.

wedding day. The book had everything its vast readership presumably wanted to read: a sullen, greedy, and sectionalist working class, a neo-Darwinian individualism, a blameless code of honour observed neither by working men nor plutocrats, but which *none the less* brings riches, and victory. Since it was published in 1925 its readers had the satisfaction of knowing that victory had almost been won. Within a year the remarkable solidarity of constitutional England throughout the general strike confirmed it.

Although the stabilization of 1920–5 did much to restore the status and confidence of the middle classes it did nothing to soften the angularity of their stereotypes of the working classes. Working men remained in endless dispute with their employers and the public; the unemployed either would not work or scrounged, or worked on the sly and thus had a wage as well as the dole. The working classes lived off state handouts paid for by the 'public', which was why taxes were intolerably high. There was, of course, a kind of truth to all this. Since the incidence of middle-class unemployment was so low and the scope of welfare before 1939 so narrow, handouts did go almost exclusively to the working classes; and, though not by much, the working classes did receive more in transfer payments than they paid in indirect taxation. After 1945, with so many more snouts in the trough, the welfare state became more socially acceptable or, at least, more difficult to dismantle. Furthermore, these assumptions were reinforced by contemporary versions of more timeless ones—the profligacy and fabulous wages of women munition workers was the classic wartime one[32]—or simply mixed up with the timeless ones themselves:

I knew only the distaste and fear with which my mother and father and their friends regarded the workers. Even Liberals were bad enough, but the workers . . . Father hated to see them drawing the dole, believing that the principle of giving money away was wrong. He had been heard to call the destitute of the town, ironically, 'our non-banking friends'.

'Non-washing, you mean,' Mother said. It was not their financial so much as their hygienic habits she loathed.[33]

[32] Florence, Lady Bell, *Landmarks* (London, 1929), 68.
[33] B. Aldiss, *The Hand-Reared Boy* (London, 1970), 102. Although this partly autobiographical novel is largely about adolescent sexuality it is also very sharp on bourgeois social mores in the 1930s. 'Father' was manager of a Barclay's bank in a Leicestershire town.

But the stereotypes were effective whether true or not. They became ideological truths, absorbed, like the finery of women munitions workers or the profiteers and their pleasure boats, into the mental world of Conservative politics and shaped it at nearly all levels.

Ideological truths about class inevitably became inextricable from ideological truths about the economy. Throughout the inter-war years British governments, and Conservative ones most of all, were slaves not of defunct economists, but of conventional wisdoms and 'common-sense' economics. This was so whether it was dressed up by the Treasury or the Bank, or more naïvely expressed by an uncomplicated member of the National Government like Walter Runciman or a Home County backbencher.[34] How conventional wisdoms were presented depended, of course, upon context: the Treasury was capable, as it did in 1929, of presenting a formidable technical case against reflation,[35] but the underlying assumptions differed little from those of the plain man in Tunbridge Wells.

No doubt the directors of the foreign issue houses (who almost exclusively made up the court of the Bank of England) were more self-serving in their adherence to conventional wisdoms, since common-sense economics probably suited their particular interests. It is also true that leading officials of the Bank and Treasury had got used to listening to the merchant bankers and had a childlike belief in their sagacity and detachment. But when these officials were required to defend themselves in public, like Ernest Harvey and (notoriously) Montagu Norman before the Macmillan Committee,[36] or commissioned to assert the Treasury's case, like Richard Hopkins to the Royal Commission on Unemployment Insurance,[37] all technical pretences were abandoned, and we are back in Tunbridge Wells. The political economy of the Blacketts, Normans, Hopkinses, Niemeyers, or Fishers was inspired by a

[34] On Runciman as an 'average' but easily frightened minister, see H. H. Henderson to R. H. Brand, 15 Feb. 1932, Brand Papers, Bodleian Library, Oxford, File 17.

[35] See the Treasury's reply, written at the direction of Churchill, to the Liberal Party's unemployment proposals: *Memoranda on Certain Proposals relating to Unemployment*, PP (1929) xvi. 873 (Cmd. 3331), 4–15, 45–52 partic.

[36] See, for example, Committee on Finance and Industry [Macmillan Committee], *Minutes of Evidence*, PP (1931), i. (Cmd. 3894), 2–31 (Harvey); 212–16 (Norman).   [37] See above, p. 216.

series of precepts (not living beyond your means, paying your way, 'safety first') and sometimes a ludicrously inappropriate code of honourable practice (as with devaluation), which are supposed to be appropriate for us all but which, in the circumstances of inter-war Britain, as rules for life meant much more to the middle than to the working classes. Above all, their economic world-view was based upon stereotypes of working-class behaviour which gave it added ideological authority. What united the merchant banker, the Treasury official, the manufacturer, and suburban Toryism was a belief that the working classes behaved in certain ways which, on the whole, the middle classes did not: class wisdoms became conventional wisdom and common sense was validated by class-pride.

We have seen that from the end of the First World War middle-class Britain was increasingly mobilized by a 'deflationary' ideology fashioned by a particular notion of the working class and characterized by an acute hostility to working-class politics. This was primarily a negative ideology—and in the end never amounted to much more than that—but it was always expressed in part via a positive political rhetoric. A rather vulgar form of a pre-war anti-collectivism was one of its essential features. It thus emphasized the ideological centrality of the individual in economic life and the family in social life while assimilating the financial practices of the family to those of the state. Furthermore, the state, by a developing system of censorship, attempted what it had never specifically done before: to reinforce the economic primacy of the family by moral and social buttresses. A succession of home secretaries, most notoriously Sir William Joynson Hicks (1924–9), whose appointment seems in retrospect almost unbelievable, attempted to perpetuate a regime under which sexual and economic orthodoxies became inseparable.[38] The refusal of the Board of Film Censors in the 1930s to allow *Love on the Dole* to be filmed, on the grounds that it was politically *and* morally unsound, is simply the most celebrated example.[39]

The Conservative Party was, as we know, the grand beneficiary

---

[38] For an example of Joynson Hicks's style, see W. J. Hicks, Viscount Brentford, 'Do we need a Censor?', *Criterion Miscellany*, 6 (1929).

[39] J. Richards, 'The British Board of Film Censors and Central Control in the 1930s: Images of Britain', *Historical Journal of Film, Radio and Television* (1981), 111. The film was not released until 1941.

of this. But there is much evidence that the middle classes were never entirely happy even with the Conservatives and sometimes felt deserted by them. Equally, on two occasions, many of them deserted the Conservatives: not, of course, to Labour, but to the Liberals. The Liberal Party, indeed, and not Labour was the greatest threat to Conservative predominance in the inter-war years, and in two ways. First, by spoiling the Conservative vote sufficiently either to allow Labour in (1923 and 1929) or even, as almost happened in 1929, presenting Labour with a parliamentary majority which was probably unrepresentative of national opinion. Second, by becoming a bourgeois special-interest party and thus enforcing a British version of continental-style interest bargaining which the Conservatives have always hated even when practising it. The 1920s Liberal Party was, in fact, as close to a *Mittelstands-partei* as pre-war Britain was likely to get. It is possible, consequently, to exaggerate the eclectic nature of inter-war Liberalism. It is true, as Michael Kinnear points out, that the Liberals won 281 seats at least once between 1918 and 1929—not many short of Labour's 304.[40] It is also true that seats *won* by Liberals in general elections were rather a rag-bag. But from the early 1920s on the social character of the Liberal party was more uniform than this would suspect. The number of urban-industrial working-class seats it could win was few and declining, and while it was still disproportionately Scottish and Welsh in parliament (23 out of 59 seats in 1929), its popular support was overwhelmingly in provincial England—in the outer suburbs, county and spa towns, and rural constituencies. In the 1920s it won many southern English constituencies it failed to win at all before 1914. In 1923 it won over half the country's rural seats and would have come close to doing so again in 1929 but for Labour intervention.[41] Over much of non-borough England the Liberal Party was frequently and often usually the second party, one of the familiar poles of English middle-class life. As late as 1927 Richmal Crompton has William, who has not realized that 'going-over' in the context of spiritualism means communion with the departed, apologizing to an offended lady-spiritualist: I thought you meant going-over, like Oxford and Cambridge, Liberal and Conservative. Yet the Liberals were rarely able to repeat these successes. Many of the

[40] M. Kinnear, *The British Voter*, (London, 1968), 120.
[41] Ibid.

281 victories were one-off and the Party failed—in 1931 failed completely—to sustain its role as a middle-class interest party. Why was this?

It is clear that the decline of nonconformity denied the Liberals much of their traditional and thus stable vote. It is true that by the end of the period the seats Liberals still held were amongst those with highest nonconformist church attendance. In closely fought constituencies a historic nonconformist vote could still carry a Liberal across the line, at Berwick-on-Tweed in 1935, for example. There were, however, now few of these. But the decline of nonconformity had not denied the Liberals a role: they were still able to compete for an aggrieved but volatile middle-class vote. As E. R. Roper Power pointed out in 1937, in much of the country the emptying of the chapels had replaced a partisan two-party system with a species of one-party politics.[42] But this system, which emerged in much of provincial and suburban England, was not so much Conservative as anti-trade union working class, though in the end the Conservative Party came to embody it. Similarly, the innumerable 'independent' councillors on urban district and rural district councils, though usually Conservative in the last resort, were not necessarily hostile to the Liberal Party and were often prepared to co-operate with it. It was perhaps less important that an independent was Conservative than that he or she was not Labour. Thus it was possible for the Liberals to come from nowhere in apparently hopeless constituencies—as R. M. Kedward did in Ashford (Kent) in 1929—by exploiting local issues and fluid political loyalties.[43] Despite the attrition of their former nonconformist electorate the Liberals after 1918 could amass a substantial vote—in 1929 23 per cent of all votes cast—but it was undoubtedly a highly unstable one.

However, it cannot be argued that the electoral system itself was a significant impediment to the Liberal Party. That the Liberals, particularly in the 1920s, were proportionately under-represented goes without saying, but this is not necessarily fatal. The system also permits a party with a cohesive electorate to be grossly over-represented. The question to be asked of the electoral system is

[42] E. R. Roper Power, 'The Social Structure of an English County Town', *The Sociological Review*, 29 (1937), 409–11.
[43] Though Kedward was himself a nonconformist minister, Ashford had the lowest proportion of practising nonconformists of all the Kent county seats.

not how and why the Liberal Party was under-represented, since it plainly was, but whether the system obstructed the development of a cohesive Liberal electorate. There are several ways in which it might have done this. It subjected the Liberal Party to the charge that a Liberal vote was a wasted vote, and it is clear that in certain circumstances voters do feel compelled to choose between the two largest parties. It was also open to spoiling, as it could spoil the Conservative vote. In 1929 Labour intervention deprived the Liberals of perhaps forty seats even though these were mostly ones which Labour had little or no chance of winning. This in turn had one possible consequence: by diminishing the Liberal Party in the House of Commons it weakened its capacity to bargain with the other parties and thus to make itself indispensable to any major part of the electorate.

There is some truth to this but not much. An electoral system which was notoriously favourable to parties with a defined social or geographical basis clearly could not of itself deprive the Liberals of a cohesive electorate. Nor is it historically clear that third parties must be 'squeezed': there is much evidence that if people feel strongly enough they will vote for third parties regardless. In any case, in those parts of the country where the Liberals were now strongest they were not usually the third party, but the second. And if the Liberals could not use their position in 1923 or 1929 to engage in interest bargaining it is hard to imagine any circumstances when they could.[44] Why, then, was it so unstable?

In fact, there *were* structural and ideological impediments to the development of the Liberal Party as a party of suburban-provincial England and it is debatable how much freedom of manœuvre the Liberal élites had. In one way, however, they probably missed an opportunity. Most of the successes of the Liberals in the 1920s appear to have been partly fortuitous or the result of local initiative. They had little to do with the national leadership or its campaigns. The Liberal Party, as an organization, would have been better served had it directed its efforts more specifically at this narrow electorate. However, while some of its leaders, like Sir

[44] In 1923 there was scarcely any bargaining at all—though this was certainly not the Liberals' doing alone. In 1929 bargaining was more apparent but the agreements with Labour were Lloyd George's rather than the Party's. See M. Hart, 'The Decline of the Liberal Party in Parliament and the Constituencies', unpublished D.Phil. thesis (Oxford, 1982), 396–408.

John Simon, or ancient Liberals like George Lambert,[45] probably would have done this, it is almost inconceivable that either Asquith or Lloyd George would have been prepared to do so. Both had an entirely different conception of the Liberal Party; both were deeply opposed to its being any sort of class party, and if it were, it would not be as a party of middle-class defence. There was thus a real tension between the programmatic ambitions of the Liberal leadership and the grievances of its likely electorate. Neither the parliamentary strategies of the Liberal Party nor its programme were single-minded enough to be acceptable to the bulk of its constituency; and supporting Labour, which the Liberals did rather aimlessly in 1924 and 1929, were almost certainly unacceptable.

This failure had an inevitable parallel. The Liberals made no obvious effort to restore their old influence in secondary political bodies like farmers' organizations, ratepayers' associations, women's unions, etc.—that great associational network of middle-class England—whose influence alone could have habituated the electorate to voting Liberal. Single parliamentary successes were always possible, but without the support of such bodies they could rarely be repeated. It might have been difficult for rank-and-file Liberals to have broken the informal Conservative hold on bourgeois associational life, which became almost complete in the 1920s, but there no evidence they seriously tried.

The Liberals faced two other difficulties which it is hard to see that they could overcome. The first was the demographic and ideological weakness of agriculture. In 1931 only 6.1 per cent of the occupied population earned its living from the land. This was a very much smaller figure than in any other 'comparable' country—the equivalent figure for Germany and the United States is about one third—and is so much smaller as to make it doubtful whether there are any other 'comparable' countries. This meant that in Britain there was nothing like those huge coalitions of indebted and increasingly impoverished farmers who had an immediate and direct interest in inflationary policies. These coalitions, furthermore, were not only electorally large, they gave 'inflation' a social and political acceptability which the working classes never could have done. Conservative parties in the United States and

[45] Liberal (after 1931, Liberal National) MP for South Molton, 1891–1924, 1929–1945.

Germany resisted rural pressures at their peril, and in both cases paid the price when they did. But in Britain agriculture was simply too small and defensive in relation to other bourgeois interest groups, and what the Liberals might have gained by exploiting the financial anxieties of an increasingly indebted farming community they could well have lost in the suburbs. While, however, that community was an essential part of the Liberal electorate, it was precisely its weakness that made viable a constitutional Conservatism.

The second difficulty was related to the first: though there there was in some sense a 'crisis' throughout the inter-war years, the crisis was never serious enough. More particularly, mass unemployment never had the same socially disintegrating effects that, in varying degrees, it had almost everywhere else. It was contained, not simply within the existing state structure, but within traditional party allegiances. Fear of what the unemployed might do is a powerful solvent: it could have diverted from the Conservative Party the loyalties of a middle class, some of whom, as was clear in 1929, were more fluid in their political behaviour than is often supposed. Yet this did not happen and it is important to understand why.

First: the dole, *inter alia*, acted in a such a way as to transform the unemployed from simply being workless to being dependent, and dependence was reinforced by the threat (rarely executed in practice) of withdrawal or reduction in payment. This did not, as I have suggested, make the unemployed politically docile, but it did render them politically helpless. E. W. Bakke argued that the dole as it developed was a 'Labour' policy grudgingly accepted by the Liberals and the Conservatives because they could think of nothing else.[46] This might be true, but in fact, despite what the Conservatives often said, the dole was undoubtedly their preferred way of treating the unemployed. Not only did it maintain them as a dependent non-workforce, it was always more admissible than 'inflationary' expenditures. It was also useful in prolonging the life of significant stereotypes—if you have the dole you must have dole-scroungers—and one of the effects of the 1931 and 1934 unemployment insurance legislation was to do precisely that.[47] Furthermore, the political energies of the unemployed were

---

[46] E. W. Bakke, *Insurance or Dole*, (New Haven, 1935), 164.
[47] For the 1934 Act, see above pp. 250–1.

expended on the manipulation of dole administration and securing a 'fair' payment; were thus confined and localized, and in a wider sense made harmless. Bakke is, however, right to this extent: in 1931 the Conservatives inherited a system of uncovenanted benefit for which the Labour Party was blamed and made responsible. But it actually suited the National government very well; it politically marginalized a substantial section of the working class while encouraging that surreptitious moblization of the employed against the unemployed which was undoubtedly one of the Conservative Party's tactics in the 1930s. It reinforced the Party's unique claim both to guarantee a deflationary political economy and to neutralize any threats to the social system which deflation might bring with it. It was thus doubly advantageous.

Second: as soon as the Labour Party became the fulcrum of British politics (which it did in 1918–19) the position of the Conservative Party became almost impregnable. The Tories, indeed, had to do remarkably little to confirm this: it is notable, for example, how easily they could regain lost agricultural seats without doing anything at all. This was partly (as I have argued) because agriculture was too weak to embark upon a sustained independent politics[48] but more because the Conservative Party was always the most acceptable ideological alternative to Labour whenever that choice had to be made—as in 1924 or 1931. The great regroupings of those two years were based on a whole universe of sentiments and primitive convictions which were instinctive and instinctively favourable to the Conservative Party. They did not even need to be articulated: it was *known* that the Conservative Party was the party of bourgeois propriety and dignity. It did not need to be said (though it was often enough) that the Conservative Party was the best defence against a politicized working class. It is difficult to see how even the most single-minded Liberal leadership could have undermined that.

The failure of the Liberal Party to transform itself into a middle-class special-interest party left the field necessarily free to the Conservatives. What they picked up was a popular majority based upon a powerful, but largely negative ideological and social unity. It was held together not by what people had in common so much as by what they had in common *against* a particular conception of the

[48] See above p. 279.

working class. Once the relationship of the organized working class to society came to define political action it was possible for the Conservative Party to unite almost certainly otherwise antithetical economic and social interests.

How was this done? We have seen that from 1919 onwards the Conservatives devised an anti-inflationary political rhetoric which, though meant for general consumption, actually suited some people's interests more than others. Yet throughout the period they were the party of both industrial and financial capital and this though it proved impossible to treat both in an even-handed way. We must now see how this happened. In the 1920s manufacturing industry was clearly subordinated to a policy which favoured finance; after 1931, with a managed currency, protection, partial exchange control, and debt conversion, the balance altered— though even much of this, particularly devaluation, was forced on the Conservative Party by the run of events. Yet despite this subordination, which much of industry keenly felt,[49] there is little sign that manufacturers as a body abandoned their allegiance to the Conservative Party. It is, of course, arguable that there was calculation in this: the Conservatives were after all the party of protection. Baldwin had sought an electoral mandate for it in 1923 (or that is what he said he was doing) and it was always understood that protection would be introduced whenever political circumstances permitted. But until 1931 circumstances did not permit and from 1924 to 1929 the Baldwin government relied upon policies which were often bitterly criticized by industry. In any case many manufacturers were still free traders, which makes their adherence to the Conservative Party even more remarkable. They adhered to the Conservative Party not simply, as W. D. Rubinstein has argued, because in the early 1920s all wealth came together as a

---

[49] See, for example, the Federation of British Industry's submission to the Macmillan Committee; *inter alia*: '(a) That British monetary policy during the last five years cannot be acquitted of an important share of responsibility for the lamentable conditions of trade and employment during this period, and for the lack of expansion of our overseas activity. (b) That the sacrifices of industry to the needs of finance which that policy has entailed have not been adequately counterbalanced by benefits conferred on other sections of the community. (c) That from the point of view of British industry and commerce the essential prerequisite of a proper functioning of the gold standard is to a certain extent a question of weighing the interests of one group against those of the others.' (*Minutes of Evidence*, I, 188.)

single élite[50]—the process was never as positive or as complete as that—but because businessmen took the same view of politics as everyone else outside the working class. They, more than most, had reason to believe that the 'working class' was a unionized working class with whom they were perpetually in conflict and for whose greed they would have to pay. Furthermore, this essentially ideological judgement was given a specifically economic rationale: the fundamental problem of British industry was not exchange or interest-rate policy but wage-costs forced up by monopoly union power. The effect of the Labour-cost doctrine, as W. Adams Brown pointed out in 1929, was largely to exculpate the Conservatives from any blame.[51] The notion that a greedy work-force had priced itself out of jobs or destroyed the competitiveness of British goods became another of the conventional wisdoms of the period, the more effective because it was at least plausible and there were many to argue it.[52] But its plausibility is less important than its character. It fell into a familiar category of inter-war truths, was easily assimilated to them, and, like them, because unquestionable. That Keynes should have questioned it was bad enough, but that he should eventually have dismissed it so brusquely—as he did in the first couple of pages of *The General Theory*—probably did more to make him unacceptable to common-sense man than anything else. Though many industrialists had done well in 1919–20 and had no particular interest in deflation as such, none the less, when faced by an organized working class, they reacted as everyone else outside the working class did. Thus the labour-cost doctrine was an essential element both in the Conservatives' ideological hegemony and in integrating industrial capital with finance. There was, indeed, a certain iron law about what happened: hardly anyone had been more critical of the deflationary policies of the early 1920s than Sir Alfred Mond, creator of ICI and one of Britain's few superindustrialists (but also a Liberal MP, a minister in the Lloyd George coalition, and a free trader), yet in 1926 he joined the Conservative Party with no sense that, at least intellectually, this was a preposterous step.

[50] W. D. Rubenstein, 'Wealth, Elites and the Class Structure of Modern Britain', *Past and Present*, 76 (Aug. 1977), 9.

[51] W. Adams Brown Jun., 'The Conflict of Opinion and Economic Interest in England' in S. Pollard (ed.), *The Gold Standard and Employment Policy between the Wars* (London, 1970), 53.

[52] See, particularly, M. Casson, *Economics of Unemployment* (Oxford, 1983), *passim*.

Such unity permitted not only a coalition of finance and industry but a second coalition of social groups which included, but went far beyond, the income tax-paying/*rentier* class in whose interests the 1920s policies were probably designed: a huge assembly of 'middle' classes, numbering 9–10 million adults, who stood between the middle classes proper and the manual working class, but who felt themselves in both their style of life and in their hostility to the union-ized working-class to be middle-class. They were the 'constitutional classes' whose loyalty to the government during the general strike was as intense as the solidarity of the strikers. In the inter-war years the 'constitutional classes' made up civil society; in their own terminology they were 'the public', and the public was what remained after the manual working class had been subtracted. Thus the *Daily Express* could write in April 1921: 'The workers may confide with perfect assurance in the generosity and justice of public opinion.'[53] Keynes used the word exactly the same way a decade later:

I am sure that a great many members of the public do not look at it that way. They are thoroughly depressed. They think that these troubles are due to very deep-seated causes . . . that Labour is greedy and is asking for a larger and larger share of a smaller product, and we are getting nearer and nearer to the abyss.[54]

Keynes's distinction between 'public' and 'labour' is absolutely explicit and the electoral hegemony of the inter-war Conservative Party is the product of this distinction.

The Conservatives are best understood, therefore, as the party of the public and as such were able to overcome historic sectional and, in most places, ethnic-religious obstacles. It was this which explains the Party's success in Scotland. Although weaker than in England, the class configuration and social traditions of Scotland were strong enough to permit a political regrouping with the Unionist Party at the centre.[55] In face of the early and rapid, but then incomplete, advance of Labour in central Scotland, older (but already declining) anti-Unionist ideologies based upon national sentiment or religion never had a hope of prevailing. Only

[53] *Daily Express*, 9 Apr. 1921, quoted Bonham, 20.

[54] Private Sessions of the Macmillan Committee, Transcript, 22 Oct. 1930.

[55] It is important to note that the desertion of the Simonite Liberals to the Unionists was significant in this process. Simon took the bulk of Scottish Liberal MPs and votes with him in 1931.

in Wales was it not possible for the Conservatives to become the party of civil society; partly because ethnic-linguistic traditions (many of them specifically anti-Conservative) were much stronger than in Scotland, partly because a viable rural anti-Conservatism was possible, and partly because the unionized manual working class was such a large proportion of the electorate anyway.[56]

There was also a sexual bias to Conservative support: the Conservative lead among women was huge. But if we see the Conservatives as the party of the public this lead becomes explicable. The social world of the organized working class was sectional, collectivist, and masculine. It was a result of a sexual division of labour, and the individualist and familial ideologies surrounding women's role-allocation, that many women should feel deeply hostile to that world, and should identify instinctively with the public and the party of the public.

But the 'public' is primarily a status-category, and the key to the success of the Conservative Party amongst the classes which constituted the 'public' was the establishment of a status-order acceptable to them. The only political way this could be *seen* to be done, however, was by a deflationary political economy which undermined the organized working class, reinforced unfavourable stereotypes of it, and gave a general authority to a number of conventional wisdoms based upon a universalized and apparently class-neutral notion of 'inflation'. It is true that within these constraints the Conservative leadership had a certain freedom of manœuvre; the party was still sufficiently hierarchical for its leaders to be able to distance themselves from their constituency for some of the time — a good deal of inter-war Conservative social policy would have been impossible were this not so. But in those areas where the opinions of the constituency were emphatic, whether in overall economic policy or (say) the policing of industrial disputes,[57] in those departments of life where the 'public' felt itself most threatened by the organized working class,

[56] But if we look at Cardiff, with its substantial English or Anglicized middle class, and a large, but not very well organized English-speaking working class—with a social structure not unlike an English industrial town's—the Conservatives did very much better, winning all three Cardiff seats in 1931 and 1935.

[57] Jane Morgan, *Conflict and Order* (Oxford, 1987), 111–228 partic. Dr Morgan's work shows just how much the rhetoric of 'one nation' was indeed just rhetoric, at least in this sphere, and should be read alongside any of the class-harmonious studies of inter-war Conservatism.

the leadership had to capitulate, whatever it thought. Nor did such a regime preclude economic growth, or even at times a mild redistribution of income, but these were permitted only so long as they were not the result, more importantly appeared not to be the result, of organized working-class activity. As ever, T. E. Gregory put into words what others thought. Commending the return to gold at par he wrote:

The great and overwhelming merit of the gold standard is just that it implies a world level of prices, and that, in consequence, changes in the position of classes and individuals, so far as they result from changes in prices, cannot so easily be attributed to the vagaries of particular politicians.[58]

Yet this remarkable preponderance did come to an end. Between 1935 and 1945 the Conservative share of the two-party preferred vote declined from 59 per cent to 45.5 per cent, by conventional standards a huge shift in opinion. What should be noticed at the outset is how abrupt the change was. There is no evidence from the by-elections between 1935 and 1939 that Labour would have made significant gains in a 1940 general election, while the Gallup polls suggest that the Conservative percentage of the preferred vote was as high in 1939–40 as it was in 1935.[59] By December 1941, however, of a Mass-Observation sample, one in six said they had changed their political views since the war, and by August 1942, one in three.[60] Gallup's first wartime poll (June 1943) showed Labour clearly ahead;[61] but the performance of proxy Labour candidates in by-elections from the beginning of 1942 on makes it very likely that Labour was ahead even by then. Rather than developing throughout the lifetime of the war, the movement of opinion to Labour was possibly complete as early as the end of that year.[62]

The second thing we should notice is that this change was almost wholly within the working class. It is, in fact, easy to overexplain

[58] T. E. Gregory, *The First Year of the Gold Standard* (London, 1926), 95.

[59] Before the war, Gallup, in effect, polled the preferred vote. The sample was asked whether it would vote for the 'Government' or the 'Opposition'. The results in Feb. 1939 were: Government, 54%, Opposition, 30%; No opinion, 16%. The corresponding results for Feb. 1940 were: 51%, 27%; 22%.

[60] A. Calder, *The People' War* (London, 1971), 337.

[61] Labour 38%, Conservative 31%, Liberal 9%, Others 8%, Don't Know 14%.

[62] See R. B. McCallum and A. Readman, *The British General Election of 1945* (London, 1947), 268.

the 1945 election result. While it is true that the ideological climate was uniquely favourable to the left, that many young men and women of the professional classes were influenced by it, and that the bourgeois vote undoubtedly frayed, most of the middle classes were unaffected. G. D. H. Cole thought that the 'wealthy and also the well-to-do voted against the Labour candidates in fully as high proportions as in previous elections.' He also believed that Labour won 'a large majority of the votes cast by "other ranks" ' in the forces but 'only a small proportion of holders of commissions'.[63] That must be right. But it must further be right that the great majority of those who were middle-class or continued to think of themselves as middle-class *had* to remain Conservative: the Party could not have got 40 per cent of the vote otherwise. There is as well much evidence that negative stereotypes of the working class and its behaviour survived the experience of the war unscathed. One reading of the evacuation surveys actually suggests that they were reinforced: the often harrowing encounters between provincial respectability and evacuee uncouthness could hardly have done anything else. To the already elaborate folklore of working-class dreadfulness was added another wisdom, almost universally believed: that their children were lousy and wet the bed.[64] And it is clear from surveys of middle-class opinion in the late 1940s and the early 1950s that the political conception of the working class developed in the 1920s was as hostile as ever.[65] The force of these stereotypes might have weakened a little during the war; what is more likely, however, is that they were simply uttered with more circumspection.

In any case, much of the middle-class Labour vote in 1945 was transitory. But the movement of opinion among the working class was not, and that alone was sufficient to defeat the Conservatives in 1945. Throughout the 1920s the Tories (probably) had a majority of the working-class preferred vote and in the 1930s (almost certainly) a majority of the actual vote—a reasonable

---

[63] G. D. H. Cole, *A History of the Labour Party since 1914* (London, 1948), 434–6.

[64] Of course, it was often true: about 50% of evacuees appear to have been verminous. See J. Welshman, 'The School Medical Service in England and Wales, 1907–1939', unpublished D.Phil. thesis (Oxford, 1989); also R. Padley and M. Cole, *Evacuation Survey* (London, 1940), 99; Susan Isaacs (eds.), *The Cambridge Evacuation Survey* (London, 1941), 127; and both *passim*.

[65] Bonham, 79–87.

estimate is 55 per cent in 1931 and 50 per cent in 1935. It was a combination of this exceptionally high working-class vote and the tenacious social unity of the non-working classes which was responsible for the Conservative Party's electoral success in the inter-war years. In 1945 the Party's non-working class vote remained largely intact, as did the ideological base of that vote. But its working-class vote significantly fragmented: it fell from 50 per cent to 30 per cent, the 'normal' level at which it remained for the next generation. What the historian has to explain, therefore, is comparatively specific: why did a significant fraction of the working class change its vote and change it so rapidly? Furthermore, that it did change it so rapidly largely eliminates structural–atemporal explanations like age, new voters or social-psychological dispositions. Younger voters, for example, might have been readier to *change* their vote, but their being young or first-time voters is not by itself an explanation.[66]

As a historical phenomenon, it is not easy to explain working-class Conservatism. We have a large literature on post-1945 working-class Toryism, but, though much of it is implicitly historical—in the assertion, for example, of 'traditional' reasons for Conservative voting—the preferred explanations are in practice structural or descriptive.[67] The characteristics of working-class Conservatism which emerge from this literature are these: it is highly deferential (though reasons for deference might differ) and it accepts that Conservative élites are without question more fitted to govern than their opponents; working people who defer are not sociologically very different from those who do not; differences depend upon tradition, region, and psychological traits. Insofar as working-class Toryism has sociological determinants they are occupational: men and women in larger workshops or factories are more likely to belong to a trade union, readier to have a conflictual view of society, more prepared to allow class or job considerations to override the belief (which they actually share with working-class Tories) that the Conservatives are better at ruling than anyone else—and, for all these reasons, are less inclined to vote

[66] For first-time voters, see D. E. Butler and D. Stokes, *Political Change in Britain* (Harmondsworth, 1971), 332–4.

[67] For the data, see partic. E. A. Nordlinger, *The Working Class Tories* (London, 1967); R. McKenzie and A. Silver, *Angels in Marble* (London, 1968); W. G. Runciman, *Relative Deprivation and Social Justice* (Harmondsworth, 1972), 210–21; Butler and Stokes, 136–49.

Conservative. The smaller or more disorganized the workplace, the more all these are reversed. We also know that many working people, even those at the bottom of the heap who are often the very embodiment of them, accept as true most of the negative stereotypes of the working class. Runciman shifts the argument a little: working-class Conservatives, he suggests, do not so much defer to the middle class as imagine they are middle-class. Class 'self-rating' is thus the prime determinant: working-class Tories, by misinterpreting their class, misinterpret social reality and crucially confuse their appropriate reference groups. The political consequence is, of course, the same.[68]

While we may concede that certain individuals are, for example, psychologically disposed to a deferential Conservatism and that these explanations of recent working-class Toryism do allow for variables, and thus change—size of workplace, for example—they do not allow for sudden transformations or admit the role of the state in shaping party allegiance: the political system is simply passive or a consequence. But we know this not to be the case. The state and its agencies, and the political parties which can manipulate them, are active and not passive social elements. The political system of inter-war Britain was not just an effect of party allegiances but dynamically helped to fashion them. Thus in this period the state, even if it did not create working-class Conservatism, helped to entrench it. It did so in three ways. First: by identifying the Labour Party exclusively with its unionized base and then (logically) identifying the political idea of the working class exclusively with a necessarily sectional Labour Party, the Conservatives made it exceptionally difficult for the Labour Party to break out from this unionized base, despite its specific attempts to turn itself into the ordinary man's party and the unremitting moderation of its governments. The Conservative Party devised, or at least hit upon, a rhetorical strategy which was, as John Turner implies,[69] remarkably effective in mobilizing a large proportion of what was a politically very inexperienced electorate. Second: it set about ensuring that everyone outside this sectional working class would define themselves in relation to it, and

[68] Runciman, 201–10.
[69] J. Turner, 'The Labour Vote and the Franchise after 1918: an Investigation of the English Evidence', in P. Denley and D. Hopkin (eds.), *History and Computing* (London, 1987), 136–43.

against. Third: by trying to weaken and then marginalize the old unionized working class. It did this directly, for example, by (more or less) provoking and then defeating the general strike or indirectly by treating the unemployed as helpless and incompetent. Discreetly but relentlessly it encouraged the notion that the working class was responsible for its own misfortunes and that any significant relief of these misfortunes would be opposed to the interests of the 'public'. The state was itself, therefore, partly responsible for the fact that so many working people should have identified with the public against others of their own class.

This regime, however, despite its impressive political success, was highly unstable. It could afford no risks; even the comparatively modest rearmament programmes of the late 1930s were putting it under strain. As the National government discovered, it was almost impossible to devise any way of rearming which did not enormously increase the claims of the organized working class on society. The policy of appeasement must always be seen in that light;[70] and the phoney war was an attempt to prolong the pre-war order into the war itself. In fact, hardly anyone supposed that that could successfully be done. On the contrary, most accepted it as axiomatic that war would mean an end to the old order. Two days even before it was declared Harold Nicolson noted of the duke of Devonshire (with whom he had dined at the Beefsteak): 'I must say I do admire a man like that, who must realise that all his grandeur is gone for ever, not showing the slightest sign of any gloom or apprehension.'[71] It was understood by all when the coalition government was formed in May 1940 that defence of the pre-war political economy would be abandoned, that it would have to take its chance along with the rest.

Once the Conservative élites had surrendered exclusive control of the state the structural and ideological bases of the pre-war system were quickly dismantled. The principal victims of this were (and had to be) that part of the middle class most openly protected by the inter-war political system—to many of them the 'euthanasia of the rentier'[72] must have seemed dangerously near at hand. The

[70] R. A. C. Parker, 'British Rearmament, 1936–39; Treasury, Trade Unions and Skilled Labour', *English Historical Review* (1981).

[71] H. Nicolson, *Diaries and Letters, 1930–1939*, (London, 1966), 418.

[72] The phrase is, of course, Keynes's. See J. M. Keynes, *The General Theory of Employment, Interest, and Money* (London, 1936), 376: 'the euthanasia of the

principal beneficiaries were (and had to be) that part of the working class which received least from the old order. These losses and gains were bound to result from the demands of the kind of war it had been decided in 1940 Britain must fight. But in certain areas, social policy for example, the state initially raced ahead of popular expectations and the working class, like everyone else, was caught up willy-nilly.

Ideologically, the weight of the state was thrown against the 'public'. The bourgeois classes whose dignity and status the inter-war Conservative Party had endlessly propped up found themselves as reduced in social esteem as the industrial working classes had been a few years before. (And the myth of the 'few', the young upper middle-class or grammar-school boys, those for whom Richard Hilary's *The Last Enemy* is the great literary memorial, who fought an individualist and heroic war deliberately contrasted to the brute mass war being fought all around them, was in part designed to save something of the respectable classes' esteem.[73]) Again this was to some extent simply a result of the necessities of war—shipwrights are thought to be more useful than accountants— and to some extent deliberate state policy. In the inter-war years the agencies of the state had been used to depreciate the social significance of the industrial working class; during the war they were used to inflate it. Towards the end of the war, the Conservative members of the government tried to undo some of this and were obviously alarmed at its implications, but by then one might say the damage had been done.[74]

The reordering of the economy, particularly the transformation of the heavily unionized but very depressed staple industries, and the marked redistribution of social esteem which the state helped to promote had both positive and negative political consequences. Positively, it enormously increased the scope of the organized working class and endowed its political aspirations and bargaining

rentier, of the functionless investor, will be nothing sudden, merely a gradual but prolonged continuance of what we have seen recently in Great Britain, and will need no revolution.'

[73] See the 20 Dec. 1940 entry in Harold Nicolson's diaries: 'Go down to Nether Wallop to lecture to the Air Force about the German character. I do not feel that the young men really like it. They are all fascists at heart and rather like the Germans.' Nicolson, *Diaries and Letters*, 131.

[74] For an interesting example, see I. McLaine, *Ministry of Morale*, (London, 1979), 171–216.

practices with a legitimacy they had not previously possessed. The political conception of the working class did not change; but the numbers of working people who thought they had an interest in embracing or perpetuating it increased rapidly. Runciman has argued that those working men and women who in 1945 voted Labour for the first time were moved by a kind of delayed anger, that wartime conditions led them to re-evaluate their own experience. But it was probably not quite so self-conscious. All general elections are plebiscites in which electors are invited to affirm or deny the status quo: this was as true of 1945 as of 1931 or 1935. The status quo in 1945, however, was profoundly different and this was largely the state's doing: it had, for example, retrospectively invalidated nearly all the timeless truths upon which the National government had built its majorities. And this it did very quickly indeed. Thus the working class which voted Labour in 1945 was ideologically and structurally in part the creation of the state.

Negatively, the 'public', the not-working class who behave differently from the working class, was numerically smaller and less self-confident. The Conservative public had not changed its own mind about the working class but it had fewer allies and a smaller audience. From the moment the Chamberlain government fell it became increasingly difficult for the Conservative Party to present itself as the party of civil society against the working class, either on prudential grounds or grounds of pure numbers. It is not surprising, therefore, that Labour won the 1945 election.

The Conservative Party's electoral predominance in inter-war Britain was not based, as Ramsden has argued it was, on a consensual mode of politics and it would have achieved precious little success had it been so.[75] It is true that the Conservative leadership did not give its followers all they might have wished—few Conservative leaders do—but they gave them nearly all, and it would be a mistake to think that Baldwin's class-harmonious rhetoric was at all representative of popular Conservatism, or even representative of the actions of successive Conservative governments. This predominance was, in fact, achieved by creating a

[75] Ramsden, 188–215, though Ramsden has recently hinted that there was more to it than Baldwin's apparent goodwill. See J. A. Ramsden, ' "A Party for Owners or a Party for Earners?' How far did the British Conservative Party really change after 1945:' *Transactions of the Royal Historical Society*, 37 (1987), 57.

coalition of classes and interests united only by a normative hostility to a political notion of the working class. Parkin, as we have seen, suggests that Labour-voting members of the working class feel themselves outside the dominant value system; more important, however, is the fact that the Conservative classes *thought* that working men felt themselves outside the dominant value system, and were thus different or threatening, and persuaded a majority of the community to agree with them. This normative hostility took the form of a political rhetoric inspired by stock wisdoms—'prudence' and 'economy' against 'profligacy' and 'envy'—and at a more vulgar level by conventional stereotypes of working-class behaviour which were absorbed into the language of popular Conservatism. The relationship of this kind of Conservatism to the self-interest of those who believed it is unclear, but it was closely related to perceived styles of life; and for those who continued to think of themselves as not-working class it was powerful enough to resist most changes in physical circumstances. How far the accident by which the Conservatives were out of office in 1930 and 1931 contributed to their electoral success must be speculation. That it was a factor is hardly doubtful; but, as I have suggested, there are many reasons for thinking that the Conservatives could have ridden out the storm in a way impossible for Labour, if only because their techniques of electoral mobilization were more suited to exploiting, or coping with, deflation.

This huge Conservative coalition, however, crucially depended upon an abnormal degree of working-class support, from people whose actual style of life was much closer to that of the organized working class than any other. The preservation of that vote, in turn, largely depended upon the continuing Conservative domination of the state and its instruments. But in 1940 the Party lost that domination and then quickly lost a large fraction of its working-class vote. Its defeat in 1945 was the consequence.

Conclusion

IN the Preface to this book I attempted to describe how its concerns developed and I suggested that although the chapters were not written in the order they appear here the argument they propose is best represented as they have been published. But what is clear to the writer may be less clear to the reader and it seems wise, therefore, that the argument should now be made explicit. This is most easily done by restating the three main themes of the book—all of which are interrelated: the nature of working-class consciousness and culture, the role of the two world wars in the development of these and class relations more generally, and, finally, the role of the state.

Working-Class Consciousness and Culture

In a paper published in 1985—though delivered in 1981—J. M. Winter wrote that I offer

an interpretation of the meaning of class consciousness which is completely at odds with a number of central assumptions embedded in the work of earlier labour historians . . . in his hands the concept takes on a profoundly revisionist character. Class sentiment, in his work, becomes the shoals against which socialist and progressive hopes foundered rather than the rock on which their potential or real power rested.

He goes on to note that 'virtually all labour historians' assume that the labour process 'breeds militancy and radicalism in the same way, in a sense, that a nuclear reactor breeds fissionable material: it may never explode, but its potential for eruption is ever present.' This assumption, he argues, I have challenged 'at its core'.

In his work, class consciousness is a term which . . . describes attitudes which are defensive, negative or apolitical. A class conscious stance thus becomes one of working-class suspicion of middle-class men and women arising out of a belief in the fundamental incompatibility of the ideas and politics of men who do not share the same life experiences or the same way of earning a living, whether or not they are your allies or ostensible partners in the labour movement.

The political Labour movement is therefore based on a kind of class 'rancour' and it 'could not but be infused by the spirit of a defensive and politically inert working-class culture'. He concludes that my interpretation is close to the one preferred by Gareth Stedman Jones in a famous article originally published in 1974.[1] This elegant summary of my position was based upon the argument—as he understood it—of *The Evolution of the Labour Party* and two of the chapters in this book, the second and the third. But it would be reasonable to suppose that such a summary could be extended to the argument of the whole book: in which case, how fair a summary would it be?

Although I recognize in it much that I believe to be true, it is, I think, none the less the most extreme interpretation that could be drawn. I would argue that the position is more complicated. It is plain that the British working class was never a revolutionary one; more than that, its political culture was undoubtedly defensive. As I suggested in the first chapter, the British industrial working class was effectively contained within a highly ritualized political and social system which was ideologically acceptable to all classes. This, if nothing else, implied that the working class would always be conducting its politics within institutions devised by others. It would, therefore, necessarily be thrown on the defensive. But no comparable working class *anywhere* has been hegemonic and all of them have had to accept political institutions devised by others, however much they might subsequently have modified them. We must ask ourselves what they extracted in return. I have suggested that the British working class extracted a good deal; before 1914, outside Australia and New Zealand, it is hard to think of one which extracted more.

The political structure of late nineteenth-century Britain turned out to be peculiarly favourable to proletarian politics. It permitted an almost unrestricted working-class political activity while severely inhibiting the ability of the non-working classes to obstruct it. It

[1] J. M. Winter, 'Trade Unions and the Labour Party in Britain', in W. J. Mommsen and H.-G. Husung (eds.), *The Development of Trade Unionism in Great Britain and Germany, 1890–1914* (London, 1985), 360–3. For Stedman Jones, see above, pp. 13–14.

must also be emphasized that this went way beyond party politics. By allowing the working class a comparatively high degree of job-control and a real freedom in its private existence it also permitted the growth—as I have argued in the fifth chapter, 'Work and Hobbies'—of a working-class culture which was as institutionally and intellectually sophisticated as it might also have been defensive. That is why I do not share Stedman Jones' view that late nineteenth-century working-class culture was 'remade' from a radical artisanal to a quasi-political non-vocational one, since his view does not admit that working-class culture could be radical and non-vocational at the same time. The working class was actually intensely political but political energies were scattered among a profusion of associations which tended to compete with as much as complement formal political activity. The important thing, however, is that they did both. In a way, the 'non-political' nature of a culture which could compete with formal politics was the price paid for a culture which was developed enough to create working-class organizations in the first place. Thus at the moment when Stedman Jones' 'non-political' working class was being formed the Labour Representation Committee was making its first real advances in the metropolis. I would also argue that much of what appears to be 'apolitical' or inert in working-class life is not so: working-class gambling, for instance, had an intellectual function usually not apparent to an outsider, while the response of the inter-war unemployed to their situation, which is easily seen to be apolitical, 'it's all bad luck', was entirely defensible and politically not ineffective. And one of the reasons why historians believe it to be apolitical (as I have argued in the sixth chapter) is that so much of our evidence is itself ideologically antipathetic to working-class life.

Furthermore, if, as I believe, 'socialism', either doctrinally or as a mobilizing rhetoric, made surprisingly few converts among the industrial working class before the First World War, this was due not so much to suspicion of a doctrine which emanated from the middle class (though it was often suspect on those grounds) as to the ideological attraction of free trade, a doctrine which also came from the middle class but which functioned, and *increasingly* functioned, to the benefit of the working class. If, therefore, the labour movement before 1914 appeared hesitant and cautious that was partly because circumstances were surprisingly favourable to the working class. Even after 1918, when circumstances were much less favourable, this ritualized parliamentarism continued to restrain labour's opponents: while the labour movement was decisively defeated in the inter-war years, it is not clear that the non-working classes decisively won.

It is also the case (in my view) that the working classes were largely unaffected by what I have called an 'official' culture and were suspicious of attempts to impose it on them. That further suggests that many in the labour movement would be hostile to 'middle-class' socialists in so far as they represented that culture. But again I have argued that the position is more complicated. Many of the leaders of the Edwardian Labour Party were by no means alien to an official culture and that is as true of an authentically working-class figure like Arthur Henderson as it is of someone who trained himself into the middle classes like Ramsay MacDonald. Equally, the cultural assumptions of most active members of the labour movement were recognizable to anyone of the educated middle or upper classes. It was not, after all, difficult for a member of those classes to gain rapid advancement in the Labour Party after 1918 so long as he or she was prepared to accept the Labour Party's codes. What is true, however, is that the total or partial adherence to an official culture by much of the leadership of the labour movement caused real tension. It meant that they saw significant aspects of working-class life through disapproving official eyes. They shared, for example, received views of working-class betting and even, as I have suggested, of the scrounging nature of many of the unemployed. That in turn had political consequences. It is arguable that Ramsay MacDonald's behaviour in 1931 is largely to be explained by this—that he associated the attitudes of the trade unions during the crisis with the kind of working-class behaviour that he had always despised.

The Effects of the Two World Wars

Although the argument of this book has been largely thematic it is clear that there were throughout the period marked chronological influences. In particular, the two world wars represented important discontinuities. In my book *The Evolution of the Labour Party* I certainly underestimated the effects of the First World War. It was partly responsible for the emergence of the Labour Party as one of the two main parties and a rapid growth of working-class organizations, and (more doubtfully, perhaps) a stronger 'democratic' impulse in British society. C. F. G. Masterman suggested that the course of the war, by discrediting much of the military caste, discredited also the pre-war social hierarchy to which it was attached, while contact with Australians, Canadians, and Americans opened up an alternative set of political relationships, much more favourable to the working class.[2] It is likely, furthermore, that the state itself was compelled to promote working-class politics, if only to secure the allegiance of the industrial working class to the war effort. It is fair to assume that what it did more powerfully in the Second World War it did in weaker form in the First.

From the point of view of both the working class and British society, however, the significance of the war lies in what it did to the middle classes. For them (as I have argued in the ninth chapter) it represented a kind of historical trauma which historians have not sufficiently recognized. We are used to the notion that the continental bourgeoisies were both pauperized and radicalized by the war—used to it indeed to the point of cliché. We are less used to it in Britain, partly because the British bourgeoisie was able to regain most of the ground lost within the existing institutions of the state. But even a casual acquaintance with the mood of the middle classes in 1919–21, both those who had done well and those who had not, the 'New Rich' as well as the 'New Poor', suggests what had happened. For the middle classes the real problems which many of them faced both during the war and immediately after it were directly proportional to the gains made (as they supposed) by the working classes. Thus at the moment when the organized working class, through the Labour Party and the trade unions, was claiming political centrality the non-working class was prepared to concede it to them by blaming them almost exclusively for their plight. Sir Harry Brittain, Conservative MP for Acton, caught this mood as well as Warwick Deeping. Commending the Middle Class Union, founded in early 1919, he wrote:

The Government . . . falls easily into the habit of remembering only, dealing only with the *vocal* working classes. Glance at the record of any

[2] Masterman, *The Condition of England* (London, 1909), 25.

six months' legislation of recent years. Labour, Labour, Manual Labour every time. Labour is flattered, battens on success and eventually achieves an arrogance which finds at last a too-complaisant Government hard pressed to make further and still further concessions.[3]

There were other bourgeois demons, 'profiteers' for example, or the Lloyd George government, or Capital, but they were always secondary demons, and the profligacy of Lloyd George was the fault of the working class anyway. The reaction was such, however, that in 1942, when the interests of the middle class were not uppermost in people's minds, Sir John Boyd Orr was prepared to argue that the prevention of a middle-class New Poor was one of the major tasks of social reconstruction.[4]

Within its own terms it was the remarkable achievement of the late Victorian and Edwardian period to exclude a political notion of the working class from the centre of politics. The First World War undid this and increasingly people were compelled to define themselves in relation to what Brittain called the 'vocal working classes', to make up their minds whether they were for them or against them. The inter-war years demonstrated the risks for the vocal working classes in doing this. While the assumption behind the Labour Party's rhetoric was that you could induce the majority of the electorate to declare themselves for, there was always the real possibility that the majority would, in fact, declare themselves against; which is indeed what happened. Britain thus developed in the inter-war years what she had never had before, a bourgeois politics, based specifically upon opposition to a political conception of the working class.

The Conservative Party was the beneficiary of this and I have argued that existing accounts of how the Conservatives mobilized its majority are largely incomplete. The Conservatives eventually assembled a large combination of classes, a kind of negative status-group which thought of itself as the 'public', with little in common except their hostility to what they understood to be the 'working class'. An essential element in this mobilization was the Conservative Party's capacity to exploit the kind of ideologically fashioned stereotypes which even before 1914, as I have suggested in the sixth chapter, had clear political implications. It turned out

[3] Sir Harry Brittain, MP, 'Middle Classes, Mobilize', *Review of Reviews* (May 1919), 316–18.

[4] See *Journal of the Royal Statistical Society*, 3 (1942), 189.

in these circumstances to be surprisingly easy to isolate the labour movement and restrict its freedom of action. The First World War and its immediate aftermath, which seemed to provide so many opportunities for the labour movement instead provided more opportunities for its enemies.

The Second World War, on the other hand, rapidly undermined the preponderance of bourgeois politics. The Chamberlainite Conservative Party could not long survive the decision in 1940 to fight a war to the end; on the contrary, it could survive only if Britain did *not* fight such a war. The formation of the Churchill coalition was thus a disaster for it and was almost instantly understood to be a disaster. Within a couple of weeks of its taking office Henry Channon, the Conservative MP for Southend, wrote of the strange people 'who have drawn numbers in this mad lottery [the coalition]. It will be years before a really Conservative Government comes in again.'[5] The Conservative Party's political strategies, so successful in the 1930s, collapsed after 1940 because the idea of the 'public' lost much of its ideological force, while the conventional wisdoms of public life became for once the wisdoms of the left. Given the nature of these political strategies, however, it is unlikely that the social policies of the Second World War—and hence the simultaneous ideological shift—were the result of a wartime consensus: rather they were 'Labour' policies reluctantly accepted by the leadership of the Conservative Party (though by some less reluctantly than by others) and possibly never accepted at all by much of its constituency membership. The stereotypes of the working class remained as powerful as ever; they were just believed by fewer people.

The Role of the State

The state was, of course, not an entity independent of social classes: its relationship with the working class, as with other classes, was always dynamic. The mere existence of the working class, particularly the organized working class, influenced the responses of the state to that class as well as to society as a whole. Nor was it always the case that in this relationship the state was the active partner. Nevertheless, the history of this period strongly

[5] R. Rhodes James (ed.), *Chips: The Diaries of Sir Henry Channon* (London, 1967), 254.

suggests that it usually was the active partner and that the fortunes of the British working class rose and fell according to its goodwill.

Can we ask, at the risk of hypostatizing the state, what it wanted? At the beginning of our period (1890, as we have seen) the German economist G. von Schulze-Gaevernitz noted that nowhere in England does one meet 'that deep-seated mistrust which makes the German workman regard every man in a good coat as an enemy if not a spy [*Geheimpolizisten* in the original— actually plain-clothes police].' At its very end (1953) Edward Shils and Michael Young wrote:

Over the past century, British society, despite distinctions of nationality and social status, has achieved a degree of moral unity equalled by no other large national state. The assimilation of the working class into the moral consensus of British society, though certainly far from complete, has gone further in Great Britain than anywhere else, and its transformation from one of the most unruly and violent into one of the most orderly and law-abiding is one of the great collective achievements of modern times.[6]

All three undoubtedly exaggerated Britain's social and moral harmony. It was not unknown for plain-clothes policemen to keep an eye on the political activities of the British working class and one arm of the state, the judiciary, was increasingly antipathetic to it. But they were not wildly exaggerating. They were, in fact, describing a social equilibrium which the British state itself did much to promote. Britain before 1914 was no paradise for the working class, nor indeed after it, but the state's anxiety to entrench a non-authoritarian social stability had the effect of relatively strengthening the working class at the expense of everyone else. Not (so to speak) positively—in hardly any other country after all was property more secure—but negatively, by undermining the ideological legitimacy of many kinds of anti-working class action deployed elsewhere.

Nevertheless, the relationship of the state to the working class over the whole period was not as neatly symmetrical as these quotations suggest. I have argued that before 1914 and after 1940 the working class did pretty well from the state and at least as well as any other class. This was less true of the inter-war period. And the reason for that was the exceptional degree of social unity

[6] For Schulze-Gaevernitz and Shils and Young, see above pp. 8, 18.

displayed by those who thought of themselves as non-working class and the simultaneous inability of the organized working class to exploit the state for its own purposes. It is this I tried to suggest in the chapter on the second Labour government. I was concerned there with the intellectual and physical constraints upon Labour ministers—what we might expect them to do and what they might be allowed to do.[7] In this sense much of the now huge literature on inter-war employment policy is beside the point. While it is clear, however, that Labour ministers were not allowed to do much, we should not overrate the degree to which the state had lost the comparative autonomy it possessed before 1914. Given the extent of the triumph of the labour movement's opponents after 1922, even more after 1931, one can easily imagine circumstances when its attitude to the working class could have been distinctly more hostile than it actually was.

The Second World War demonstrates how active the state could be, and how important it was for the organized working class. While it would be wrong to argue that the working class was simply passive throughout the war—the Chamberlainite state gave way because it knew it could not fight the war as it thought it had to be fought without that class—it is clear that much of the working class which voted Labour in 1945 was the creation of the state and not of the labour movement itself. Equally, the change in ideological mood, which occurred so rapidly after 1940, was largely determined by the state. It proved, therefore, not possible for the organized working class to assimilate civil society to its own political hopes without the agency of the state. The state, therefore, made possible the Labour victory of 1945; by undermining the political economy of the inter-war years it, in a way, completed the circle.

[7] See the discussion of this chapter in S. Lukes, *Essays in Social Theory* (London, 1977), 21–4.

INDEX